Newswriting

Newswriting

GERALD STONE
Southern Illinois University at Carbondale

HarperCollins*Publishers*

Photo Credits: p. 6, Reuters/Bettmann; p. 27, Kagan, Monkmeyer Press Photo; p. 47, © Mahoney/The Image Works; pp. 71, 351, Southwick, Stock, Boston; pp. 94, 279, Grant, The Picture Cube; p. 122, Daemmrich, Stock, Boston; p. 154, © Winter/The Image Works; p. 170, © Paul Conklin; p. 195, Strickler, Monkmeyer Press Photo; p. 227, Conklin, Monkmeyer Press Photo; p. 253, Sygma; p. 301, © Wells/The Image Works; pp. 329, 382, Rogers, Monkmeyer Press Photo; p. 405, UPI/Bettmann.

Sponsoring Editor: Melissa A. Rosati
Project Editor: Diane Rowell
Design Supervisor: Lucy Krikorian
Text Design: Circa 86, Inc.
Cover Design: Kay Cannizzaro
Cover Photo: William Whitehurst
Photo Researcher: Mira Schachne
Production Administrator: Paula Keller
Compositor: Circle Graphics Typographers
Printer and Binder: R. R. Donnelley & Sons Company
Cover Printer: The Lehigh Press, Inc.

Newswriting

Library of Congress Cataloging-in-Publication Data

Stone, Gerald (Gerald C.)
    Newswriting / Gerald Stone.
        p.   cm.
    Includes index.
    ISBN 0-06-046457-7
    1. Journalism—Authorship.   2. Reporters and reporting.
I. Title.
PN4775.S74   1991
808'.06607—dc20   91–19972
                                                                              CIP

91 92 93 94   9 8 7 6 5 4 3 2 1

To Donna, Alec and Leah

Contents

Preface

Newswriting is a beginning newswriting book with one major advantage over some of the other successful offerings in the field. This book is designed specifically to take a novice writer from no knowledge of newswriting to a level of proficiency acceptable in the more advanced journalism courses. It is based on extensive study of just what is required to achieve success in the first newspaper newswriting course.

The author spent 12 years coordinating multiple sections of the beginning newswriting course with 8-to-12 sections of the class per semester, for majors and nonmajors, using full- and part-time faculty. Without close coordination of content among the sections, we found that many of the students getting into the more advanced journalism writing classes didn't have the skills they needed to cope with the writing demands. It didn't matter whether those more advanced classes were in newspaper, magazine, broadcast, public relations or advertising copy writing. Complaints by faculty in higher-level classes were bitter and well-founded.

Typically, we enrolled 16 students per section in the beginning newswriting class, and by the fourth week of class there were 12 or fewer. At the end of the semester, 9 or 10 successful completions were about the average. As we searched for ways to improve student performance, we found these to be the most important items to consider:

1. Writing skills of those entering the basic newswriting class were, on average, not up to our expectations. This impression was confirmed by full-time faculty members who had been teaching the beginning class for more than 20 years.

It's a sad commentary on the state of preparatory programs in English, but it's a fact we live with in our beginning newswriting sections. Colleagues assure me that this impression is accurate across the country.

2. A variety of approaches to teaching basic newswriting can work. It isn't necessary that every teacher cover exactly the same material in the same order. But certain material must be presented in the class to ensure that students will have mastered the basic skills expected at the outset of the more advanced classes.

3. People learn how to write by writing. The more writing they do, the more proficient they become at it.

As a measure of control among the several sections, we instituted a mandatory final writing exam graded by a committee of faculty teaching the class. The idea was to ensure a minimum level of writing ability coming out of the course and to prevent those "mercy C minus students" (the ones who did all the work and attended all the classes, but still didn't reach minimum standards) from passing into the advanced writing classes. This final exam hurdle stopped another two students per section from getting through the filter-to-the-field class. Now we were enrolling 16 students per semester and passing 9–10: a frustrating situation for teachers and a resource drain. Perhaps a greater percentage per section would succeed if there were a more "programmed" course textbook.

So the next step was a national study of successful journalism schools, measured in terms of their students' winning national writing competitions. The rationale was that if their students could write well enough to win national awards, they must be doing something right, and they are probably doing it in the first newswriting course.

This book encompasses what was learned through close scrutiny of our newswriting sections plus the outcomes of the study of journalism schools. It isn't the only approach, but it is a well-proven one. *Newswriting* differs from the other basic newswriting texts by attempting to do *no more* than prepare students for the second-level journalism writing courses. The chapters are relatively short and loaded with examples. Writing exercises follow each chapter and are geared for in-class use or homework assignments. The exercises drive at the chapter's main points.

The content is designed in what we found to be an effective progression of just the necessary basic concepts for teaching beginning newswriting. Teachers aren't expected to march their students in lock step through the book, but *that will work* for many. Others might reverse the presentation of a few chapters or pick and choose among the later chapters to emphasize what they believe is most important. This is also part of the design because not every class will progress far enough during the semester to get through the entire book. Still, the chapters are ordered to present the crucial basic information in logical progression.

In all, *Newswriting*'s objective is to provide students an easy to use, strategically structured textbook to bring them from novice to capable beginning journalistic writer.

Other than taking students from neophyte to competent, pluses for *Newwriting* are:

1. Students will use almost the entire book during their course term. Instead of paying extra for a variety of chapters on advanced writing and specialized reporting that nobody seems to cover in 10 to 16 weeks of class, students shoud be able to complete all 17 chapters.

2. The text includes a city directory of names and addresses of people named in the exercises and a close-up map of the metropolitan area. Including a city directory is not novel, but our experience and the survey outcomes indicate that students fall short on accuracy. Teachers who use their own exercises report they expect students to know the names and spellings of local officials, but schools don't provide easy access to copies of local directories or telephone books in the newswriting classroom.

3. A teacher's manual is available with suggestions for instructors using the book, and the manual includes examples of completed story exercises written by practicing journalists.

ACKNOWLEDGMENTS

On a more personal note, the author is greatly indebted to many colleagues who contributed comments and suggestions throughout the three years this text has been in progress. John Lee, at Memphis State, suggested me as a possible beginning newswriting text author. Former Editor Barbara Cinquegrani stuck by me through several early drafts, my initial attempts to pass muster, which finally led to a contract. Current College Communications Editor Melissa Rosati spent the next two years seeing the project to its conclusion. Editor-in-Chief Anne Smith kept a watchful eye through the entire period. Project Editor Diane Rowell and copy editor Lee Paradise, unrivaled in the nation's newsrooms, fine-tuned for the finishing touches.

Along the way, six exacting and outspoken text reviewers—colleagues in journalism education—spent countless hours at my drafts with scathing but keen editing pencils. These cantankerous curmudgeons kept blue-penciling my prose through half a dozen rewrites until it reached its present state. Apparently they believed that a newswriting text ought to contain flawless writing. Reading their editing comments was frequently painful, but I agreed that their standards should be my goal. Any failings that remain are my own.

The following reviewers deserve credit for their contribution to the best writing this text may have achieved: Jack Botts, University of Nebraska–Lincoln; Barthy Byrd-Savino, University of Texas–El Paso; Robert Daly, Kansas State University; John C. Doolittle, American University; Martin Gibson, University of Texas–Austin; W. Wat Hopkins, Virginia Polytechnic Institute and State University; Marian Huttenstine, University of Alabama; John D. Mitchell, Syracuse University; Robert M. Ours, West Virginia University; and Alf Pratte, Brigham Young University.

Elinor Grusin at Memphis State made suggestions on the law section; Virginia Roark of Southern Illinois University at Carbondale built the index; and Donna Besser Stone critiqued the ethics section and frequently assured me that in spite of my misgivings the three years were being well-spent.

Gerald Stone

To the Student

The Joy of Journalism

A crime beat reporter was called to the scene of a tense stand-off between police and a man in a parked car who had a .32-caliber pistol held against the head of a screaming woman.

"It's Charlie Green," police told the reporter. "He's never done anything like this before... said he'll kill the woman if we don't let him drive away. We said no, and he asked to talk to you. Want the bullhorn?"

Waving off the officer, the reporter stood out in the street and raised his arms. "Charlie, it's me. Let the woman go. I'm coming in."

The exchange was made, and the reporter sat in the back seat of the car. He lit a cigarette and handed it to the man behind the wheel. "Well, Charlie, looks like you really messed up this time."

"I know, man. What am I gonna do?"

* * *

Nothing quite captures the thrill of being a journalist. What other profession lets you:

- be where the action is
- know the powerful and famous
- learn about new ideas
- influence public opinion
- occasionally right a wrong
- feel your creative juices flow
- see your byline and
- have such a wide variety of daily job experiences?

Here's a closer look at these daily benefits of being a journalist.

Being where the action is.   When news happens, the journalist is among the first on the scene: at a fire, a drug bust, an election, the Kentucky Derby, a trial, an earthquake, a press conference. If it's newsworthy, the journalist is there to report and write about it.

The head football coach in your college town is indicted for allegedly selling blocks of game tickets to undercover agents. The sports department is all over the story, but as the news side court reporter, you have the front-row seat at the trial. Everywhere you go—at fast-food counters or the laundromat—people ask you what's happening with the coach. They know you're right there as events unfold.

Knowing the powerful and famous.   Much of a journalist's daily activity is the routine coverage of a beat such as education or the police. But the people being covered often are the movers and shakers of society: political leaders, the wealthy and influential, even celebrities. Many journalists are on a first-name basis with their city's mayor, star athletes, corporate heads, university presidents and society's elite.

Of course, journalists also know the people who live a less public but equally interesting life, such as detectives, horse trainers, fortune tellers, hotel desk clerks and morticians. Interviewing important or interesting people probably accounts for most of the time a journalist spends out of the newsroom.

Learning about new ideas.   Gathering information demands even more of a journalist's time than writing. Journalists must be avid readers of books, magazines and newspapers to stay on top of current developments across fields from anthropology to political science to social work.

Journalists develop this store of knowledge by reading and by talking with their sources in the specialty field. If you report on crime, you need to know about criminology, psychology, law, drugs, prison reform and the court system.

As a police reporter, you decide to do a story on witness identification lineups. A psychology journal carries a story about memory and recall under stress situations. You talk with attorneys, some prosecutors, a criminology professor, a couple of judges you know and a few petty criminals. You discover that lineup evidence has been ruled inadmissible by some European courts. In your own state, several convictions based primarily on lineup testimony resulted in innocent people going to jail. Pretty soon you have a three-article series, loaded with facts and quotes from experts, that suggests there are dangerous flaws in the lineup identification system.

Influencing public opinion.   Unlike a set of encyclopedias that might gather dust on a bookshelf, journalists share information with a mass audience. That's really the whole purpose of the profession. After people complete their formal education, they rely on the mass media for most of their new knowledge. By providing that knowledge, journalists ensure an informed citizenry, the foundation for the representative government our forefathers established.

As a political reporter, you have a responsibility to inform the public about local candidates' positions on major issues, and the further duty to present the candidates' experience and personalities: anything that might affect their ability to hold public office. You won't try to influence an election by promoting your favorite candidates, but you are obliged to report that one of the contenders for city auditor pleaded no-contest to a tax evasion charge.

Righting wrongs.   It doesn't happen frequently, but it does happen. Journalists uncover information about some social or political wrong-doing and air the problem in the mass media. Being a "watchdog" is one of the traditional journalistic roles. It means that the press functions as the public's unofficial eyes and ears to report infractions of law, ethics or policy. Sources who know of injustices being committed at their work places, in government or in law enforcement rely on a journalist to bring media attention to the problem. Most journalists experience at least one instance of news makers involved in corruption, and many journalists have the satisfaction of seeing the perpetrators brought to justice through the established legal process.

Feeling the creative juices flow.   Journalists enjoy the creative aspects of their jobs that appeal to people who like to write. Writing a story or editing it, doing a broadcast segment, creating an advertisement or public relations campaign brings pride of accomplishment.

If you're a wordsmith, a creator of prose, you care about clarity and the flow of ideas. Your stories become compelling; they carry impact. Few other professions let practitioners see the results of their labor so regularly, and to know that so many others are paying attention to the finished product.

Seeing your byline.   Your name in print...is there a greater thrill? It's one thing to know you've done a good job, but an even better high is looking at your work, with your name on it, and knowing that perhaps 100,000 people also saw it.

Like the actor or comic who is rewarded with applause, you can't help but glow over that byline. It compensates for some of the lows: the pay, long hours, deadlines and hassles that go with this job, as with most others. Seeing your byline can make them seem insignificant.

Never a dull moment.   Perhaps the most joy a journalist experiences is the excitement of doing something new and different. Of course there are plenty of routine tasks, but journalists are never sure what the next day may bring.

You report to work anticipating doing some rewrites or maybe having time to polish that news feature you've been working on this week. Then the editor sends you to cover a mayor's press conference. Three hours later, the police radio monitor prompts an assignment to a SWAT mission at a riverfront warehouse. It's a false alarm, and you call in to learn that the music writer is sick today and you'll be covering the symphony tonight. Go change into your evening clothes, pick up the tickets at the box office at 7:30. Hope you like Tchaikovsky (and hope you know something about classical music). Have your article in by 11 p.m., then take the rest of the day off.

This scenario is not too unrealistic. At smaller papers, it may be a typical work day. It's hectic, pressure-packed and anything but dull.

*   *   *

What about Charlie Green, the crime reporter in the back seat of the car? Well, that was an extremely unusual journalistic undertaking, not recommended under any circumstances, and one you won't have to face. In fact, the reporter said *he* wouldn't have done it if he hadn't known Charlie for five years and known him to be a petty thief, not a killer.

Charlie shed a few tears, gave his gun to the reporter, finished the cigarette and then was taken to jail.

Newswriting

... how the ... are ...
... policing an educating

Lawyer ... Opposition

Reaction to the proposal has been mixed. Those most staunchly opposed to it are trial lawyers, who now argue the malpractice cases in court.

"This will take away the right to a jury trial," said Martin Maher, president of the Association of Trial Lawyers of America. "To put caps on an injured victim's right to recover are wrong. To limit an injured victim's widows' and widowers' rights to recover fair and adequate compensation by an American jury is wrong."

The association representing hospitals, the American Hospital Association, also objects to the measure, chiefly because of the way it is financed: the association fears hospitals will lose Medicare and Medicaid payments if the states cannot make the changes.

"This proposal makes hospitals a special target, even though the problem permeates the entire health care industry," said Gaelynn DeMa... Washington counse...

... But Senator ... the Republican ... by that the Pres... to the waiting-period ... Senate passed his ant-...
...tion.

...dy bill itself would be tough ... but that's not going to happen ... view," he said on "Meet the ... Mr. Reagan's dramatic en-...orsement of the bill in March clearly aided its cause among House Republicans and could set the tone for a warmer reception in the Senate among Republicans and Democrats alike.

Senator Joseph R. Biden Jr. of Delaware, the Senate Judiciary Committee chairman, has introduced the Demo-cratic version of the anti-crime bill, ...ich would ban the assembly and manufacture of 14 types of domestic assault weapons and provide $1 billion in aid to state and local law-enforce-ment agencies.

The National Rifle Association president, Wayne LaPierre, said he ... both the Bide...

... wh... char... comf... tail... own... 25 sta... pract... the ... ce...

...e ...estic raise... rai... f or ... cha...

A Nose for News

A superior newspaper journalist knows which questions to ask, doggedly pursues sources and digs until the story is complete. Such a journalist is not born, but blooms after study, practice and later maturing through on-the-job experience.

Inquisitiveness is a natural, human trait accessible to fine tuning. The inquisitive impulse—journalists call it a "nose for news"—can be learned. In fact, a nose for news is simply knowing what makes news, what generates interest when people read newspapers or listen to radio or television news.

This section offers several general principles important to news values; however, news values are relative. No single element always takes precedence over another. Working journalists consider the particulars of each news event, and they weigh events as a whole without making judgments among discrete news values. Still, the ability to recognize news values benefits beginning journalists.

CONSEQUENCE

News events that affect the largest number of people have the most consequence. The news value of consequence should be considered at every level, both for good news or bad.

A hurricane ravaging homes across a four-state coastal area has more consequence than a tornado touching down in one town (unless it's your town). Plans to build a factory offering job opportunities for 1,500 unemployed residents creates more excitement than a small business expansion that may add 50 employees. And the consequence principle is applied easily to money: A $1 million bank heist generates much more reader interest than a $10,000 robbery.

Remember consequence as the rule of "greater" effects. The greater the numbers—the more people, places or things affected—the greater the consequence. Greater consequence means more reader interest.

PROMINENCE

A second news value is called eminence-prominence, referred to here as prominence. Eminence actually deals with titles: important people and people in high positions, regardless of whether they are in the limelight. Prominence means people who are known or conspicuous. A prominent person, even one without title or high rank, has a name most people recognize.

A medical doctor who is a kidney specialist would be eminent because the person is an M.D. and a specialist in treating kidney disease. This person may be known only to patients or to the medical community. While the general reading public may not know this person, the title of doctor and kidney specialist suggests a higher news level than if the person were a paramedic. More people enthusiastically read about Bruce Springsteen than about a lesser-known rock star, and about the lesser-known rock star than about the stage hand. This level-of-performance guideline holds true in almost every social or occupational category.

Eminence is closely associated with prominence, and for news value considerations, the distinction between the two is minor. Remember, people in the spotlight—whether government officials, educators, business people, labor leaders or movie stars—rate higher in general reader appeal than less conspicuous people.

PROXIMITY

The location of the news event, its proximity, also affects its news value. The closer to home (the area in which the news story will appear), the greater the news value. Anything in the reader's own neighborhood is likely to be of more interest to that reader than similar events occurring in other neighborhoods. Happenings in your city will probably be of greater interest than those in another part of the state or neighboring states.

Proximity explains why some really major events have low news value for U.S. readers. Our nearest neighbor nations are Mexico and Canada, but neither country is very close to most U.S. residents. Other nations are even farther away. A news platitude is that an earthquake in India that destroys three cities and kills thousands of people gets only a brief mention in a back-page story of U.S. newspapers while a flood in Kansas with a relatively low death and destruction rate makes front-page banner headlines. Proximity suggests that the closer the news event is to the reader, the more likely it is to touch the reader's life.

Proximity also explains the rise of suburban daily papers. The big city metro dailies can't adequately cover all news in each surrounding suburb. The proximity news value also indicates why "hometown" weekly papers and rural radio stations continue to survive. Rural residents want news about their friends and about the government decisions affecting their town and country. The smaller media outlets give this local information that is unavailable elsewhere.

Consider that the priority level of news values, even among the three mentioned so far, is not a hard, fast rule. Prominence doesn't always come before proximity. For instance, if the mayor of a neighboring town is impeached, that might be interesting. If your own local city clerk is fired, that might be more interesting. And the firing of a local city clerk may not command as much attention for many readers as the news that a famous Hollywood actress has died. Every U.S. paper and television station gave conspicuous and extensive coverage to the death of John Wayne. This famous actor's death must have lowered the news budget priority of a lot of more-local stories at many papers and stations.

TIMELINESS

Many journalists insist that timeliness is the single essential element in the definition of news. Some mention of when an event occurred will be present in every story, usually high in the story. The more recently an event occurred, the greater its news value. Something that took place last night at 10:30 might first be reported in the morning newspaper and announced on morning radio broadcasts. By that afternoon, the item may no longer be newsworthy.

Under the same guidelines, an event that begins something, such as the opening of a local play or the start of an election campaign, has more news value than later, similar elements of the same event. The Wednesday matinee of the second week of a local play isn't news unless something unusual happens during that performance.

Timeliness often presents difficulties for news writers because as a news value it must be established early. The reader needs to know when

International transmission of major news events, such as Chinese students carrying a model of the Statue of Liberty during a 1989 march for democracy in Shanghai, makes front-page headlines around the globe in a matter of hours.

the event occurred or at what point in a series of unfolding events this story takes place. Timeliness is one of the more critical news values, but it too must be weighed in importance against others. There is no rule that says the time factor belongs in the first paragraph or even in the first four grafs (*graf* is journalese for *paragraph*). However, in almost every news story the timeliness news value should be provided and usually the higher in the story the better.

ACTION

News has been defined as a change in the status quo. Though that definition is too simplistic, certainly definite actions taken are more newsworthy than mere contemplation of future action.

When government bodies meet for decision making, they discuss some issues and vote on others. Their discussions may be reported in the news media. Their decisions, the items on which they vote, almost always will be reported, even if the topic is only a vote to buy a new fire truck. Items discussed but not brought to a vote may be much more consequential than the actions actually voted upon. But the action news value suggests that any definitive decision made by the governmental body should be reported.

Most other "action" decisions are easier to make. The body of a known gangster is washed onto the deserted bank of a nearby river. Certainly, this is news. But a shoot-out between gangsters and police at a downtown restaurant, without question, makes the front page or lead story of the evening newscast.

Disruption of the status quo is news. The more disruptive an action, the more likely it will grab attention. But the "action" news value is also at play when a definitive action preserves the status quo.

NOVELTY

Novelty can be a news value similar to action. Here the oddity makes news simply because of an intrinsic, unique characteristic. Readers like to know about the "first" and the "biggest" and the one-of-a-kind. The first baby of the year in your home town, the biggest pumpkin of the season and the most decorated war veteran all qualify. Ripley's *Believe It or Not* was a success in the Sunday comic sections for many decades; the *Guinness Book of World Records* boasts sales of more than 42 million.

Television has capitalized on novelty in "That's Incredible" and a host of similar series: the most-wanted criminals, the fantastically wealthy and the daredevil adventurers.

But the "biggest" or the "first" don't have a monopoly on the novelty news value. Myriad not-so-common events fit these guidelines. The decision to close the oldest all-girls' school, to open a sealed time capsule or to pave over the last cobblestone street left in town qualify for news play under the heading of novelty. That list, however, is chiefly feature material.

Novelty can be a news value in straight news stories. Robberies occur in most medium-sized cities every day, but seldom does a thief mistakenly break into a police precinct. A local hotel owner defies superstition and numbers the 13th floor. From that time forth, every misfortune that occurs at the hotel happens on the 13th floor, including fires, police raids and leaky plumbing. A woman has a baby in a local cab, and although that's happened before, this is the third time she's had a baby in a taxi.

Many more-serious incidents are newsworthy because of novelty. Reporters chronicle novel ways of committing crimes, from larceny to murder. Political leaders offer novel approaches to solving public problems. Teenagers and oldsters invent new technological devices. Hospitals provide a multitude of both miracles and inexplicable tragedies.

Virtually anything that seems at least a little unusual to a news writer will probably be received by the audience as an oddity worthy of attention.

HUMAN INTEREST

Human interest is a news value that defies easy definition because of its nearly all-inclusive nature. It is so encompassing that many journalists rank it with timeliness as an essential element in the definition of news.

Stories fitting this category contain strong emotional appeal that may or may not involve news happenings. They always include people or things that happen to people, their families, friends, pets or possessions. Human interest articles report occurrences that involve the reader by arousing feelings such as joy, hatred, sorrow, understanding or sympathy. Instead of something unusual, the human interest element often involves common experiences with which people identify. The classic form of human interest article, called a tear-jerker, literally moves the reader to tears, but tragedy is not a qualifying prerequisite to human interest stories. We can feel warmth when a puppy is returned to its owner, happiness with a cancer success story or pride for a person who triumphs over any adversity or unusual situation.

The chief difference between human interest and other news values, especially novelty, is in the arousal of people's emotions. This arousal in the reader is the key element in the human interest category.

One other aspect about human interest: These stories can be powerful. A person reading such an article might consider it the most gripping news in the paper or on television that day. And that person is likely to remember this story the longest. Readers identify with the people reported about, and reader feelings linger.

HUMAN INTEREST—SEX

Another aspect of human interest is sex, whether it's titillating, shocking or shameful. And sex can be all three. This news value has been recognized as a separate category, although it frequently accompanies other discrete news values, but it also can be identified as a major aspect of human interest. The embezzling of bank funds might be just another theft except that the vice president falsified the books to keep a lover. Police raids resulting in a drug bust are common until linked with a couples-swapping club.

Despite, or perhaps because of, any moral views, the element of sex is more often than not relevant to *why* the story occurred. If it helps explain the why of a news story, sex can be a legitimate human interest news value. However, journalists must not pander to audience titillation. For instance, most professional journalists know more about the sexual activities of news makers than they wish to publish. Married governors and even presidents have kept lovers, a fact known to journalists who never reported such moral indiscretions unless, perhaps, the lover was placed on the public payroll. Sex is one of the basic human needs, one that very often explains why people do what they do, but its newsworthiness can test a journalist's ethics.

HUMOR

Everyone enjoys a good laugh. Funny incidents happen all the time and should be reported. Often, humor in an incident must be discerned by the reporter and will come through to the reader in the way a story is written or edited. Writing humor is difficult, especially when forced from the facts to which a news writer is forever bound. But just as often, the incident itself is funny and merely writing what happened provides the best effect.

Of course, what is funny to one person is not always humorous to another, but the chances are that if you find humor in the incident, so will your readers. Recognize that the single, short, humorous piece in the newspaper might be the most widely read and often repeated story of the day.

To recap, here are the major news values, in what is probably their order of decision making use by news writers:

1. consequence
2. prominence
3. proximity
4. timeliness
5. action
6. novelty
7. human interest
8. human interest—sex
9. humor

Some seasoned journalists might argue that the list is too detailed: that timeliness, prominence, proximity and consequence form the complete set of news values. Others might contend that novelty, sex and human interest are subsumed in the human interest category. Another view is that there are more discrete news values than the nine on this list, probably a lot more.

Still, the list of nine items provides a good start for recognizing the many news elements a reporter encounters. The values also serve as a link to a journalistic concept called the *five W's and H* of news: *who, what, when, where, why* and *how.* These elements are the building blocks of news stories. Veteran reporters and editors maintain that if you answer these six questions for the reader, you've completed your newswriting job.

You will again see the five W's, but now consider how they fit with the basic news values. "Who" goes with prominence, "what" goes with consequence, "when" goes with timeliness, "where" goes with proximity, and "why" and "how" are refinements related to the other five news values.

ACCURACY, FAIRNESS AND OBJECTIVITY

Going beyond an introduction to news without mentioning journalism's traditions of accuracy, fairness and objectivity is akin to scaling a rugged mountain peak barefoot. That climb won't be successful, and the attempt is likely to be painful.

Accuracy, fairness and objectivity are the distinct elements that define newswriting for the media and that separate it from fiction. Writing news is recording and interpreting *facts*.

When journalists gather news from sources, they soon learn their work is constantly on trial. Sources are concerned about how the information will appear in print. Reporters must be alert to potential mistakes from their first scribbled notes through their final reading of the article. Editors then scan the piece, questioning anything that might not be accurate. Other news room personnel also check for errors. The entire journalistic process is designed to ensure that everything published will be as correct as humanly possible in every respect. But the burden of accuracy belongs first to the reporter-writer. There is no room for doubt, and no excuse for factual mistakes.

Accuracy includes the exact spelling of names, the right locations, correct dates and times, proper addresses, the right person quoted with the source's exact title, and only those words actually spoken placed in quotes. Every fact must be exactly right. Precision is an imperative because accuracy forms the basis of objectivity and fairness. Without accuracy, the entire news enterprise loses its credibility and dependability with the public.

Fairness is closely related to objectivity. A journalist has a responsibility to report and write the truth, or to come as close to the truth as is humanly possible. While writing your article, imagine yourself going back to your sources the next day with a copy or tape of the finished product, allowing each source to evaluate your work. Of course, you *won't actually do that,* but if you visualize doing it while you're writing, you shouldn't have a problem with fairness. You will upset some people, but that is part of doing the job properly. If you report and write with fairness, you attain professionalism and a clear conscience.

"Objectivity" is actually a state of perfection that can never be reached. But knowing that objectivity is an impossible goal doesn't prevent the journalist from always aiming for it. In practice, reporters try to keep their opinion out of the story and to adopt as neutral a view as possible in every reporting situation. If you cover your team's championship playoff game, it's no longer your team: it's one of the two teams vying for the title. You may secretly hope your team wins—in fact it's difficult to imagine how anyone could avoid those feelings—but as you report the game and as you write what occurs on the field, you do so as if you were in no way connected to either group of players.

A journalist's objectivity is constantly under pressure. Virtually every story covered has an aspect that pulls the writer toward a particular viewpoint. Two sources are engaged in controversy and you find one quite attractive while the other is repulsive to you . . . even antagonistic, resentful, skeptical of your motives and downright unpleasant to deal with as a source. Still, when you gather the facts from these two sources, you must treat them equally. Each source deserves the same hearing; each the same opportunity to have that side of the controversy known. Readers deserve an unbiased report. Remaining objective under such conditions is a chore for the journalist; still it's a necessity. Let the facts determine how the story will be structured. Don't allow your personal feelings about the sources to influence your view, judgment or treatment at any point during the reporting-writing process. Accomplishing neutrality is an absolute requirement for journalists.

The themes of accuracy, fairness and objectivity merge with every aspect of journalism. They can haunt or reward you, but just as an attorney or a physician makes critical decisions, so does the journalist.

SUMMARY

Luckily, a nose for news, the journalist's foremost characteristic, isn't innate. It can be learned by understanding the nine basic categories of news values, those aspects of changes in the status quo that people want to know about. Reporters and writers base their information gathering on these news values and use them to make their articles interesting.

- *Consequence.* News events that affect the largest number of people have the most consequence.
- *Prominence.* People in the spotlight rate higher in general reader appeal than less conspicuous people.
- *Proximity.* The closer to home (the area in which the news story will appear), the greater the news value.
- *Timeliness.* The more recently an event occurred, the greater its news value.
- *Action.* Disruption of the status quo is news; the more disruptive, the more attention-grabbing.

- *Novelty.* Oddities make news simply because people find them fascinating.
- *Human interest.* Stories fitting this category contain strong emotional appeal to readers.
- *Human interest—sex.* Whether titillating or shocking, sex is a human concern that often explains why people do what they do.
- *Humor.* Funny incidents happen all the time and should be reported. Everyone enjoys a good laugh.

Three other basic considerations in journalism are accuracy, fairness and objectivity. Accuracy is simply mandatory to the profession, always. Objectivity is an ideal that can't be reached, but it remains a journalist's goal. And fairness is the golden rule quality that makes it possible for a journalist to smile into the mirror.

Thinking it Through

EXERCISE 1.1

News Values

For each pair of items mark which is the more newsworthy by circling the letter (either A or B). Then use the following list of news values to write the **best** reason for your choice in the blank provided. [Exercises may be done on a separate sheet of paper or VDT screen by writing the pair number, letter choice and news value, e.g.: 1. A. prominence.]

a. consequence   d. timeliness   g. human interest
b. prominence   e. action   h. human interest—sex
c. proximity   f. novelty   i. humor

1. _____ A. Man is arrested outside local nightspot following a brawl among customers in parking lot.

   _____ B. Man is arrested outside lumberyard while loading planks onto his truck at 3 a.m.

2. _____ A. Mother of four arrested for driving while intoxicated.

   _____ B. City council member arrested for DWI.

3. _____ A. Couple who met in an elevator are married in an elevator.

   _____ B. Couple on way to their wedding get stuck in an elevator for an hour.

4. ____ A. Political convention slated for nearby city.

   ____ B. Festival for political hopefuls slated here.

5. ____ A. Burglar found locked in storeroom of business at midnight.

   ____ B. Burglar caught after setting off silent alarm of business at midnight.

6. ____ A. Local beauty returns from winning national pageant.

   ____ B. Local beauty pageant set here tonight.

7. ____ A. Bus drivers go on strike.

   ____ B. Grade school teachers go on strike.

8. ____ A. Police arrest speeder after downtown chase.

   ____ B. Police arrest car thief in used car lot.

9. ____ A. Philanthropist wills estate to young housemaid.

   ____ B. Philanthropist wills estate to local charity.

10. ____ A. Private jet crashes into mountain.

    ____ B. Commercial passenger jet crashes into mountain.

11. ____ A. Local man named in paternity suit.

    ____ B. Local man arrested for alimony non-payment.

12. ____ A. Local firm manufactures automatic coffee brewers.

    ____ B. Local firm manufactures barrel hoops.

13. ____ A. School Board votes teacher pay raises.

    ____ B. City Council hears tract rezoning proposal.

14. ____ A. Youngster who flunked high school choir gets soloist position with civic opera cast.

    ____ B. Youngster who won writing essay gets scholarship to college.

15. ____ A. High school principal has novel published.

    ____ B. High school English teacher has novel published.

EXERCISE 1.2

News Values

For each pair of items mark which is the more newsworthy by circling the letter (either A or B). Then use the following list of news values to write the **best** reason for your choice in the blank provided. [Exercises may be done on a separate sheet of paper or VDT screen by writing the pair number, letter choice and news value, e.g.: 1. A. prominence.]

a. consequence
b. prominence
c. proximity

d. timeliness
e. action
f. novelty

g. human interest
h. human interest—sex
i. humor

1. _____ A. Four women have twins in local hospital during month.

   _____ B. Woman has quintuplets in local hospital.

2. _____ A. Ex-convict Tim Manfred slain by gunmen during opera performance.

   _____ B. Body of ex-convict Tim Manfred found in cement piling.

3. _____ A. Hurricane due within 50 miles of city.

   _____ B. Alaska blizzard causes 15 lives lost.

4. _____ A. Truck kills mother hurrying to phone doctor for dying daughter.

   _____ B. Truck kills mother hurrying to phone beauty parlor for appointment.

5. _____ A. Lions Club donates $300 to United Givers Fund recently.

   _____ B. Rotary Club donates $300 to Heart Fund to kick off drive.

6. _____ A. Government's irrigation projects will ensure farm drought control.

   _____ B. Scientists discover serum to extend human life span by 10 years.

7. _____ A. Thieves loot cash register of a hardware store.

   _____ B. Burglar alarm system stolen from hardware store.

8. _____ A. Mayor sued for divorce on grounds of adultery.

   _____ B. Taxicab driver wins divorce from unfaithful wife.

9. _____ A. 200 World War I veterans to convene here.

   _____ B. 200 accountants to attend convention here.

10. _____ A. Shoe clerk and waitress arrested for petting on park bench.

    _____ B. Banker arrested during police raid on love nest.

11. _____ A. Indian raja to marry local stenographer.

    _____ B. Broadway actress to divorce her second husband in Reno.

12. _____ A. Price of milk advances 5 cents per quart.

    _____ B. All sales of yachts to be levied a 10 percent tax.

13. _____ A. City council commends police chief for department efficiency.

   _____ B. City council fires police chief because of department corruption.

14. _____ A. Twin girls born in hospital to banker's wife.

   _____ B. 5-day-old twin girls found abandoned on church steps.

15. _____ A. Harvey L. Brock elected governor of New York.

   _____ B. Dale H. Merrywell elected governor of Utah.

16. _____ A. 12 cases of polio reported here during week.

   _____ B. Plague kills 5,000 in Peru.

17. _____ A. Widow contests millionaire husband's will of $1 million to charity.

   _____ B. Widow contests millionaire husband's will of $500,000 to chorus girl.

18. _____ A. Six persons receive minor injuries in local two-car collision.

   _____ B. Four persons receive minor injuries in local hotel elevator crash.

19. _____ A. Fan dancer shoots lover after learning he is married.

   _____ B. Bartender's wife shoots him during domestic quarrel.

20. _____ A. Man hanging on monkey cage bars at zoo, mimicking monkeys to impress girlfriend, gets four stitches at hospital after being bitten by monkey.

   _____ B. Worker at zoo receives eight stitches at hospital after being bitten by cougar.

Simple, Summary Leads

THE FIVE W'S AND H PRINCIPLE IN LEADS

A "simple," or summary, lead can be thought of as the first paragraph of a news article. It should tell as many of the five W's and H as necessary for that particular news story. It should give the five W's and H in the proper order, and it should do so concisely, usually in a single sentence. Superior leads present the necessary facts in the correct sequence and in a succinct manner that encourages readers to continue the story.

IMPORTANCE OF LEADS

Everyone making a living at news writing would agree that the lead is the most important part of the story. The first justification of that statement should be obvious: If a lead doesn't motivate the reader to continue, there *is* no rest of the story for that reader. Dull or confusing leads waste the rest of the writer's work. Other rationale for the importance of the lead deal with theme and tone, pace and establishing the five W's and H. The most revealing evidence for the importance of leads is documented in findings of a research study.[1] Three practicing journalists were part of a case study in which each talked aloud, into a tape recorder, while writing articles for their newspaper. These professional writers spent fully one-third of their article-writing time doing the lead. These weren't beginning writers

[1]Beverley J. Pitts, "Protocol Analysis of the Newswriting Process," *Newspaper Research Journal* 4:12–21 (Fall 1982).

but reporters with several years on the job. They didn't have writer's block. They merely understood that each story deserves an excellent lead. So they spent a third of their writing time writing, rewriting, then editing the lead to make it as good as possible. With the lead in place, the rest of the story, even of a longer story, seemed almost to write itself. The remainder of the article was primarily a task of organizing and transcribing notes.

Practicing reporters confirm that time spent writing leads is well-spent. It must be assumed that the lead writing process is dynamic; a beginner will get better with practice. But even experienced news writers will spend a disproportionate amount of writing time perfecting their story leads.

SIMPLICITY AND SUCCINCTNESS IN LEADS

Satisfying all the points in the definition of a simple lead requires making every word count. Often, several rewrites are necessary to achieve just the lead you want, just the way it should be. Your initial efforts may seem difficult, but your writing will become better with practice.

To develop this talent, a beginning writer should examine carefully the characteristics of an effective lead. The first element is that the lead should tell as much as necessary of the who, what, when, where, why and how of the story.

Crowding all these W's into the lead of the article is too simplistic a technique and a pretty dull way of presenting a news story. By definition, a lead should not be dull. If it were necessary to include all of the five W's, each lead would be too long, violating yet another goal of the lead: be concise. Writing the lead is a process of selecting necessary elements among the five W's for the lead. All depend on story content. Begin writing the lead by determining which of the five W's best emphasizes the important story content.

FOCUSING ON IMMEDIACY

Remember the Chapter 1 discussion of news values. Almost every story can be described in terms of its news values. Some stories really stress only one of the W's or H. For instance, if you are reporting that a rock concert star is performing tonight, you write a "who" lead emphasizing the performing celebrity: Madonna, the sultry pop singer whose controversial lyrics and attire draw national attention, will perform at 8 p.m. at the City Coliseum.

What makes the preceding example a "who" lead is not that it contains *only* the who element. Obviously, it also includes the "what," "where" and "when" elements. It is a "who" lead because it begins with and emphasizes the "who" by giving the singer's name and some more information about her.

If a celebrity is performing in town tonight, expect your readers to be *most* interested in the performer, who he or she is, rather than when or where the concert will be. Consider an example in which the wrong element has been selected for the lead:

> Rusty "Fingers" Thomas, a Coaltown burglar with two previous theft convictions, was apprehended Sunday night while carrying an art treasure from Coaltown City Museum.

Unless Fingers has attained unusual local notoriety for his past exploits or has been the subject of a police manhunt during the past several days, the lead is wrong for the story. Instead of a "who," this should be a "what" lead, such as the following:

> A man holding Coaltown's most valuable art treasure was arrested Sunday night on the steps of Coaltown City Museum.

The facts as given call for an emphasis on the crime itself, the "what" of this story. There's room later in the article to actually name Fingers as the arrestee. In fact, Fingers' identity might not be given until the third or fourth paragraph if

- he was carrying a painting by one of the old masters
- the painting was worth $1 million
- there had been considerable publicity surrounding the purchase of the painting for the museum
- the painting had been purchased only a few days before the arrest.

As the writer, you need to decide which element of the story is the most newsworthy and which element readers will want to know about first. That's the mind set essential in evaluating story facts and determining the lead element. This introduces the inverted pyramid structure of newswriting, in which a news story is pictured as an upside-down pyramid. The most important facts are offered first (in the lead), and the least important facts are relegated to the inverted pyramid's point (the bottom of the story).

EDITING FOR LEAD IMPROVEMENT

If the story is arranged properly, each fact you introduce will be of greater importance than any subsequent ones. The lead will begin with the most important element of the story and proceed through the progressively less-important pieces of information to the end of the first paragraph.

Once that structure is used in the lead, the outline of the story is established. You need only to present more details of the lead, in descending order from the second paragraph through the end. Chapter 4 discusses the inverted pyramid in greater detail, but knowing why journalists order news values in the lead is worthwhile at this point.

Given the following set of facts, which should the lead emphasize?

1. City Council is divided between conservatives and liberals—a situation known to those who follow council news
2. proposals for a new fleet of police squad cars have been discussed the last three weeks
3. in council meeting last night, member Edith Frank, a liberal, moves to accept proposal for $2 million fleet of squad cars
4. conservatives speak against the proposal because of cost; rebuke liberals as reckless spenders
5. after lengthy and heated debate, including some angry name calling, council agrees to a $1.2 million fleet

You might begin with a "what" lead:

City police will get a $1.2 million fleet of new squad cars following heated debate by the City Council Wednesday night.

Pause to consider that this lead focuses on what *will be* rather than what *was*. A lead focusing on what *was* might read:

City police <u>were voted</u> a $1.2 million fleet of new squad cars following heated debate by the City Council Wednesday night.

This kind of lead would have been accurate, but not nearly as good as the first, which keyed on the coming fleet rather than on last night's vote. The better lead is in active voice; the other is in passive voice.

But neither is the best lead for the set of facts presented. The facts call for a "why" lead:

Angry debate by City Council factions ended in a cost compromise Wednesday night for a $1.2 million fleet of new police squad cars.

Such a lead is superior to both earlier leads because it correctly incorporates the key emphasis of what happened: the compromise between fiscal conservatives and liberals on the council. We can assume that the paper already has reported the several police car proposals along with dollar figures, so these lead elements are given a lesser role. Note that the superior lead begins with the angry debate, moves to the compromise, and then incorporates the immediacy of the active voice principle.

How will this story continue after the lead? The logical next paragraph probably would be that a fleet of squad cars had been proposed but that its cost, at $2 million, led to counter proposals by financial conservatives, ending in the decision to go with a less-expensive fleet. Then some quotes and the names of the council members leading the debate might be mentioned because the "who" in this instance is of relatively minor importance.

Here's another set of facts:

1. an early-morning Ravenwood house fire results in the death of Emily Skipworth, 54, a local resident
2. the house is destroyed by the fire, which also causes some damage to two neighboring houses
3. four other members of the family escape the blaze, but Ruth Skipworth, Emily's daughter, is taken to the hospital to be treated for minor burns and smoke inhalation
4. two fire trucks from Precinct Six were called to the scene at 4 a.m.
5. neighbors and firefighters fought the blaze for nearly an hour
6. cause of the fire is unknown at this time

If you decided this should be a "who" lead, you're right. But this lead also demands the "what" element. Although the facts are tragic, in every city of any significant size homes occasionally burn, and people die in such fires. Here's an acceptable lead for the story:

Emily Skipworth, 54, died early this morning as fire destroyed a Ravenwood home.

It is possible not to mention Emily Skipworth by name in the lead, but to begin the second paragraph of the story with the woman's name or hold her name for later in the article. That might be the case in a metropolitan paper, and the lead might be: "A 54–year-old woman died early this morning. . . . " It would still be a "who" lead even if it didn't contain the person's name.

Note that the lead includes few embellishments. This simple, straight news story lead focuses on the two chief elements from the set of facts: a woman died in a house fire. The lead might have been:

> A 54-year-old woman died early this morning as fire ravaged a Ravenwood home in a four-alarm blaze of unknown origin.

But this is crowding the lead with unnecessary elements of the five W's. Also, writers should avoid the urge to add screaming sirens, licking flames or weeping families ("destroyed" is better than "ravaged"). The force of facts carries more impact than do dramatic attempts to create suspense or relate tragedy, although action verbs are a plus.

The reason the fire story must include the "what" as well as the "who" in the lead is that the majority of the early part of the story will deal with the house fire rather than with the woman's death. If there is more to say about the woman—and a good reporter will find and write it—this will probably come at the middle or end of the article. The principle of news value assures us that any person's death is far more consequential than the loss of property. On the other hand, this news story cannot be written around the woman. It must be written about the fire while including the loss of life associated with the fire.

The fire story emphasizes one other point about simple leads. Rarely will a lead contain only one of the five W's and H. In the fire story there are four: "who," "what," "when" and "where." Neither "when" nor "where" is very specific in the lead, but they are present. The order of these elements in the lead is really critical only in the presentation of the two main elements, "who" and "what." The other two elements, "when" and "where," are placed where they fall naturally, to maintain the order of the two most important elements.

Let's tackle another set of facts:

1. a local organization, Moms of Mercy, will hold a fund-raising event next week
2. group is sponsoring a picnic in Merrywood Park featuring, among other events, a balloon face-painting contest
3. entry fee is $5 per contestant, open only to children under age 15
4. contest begins at 9 a.m. Saturday and ends before the picnic lunch, winners announced at 2 p.m., prizes given

5. beginning at noon, the group will sell prepared family picnic baskets and cold drinks
6. Moms of Mercy group has more than 100 local mothers whose main cause is providing funds for needy families

This is the kind of news opportunity most beginning writers are offered. For our purposes, there is no special handling required, just proper arranging of news values in the lead. It is a "what" lead that requires assembly of as many pertinent W's as possible in the lead:

Painting faces on balloons will be the main contest event at the Moms of Mercy fund-raising picnic in Merrywood Park Saturday.

That gets in the "what," the "when," the "who" and the "where." It also orders facts on which the rest of the story can be built simply by amplifying these news elements in later paragraphs. The lead includes the novelty of painting on balloons rather than on canvas, a fact that may entice readers to continue the story rather than looking for another article. The lead could have begun with "The Moms of Mercy will hold . . . " but this has little attraction unless the reader happens to be a member of the organization.

Remember not to impede the reader with unimportant details. For example, a seemingly needed item was omitted from the lead: that only children under age 15 will be allowed to paint balloons in the contest. This point is not critical to the first paragraph. It can be included in the second paragraph, where the writer will add more facts about how the contest is to be handled. A good reporter will have found out specifics such as whether the art is to be done with brushes or finger paints; whether the balloons are to be provided by the Moms or donated; size of the balloons and how the judging will be done; whose idea the contest was; and what the prizes will be. All of these details can be worked into the body of the story. If the article has little consequence for the community, the editor can omit some or all of these details.

We've looked at several lead types using the five W's and H, but "how" leads are different. They almost always begin with an introductory clause, and they are used infrequently. This is because the "how" of a news story is seldom the most important part, or the "how" just may be too complicated to try to work into the story's lead. Here's an example of a "how" lead:

Reunited by an anonymous benefactor, a pair of twins embraced for the first time in 50 years Sunday at Oakdale Manor's lunchroom.

A rare happening, indeed. Beginning the article with the benefactor focuses the lead, and the rest of the story, on how this reunion occurred. It should be a story about bringing the twins together.

This example provides an interesting sidelight to the discussion of simple leads. The twins story lead might begin differently. You might start with the first words uttered when the two recognized each other. Or you could recount the incident resulting in their separation. Those might have been more appropriate and interesting ways to begin this story. The point here, however, is to demonstrate an instance of using the "how" as the major news element in a simple news story.

Journalistic writing requires the ability to place important facts of any news story in the proper order. Every time you start to write, remember to arrange your information in descending order, with the most important news values first. If you work on a few dozen of these simple leads, you may only begin to get the hang of it. Don't be discouraged. Remember those three working journalists who still spend one-third of their writing time on the lead.

Recalling the simple, summary news lead definition, it is evident that there's more to writing a lead than deciding which elements to include and how to arrange their order. Being "as concise as possible" is another aspect of a good lead. Even good writers rarely master (and frequently forget) concise writing.

A rule of thumb in lead writing is to keep this first paragraph within a 30-word maximum. To some writers, 30 words may seem downright verbose because at that length the one-sentence lead might be the longest sentence in the entire article.[2] However, if several facts deserve prominent play in a news story's lead, 30 words aren't many. Beginners should learn to keep their first-paragraph lead well within the 30-word maximum. After years in the business, too often writers forget the excellent reasons for that rule. The journalist's most important reason to limit length in the first paragraph is to avoid cluttering the lead. A jumble of facts thrown at the reader all at once is confusing. There is only so much the mind can comprehend at once, and most readers won't want to work at trying to understand what you've written. They shouldn't have to. If the writer insists on cramming the first paragraph full of every worthy fact, readers won't make it through the lead. All the work put into the rest of the story will be lost. The 30-word guideline reminds writers to select carefully only what is essential. The other important facts can follow in the second or third paragraph.

There is also a visual reason to keep the lead short. A large block of

[2]Harry Stapler, "The One-Sentence/Long-Sentence Habit of Writing Leads and How it Hurts Readership," *Newspaper Research Journal* 7:17–27 (Winter 1985).

type at the beginning of the article strains the eye. The mass of gray type suggests drudgery and work. Readers turn to other, less demanding stories. In broadcast newswriting, a long opening is as discouraging to listeners as the long block of type is to readers.

You should be able to write a lead in fewer than 30 words nearly every time you begin a story. While still learning, count the words of your lead. If you've gone over 30 words, look for ways to decrease the number. Try one of the following three ways.

First, consider which elements of the five W's and H have been included but can be saved for a later paragraph. Maybe you've given too much "who." Can you omit the names and instead use a title or other shorter reference? How much of the information in the next example is critical to the lead?

> John G. Adams, a professor of history at Blackburn University and author of three regional history books, will speak at the Sunshine Presbyterian Church on Second Street tonight at 8 on the topic of Indian relics.

This isn't a long lead, but it certainly packs more than enough information into the first paragraph. Either omit the professor's name or reduce the lengthy identification. The lead is probably not right anyhow. A more appropriate beginning might be: "Secrets to finding Indian relics will be shared by . . . "

A second way to reduce the number of words in the lead is through reorganization, alluded to previously. Often, slightly rearranging the elements produces a lead that is both smoother and less cluttered. You should not move the elements around just to reduce length. If the W's are in the right order, they should stay that way. But unless Adams is at least a local celebrity, this lead should emphasize "what," the topic of the presentation, and should follow with "who," some indication of the person making the presentation.

The last way to reduce words in the lead is the easiest. Delete unnecessary words. Even little words count. In the Adams speech lead, change "a professor of history at Blackburn University" to "a Blackburn University history professor." More words are saved by writing "the Second Street Sunshine Presbyterian Church" or by omitting "Second Street." Save it for later in the story. A more concise lead is:

> A Blackburn University history professor will share his Indian relic-finding secrets in a talk at the Sunshine Presbyterian Church at 8 p.m.

Now concise with fewer than 30 words, the lead gives your reader a feeling of immediacy. This is a tone you'd like to capture in your news articles. Better yet, if the story begins with "what," the lead is even more improved:

> Secrets to finding Indian relics will be shared in a Blackburn University history professor's talk at the Sunshine Presbyterian Church at 8 tonight.

Again, shorter is better. We can get the same information across—the necessary information for the lead—with just a little omitting, reorganization and word deletion. But be careful. Don't delete so many words that your sentence becomes grammatically incorrect. Some pronouns, articles and prepositions are needed to make complete sentences. Remember the three working journalists striving to improve their leads. They are trying to include just the right news elements, to put those elements in the proper order and to ensure that every unnecessary word is deleted. This process is repeated with each lead they write. They concentrate on the first 30 words (or less) because they know how important the story lead is.

IDENTIFYING NEWS SOURCES

Leads presented so far haven't dealt with a particularly important element news writers must consider in all stories. News is nonfiction. News relates to something that actually happened, is happening or will happen. In virtually every case, the journalist is a reporter rather than merely a writer. Reporters are not usually at the scene of an arrest, not in the room when governors make decisions, not in the building when it catches fire or at the lake when the largest bass is caught. This information, and hundreds of other such stories, must be obtained after the fact. Talk either with people who were at the scene or with those in authority whose business it is to have the needed information: the police sergeant on duty when the arrestee is brought in, the governor or governor's press secretary, the fire chief. Although by necessity the reporter interviews the fisherman who caught the largest bass, it's a good idea to talk with the dock owner, the fish-and-game agent or some of the old-timers at the bait store who may be more objective about the monster bass. A "big fish" story is a prime example for not relying only on witnesses at the scene.

The reporter obtains much of the story information secondhand, from someone in authority who ought to know the facts. Telling readers where

Reporters interview a metropolitan police commissioner, an authority on local crime conditions and specific criminal acts. This source will be identified early in the resulting news story.

or from whom the information came is called attribution. Attributing the source of information is a cardinal journalistic rule.[3] Try to include the source in the lead, especially when readers must realize that the reporter could *not* have obtained the information without a source. Because the source of news usually is not as instrumental to the story as the five W's and H, the source often is the last element of the lead:

> Hillsboro will be the site of a $5 million tire plant, the mayor's office announced today.

A medical announcement lead might be:

> The nation's oldest liver transplant recipient was listed in satisfactory condition at noon today, according to Barnes Hospital chief surgeon Dr. Herbert B. Morton.

---

[3]In extreme circumstances reporters may "protect" sources by refusing to divulge the source's name. Those situations involve legal and ethical considerations discussed in Chapter 17.

Although in most instances the source should be given in the lead, a full identification is not always necessary in the first paragraph, particularly if source identification generates clutter. For instance, in the liver transplant lead it is permissible to omit the doctor's name:

> The nation's oldest liver transplant recipient was listed in satisfactory condition at noon today, according to a Barnes Hospital surgeon.

Readers will have no doubt that the source is an official at Barnes Hospital, so the surgeon can be named in a later paragraph.

Here's another example of partial identification in the first paragraph, followed by full identification immediately thereafter:

> The largest heroin bust in the city, netting drugs valued at $28 million, was completed by dawn this morning, police reported.
> Capt. Darwin Edwards of the vice squad said his unit had been following the case for nearly six months before closing in on . . .

Proper punctuation usually requires that a comma be used to separate attribution from the rest of the lead, depending on the construction of the lead paragraph. Here are some examples illustrating both attribution forms:

> A murder indictment has been returned against a local pharmacist held in the drug overdose case of an Iona teenager, according to the Grand Jury's report.

> School Board member Edgar Rosen announced today he will retire from his position at the end of the current school term and "go fishing in the tropics."

> A recount of Ward Six ballots has been authorized to settle the disputed mayor's race outcome, City Election Commissioner Angel G. Simon said.

> Fire officials have ruled arson in the case of last month's wharf warehouse blaze that resulted in the death of a night watchman.

The only aspect of an effective summary lead still to be discussed is how it should entice readers to keep reading the story. Of course, many concepts already introduced are designed to lure readers into the rest of the story. But there should also be an element of action, intensity or brightness in the writing that makes the lead more compelling. This is the single concept of lead writing that rules can't help cultivate. The best tip that can be given as you begin your lead writing practice is *keep your leads simple*. Not every lead has to be brilliant.

Most often, an effective lead includes the news values in the proper order and is short. Order and brevity encourage readership. Unusual "devices" to increase reader interest are not recommended for simple story leads. Leave the devices for the more complicated articles requiring complex lead treatment.

Some beginners may have the idea that a way to get readers into the rest of the story is to omit something important from the lead. The "teaser," a more advanced form, does just that. However, the story must warrant this kind of treatment. Simple news stories don't. Never withhold an important element from the five W's and H as a ploy to draw in the reader. Chances are it will do the opposite.

The impossibility of neatly describing ways of drawing the reader into the story with a lead doesn't take the writer off the hook. Try always to write your lead in a way that encourages the reader to stick with the rest of the story. Take the time and care to make your lead as good as it can be, and you will have achieved enticement, the last aspect of lead writing. Spending some time with the writing exercises will help you reach your goal.

SUMMARY

Everyone making a living at news writing would agree that the lead is the most important part of the story. If a lead doesn't motivate the reader to continue, there *is* no rest of the story for that reader.

Simple, summary leads are the most frequently used news story lead types. They should accomplish the following goals:

- tell the reader as many of the five W's and H as necessary for the news story being written;
- order the five W's and H from the most important to the least important news value;
- be concise—probably fewer than 30 words;
- encourage readers to continue reading the story.

In practice, the most difficult aspect of simple, summary lead writing is ordering the five W's and H by news value importance. Almost every story can be described in terms of its news values. Decide which element of the story is the most newsworthy and which element readers will want to know about first. A lead that is arranged properly begins with the most important story element and proceeds through the progressively less-important pieces of information to the end of the first paragraph. Using that structure in the lead establishes the outline for the rest of the story.

To make the lead more concise, try these three procedures:

1. remove elements of the five W's and H that can be saved for a later paragraph;
2. without sacrificing news value order, rearrange lead elements to produce a smoother and less cluttered lead;
3. delete all unnecessary words, but not so many words to thwart the sentence's grammatical integrity.

The journalist's final lead consideration is attribution. Because reporters seldom are eyewitnesses to news, sources provide most information. Telling readers where or from whom the news came is called attribution. Include the news source in the lead, usually as the last element, and usually set off by a comma.

Thinking it Through

EXERCISE 2.1

Leads One

The following are *rough* notes for story leads. For each set of notes, list the five W's, then number the first *three* for order of importance ("1" is most important). [Exercises may be done on a separate sheet of paper or VDT screen by writing the example number, listing the five W's and then ranking the three most important ones.]

Write a summary lead sentence for each example after verifying facts for "local" stories in the City Directory (page 439). Anything that cannot be found in the directory should be considered correct as given.

A   private plane crashes into Green Mountain in blinding rainstorm Friday night; two passengers, A.D. Brown and Walter R. Smith of Lakewood, Calif., found dead in wreckage early this morning; state police removed bodies this morning.

Who: _____   _____

What: _____   _____

When: _____   _____

Where: _____   _____

Why: _____   _____

Source: _____

LEAD:

B Herman Scruggs, 84, hospitalized at Lady of Mercy Hospital with fractured collarbone; suffered injury in City Park; fell making touchdown; playing quarterback in football game between school youngsters; "drafted when one team lacked a player," Scruggs said

Who: _____   _____

What: _____   _____

When: _____   _____

Where: _____   _____

Why: _____   _____

Source: _____

LEAD:

C Helen Grimes, 9, chosen city's Junior Miss in contest finals Saturday night at Bayside Auditorium; 30 finalists competed after field of nearly 200 entrants reduced past weeks; wins $1,000 prize and new wardrobe from local department store; talent was blues singing; parents C. William Grimeses, 535 Riverside

Who: _____   _____

What: _____   _____

When: _____   _____

Where: _____   _____

Why: _____   _____

Source: _____

LEAD:

D   fire destroys home of Mr. and Mrs. C. Robert Dulles, 222 Birch St., while couple at movies Thursday night; dog, Spottie, left in basement, perishes in fire; Mrs. Geraldine Dulles collapses upon return from movies; frame house enveloped in flames when firefighters arrive; faulty electrical wiring believed cause Fire Chief Arnold Limpert says

Who: _____   _____

What: _____   _____

When: _____   _____

Where: _____   _____

Why: _____   _____

Source: _____

LEAD:

Writing Practice

EXERCISE 2.2

Leads Two

Write a simple lead for each of the following fact sets without *adding* any information to the lead. Verify "local" story facts in the City Directory. Anything that cannot be found in the directory should be considered correct as given. The lead you turn in should be your best effort, so rough it out first and polish it before submission. All leads must be fewer than 30 words.

A   two men fleeing from a quick-stop market are arrested by police officers Will Jennings and Dean Robinson after a short chase outside the building; arrested are Oliver Priceton, 22, and Dale Richardson, 19; market manager G.R. Raleigh, 53, said the two were robbing him when officers arrived; about $300 found stuffed into the shirts of the two men arrested.

B new firm to open here in Cherryvale next month; it is the first branch of Exquisite Candies to open outside New York City as Exquisite Candies starts franchising 100 stores across the nation this year; franchise rights cost $50,000 each—the entire 100 are already sold; local store is first slated because parents of founder live here; they are Mr. and Mrs. Eddie C. Smythe; store to employ five.

C 40-foot trailer truck carrying load of live chickens jackknifes on Interstate 90 loop in town; driver injured, taken to local hospital; chickens strewn across all lanes in 5:30 p.m. rush hour; traffic backed up five miles; scene chaotic as police, city work crews and some local motorists try to round up chickens.

D blaze at warehouse on outskirts of town destroys estimated $500,000 in new color television sets and causes about $200,000 damage to warehouse; Fire Chief Arnold Limpert says fire was arson; empty gasoline containers found outside building; tv's were import models; recent strikes in city about U.S. versus imported goods; fire began about 2 a.m., now 7 a.m., need story by 9 a.m. for first edition of this afternoon's paper.

E City Council meets and takes following action: (a) approves purchases of three new city dumpsters; (b) sets date of City Father's Festival; (c) approves consolidation of city's three high schools into a single high school . . . all to be in Central High's building starting with fall term; (d) purchases land for $450,000 as possible new airport site; (e) seats Wilma O'Malley as new member of council; meeting ends at 9:45 p.m., write for morning paper.

F U.S. Air Force to double size of base near city; Col. Richard Janes announces personnel to go from 5,000 to 10,000 as base adds testing of experimental fighter jets to present mission of training maintenance personnel.

EXERCISE 2.3

Simple Leads Three

Write simple leads for each of the fact sets without adding any facts to those given. Write the best under-30-word lead you can after polishing your effort on scratch paper or in trials using typewriter or VDT screen.

A police identify body of young girl as Sue Ellen Higgins, 12, missing for three days; boys find body near drainage ditch about two blocks from St. Mary's School where Higgins went to school; no cause of death known at this time; body found at 9 a.m., write for this afternoon's paper.

B touring circus to open tonight at 7; Ringling Brothers Barnum & Bailey; comes to town once a year, stays five days; tickets $5 adults, $2.50 children under 13; located at Warwick Park, corner Walnut and Second.

C American Medical Association Committee on Drug Abuse meets here at 8 tonight and approves report linking marijuana with traffic fatalities; will recommend to AMA national convention that major study be undertaken nationally; write for tomorrow morning's paper.

D you are city hall reporter for afternoon paper in Del Rio, Texas; Mayor Alvin C. Baker calls you in this morning in September and says he has a story for you. Jose G. Verde, who has been assistant city manager for four years, has resigned to accept post as city manager of Dallas, Texas, effective Oct. 1.

E you are an education beat reporter for the morning paper. Your friend Dr. Henry Jackson, head of the Department of Geography at State College, suggests you contact one of his faculty members about a new book. You meet Dr. Clinton H. White, associate professor of geography, who says he recently finished writing a college text, "Geography of the Western States." He says word has come from Universal Publishing Co. of Chicago. Universal will publish his book. It will be on the market in time for this spring's classes.

F Patrol Officer Fred Dennam of the Los Angeles Police Department tells you a car was damaged Saturday night; lucky it didn't result in multiple deaths on the freeway. Peter S. Glaviano, 3819 N. Clay St., was driving home on the Santa Ana Freeway about 5 p.m. when his windshield was smashed by a brick. Glaviano said he saw two boys peering down from an overpass as his windshield shattered. He said he lost control of the car . . . it may have spun several times . . . and finally smashed into the innermost lane guardrail. No other vehicles hit his car and Glaviano was unhurt as Dennam's patrol car arrived at the scene. Write story for your afternoon paper.

Advanced Leads

With practice, the straight five W's and H news lead is relatively easy to handle. However, you may write several dozen before becoming proficient. *Proficient* implies that you've conquered the technical and creative aspects of lead writing. You can sit at your VDT or typewriter to begin a story and feel confident you'll be able to arrange the elements in the right order following all rules of simple, summary lead writing.

You know you're going to have a good lead by the time you've had a chance to edit it once or twice. Reaching that stage is quite an achievement, but total success is more difficult because a simple five W lead fits only about three out of four news stories.

Fortunately, journalistic writing is more than merely hammering out five W leads. You can imagine how dull and repetitious each news story would be for the reader, viewer or listener and, just as importantly, for you, the writer. The subtle complexities of journalistic writing make the process interesting, although more difficult for beginners. Each set of story facts suggests its own lead treatment which, in some instances, emerges as something other than a simple, summary lead.

One principle in moving beyond simple leads, then, is that the set of facts in each story suggests a lead treatment type. If you select a simple lead for a story that should have a more advanced lead treatment, your lead will have less impact, less sparkle, and it will trigger less reader interest than one of the more advanced treatments outlined in Figure 3.1. If you err by using an advanced treatment for a story that should be a simple lead, your lead may seem forced or may confuse readers.

Advanced Lead Treatments:

- **Quotes** – direct, indirect and fragments
- **Narrative** – story-telling device
- **Descriptive** – scene-setting device

Advanced Lead Gimmicks:

- **Question** – usually an unnecessary crutch
- **Teaser** – potential problems with truth
- **Freak** – oddity lead for unusual stories

Complex Leads:

- **Multiple-events** – joins several equal news elements
- **Tie-back** – reminds readers of related past event
- **Point-counterpoint** – controversial views contrasted
- **Still-to-come** – most recent event in an ongoing story

Figure 3.1   Advanced and complex lead types

Another principle of advanced leads is that journalists do not always use the same category title for a particular lead type. For instance, both *simple* and *summary* have been used here to indicate a lead with story facts presented in the first paragraph in descending order of importance.

The variety of terms used to describe leads is a reflection of the richness and the intricacy of advanced lead types. These are not distinct or fixed, and there are recognized combinations of several types. You may develop a new lead type someday or write a lead that defies categorization. The advanced lead categories provided here can help you recognize basic distinctions that should aid your early efforts. But they aren't intended to lock you into strict patterns.

A final characteristic of advanced leads is that they may extend deeper into the story than merely the first paragraph. Lead elements can run into the second, third or even fourth paragraph of the article. This certainly is different from the simple lead, which normally includes all of the necessary W's and H in the first one or two paragraphs.

QUOTES AS LEADS

Because so many news stories emerge from live sources through interviews, press conferences, speeches, etc., reporters have ample opportunity to consider using quotes as leads. The following are two schools of thought about quote leads:

1. So few quotes satisfy the requirements of an effective lead that journalists should never use a quote lead.
2. Few quotes result in effective leads, but those that do should certainly be used.

This presentation acknowledges the rarity of effective quotes for leads, but it reviews three lead forms that might be considered when a potent quote emerges: direct quotes, indirect quotes and fragmentary quotes.

Direct Quote Lead

Direct quote leads are used primarily on speech stories. They can be good if the quote is succinct and effective. As these hedging remarks imply, few quotes meet the criteria of being both succinct and effective. Here is an example of one that is *neither:*

> "Our own community has some of the finest farmland in the country and we should all be more cognizant of the fact when we speak with business colleagues from other counties and other states," Johnny Whitehouse said in a speech to the Lions Club here Wednesday.

Never mind that Whitehouse's statement is dull and probably not fully reflective of the *theme* of his speech to the Lions. It is not succinct. The lead would have been better had the statement been paraphrased rather than quoted directly. If Whitehouse talked to the Lions Club—a community group of business leaders in most cities—and this statement was the most notable point he made, chances are the speech wasn't worthy of reporting at all. If we give Whitehouse the benefit of the doubt and concede he probably had remarks worth quoting in a news story, then surely this is *not* the quote to use. Here's a better selection for a quote lead:

> "Agriculture is Maywood's largest employer and the industry that provides the most tax dollars to this county," Johnny Whitehouse told members of the Lions Club Wednesday.

If there is a *strong, succinct, theme-setting* quote for the lead, use it. Listen for such a quote in reporting other news events. If a council member uses one at a meeting, a company vice president uses one during an interview or a witness uses one about an event on the street, lead with it and do so proudly. Just be sure the quote meets all three criteria for a quote lead.

Besides selecting the effective quote, the news writer must decide how to structure the attributive statement. There's a tendency to record the quote alone and then to write something like "So said Johnny Whitehouse in a speech to the Lions Club Wednesday." Overcome the "so said" urge. It's a poor construction for attribution. Consider the following structures instead:

"It's the brightest light in my life," said Jane Elmore, a blind skydiver, as she climbed into the Piper Cub this morning to open the Handicapped Athletes Sports Spectacular.

"Some guys frame the first dollar they ever made in a business. I still wear my first penny in my loafer."
Ralph S. Troth, owner of Trothstep Leisure Shoes, clicked his heels and pointed to a bright copper penny wedged in the slot of his right penny loafer as Chamber of Commerce members craned their necks for a peek during today's luncheon meeting.

"The best therapy for adults over age 70 is to care for a pet," Dr. Waldo T. Stahl, City Hospital's Geriatrics director, said as he stroked one of his patients' cats.

"I won't tolerate 50 homeless families," the head of Chicago's housing authority told Mayor George Brown. "If the city doesn't find a place for them by 5 p.m., it can pay their hotel bills tomorrow."

Indirect Quote Lead

Since people usually don't say things that provide strong, succinct, theme-setting quotes for your lead, the more likely lead presentation is an indirect quote lead such as the following:

A skydiver who was blinded in an automobile accident said her sport epitomized handicapped people's triumph over physical adversity.

Mayor Art Dupree chided city contractors for what he termed excessive bid figures on street improvements the city will need this fall.

The examples suggest that indirect quote leads are similar to simple or summary leads. Both provide an overview of the essential elements of the story. What makes them advanced lead types is that they focus on the essence of the quote without providing what usually would be considered necessary W's. Emphasizing the statement gives the reader key information and avoids crowding the story's first paragraph. In these two examples, and in most indirect quote leads, the "when" and "where" may have to wait until the second or third paragraph.

Fragmentary Quote Lead

Occasionally a portion of a quote satisfies the requirements of an effective lead. Examples are:

> Lt. Gov. Janice L. Gwin used her office "as a magnet for personal materialism," according to her opponent in the November governor's race.

> Rodney Fuller "left a legion of activists for the handicapped that will alter American corporate policy," the Rev. Stanley Kerr told mourners at Grace Episcopal Church this morning.

Quote fragments have the advantage of retaining the speaker's unique phrasing while omitting unnecessary verbiage that would render the complete quote unusable because of its length. However, writers must work quote fragments into the sentence smoothly so readers aren't confused by the juxtaposition of quoted and non-quoted elements in the same passage.

Remember that any of these quote lead forms should be used with discretion. The most common journalistic use of quotes is after the lead, to elaborate and amplify a summary or paraphrase in the story lead.

NARRATIVE LEADS

Often neglected, evidence shows that narrative leads could be used more frequently.[1] Readers indicate that narrative story treatment is perfectly acceptable, easily understood and sometimes more interesting than the traditional five W lead.

Narratives begin the story the same way a person relates the story to a

[1]Lewis Donohew, "Newswriting Styles: What Arouses the Reader?" *Newspaper Research Journal* 3:2 (January 1982):3–6. See also, R. Thomas Berner, "Commentary: The Narrative and the Headline," *Newspaper Research Journal* 4:3 (Spring 1983):33–40; Gerald Stone, *Examining Newspapers: What Research Reveals About America's Newspapers* (Newbury Park, CA: Sage Publications, 1987), pp. 49–51.

friend. Instead of beginning, "John got four stitches as the result of a car accident at the corner of Elm and Segwood Monday at 4 p.m.," the narrator of the tale might begin, "John was on his way to a downtown appointment yesterday and was running a little bit late, so he . . . " While omitting trivial details, the narrative lead presents the news article in story form. Beginning with the action of the story, it relies heavily on that action to quickly draw the reader or listener into the story. Some, but not all, of the five W's are present. Here are examples:

> The courier told the chauffeur not to stop for roadblocks or military patrols but to take him to the embassy by the most immediate route available.
> His leather briefcase, handcuffed to his wrist, contained an executive order that might save the lives of thousands of Americans in war-torn Beirut.

> If all went well, a single radio command would be given and more than 40 detectives and uniformed police would converge on the targeted apartment building.
> Moments later this would be remembered as the city's largest drug bust, or forgotten as one more waste of time and tax dollars on false tips from street informants.

Either of the examples could have been handled with a simple lead focusing on outcomes, but neither would have been as reader-involving as the narrative structure presented. Some news writers shun the narrative because it relies on a writing style associated with novels or thrillers. But it's difficult to imagine a stronger lead than the narrative for the set of facts given. Research shows that readers find this presentation clear and appropriate.

DESCRIPTIVE LEADS

Similar to the narrative, a descriptive lead uses the story-telling approach but focuses on the setting instead of the action. Though seldom used, the descriptive lead paints a word picture as either an important news element or a device to increase reader interest. When appropriate to the tone of the story, descriptive leads can be extremely effective. Here are examples:

> Fashionable rattan chairs and tables bobbed like corks on a fishing line in the lobby's waist-deep water. Ceiling sprinklers still

dripped intermittently into the pool below with a bip-bip-bip . . . the only sound in a sea of expensive debris.

It was nearly 12 hours after fire gutted the plush Twin Towers office complex on Biltmore Road. No lives were lost, but the bill has been estimated at $15 million.

Three small children, each with close-cropped hair growing in irregular clumps, play on the porch. A fourth is held in her arms, and she pats its back when it coughs.

The children are the only signs that this quiet suburban street is the center of the latest toxic waste controversy, and Anita Grace's story is the most traumatic in the neighborhood.

Descriptive and narrative leads might very well exceed the recommended 30-word first-paragraph limit. Action building and scene setting require more space than most other lead types, but they are no excuse for 100-word openings. However, these two advanced lead types are not likely to perform their tasks in 30 words or less. Break the information into smaller paragraphs (as in the examples) or let them run a little longer in the first graf. Because the descriptive and narrative are unusual forms, the reader will probably regard them as novelties rather than cumbersome impositions.

QUESTION LEADS

One of the least frequently used advanced lead types (and one of the most controversial) is substituting a question for the normal simple lead. The opening question is followed by elements containing the five W's and H, and the normal simple lead may actually be in the second paragraph, as in the first of these examples:

What do you say when the Internal Revenue Service pays you a house call?

James B. Cortland, 44, answered his door toting a pistol that left IRS investigator Iris D. Treadwell, 32, with a wound in her right hand.

Where does the umpire keep all those shiny, new baseballs he provides during a big league game?

The first example is called a "direct address" question lead because of the specific "you" reference to the reader. This IRS lead emphasizes the main problem with question leads: They are usually unnecessary contrivances that hamper rather than help the story. In the IRS story, the second graf really makes an acceptable lead by itself, or the lead might have been: "An Internal Revenue Service agent was shot in her outstretched hand when she paid an uninvited house call on a local man Tuesday." The farcical element can be captured in a short summary lead without the opening question.

The baseball example is an "indirect address" lead because the word *you* is implied. The question really asks, "Where do you suppose the umpire keeps all those shiny new baseballs . . . ?" This example suggests that a question lead is used best as a device to tweak the reader's curiosity, to pull readers into a story of marginal interest.

Rarely seen on hard news stories, the question lead appears most frequently in features, and especially in broadcast media writing, where it can perk the listener's attention as a prelude to the hard facts of the news story.

TEASER LEADS

The writer of a teaser lead purposely teases the reader by omitting an important element. Most writers go even further by drawing the reader's attention to the omission. Here are a couple of teaser examples:

> Today he destroyed more than $20 million in property, a figure surpassing his previous record and more property value than he ever dreamed he'd be paid to obliterate.

> Candice Landry testified that married men who visit prostitutes constitute the nation's largest market of victims for con artists and blackmailers.

Either of these two leads is guaranteed to draw the reader into the story just to find out what it's about. Is the property destroyer a demolition derby winner, a dynamite expert, a building dismantler or something else entirely? The reader must continue to find out.

The combination of sex, crime and a teaser lead in the second example presents an almost irresistible lure to readers. Why are married men the largest victim market? What does prostitution have to do with it? How do con artists and blackmailers fit in? Who is Candice Landry, and how does she know?

Although the teaser lead can be a powerful device to hook the reader, there are some drawbacks. The teaser is definitely a contrivance: a purposeful ploy to engage the reader by withholding important story facts from the lead. Teasing the reader can backfire when the ploy galls rather than goads. If the tease is not deftly executed or the payoff (the information withheld from the lead) not worth the wait, readers may feel tricked or cheated.

Another entire area of newswriting considerations must be mentioned with teaser leads. Throughout the article, journalists must adhere to their responsibility of telling the truth. A news writer does not have permission to trick or to lie to the reader. Facts can be embellished only within the limits of honesty. News writers may not cross the thin line between teasing and lying.

In the example of the man who destroyed $20 million in property, a change in one word would cross the barrier between teasing and deceit: "Today he <u>confessed</u> to destroying more than . . . " Inserting "confessed" in that lead may seem only a subtle difference. After all, the lead is a teaser. But "confessed" carries the connotation that the man is engaged in an illegal activity. If the property destroyer performs a task for which he earns a fee legally, the writer is *not* permitted to suggest something else.

FREAK LEADS

The term *freak lead* applies to any lead type so unusual that the reader is actually challenged to read on. A host of possibilities fall into the freak lead category, from beginning the article with a riddle to starting with a line from a song or poem. Here are a few examples:

> If a tree falls in the forest and nobody is there to hear it, does the fall make a noise?
> The answer to this philosophical question may be learned from International Paper Co.'s innovations combining robotics with its lumberjacking operations.

> Girls just like to have sun.
> Evelyn Wellen, the Los Angeles fashion designer credited with Americanizing the string bikini, said her new line of women's bathing suits will be made of fishnet material over a flesh-colored fabric.

"Here lies
Seil Ereh
1891–1981"
If this mirror-image epitaph seems too eerie to be real, rest in peace.

The tombstone was found by a caretaker at Boston's Northside Cemetery last week, but is being chalked up to either a poor-taste prankster or a fraternity initiation ritual.

Z-A-N-Y. Ten-point Z on a double letter score; four-point Y on the triple word.

That was the 78-point play that capped Tuesday's high school Scrabble tournament and gave Woodridge its first trophy in the playoff held locally for nearly a quarter of a century.

These examples only show the wide range of freak lead possibilities. The first two are obvious tactics used to pull the reader into these stories because a different presentation might not have enough drawing power. The last two examples are better freak techniques because in each instance the set of facts lends itself to a freak lead: Oddity stories encourage odd lead treatments.

The six advanced lead types covered in the preceding discussion are the most easily identifiable alternatives to the simple five W's and H lead. More difficult sets of news story facts suggest complex lead alternatives. While simple leads normally include all the necessary W's and H in the first or second paragraph, advanced leads permit delaying some news elements until the third or fourth paragraph. Complex leads may stretch the necessary news elements even deeper into the story.

Complex leads are the right choice for complicated stories or for stories in which time impinges on the news element. We can look at a couple of complex leads derived from related incidents occurring at about the same time.

MULTIPLE-EVENTS LEADS

Here is a set of facts with closely related incidents but with one incident deserving a little more prominence in the story than the others:

In its weekly meeting, the City Council approves the annual budget. Controversy surrounded several budget provisions during the past

Flames erupting through the roof of a building force Boston firefighters to retreat down a ladder. Stories about major fires that burn through the night are likely to receive complex leads, possibly a still-to-come, multiple-event or even a tie-back if a rash of such fires has plagued a city.

few months, with the pro and con arguments debated by the council and reported by local media. Because the city charter's budget approval deadline is tomorrow, council members reached consensus at the meeting to avoid possible legal entanglements of missing the deadline. Controversial points included $5 million for a city services contract; $8 million for city employee pay raises and $14 million as the city's contribution to a federal highway renovation program.

If you tried to include all of these points individually, you'd have a 50-word lead that would confuse the reader. Instead of offering all major points, write an overview of the situation, stressing the most important news element:

The City Council met its budget deadline Thursday as members reached consensus to approve $27 million in controversial line items.

In one respect, this appears to be a simple lead. Several necessary news elements are included: (1) the approval deadline was met; (2) the controversy was settled; (3) $27 million in appropriations were approved. The who, what, when, where and elements of why and how are there. But the lead is actually a multiple-event lead, an umbrella of events that occurred at the meeting. Since there isn't room in the first paragraph to list three major line items in the City Council's controversy, work them into the second or third paragraph.

The writer will probably devote one or more paragraphs of the story to the consequences of not meeting the budget approval deadline. The story will include quotes from individual council members, particularly those who led the consensus move. Although the reader learns the essence of the story from the first paragraph alone, many individual lead elements must wait until several grafs into the story. The City Council story is complicated. While the lead may seem short and simple, it is actually complex.

Another example providing outcomes of a chain of related events follows in this set of story facts:

> A two-day-old labor strike at Premium Parts Inc. has resulted in these events of the afternoon and evening: two fires were started in storage buildings owned by the company; there was a fight in front of the plant's gates between pickets and newly hired security guards; police were called to stop strikers from destroying the firm's boxed products at a railroad loading site on the other side of town; two corporation officers resigned at the close of business; the mayor announced she is considering asking the governor to call out the National Guard; the chief of police ordered a 10 p.m. curfew in the plant's immediate area.

> City law enforcement and fire fighters worked through the night Friday to combat an outbreak of violence and vandalism related to the strike at Precision Parts Inc.
>
> Developments during the day included resignations of two Precision officials, a 10 p.m. curfew called for the plant area and a suggestion by Mayor Carol Howard that the governor might be asked to send the National Guard.

Note that this multiple-events lead mentions no specific incidents at all until the second paragraph. Enumeration of the acts of violence and vandalism may extend to the third graf or even later in the story. A real tragedy, such as a death during the fight or fires, would change the lead considerably. In that event, begin with the death in a first paragraph, similar to a simple lead, and use part of the overview treatment in the second graf. A death alters the set of facts presented, adding an element that deserves more attention than others in a relatively equal set of facts. Such a lead might have been:

> A local man was killed Friday during a fight outside the gates of strike-ridden Precision Parts Inc.
> Frank O. Reeves, 56, an assembly plant foreman, died in one of the stormy incidents that brought city police and firefighters to scenes of violence and vandalism.
> Related strike actions included the resignation of two company officials, a 10 p.m. curfew in the plant area and the suggestion that the National Guard might be called in.

Although this story begins with a simple five W's lead, elements extend through the first three paragraphs, forming an overview after the five W's focusing on Reeves' death.

As seen in the two examples of multiple-event leads, a variety of news happenings from a minor accident to a major hurricane may suggest using such leads.

Here is another multiple-event set of facts with a slightly different twist. The writer must synthesize an outcome for the reader:

> Zoning board approves rezoning a square block of dilapidated downtown buildings from offices to retail sales and multiple housing. Rezoning was sought by a New York City investment firm that has indicated it will build a $60 million hotel and ground-level shopping mall. The firm has already received city investment tax credit approval for the project and has announced it will begin demolition and construction when it raises $15 million of the total price from local investors.

> Milwaukee is one step closer today to a $60 million downtown hotel and mall following rezoning of a square city block of old buildings.

Again, this resembles the simple lead, but is really much more complex. The news is not property rezoning approval, although that was the only discrete event occurring today. The lead should reflect that another link was added to the chain of events culminating in a face lift for the downtown area. The next graf would recap previous events that cleared the way for the development and would mention the remaining hurdle of local financing. A third graf might disclose demolition and construction schedules or detail the day's rezoning decision. The construction start is saved for later in the article. This multiple-event lead differs from the two preceding examples because the writer provides an overview to give the reader needed perspective. Instead of merely learning that rezoning was approved, the reader gets the full scope of how today's news event is part of a larger, continuing event. Providing perspective is another way of saying that the journalist helps interpret events for the reader. Interpretation doesn't hinder fairness or objectivity; it is part of a journalist's responsibility to accuracy.

The idea of continuing events prompts mention of the other types of complex leads. They are complex because the facts on which they are based must be juxtaposed with time.

TIE-BACK LEADS

Often called a "second-day" lead, a tie-back is a lead that updates news developments tied to a previous event. The event may have occurred as recently as yesterday or as long as a year ago. Many possible news stories fall into this tie-back category: the arrestee who comes to trial months later; measures that official bodies discuss and then vote on after the bills come from committee; projects announced, begun, then completed; criminals caught long after the crime was reported; businesses that open and either fold or flourish. Here are examples:

A teacher pay raise was signed into law today by Gov. Liz Clinton, whose campaign included a promise to veto any measures that might result in higher state taxes.

Opponents of the pay raise have said it will result in a 5 percent tax increase.

Following two previous unsuccessful attempts to cross the Atlantic Ocean in a 16-foot sailboat, Angela Sorrells docked Saturday at a sunny Spanish shore.

Soybean prices, which nearly tripled during the summer drought, tumbled the maximum daily allowable 25 cents in the opening moments of today's commodity market trading.

A 38-year-old man who spent more than half his life in prison on robbery convictions was shot and killed today during a holdup at Joyland Liquor Store, police said.

In these examples, readers might be given the current news (soybean prices dropping or a holdup man being killed) without any tie-back information. But journalists who know that their purpose is to help readers fully understand the news will agree that the tie-back elements belong in the leads of these stories.

POINT-COUNTERPOINT LEADS

Often called a "contrast" lead, the point-counterpoint lead involves a controversy with at least two clearly defined points of view. Many stories involving controversy require the writer to include both sides of the argument in the lead. This approach is superior to giving one side in the first graf and saving the other side for the second or for a later portion of the story, which destroys objectivity. Point-counterpoint leads can, however, continue through several opening paragraphs, depending on the complexity of the views presented. Here are two examples of point-counterpoint leads:

School bus drivers called in sick instead of reporting at their scheduled pickup routes this morning to protest the school district's refusal to allow them to form a union.

School Superintendent Barbara Porter said she will meet with the School Board today and urge job termination of every driver who cannot produce evidence of seeing a physician.

"Organized demonstrations such as this sick-in are exactly what we promised parents would be prevented," Porter said.

Dean H. Jones Jr., spokesman for the drivers, called the sick-in a legitimate use of non-violent protest.

The Game and Fish Commission today delayed deer hunting season until the Legislature votes on a measure requiring all hunting license applicants to prove they own an orange safety vest.

Still in committee in the State Senate, the orange vest bill has the backing of wildlife officials and state troopers but is being opposed by both the National Rifle Association and the American Civil Liberties Union as a measure that stifles freedom of choice.

These leads are complex because the writer needs to clue the reader in to a controversy-in-progress as early in the article as possible. Presenting both viewpoints avoids the perception of bias if the writer selects one rather than the other view as the lead. Point-counterpoint leads are not used on stories with more than two distinct views. Three or more viewpoints would produce confusion and crowd the lead.

STILL-TO-COME LEADS

A continuing story with incomplete events presents special news opportunity. The journalist must bring readers up to date on recent developments and relate through the still-to-come lead that all the action is not yet over. Such story treatment often results from news deadlines. Journalists don't receive a news package tied in a neat bow when the presses are ready to run or when the producer gives the on-air cue. Writers necessarily anticipate deadlines and provide the latest happenings while acknowledging that more are likely to come.

>   Police were still searching the woods behind Booneville Park early this afternoon for two armed gunmen who robbed a pawnshop at Fifth and Main today.

>   The jury remained in deliberation at midnight in the case of a local mother accused of abandoning her 3-week-old child in a ladies room at a fast food restaurant.

>   Randy Johnston, 32, who refused treatment for a stab wound he received in County Jail Tuesday, remained in critical condition Friday night as hospital authorities seek a court order to treat him.

>   Samuel R. O'Roark has state lottery officials in a quandary after announcing earlier today he will refuse his $1.25 million sweepstakes prize to keep his present job as a racehorse trainer.

In the still-to-come lead, as in all complex lead treatments, the writer looks objectively at story facts and puts them in perspective for the reader. Sometimes writer decisions involve deadlines, as in the last three lead types. Sometimes decisions require including previously reported information, and sometimes they involve early presentation of certain story facts while saving other facts for later in the story. Complex leads are challenging because they require more writer initiative and judgment.

SUMMARY

Fortunately, there's more to newswriting than merely hammering out five W's and H news leads. Each story's facts suggest an appropriate lead treatment type, and some of these types are advanced leads. Although the nomenclature isn't standardized, journalists recognize several advanced lead types that can be categorized as follows:

Advanced treatments:

- *quotes*—Using a quote is rarely the most effective lead approach, but when the quote is *strong, succinct* and *theme-setting*, use it.
- *narrative*—The narrative lead presents the news article in story form, stressing action.
- *descriptive*—The story-telling approach is used, but it emphasizes scene setting rather than action.

Advanced gimmicks:

- *question*—Seldom used (and controversial), a question is substituted for the normal simple lead, with the five W's and H lead following in the second paragraph.
- *teaser*—The writer purposely teases the reader by omitting an important element from the lead. However, responsible journalists never lie to the reader.
- *freak*—This lead is designed to be so unusual that it challenges the reader to read on.

Some of these advanced lead types extend beyond the first paragraph of the story. The necessary W's and H can run into the second, third or even fourth paragraph. This is certainly true for complex leads:

- *multiple-events*—The story contains several closely related incidents, but one deserves a little more prominence. Lead with an overview stressing the most important news element.
- *tie-back*—The lead offers new developments while including previously reported events to which today's news is linked.
- *point-counterpoint*—This complex lead type includes at least two clearly defined points of view in a story involving controversy.
- *still-to-come*—The lead must bring readers up to date on recent developments and indicate that all the action is not yet over.

Many complex stories embody a time element due to either continuing events or an approaching deadline. Lead writing for complex stories demands journalistic interpretation, the duty to put a story in perspective for readers.

Thinking it Through

EXERCISE 3.1

Advanced Leads One

A In each of the 15 items, determine which type of lead is given. Select among the following lead type designations:

simple	narrative
question:	descriptive
direct address	teaser
indirect address	freak
quote:	multiple events
direct	tie-back
paraphrase	point-counterpoint
	still-to-come

1.   Police say they have narrowed the search for an arsonist to New Orleans' Garden District but are unable to predict when this city's longest series of arson fires might end.

Lead type: _____

2.   It was a scene right out of the Scopes trial, including a heated debate between an evangelical preacher and a biology professor.

Commissioners and onlookers applauded points as the protagonists quoted Scripture or medical texts in a show equal to Perry Mason's finest television cross-examination.

The New Testament has rarely gotten so much attention at a City Planning Commission meeting as it did Wednesday night when hearings began on the zoning code distance between churches and family planning clinics.

Lead type: _____

3.   Police and demonstrators clashed Tuesday in Washington, D.C., as the Refugee Coalition staged a 5,000-member protest of recent State Department rulings on identification cards for illegal aliens.

Lead type: _____

4.   Four members of the Mayor's Office stood in the hallway outside Judge Edgar Thorpe's chambers and waited nervously for the final hearing to determine if they would retain their jobs.

The youngest snuffed out a newly lit cigarette as a bailiff opened the door and motioned the group inside.

Lead type: _____

5.   "CAR-RT SORT"

If you don't recognize this recent nom de plume, you probably haven't been reading your junk mail closely enough.

Lead type: _____

6.   Who in his right mind would give up the board chair position with a major airline to become a conductor on Amtrak's New York-Boston run?

Lead type: _____

7.   Five persons are dead and hundreds more suffered injuries as near-zero temperatures brought Fort Worth to its knees at noon Monday.

Winter rains combined with the record cold left a sheet of ice covering much of the city and cut both heat and water supplies to homes. Police and hospital personnel worked through the night to aid the injured and find shelter for those without warmth.

Lead type: _____

8.   The air inside Cadder's Mine is cold and dank. Puddles on the floor of the shaft invite falls and the perils of gashes from jagged rocks. When the door is sealed, no light or shadows exist, only blackness.

This den was a two-day prison nightmare for the John Marquette family while the Federal Bureau of Investigation worked to solve the largest known ransom attempt in this area.

Lead type: _____

9.   "It takes wild gimmicks to succeed in today's toy market, and Familytime Games will no longer risk the whims of a fickle public," James R. Marcum said today in announcing the firm will close next month.

Lead type: _____

10.   Convenience stores that have relied on the services of Joseph Kallup have a perfect anti-theft record: 14 arrests, no employee injuries, and not a single dollar lost from the till.

Police are so impressed with Kallup's new "old" remedy they are recommending all businesses give him a call.

Lead type: _____

11.   Directors of the May Festival have threatened to sue promoters of Spring Fling if the new organization receives city funding, although both groups have been endorsed by the local Convention Bureau.

Lead type: _____

12.   Albert Wheaterby, a Detroit pharmacist implicated in the drug-related deaths of two teenagers in June, was indicted today by the Grand Jury on four counts of second-degree murder.

Lead type: _____

13.   Members of the pipe fitters union are expected to reject Thursday's wage increase offer by Wilson Fabricating as the contract renewal deadline nears.

Lead type: _____

14.   A 10-story glass office building will be started at the corner of Elmwood and Second Street next week to house locally owned First National Bank, officers announced today.

Lead type: _____

15.   Den mother Wanda T. Smith told her pack of Cub Scouts she could no longer lead them because the area Scout Council has ruled single parents ineligible to lead a troop.

Lead type: _____

Writing Practice

EXERCISE 3.2

Advanced Leads Two

A   Carlton G. Langsford, vice president of Finance at State College, announces this morning that the university administration has decided not to give salary increases to employees, either faculty or staff, some 800 people. He says the decision was based on financial constraints due to reduced revenues from lower student enrollment at the university this year. "Our choice was to fire some employees or to give no raises across the board. We chose the latter as the more humanitarian alternative of two poor choices."

You get a call from Virginia Waxman, dean of the Faculty Senate, who tells you the no-raise decision is "an insult to every faculty member at State College." She says, "It's time for the university administration to fold some of its pet projects and to use portions of the school's $40 million endowment to fund raises." She says the senate's position is to cut the athletic program before denying necessary cost-of-living increases.

You call Angela Netters, senior physics major and president of the State College Student Government Association. She says the SGA has opposed any measure that might result in reducing educational benefits for students. "In this case," she says, "we expect the best teachers to begin seeking employment at other schools. The SGA favors reduction of unnecessary instructional programs such as choir, band or ROTC rather than risk losing State College's best teachers."

Write a lead for this afternoon's paper.

B Your contacts at the District Internal Revenue Service inform you that the IRS will be moving more toward computerized tax returns in the next several years, and that by the end of the decade all American tax returns will be audited by computer. In 95 percent of audited individual returns today, the taxpayer who is told he owes more tax dollars pays the amount without an argument. In the other 5 percent of audited cases, an individual will argue the point but is likely (again, 95 percent of the time) to pay the sum the IRS says is owed without taking the matter to tax court.

Write a complex lead.

C Tommy Penwaite, head coach of the State College Red Raiders, speaks at the annual banquet of the Lettermen's Club, a local group of former athletes and others who make contributions to State College teams. He makes the following remarks during a 40-minute presentation:

"I'm convinced the head football coach today has less to do with teaching players the game and more to do with selecting the best players for the team. My job begins when the season ends and ends when the season begins because my main job for the team is recruiting future players. I try to leave most of the field coaching to my staff.

"Recruiting has changed a lot in the past 10 years since it's become evident to league officials as well as all us coaches that the game is won and lost on recruiting trips. Of all the league's rule changes during that time, I'd say three out of four have dealt with recruiting and only one out of four concerned changes in game rules.

"I have no quarrel with the strict guidelines that now govern recruiting. I'd like to be known as the strictest coach in the league when it comes to recruiting. I'm convinced that we owe it to the young man we're interested in to be forthright, and I mean completely honest, even if it means losing him. This is the order of concerns I believe in: the individual's life interests come first; education comes second; and the team comes third. If we follow these principles, we're going to lose some good players but the Red Raiders will always have a winning season in ethics."

Write a (1) direct quote lead; and (2) an indirect quote lead.

D Harry D. Elrod, owner of the Diet Deli and Health Restaurant at 616 Center St., was the winner last night of the annual eating contest sponsored by Gamma Mu Sorority. Elrod consumed 15 Twinkies, nine bottles of soda pop, four bags of potato chips, two pizzas and eight assorted candy bars during the three-hour Junk Food Jubilee. He won $200 and a year's supply of microwave popping corn.

Write a lead for tomorrow morning's paper.

EXERCISE 3.3

Advanced Leads Three

A You are the arts writer for a morning newspaper. You attend an opening performance of the Civic Symphony in Barlow Auditorium to hear a Beethoven concert. Early in the performance, there's a power failure in the building and some fright as startled patrons begin to leave their seats. But Conductor Simon Altimer quiets the crowd and calls for candles. Reading music by candlelight, the orchestra completes the performance and receives a standing ovation from the capacity crowd of 4,000. Patrons leave the theater calmly with no incidents occurring. Though you thought the performance quite good, you are particularly struck by the charm of hearing a two-hour Beethoven concert by candlelight. You think the audience enjoyed that aspect immensely also.

Try to capture the experience in a lead.

B As a county reporter, you notice an oil derrick in the distance off a farm road you're driving on. Although you are aware oil companies have been drilling in this part of the state, you didn't know of any drilling going on in your county. You talk with a farmer who owns the land and find out these facts: (1) the company drilling is General Oil; (2) farmer is Olin Worstead, 55, of Summervale, who has sold the mineral rights on his property for 15 percent of profits plus $250 per month lease during drilling; (3) drilling began two months ago with a "portable rig" and a three-person crew from General; (4) company expected drilling to take only six weeks, so they expect to know any day now; (5) Worstead thinks some of his neighbors have sold mineral rights to General also. When you return to your office, you confirm all these facts with Gretchen Halstead, public information director for General. She tells you also that eight other mineral leases have been taken, all in Summervale and all adjacent to Worstead's farm.

Write a lead for tomorrow's paper.

C Scandal at town's largest industry, Terry Manufacturing, revealed this morning at press conference held by Ted Terry, plant owner. Audit reveals nearly $1 million has been embezzled by Comptroller Betty Osborn during past three years. Osborn now out of country on what was supposed to be a vacation. She left with another Terry employee, Wayne G. Baxter, vice president of purchasing and Osborn's fiancee. Evidence indicates fund siphoning related to purchases of raw materials, hence gas pipe the firm makes is being recalled for safety inspection. If a problem exists, the firm will have to inspect all pipe it has sold during the past five years, even if it's already in the ground. The plant will close indefinitely as of today. Auditors also concerned about tools inventory, expense accounts of several managers and receipts involving some $300,000 in sales during the past two years. These items to receive further inquiry during plant closing.

Write a lead for this afternoon's paper.

D Samson T. Everett is recovering at City General Hospital here following a fractured rib he received yesterday while trying to rescue a young girl who almost drowned at Bear River when her family's canoe was swamped in one of the rapids. Her parents, Ronald and Vivian Adler, began yelling as the three were thrown into the swift, rock-filled rapids. Everett, who had been hunting deer in the woods downriver from the accident, heard the shouts and saw the girl being swept downstream. He ran to the shore and dived into the icy water. Everett said the current took him downstream nearly half a mile as he clawed for the girl. He said he remembers touching her life jacket once or twice, and a strap on the jacket may have twisted around his wrist. But he was thrown against rocks in a downstream rapid and was knocked unconscious. The river washed both him and the girl onto a sandbank. Rangers coming on the scene found the two unconscious, and Rebecca, who quickly recovered with mouth-to-mouth resuscitation, suffered no injuries. The two Adler parents also were uninjured.

Write a narrative lead for this morning's paper.

E Jennifer E. Bryant, 38, a local woman, is named to head Gov. Bobbie R. May's new task force on Consumer Affairs. She has been a reporter specializing in consumer information for WKNW-TV locally as recently as last year and was a public affairs specialist during the recent May campaign for re-election. Your files show Bryant's career has always been related to either journalism or consumer advocacy. She is perhaps best known locally for being the chief spokesperson against the interstate highway system being completed through the city. Her group, Save Our Zoo, fought local, state and national highway officials for nearly 10 years. She began SOZ while still at City College and headed it full time until the issue was settled with branches of the interstate being built on the outskirts of town.

Bryant's husband is Earl A. Bryant, a local attorney. The couple has two children.

The governor's Consumer Affairs Task Force is a group of some 20 volunteers and a paid staff of five. It has a budget of $2.5 million for the current fiscal year. The idea to create such a task force was one of May's major campaign promises.

Write a lead for this afternoon's paper.

Inverted Pyramid

PRINCIPLE OF THE INVERTED PYRAMID

Arranging the content of news stories in an inverted pyramid or upside-down triangle shape has been the format of most journalistic writing for more than a century. This story structure offers organizational benefits for the news writer and reader alike. The journalist can engage in a similar exercise in logic before writing each article and can use a similar pattern of presentation for virtually any story. Readers benefit by being able to learn what happened in the first few paragraphs, if not the single first paragraph or lead, of a news story.

It is basically true, then, that the entire news story is organized in a manner similar to the organization of a simple or summary story lead. In fact, as mentioned earlier, when the summary lead is in place, it serves as an outline for the rest of the story. We'll see in a moment why this is the case, but first let's work a little more with the inverted pyramid idea.

Say you had an experience on the way to class this morning and you tell your friends about it at lunch. Your story might go something like this:

> "You won't believe what I saw this morning! I was walking to my biology class when I noticed a couple sitting on one of those concrete benches by the parking lot. The guy was dressed in a coat and tie, which I thought was strange for a student . . . maybe he had to give a speech in one of his classes or something. Anyway, the girl's face was sunburned, I thought at first, but then she jumped up and started shouting at the guy,

so I knew they had been arguing. He got up too, and they were both yelling pretty loud. Then she slapped him . . . knocked him back a couple of steps. Then he shouted at her, and he slapped her.

I thought it must be some kind of gag, like they were practicing for a play or doing a mime routine in public. But the woman fell down and her books spilled all over the place and she started crying. He shouted at her again and then began walking away slowly, without looking back.

I thought I should go over and help her, but it all happened so fast I couldn't. She got up and ran to a blue Mustang convertible in the lot a few feet away. She started it and gunned the engine. The car shot out of the parking lot, broke through the chain railing and started barrelling toward the guy. Luckily he heard it in time and dived out of the way just as the car smashed into the side of the library.

By this time a bunch of other people were running toward them to see if they were okay. The guy had been hit and had a broken leg. The woman in the car was all right, but she had a gash on her head and was bleeding. But that car was totaled, and it took a section of brick 6 feet wide out of the library. The police showed up and told everyone to leave, except the people who had seen it. They took my statement. I'll probably have to go to court as a witness.

Now there's nothing wrong with this story in its readability or interest level. It's the kind of story that probably would be told over lunch, followed by several questions from the listeners, and it might be told in just about the same way it was here. This is a narrative presentation, the usual story-telling structure used in novels, done in chronological order: first the couple was sitting on the bench, next they got up and shouted at each other and so forth to the incident's conclusion.

If this story were diagrammed, it might look like the pyramid shape shown in Figure 4.1, with a slow and narrow beginning building up through the action to the more dramatic outcome at the conclusion.

With the narrative writing style, the reader is drawn into the story as the suspense and action build, and is rewarded for continuing with the story by the outcome. The only problem with this story is that it takes too long to find out what happened. If many news stories were written in this manner, most readers wouldn't linger long enough to find out what happened, or they'd skip to the end to find out what happened right away.

Journalistic style inverts the pyramid so the "what happened," the outcome, comes first in the story. Figure 4.2 shows this inverted pyramid style, which aligns the story elements in nearly the opposite manner,

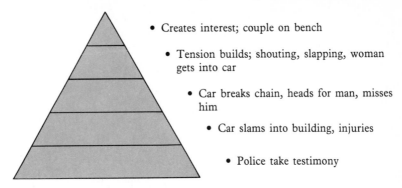

Figure 4.1 contents:
- Creates interest; couple on bench
- Tension builds; shouting, slapping, woman gets into car
- Car breaks chain, heads for man, misses him
- Car slams into building, injuries
- Police take testimony

Figure 4.1   Narrative story presentation

although there might be some chronology if that will improve reader understanding, as it might for this story.

MOVING FROM LEAD TO EARLY STORY BODY

The "base" of the inverted pyramid, which is now the top, is the story lead. It contains all of the necessary W's in a concise manner, in their order of importance. A lead for this story in the afternoon newspaper might be as follows:

> Two students were injured at State University today when a woman drove a car at her boyfriend after a violent argument and slammed the car into the university library building.
> Jay G. Drexel, 20, was treated for a broken leg after being hit by

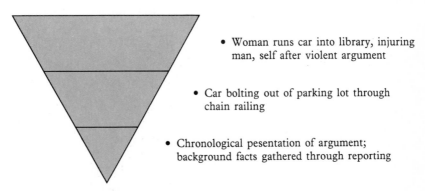

Figure 4.2 contents:
- Woman runs car into library, injuring man, self after violent argument
- Car bolting out of parking lot through chain railing
- Chronological pesentation of argument; background facts gathered through reporting

Figure 4.2   Inverted pyramid news presentation

the vehicle driven by Roxanne B. Kingsley, 19. Kingsley was treated for head lacerations and is being held by police on charges of attempted manslaughter and reckless driving.

The State University library building received damages estimated at $10,000 when Kingsley smashed the car into its north wall. The vehicle was destroyed in the crash.

Kingsley said she and Drexel had gotten into an argument Wednesday about her dating other men. The two tried to talk it out on campus this morning before their classes, but the discussion evolved into shouting and slapping. She said after he knocked her down, the next thing she remembers is slamming the car into the library building.

Drexel said, "I was lucky to hear the car before it hit me and jump away far enough to get only a broken leg."

Witnesses said they saw the two students sitting together on a bench next to the main campus parking lot. Then the two began arguing loudly and slapped one another with Drexel knocking Kingsley to the ground.

As Drexel walked away, Kingsley got up and ran to a blue Mustang parked in the lot. . . .

And the story will wind along from that point as it includes more details of the incident, more quotes from the couple and some comments from witnesses. Depending on how newsworthy an alleged manslaughter attempt in front of witnesses is on this college campus, the story might include several more paragraphs with quotes from university officials about the library damages and from people in the library about the impact when the car hit the building. The last paragraph might even include how long the couple have been together and whether they intend to be a couple any longer.

But note that all of these details would follow all of the more important elements of the story: (1) the injuries; (2) the library; (3) the manslaughter attempt with a car; (4) the argument; and (5) where and when the incident occurred. These are the main news elements of the story and should be included before any of the lesser details are given. Also, these five elements should be presented in nearly the order given.

STRUCTURE FOR READER UNDERSTANDING

After the five elements are included, the next step in inverted pyramid style should be to give more details about the main elements. A narrative style might begin the chronology immediately after the story's lead, but this would be a mistake. It's more important to give the reader full and necessary details about who the people are, the extent of injuries sustained, the damages to the library (readers might think the building collapsed) and the car, and generally why the two were arguing. Should readers decide they've learned all they need to know about the event at this point, they could stop now and still have the gist of what happened.

But the story ought to continue until all of the newsworthy details are presented. In this particular story, readers will understand the incident more fully if the writer moves into chronological presentation after including those necessary facts that support the lead. We see the chronology begin in the sixth graf of the article, as the writer shifts to, "Witnesses said they saw the two students sitting together on a bench. . . . " But the chronology doesn't begin until the writer has provided all of the main news elements, as the inverted pyramid style demands.

USE WITH DIFFERENT STORY TYPES

To use the inverted pyramid for the preceding story, all the writer has to do is to determine what happened—what is the important news readers will want to know—and start with those elements, including more details until they've been presented fully. The example may seem simple because the story is pretty straightforward. But we can look at a few more stories to get a feel for some of the logic decisions a reporter makes when writing an article in the inverted pyramid style.

Robbery Story

Here's a fact set in numbered sentence format:

1. A masked robber enters a convenience store at 10 p.m.
2. It's a male in his 20s, about 6 feet tall.
3. His face is hidden by a Halloween mask.
4. He tells the cashier to give him all the money in the register.
5. He pulls a pillowcase from his jacket and begins emptying shelf products into it.
6. He stuffs the money—about $300—into the pillowcase.
7. He fires his pistol into the cash register and tells the cashier to hit the floor.
8. He flees from the store.
9. The cashier buzzes the police alarm.
10. Police arrive and search the neighborhood without finding the man.

Okay, what happened? What are the important news elements a reader will want to know? Consider the lineup of sentences that will result in an inverted pyramid news story. They might go like this:

1. An armed robber is still at large.
2. After a holdup at an Elm Street convenience store.
3. He took $300 in cash and some shelf products Friday night.
4. He was armed with a pistol.
5. He wore a Halloween mask.
6. He was in his 20s, about 6 feet tall.

The first three items are the main news elements. They should be presented in the 1-2-3 order given because the fact that the robber was not caught is more important than another convenience store robbery, and the minor sum of money and goods taken is less important still.

Points 4-5-6 are more details about the robber and the crime. These should be in the second paragraph, after the lead.

If police have anything to add about recent similar robberies, any ideas about who the robber is or any plans for continuing the search for the suspect, that information should be included in the third or fourth paragraph.

The remaining facts about how the crime was committed, including shooting the cash register to frighten the cashier, can be told in brief chronological order in the last paragraph or two, and the article—now in proper inverted pyramid news style—is written.

Election Story

Another numerical fact set:

1. Two candidates in a runoff election for city commissioner: Henry Balsum and Margaret Winkleman.
2. Winkleman wins a close election 15,870 to 15,562.
3. Balsum concedes at 10:30 p.m.
4. Winkleman gives a victory speech to her campaign supporters and other well-wishers at 10:45. She says she'll ask Balsum to serve as her chief deputy. "Obviously the voters thought both candidates were well qualified to be commissioner," she says. "I was impressed with Henry's clean campaign, and we see eye to eye on most of the major issues facing the city."
5. Balsum and Winkleman were split during the campaign on a new city tax proposal. He opposed it; she favored it.

6. Winkleman introduces her family to the crowd and thanks Mayor Archie Sanburn for his support through the campaign. She says she'll take off for two weeks for a post-campaign rest, but will be on the job immediately after she and her family return from the Virgin Islands.

In an election story like this, there's no need for any chronological presentation. Handle it in straight inverted pyramid style by first asking yourself what happened. The answer is simple: Winkleman won the election; it was a close election; she will ask her opponent to serve as her chief deputy. The lead might go like this:

Margaret Winkleman was elected city commissioner Tuesday in a close victory over her opponent, Henry Balsum.

The fact that Winkleman was elected in a close vote is the major news element. Who she defeated also should be in the lead to remind readers of the exact event and to let Balsum supporters know their candidate lost.

Next, further details about the vote should be included as a continuation of the inverted pyramid style of more important story elements preceding lesser elements:

The vote was one of the closest in recent city election history: 15,870 to 15,562, a difference of only 308 votes.

Then the next most important piece of news should follow, that the new commissioner will ask her opponent to serve as her deputy. Had she asked him before her speech, and had he accepted the position, this element might qualify as part of the first paragraph, or it certainly would have preceded the vote count paragraph. But because her intention may only be a gesture at this point, it loses some news value.

Winkleman told supporters in her 10:45 p.m. victory speech that she will ask her opponent to serve as her chief deputy, the highest appointed post in the commissioner's office.

The commissioner's quote about Balsum can serve in the news article as the best explanation of her unusual decision. It should be included next:

"Obviously the voters thought both candidates were well-qualified to be commissioner," she said. "I was impressed with Henry's clean campaign, and we see eye to eye on most of the major issues facing the city."

It is important to give a further detail immediately after the quote. A journalist ought to explain to readers that the two candidates were not in complete agreement on the issues during the race, in spite of what Winkleman told her supporters.

In fact, the two candidates did stand on opposite sides of the current proposal to raise city taxes, with Winkleman favoring the measure and Balsum opposing it.

Even the last two paragraphs of the story should be arranged in order of their descending importance. This far down in the story, there may be some question about whether the vacation is more important than the mayor's campaign support or whether the difference matters, but it should be recognized that her Virgin Island trip is a new piece of information whereas the mayor's support is old. Put the vacation first:

Commissioner Winkleman said she will take a two-week, post-election vacation with her family in the Virgin Islands but will begin work in her new office when she returns.
She thanked Mayor Archie Sanburn for supporting her during the campaign and introduced her family to the victory celebration crowd.

If Winkleman made important announcements or divulged new plans during her victory speech, these would definitely precede both the vacation and mayor's support paragraphs. If her speech was the usual "thank you for your help" variety, perhaps some comments might be included after the mayor's support paragraph. Including "thank yous" would be done at the end of the story if at all.

CUTTING FROM THE BOTTOM UP

We can pause here to consider another reason the inverted pyramid newswriting style is so popular in news rooms. Whether it's a broadcast story or a newspaper story, it has to fit. A broadcast story has to fit a designated time slot; a newspaper story has to fit the allotted space on the page. If the story is too long, it has to be edited, or cut, to fit the space.

The easiest way to edit a story for fit is to lop off the ending. Cutting

Television news writers, editors and producers form a team to coordinate the story, video and graphics packaged as a unit so viewers can understand the news event in a report that might last only 30 seconds.

elements from the middle of the story is more time-consuming and runs the risk of omitting information needed to make sense out of something later in the story. For instance, the fourth paragraph, containing a person's name and identification, might be deleted, and the editor might not notice that there's another reference to "Smith" in the seventh paragraph, which is to be retained. Readers wouldn't know who Smith was.

The inverted pyramid writing style maximizes efficiency in writing, in reading and in editing. If every paragraph from the story's beginning contains more important information than material in any lower paragraph, then every story can be edited to fit simply by deleting sentences or paragraphs from the bottom up. Look at the election story again. If you delete the last line, you still have a complete story. In fact, if you delete any lines in succession from the bottom up, the remainder of the story still makes sense and it still includes the most important story facts. Figure 4.3 illustrates the successive cuts from the bottom up that could be made to shorten the election story.

This story has offered all the real news by the end of the third paragraph. Readers have been told who won, that it was a close election and that Winkleman said she will offer Balsum the deputy chief post. Her

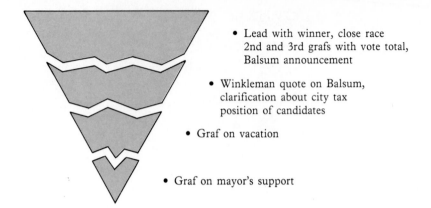

• Lead with winner, close race
  2nd and 3rd grafs with vote total,
  Balsum announcement

• Winkleman quote on Balsum,
  clarification about city tax
  position of candidates

• Graf on vacation

• Graf on mayor's support

Figure 4.3   Cutting the pyramid from the bottom

quote and the explanation about the two candidates' views on taxes aren't absolutely necessary, but they will help readers understand the news. The last two paragraphs, however, might be eliminated entirely without affecting any of the necessary news values and the complete explanation. If this is true, why include them? At what point should the writer determine that enough has been said, and stop?

WHEN TO END

Beginners make two mistakes. First, they stop too soon. They determine that they've included the important news elements, so they stop. The second mistake is the opposite problem of including everything, even when the last several sentences contain only trivial information with no news value whatsoever. The trick is to hit the middle ground between leaving out something that may be important and including something that definitely isn't.

For instance, the election story could end at the third paragraph, but the fourth and fifth paragraphs contain necessary additional information for reader understanding. Yet the story continues through two more paragraphs of minor detail. Should the last two paragraphs be included? In this case, the answer is yes. Winkleman's vacation and her thanking the mayor aren't necessary, but they do contain minor news elements. The first tells the reader what the new commissioner will be doing immediately after winning the election; the second reminds the reader that the mayor was in her corner during the campaign. Including them is a narrow call, so it's a call the editor should make. An editor might need both of the last paragraphs to fill space . . . otherwise the story might be too short to fit the allotment. If the editor needs only one paragraph, the last can be dropped, or both can be dropped to fit the space.

But fit isn't the writer's primary concern in deciding how much of the story to include. The real decision is: Does the news value of the information warrant its being included? The best rule a writer can go by is that all the information with any news value should be included. Of course, as its news value diminishes, the information becomes a candidate for placement at the end of the story. If the rule is applied for all news stories, the outcome has the following benefits:

1. Writers keep writing the story until they reach a point at which they're absolutely confident that few readers would have any interest in the rest of the information. Usually their stories will be one or two paragraphs longer than necessary.

2. The very close decisions are left to editors who must depend on their reporters' information. An editor can't know whether the information is important to the story unless the writer puts it in the article. Editors can always cut the last portions of the article if they think the information is too trivial, but they can't add the information a writer decides to omit.

3. With all the possible relevant facts included, editors have the prerogative to delete some of it to fit space limitations. But editors can't add another two paragraphs themselves to fill the available space.

USE WITH MORE COMPLEX LEADS

Let's consider some other aspects of inverted pyramid newswriting style with a more complicated story.

New Building Story

As a reporter for Riverview's afternoon paper, you are sent to the mayor's office for a story. You show up at 9 a.m. Mayor Sandy Juarez introduces you to James Eagleton, who heads your city's largest mortgage company, and she tells you:

> "Mr. Eagleton's announcement means Riverview has met the annual goal of new construction I set when I ran for office last year. This new building sets a precedent for recognizing Riverview's potential as a center for the financial industry's emerging technology. We appreciate the confidence First Mortgage has shown in Riverview by cementing its future success with that of this city."

Here is the fact set, in the form of your notes, as told to you by Eagleton:

His company, which has its headquarters here but has branches in every major city in the state, intends to build a $45 million headquarters facility in the downtown Riverview area, two blocks south of its old headquarters building at Court Street and Main. New facility will be on the site of the old Grant Produce Market building, which covered an entire city block . . . remains of warehouse to be torn down beginning next week. Construction of new building will be by Johnson Construction Co. and will be that firm's largest undertaking. Scheduled building completion date is next Jan. 1.

New building to be a 25-story concrete and steel structure with blue-tinted glass windows as the dominant feature. An eight-level underground parking garage will hold 3,000 vehicles . . . top floor will be a gourmet restaurant open to the public but owned by First Mortgage.

In all, 2,400 employees will be located in the new building (old building now has only 400). About 1,000 current First Mortgage employees will come from other mortgage locations in the state, the 400 employees in the old building will move to the new building when it's finished, and 1,000 new employees will be hired to operate a new computer transfer system, the core of this new facility. Hiring will begin in about one year.

Eagleton says the computer transfer system is an expansion of the firm's current system. Instead of having a statewide capacity, it will have an international capacity. "It will be equal to anything that now exists in the financial capitals of the world." He says he expects other mortgage and banking institutions to lease time on the new system.

While all upper levels of the building, except top-floor restaurant, will be used by the mortgage firm, the street level will be leased to local retail shops. There will be room for about 50 stores and space for shoppers' cars in part of the paid parking garage.

You're back at the office now, about to write the story on your 40-minute deadline. Always begin by asking yourself what happened. What will your readers want to know most? What's next in importance and so on?

If you selected the fact that the new building meets Mayor Juarez's campaign goal for new construction, think again. That may have happened first, but it's one of the least important news values. Here are some possibilities:

1. A new $45 million building will be constructed in Riverview.
2. 1,000 new jobs will come to the city.
3. A high-technology computer transfer system will be linking Riverview to the rest of the world.
4. Riverview will continue to be First Mortgage's headquarters.
5. 50 new retail stores will open.
6. A new restaurant will open.

Among these half-dozen likely news values, one or two overshadow the others based on consequence: the new building and the 1,000 new jobs. In some cases the two might be a close call. If local unemployment has been unusually high and the job crisis is a current news topic, the 1,000 new jobs may deserve mention in the lead. However, new hiring doesn't begin for a year, so if unemployment is not at crisis levels the clear lead for the story is this new building: a beautiful blue-tinted glass, classy $45 million, towering 25-story skyscraper climbing gracefully toward heaven right here in Riverview, visible to every reader's eye, that will change the current skyline of the entire downtown area. Of course you won't write that, but it does emphasize what your readers will want to know about first. If you go through the ordering of news elements for a lead, you should come up with something along these lines:

A $45 million skyscraper housing 2,400 First Mortgage Co. employees will begin construction in downtown Riverview next week.

The lead focuses on the building, includes the employees (possibly suggesting new jobs), names the building's owner, says where the building will be and when it will begin happening. It does all of this in 18 words, because a major news story like this one in Riverview will have more impact with a shorter lead. Much more could have been added, but then the news value of this major story would lose some of its emphasis by including too much detail in the lead.

Because the writer decides to lead with the building, inverted pyramid style suggests more details about the building ought to be the next element following the lead:

James Eagleton, First Mortgage's president, said the 25-story concrete-and-steel structure will contain retail stores, a gourmet restaurant, underground parking, a sophisticated financial computer system and 1,000 new employees.

Blue-tinted glass windows will be the dominant feature of the building, with construction by Riverview's Johnson Construction Co. scheduled for completion Jan. 1, Eagleton said.

The skyscraper will be on the site of the old Grant Produce Market, a tract two blocks south of First Mortgage's present Court and Main headquarters. Eagleton said the market building's remains will be razed beginning next week.

Eagleton said the street level of the new building will have space for about 50 leased retail outlets. The top floor will contain a gourmet restaurant owned and operated by the mortgage firm but open to the public. An eight-level underground parking garage will hold 3,000 vehicles for shoppers and employees.

Note that the new building remains the focus of attention throughout these four paragraphs. Virtually every aspect of the building readers might want to know about is included, and all of these details are given before moving on to the next news value.

Additionally, something in the second paragraph should strike a familiar chord with writers. The line about the building containing "retail stores, a gourmet restaurant, underground parking, a sophisticated financial computer system and 1,000 new employees" is the same sort of statement that would be identified as a topic sentence in an English theme. Here it serves two purposes: (1) it provides readers a quick overview of what will be in the building and (2) it lists the order of topics to be covered in the remainder of the story.

As diagrammed in Figure 4.4, the writer decides what information readers need to know most, and places news values in that order:

- what members of the general public will see as they pass the building's downtown location
- all the public-interest features the building will contain, including retail stores for shopping, a gourmet restaurant for dining and underground parking spaces
- building contents of less concern to the general public, such as the international banking computer system and the new employees to operate it.

The only rule being applied in determining this particular order of presentation is the news value of consequence. Not knowing more about

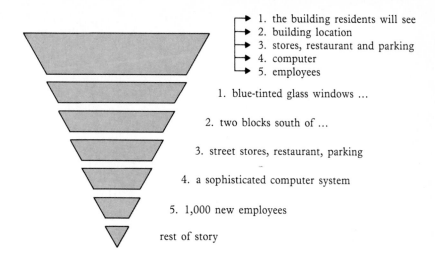

1. the building residents will see
2. building location
3. stores, restaurant and parking
4. computer
5. employees

1. blue-tinted glass windows ...

2. two blocks south of ...

3. street stores, restaurant, parking

4. a sophisticated computer system

5. 1,000 new employees

rest of story

Figure 4.4 Inverted pyramid by "topic" sentence

Riverview's size, the impact of 1,000 new jobs or the novelty of a computerized banking system, it is reasonable to order story facts by their probable interest to the widest number of readers.

One other major aspect of newswriting can also be seen in the second paragraph. It begins with an attributive statement: "James Eagleton, First Mortgage's president, said . . . " Attribution normally is included in the lead paragraph. This story omitted it to reduce clutter and increase impact with a short lead. However, gaining impact is no excuse for leaving the reader guessing where this new building information came from. News doesn't fall onto the writer's page from the sky. Journalists must name their sources in stories, but the beginning of the second paragraph may be an early enough place to meet that requirement.

So the writer is now five paragraphs into the story, and though several of the news values have been mentioned, the primary focus of all five paragraphs is to continue providing details about the major news value, the new building. After that has been accomplished, the writer shifts to other major news elements in the lead and the topic sentence of the second paragraph. The rest of the story follows:

> First Mortgage will expand its current computer network from a statewide to an international system, Eagleton said. Other financial institutions are expected to lease time on the new system which, Eagleton said, "will be equal to anything that now exists in the financial capitals of the world."

The bank will hire about 1,000 new employees to operate the expanded system and will begin hiring in about a year, Eagleton said.

Some 1,100 current First Mortgage employees at locations throughout the state will be transferred to the new headquarters building, Eagleton said. The 400 employees in the present headquarters building will be moved to the new facility when it is completed.

Commenting on the announced new building, Riverview Mayor Sandy Juarez said the new facility completes the annual new construction goal her administration set.

"We appreciate the confidence First Mortgage has shown in Riverview by cementing its future success with that of this city," Juarez said.

Three of these last five paragraphs of the article offer details on the second and third major news values: the jobs and the new computer system. Although these two remaining news values are somewhat mixed through the presentation in the paragraphs, each paragraph does follow the inverted pyramid style of offering lesser and lesser news values as the story continues to its ending.

The ending is another example of providing a little more information than might actually appear in the printed article. Mayor Juarez's comments in the last paragraph could be omitted if the story is too long or if an editor believes those comments are too inconsequential for inclusion.

Two other points can be made about the body of the story. One reiterates the naming of sources or attribution. We find Eagleton mentioned several times throughout the article. His name is not dropped into the story randomly but is used purposely with certain key sentences. For instance, sentences that forecast a coming event such as when construction will begin and when the building will be completed contain these attribution statements. And including Eagleton's name throughout the article serves as a constant reminder to readers that the story comes from Eagleton, not the reporter or the newspaper directly. More information about journalists' use of quotes and attribution is contained in Chapter 6.

The second point about the body of the story deals with its visual structure. The paragraphs of a news story are short—much shorter than those in an English theme. In fact, newspaper news story paragraphs should average about four typewritten lines. That means some of the paragraphs may be only two lines long and some may be six lines long. But when a paragraph begins to run longer than seven or eight lines, it's time to consider beginning a new paragraph or breaking the present one into two paragraphs. There are two reasons for keeping paragraphs short. First, readers view a dense clump of type in a newspaper as forbidding: It looks like work to read. More important, however, is that long paragraphs—just like long sentences—tend to become complex. The ideas they contain are difficult to follow. Shorter paragraphs contain fewer ideas and are easier for readers to grasp.

SUMMARY

The inverted pyramid story is the most frequently used method of writing a news story. It requires that a writer first decide what happened—what are the event's main news values—and then write the story with the most important news values always preceding lesser news values throughout the article. This story structure is contrasted with narrative story telling that builds up to the outcome; the inverted pyramid begins with the outcome.

Inverted pyramid style is an extremely efficient newswriting method with advantages for the writer, the editor and, especially, the reader. Readers stopping at any paragraph in the article still take the most important news from that story because anything left unread is less newsworthy than everything already read. The writer benefits because the entire news story is organized from a simple or summary story lead. When the summary lead is in place, it serves as an outline for the rest of the story.

Some rules for inverted pyramid writing are:

- Order news values in the lead, then give all necessary details on the first news value in the story before moving to lesser news values;
- Give the full story details for news value No. 2 before beginning those for No. 3, and so forth through the end of the story;
- Write the story so an editor could delete paragraphs from the bottom up and—regardless of how many paragraphs are deleted from the bottom—everything remaining in the story will be more newsworthy than anything deleted;
- Include all the information you think is even remotely newsworthy, and let the editor decide if you've written too much;
- Use attribution early in the story, and use it purposely throughout the story, particularly on statements that require attribution (see Chapter 6);
- Make paragraph length in a news story about four lines, on average.

Writing Practice

EXERCISE 4.1

Inverted Pyramid—Wells

This is a fact set in the form of rough notes a reporter might make for a news article. **Use this textbook's City Directory to check all facts before writing the article.** Any direct quotes you may use are included in quotation marks in these notes. Check spelling and AP style before turning in your story.

Barry Sherman Jr., Huron Petroleum Corp.'s public relations director, calls you with this information: Huron is back in production with a well that was capped in 1962. The well is located eight miles from the city limits on the south side, about one-third mile southeast of the intersection of U.S. Hwy. 85 and Route 3 in a field owned by Jasper C. Neil.

Sherman explains that the well is producing about 50 barrels of crude oil per day and has been back in operation a week now. According to Huron's records, when the well was capped it was producing about 40 barrels a day, an amount that wasn't worth production costs with gasoline selling at about 35 cents a gallon at the pumps. Then a barrel of crude was worth about $7.50 at the well. Now it's worth nearly $20 a barrel. He says Huron expects the well to slow to about 40 barrels a day, "but it should maintain the 40-barrel-a-day rate for at least five years. Uncapped wells have more pressure initially, but that levels off after a few months."

Neil still has his 10 percent production rights to the oil produced; Huron has 90 percent rights, the usual secondary production contract that was made with landowners in this vicinity during the 1950s and '60s, Sherman says. He adds that there are about 200 capped Huron wells in the county, many of them within 10 miles of the city. Huron expects to begin uncapping operations at no fewer than half those sites, at the rate of about 25 wells per year beginning right away. Huron hopes to average at least 50 barrels a day from all the reclaimed wells, Sherman says.

You call Neil, who tells you: "We did pretty well on our gas royalties back in the '50s, though nobody really got rich. But you got to remember that back then a barrel of crude wasn't worth as much and nobody in the county hit a real gusher. Still, there were a couple of families that owned a lot of leases, and I guess some of them will start doing pretty well now. I've only got four leases myself."

You call Huron's local general manager, but he's out of the office until after lunch, so you speak with Donna Gillespie, vice president of operations. She says the well reclaiming operation is budgeted at $2.5 million per year or a total of $10 million to uncap 100 wells over a four-year period. "It takes about a month to uncap a well, and it costs $100,000 on average per well. We have to drill back down into the pipe to get the concrete plug out. It requires at least a portable drilling rig, and it can be a tricky procedure. Once you get one open, there's no guarantee it will produce, but we think all the wells we've selected to uncap will be producers." She says Huron figures it will make $100 million from these wells in the next five years, considering some won't be on-line for the first few years. Local residents who hold leases should earn nearly $10 million from the operation, maybe more. There are some 40 residents still in the area who hold leases, Gillespie says. Most are the children and grandchildren of county landowners.

Write an inverted pyramid story for this afternoon's paper.

EXERCISE 4.2

Inverted Pyramid—Carnival

This is a rough-note fact set. Check all facts in the City Directory. You may use the direct quotes in quotation marks. Check spelling and AP style before submitting your story.

Checking the police log at the local precinct, you come across a story that deserves some news space. Seems one of those traveling carnivals is in town for the week, located in a big shopping mall parking lot about a mile from the university. Vice squad Detective Sergeant Thomas Dozier took the report of three college boys tonight who said they lost $125 playing one of the midway games at the carnival.

They said they played a game with six marbles that rolled into randomly numbered holes in a board. The numbers were all single-digit ranging from 1 to 9. The carnival man at the booth totalled the points quickly and the object was get a score below 20 or above 40. According to the police report, playing the game cost 50 cents at first, and the boys won on their first five consecutive rolls. Each time they won, they earned 2 game points toward a stereo set they would win if they reached 13 game points. But when they hit 10, the game began to cost $2 a play. Several turns later they won again and hit 12; then the game cost $5 to play. Because they were only one point away, they kept playing, but they never won again. Within 15 minutes, they had lost all the money they had with them, about $125 altogether.

Detective Thomas said the boys got angry when they realized they had been cheated. They came to the precinct to lodge a complaint and try to get their money back. Thomas took them back to the carnival in an unmarked car, but as they were approaching the midway, the man at their booth saw them and leaped over the counter and disappeared into the crowd. Thomas said he spoke to the manager about the incident, but was unable to get the boy's money back.

Thomas tells you it's the oldest gambling trick in the world. It's a game you can't win. With six marbles falling into holes numbered randomly from 1 to 9, the chances of getting six numbers that add to less than 20 or more than 40 are just about zero. But, he says, you don't bother checking the numbers at first while the man is adding and telling you you've got a winner. Then later, when you're losing, you can count as closely as you like, but you won't ever win again.

Thomas says, "Tell those college kids to be careful on the midway. We've had reports of pickpockets, some fights and the usual complaints about several of those gambling games. The boys said this guy told them he hoped they would win because his son is in college too. They should have realized who was going to be paying the tuition."

Write an inverted pyramid story for tomorrow morning's paper.

EXERCISE 4.3

Inverted Pyramid—Housing

This is a rough-note fact set. Check all facts in the City Directory. You may use the direct quotes in quotation marks. Check spelling and AP style before submitting your story.

Underwood Housing Development was built in 1968 as low-income housing for the urban poor. It covers a 35-acre site near the downtown area and houses some 3,200 residents in 1,000 apartment units in 20 buildings, although three of the buildings are vacant and boarded up. The project has been the center of controversy for a variety of issues: drug dealing, street gangs, several murders and rapes, and charges that maintenance funds were paid to city contractors who didn't perform the work or whose work didn't meet minimum standards.

Residents of the Underwood Housing Development held a meeting at 8 tonight to form a tenants' governing association. Some 400 people showed up for what was the first attempt to have UHP residents act as a bargaining force with the city's Central Housing Authority that manages the project.

Along with bitter accusations that none of the CHA members lives in any of its project units (a fact that you verify), comments from the residents included:

Marybeth James, 37, "I've been living here nearly all my life and I never remember things getting any better . . . they always get worse."

Eulah B. Simms, 24, "It's our children that need protection, not us. We keep shotguns to stop break-ins, but who's gonna stop the dope and the shootings out on the streets and in the playgrounds at night?"

Jerome Raintree, 50, "Let the Central Housing people come live in my building for one week. Then we would see some action on the building maintenance. I've been waiting six months for them to fix my roof."

James is elected to head the new group to be called Underwood Residents' Union. Four other officers were elected. Dues were set at $1 per month per residential unit. A list of demands will be presented to the CHA at its meeting (three days from today). Included are: (1) double the number of police patrols for the project; (2) make public the maintenance schedule for the remainder of the year, including projected expenditures and contractors; (3) convert an abandoned building in the center of the project to an assembly hall and URU headquarters; (4) remove any abandoned buildings that are not scheduled for renovation within the next two years; (5) repair the chain-link fence around the playground; (6) make the URU's president a voting member of the CHA board immediately.

Central Housing Authority Director Patrick Clemmons tells you by phone that the CHA doesn't have the authority to appoint another board member . . . members are elected citywide on a two-year rotating basis. He says the CHA doesn't intend to destroy any of the vacant buildings, and "the CHA might have a problem with charging dues to project residents." But, "We will be happy to receive a list of grievances from the residents and will try to work with them to help improve the Underwood Development as we always have done in the past."

Write an inverted pyramid story for tomorrow morning's paper.

EXERCISE 4.4

Inverted Pyramid—Teen Party

This is a rough-note fact set. Check all facts in the City Directory. You may use the direct quotes in quotation marks. Check spelling and AP style before submitting your story.

There's been a raid at a teen party in the Worthington suburb. Thirteen teenagers were arrested and charged with possession of illegal substances. They were released into the custody of their parents or guardians, who picked them up at the police station. One of the teenagers arrested was Daniel R. Warren, 19. Police refused to release the names of the other 12, who were juveniles, but said all the minors attended Westside High School. Two of the teens were also charged with drunk and disorderly conduct. Police Detective Aston Trent, the arresting officer, said the two were intoxicated and unclothed at the time of arrest. They were found unconscious in the front yard of a neighbor two houses from where the party was being held. Neighbors had reported the two were running naked down either side of the street smashing mailboxes with baseball bats.

Also arrested and charged with contributing to the delinquency of a minor were Dr. and Mrs. Eugene D. Arthur of 2183 Lexington. Detective Trent said the Arthurs were arrested in their upstairs study at 9 p.m. "They said they hadn't been downstairs for an hour and didn't know the teenagers had alcohol or other drugs. That might be true, but the law says adults on the premises are legally responsible in such cases. The police chief has warned parents in the past that another incident of this sort would result in arrests and charges. This is the third teen party we've been called on this month."

The raid was called when complaints of loud music and shouting at the Arthur back-yard swimming pool were called in beginning at about 8 p.m. Detective Trent said his officers found most of the teens in the pool or in the downstairs rooms of the house. "There might have been more than the ones we caught because we saw a few running through the bushes in the back yard when we came in the front door." He said police confiscated about $2,000 in illegal drugs, several bottles of liquor and a keg of beer.

Write an inverted pyramid story for tomorrow morning's paper.

EXERCISE 4.5

Inverted Pyramid—Coliseum

This is a rough-note fact set. Check all facts in the City Directory. You may use the direct quotes in quotation marks. Check spelling and AP style before submitting your story.

People have been unable to purchase tickets to college basketball games in the city. Although the games are televised locally, recent winning seasons and invitations to the National Collegiate Athletic Association championship tournament have resulted in a 2,000-person waiting list for season tickets.

The Board of Regents announces this morning that it has approved a plan to increase seating at your town's college basketball arena, the Danfourth Coliseum.

It now holds 9,000 people. Under the plan—which was chosen from among three architectural designs—the playing floor of the coliseum will be lowered nearly 20 feet and the internal concrete risers that form the bowl for spectator seating will be made steeper. Seating will be increased to 12,500 by a variety of means including slightly narrower aisles, narrower chairs, fewer entrances and better placement of seating sections.

Danfourth Coliseum was built in 1974 and was considered an architectural masterpiece that was one of the most spacious arenas in the nation.

"We thought 9,000 seats was enough to last the school well past the year 2000," said Dr. Virginia Lehman, the city's representative to the Board of Regents. "Luckily, when it was constructed, the planners emphasized comfort. Our problem here was money. This was the only design that avoided major changes to the exterior walls and dome of the building. Our renovation will cost about $5.5 million, but that's cheaper than building a new coliseum."

Board Chairman Peter K. Marshall of Cedar Springs said another design called for the roof to be raised and the walls heightened 20 feet, a plan estimated to cost $11 million and increase seating to about 13,000. The last design required cutting the walls into sections, moving them outward, reconnecting them with new walls, then redesigning or replacing the dome. That plan was estimated at $15 million, but it would have increased the seating to 15,000. The board also considered building a new coliseum, but costs began at more than $25 million.

Parking around the coliseum will be increased from 4,000 to 6,500. There is enough vacant space on two sides of the coliseum to accommodate most of the new spaces, and the school owns some land and houses adjacent to the present lots.

There were 5,000 fewer students at the university in the early 1970s when the coliseum was built. Most games before 1985 drew fewer than 6,000 people. Today, according to your university's president, basketball is a major money sport. "We have 2,000 commitments to purchase season tickets at prices ranging from $500 per ticket for the lowest level of premium seating to $1,000 for the highest. We believe our basketball program can provide enough income in the future to underwrite the rest of our sports program except football. A lot of tax dollars will be funneled into our academic program with this increased seating plan."

Lehman said spectators will still have a comfortable coliseum. "We'll have cushioned theater-type seats rather than the present plastic ones, and the extra seating won't affect the fire codes or any other safety features. Actually, the increased seating angle should make it easier to see the action on the floor."

Write an inverted pyramid story for this afternoon's paper.

EXERCISE 4.6

Inverted Pyramid—Food Poison

This is a rough-note fact set. Check all facts in the City Directory. You may use the direct quotes in quotation marks. Check spelling and AP style before submitting your story.

A local restaurant, the Gourmet Cafe, has been doing business in your city for more than 60 years. It's been owned and operated by three generations of the Boritoskie family and is now managed by Benjamin Boritoskie and his wife, Ginger. The restaurant has always had A-ratings from city inspectors and is listed on numerous visitor tour guides as a good place to eat in this town. There's usually a line of people waiting to eat there during the three daily mealtimes. The place holds 125 patrons.

Tonight at about 7:30, 14 people at the restaurant had to be taken to Our Lady of Mercy Hospital by ambulance. They were treated for food poisoning. All are in satisfactory condition, although they are remaining at the hospital overnight for observation. Irene Hardgrove, a spokesperson for the hospital, said emergency room doctors pumped the stomachs of all 14 people who were exhibiting symptoms ranging from fainting to vomiting. "All of the patients are doing fine now," Hardgrove said, "but the doctors want to keep them under observation the rest of the night. The doctors said all of the patients had recently eaten lamb."

You talk with Benjamin Boritoskie, who says there were two specialty items on the menu tonight: lamb and beefsteak. "The lamb was kept in our newest freezer, but we found out tonight that it had an electrical short and has not been keeping food at the right temperature, although the thermostat was registering okay. We've thrown out all the food in the freezer and we'll get the repair people out first thing in the morning."

Ginger Boritoskie said there's never been a similar incident in the history of the Gourmet Cafe. "I called Ben's folks and asked," she said. "We check everything in the food area carefully, but the heat from the stoves in the room prevents us from judging if a freezer is working. We have to rely on the thermostat."

Ben says his restaurant will pay all medical expenses and will try to compensate his patrons for their injuries and the inconvenience. "Our insurance will cover everything," he said. "It's an unfortunate accident, but at least it happened early in the evening before many people had eaten the lamb. Our dinner crowd started coming in at 5:30 and these people started getting sick about 6:30 p.m. It caused a lot of confusion in the place when one woman told a waitress she didn't feel well, and a man passed out on the floor across the room. I called the hospital right away."

The restaurant will be closed tomorrow for a complete inspection of all freezers and refrigerators. It will reopen for business the next day.

You check the paper's files and find two stories. In 1946 three Gourmet Cafe patrons were treated for food poisoning after drinking a bottle of Burgundy wine; in 1960 there was a minor fire in the cooking area that caused the restaurant to be evacuated, but no one was hurt.

Write an inverted pyramid story for tomorrow morning's paper.

EXERCISE 4.7

Inverted Pyramid—Train Station

This is a rough-note fact set. Check all facts in the City Directory. You may use the direct quotes in quotation marks. Check spelling and AP style before submitting your story.

Pattie O. Conner, director of Tourist Development in your city, asks you to come to her office for a story. She tells you that after a year of secret negotiations she can now announce a major accomplishment for tourism in this city. The Illinois Central Depot was sold to the Tourist Development office today for $1 million. "It was IC's intent to preserve the landmark that was so much a part of its history. We couldn't be more pleased."

According to terms of the sale, $500,000 in bonds will be sold for the Tourist Development Office by the city, and the IC Railroad will take back a note for the other $500,000 at a 6 percent interest rate for 50 years.

Conner says plans for the building are not finalized at this time, but the development office has talked about rejuvenating the downtown area, using the depot as a cornerstone of several other renovation projects. She says the building might be converted into a shopping mall with a turn-of-the-century theme. Another possibility the tourist office has discussed, she said, is making the building a museum dedicated to trains and building the downtown area around it toward a similar theme.

"The Tourist Development Office will have more to say about plans for the depot at the next City Council meeting," she says. "In any event, we consider this purchase a cause for celebration." She urges city residents to attend the City Council meeting next Monday night to hear the report.

You call the IC Railroad's headquarters in Chicago and talk with Hampton Albright, public relations director for IC's Properties Division. He says members of the IC board have been negotiating with your city's tourist office for nearly a year on the sale. "We hoped to get more for the building, which has an appraised value of $5 million. But we're very happy with the way this has turned out. If IC can continue to be a positive factor in people's lives, such as being a catalyst for downtown development or preserving a railroad theme museum, that's what we want to do. We believe we've made the most of this property by helping the tourist office acquire it on such easy terms."

You check your paper's files and find out the following facts about the building: (1) it was completed in 1905 and was a regional station for passenger train service until 1977, when it was closed; (2) it's a five-story structure with more than 60,000 square feet of floor space and a high, vaulted ceiling with fresco paintings depicting scenes of native American Indian villages in the region during the early 1800s; (3) building was where political rallies and social events were held in the city until World War II; (4) five former U.S. presidents gave whistle-stop speeches there during their candidacies for office; (5) it was declared a National Historic Landmark in 1980; (6) put on the market by IC in 1985, but not sold; (7) handled more than 50,000 passengers a day at its peak in 1945.

Write an inverted pyramid story for this afternoon's paper.

Writing Tips

Journalistic writing is different from other writing forms for several reasons: (1) it must be more concise; (2) it must be easily understood; and (3) it's usually done on a tight deadline. Still, there are few differences between good journalistic writing and good writing generally. Most of the rules for journalistic writing follow the standard rules for writing in the English language, although there are a few "conventions" or wrinkles peculiar to journalism.

This chapter offers examples of common errors made by beginning journalism writers. It next moves to examples of slightly more complicated writing problems, including grammar and style. Lists of commonly misspelled words are offered, and the chapter ends with some exercises keyed to Appendix A on newswriting style.

COMMON ERRORS

All teachers are likely to list a few beginning writing errors that really get on their nerves. Here are some of the more common problems that may serve as basic guidelines of what to avoid.

Its vs. It's Error

Beginners have difficulty distinguishing between the contraction form *it's* and the possessive pronoun *its*, without the apostrophe. This might be the single most frequent beginner's error. Remember that the apostrophe is used in contractions to indicate that some letter or letters of words are missing. In the case of *it's*, there are two possible meanings: "it is" or "it has." The apostrophe shows that the letter *i* or the letters *ha* are missing. So *it's* is a pronoun contracted either with the verb *is* or the verb *has*:

> She said it's her decision.   (it is)
> She said it's been a difficult decision.   (it has)

The possessive pronoun form *its* is a neutral gender word similar to *his*, *hers* or *theirs*. *Its* is a possessive pronoun meaning "belonging to it," and there is no apostrophe. Some examples are:

> The bike was chained by its wheel.
> Its bricks were beginning to crumble.
> The jury rendered its verdict.

Pronoun Reference Errors

Another common error in writing is the pronoun reference error that leaves readers wondering which noun is the antecedent of the pronoun:

> Hank was her lover, and she told Jim she would never see him again.

To whom does the "him" refer? Is it Hank or Jim whom she said she wouldn't see?

> Smith got into the car, put the gun in the glove compartment and lit a cigarette. It belonged to his boss.

Here the reader doesn't know if "It" in the second sentence refers to the car, the gun or the cigarette.

The way to avoid pronoun reference errors is to replace the pronoun with the noun to which it refers. In the first example, use either "Hank" or "Jim" instead of "him." In the second example, write: "The car belonged to his boss." Don't be afraid of using pronouns, just reread your work to ensure that all the pronouns clearly refer to their intended nouns.

In Order To

It's amazing how frequently *in order to* is used in news stories. Actually, 99 percent of the time the *in order* isn't needed. Using only the word *to* is sufficient to get the idea across.

Affect and Effect

Affect is the verb form. Remembering that will provide the right decision in virtually all cases. "Their argument did not <u>affect</u> her decision, but her new policy had a far-reaching <u>effect</u>."

Cite, Site and Sight

Cite and *site* are used frequently in news stories and are often confused. *Cite* is like *citation* and means "to name formally; or to use as an example" as in, "He was cited for bravery." *Site* refers to a place as in, "The warehouse was the site of the arrests." And *sight* relates to vision.

As Far as . . . Is Concerned

The most frequent problem in using "as far as . . . is concerned" is the tendency to omit the second part of the phrase. Novices will write: "Smith said that <u>as far as</u> marriage, she had no use for the institution." The sentence should begin: "Smith said that <u>as far as</u> marriage <u>is con-</u> <u>cerned</u>, . . . " A better approach is to avoid using "as far as" in your news stories. The phrase is weak and unnecessary.

That vs. Who

People are "who"; inanimate objects are "that." The form is: "The burglar who used the elevator was caught." But, "The elevator that caused the injury was repaired."

That vs. Which

Which introduces non-essential information. Clauses introduced by *which* are almost always separated by a comma or set off by commas:

> Strikers set fire to a truck, which was near the gate.
> The bill, which was the first introduced, passed unanimously.

However, *that* is used to introduce essential information, and its clause is not separated by commas:

> They found the body that had washed up on the rocks.
> This was the dog that had bitten a 6-year-old child.

Overuse of "That"

While the word *that* is frequently used and often is essential to clarity, novices tend to load their sentences with too many *that*s. Using too many is less concise and interferes with readability: "That was the last time that the legislature voted on that bill that deals with taxes." This, of course, is an exaggerated example. Simplified, the sentence should be, "It was the last time the legislature voted on the bill dealing with taxes." But the most flagrant overuse of *that* in journalism is in attribution: "She said that the car is hers," should be merely, "She said the car is hers."

Overuse of Beginning "The"

Another journalistic convention used for conciseness is an effort to avoid using "The" to begin a sentence. While "The" is needed to begin many sentences, journalistic writers are advised to delete it where possible without interfering with sentence clarity. For instance, these sentences would read just as well without the beginning "The":

> The police apprehended a murder suspect.
> The policies of the liberal candidates were challenged.
> The drivers averaged 200 mph on the race course.

Due To vs. Because Of

Whether to use "due to" or "because of" is a choice between a more stilted and a less stilted usage. The general rule in news writing is to be less formal, so "because of" is preferred. "Bridges in the city will be hazardous due to ice storms" is more formal than " . . . because of ice storms." Novices also find themselves using "due to the fact that." This phrase should always be deleted and replaced with "because."

Principle vs. Principal

An ideological view is a principle. It's a noun. A principal is the director of an elementary or secondary school, and it is also the foremost, most important or first thing. *Principal* is usually a noun but can also be an adjective as in, "Protesting is the organization's principal activity."

We're vs. Were

We're is a contraction with the apostrophe indicating a missing letter. The missing letter is from "we are," and the word is a verb form. *Were* is also a verb form, the past tense of *are*.

Then vs. Than

Then deals with time sequence or being next in a series: "She first earned $25,000 but then received a $3,000 raise."

Than is a comparative used to show relationships between two or more things: "She earned more money this year than last."

Above and Around

Above means "higher than," but it should be used only as a height dimension as in, "The palm trees reached above the street lamps." But a common mistake is using *above* with figures as in, "Damages were estimated at above $150,000." *Above* should not be used for figures; the sentence should be " . . . more than $150,000."

Mistakes with *around* are similar. *Around* means "in a circular manner," as in: "The bicycle track wound around the park." But *around* is not a synonym for *about*, when the writer means "approximately." A common mistake is to use *around* this way:

Security forces arrived around 10 p.m.
The arsenal held around 50,000 automatic rifles.

In both cases, the word should be *about* instead of *around*.

Feels

You feel something with your hand. Try to avoid using *feels* in sentences where words such as *believes* or *thinks* are more accurate to describe people's attitudes. Also, in journalistic writing, a reporter or writer can't know what a person "feels" or believes unless the person tells the reporter. So proper usage is: "<u>He said</u> he thinks the law is vague."

Up and Down

Up and *down* are best reserved for use as directional prepositions. Otherwise, they are extra baggage in many instances. The house doesn't "burn down" or "burn up"; it burns. Legislators don't "head up" the committee; they "head" it. Also, prepositions shouldn't be used as verbs. Use "increases" or "raises" instead of "ups the ante"; use "drank" rather than "downed the beer."

MORE SOPHISTICATED POINTS IN WRITING

Journalistic writing is designed to be read quickly and probably only once. If a reader is personally involved in the story, or if the subject matter is extremely high on the reader's interest list, paragraphs of the article might be read a second time. For most readers, however, any need to double back is instant grounds for moving on to another story. Needing to reread usually means something is wrong with the writing . . . some error in presentation clarity has confused the reader. Conciseness and ease of understanding are paramount in journalism, and both goals usually have to be met on deadline. Here, then, are some points about being concise and writing for easy understanding.

Choose the Short Word

Actually, the rule should be to "choose the right word," but the short word is usually the right word. There may be a hundred words that mean a person's "work." Consider *vocation, profession, trade, responsibility,*

Amid a bank of word-processing terminals, a Detroit *Free Press* copy editor reviews the "hard-copy" printouts of news stories strewn across her desk. Copy editors review news writers' stories and serve as a second line of defense against errors in fact, grammar and style.

business and *occupation*. Yet the shortest word and the most easily understood is *job*. Journalistic writers fight any temptation they might have to make a sentence flowery or grandiose. They know the words will become stilted or pompous sounding, and the sentence will become a stumbling block rather than the fluid, easy read it should be.

However, journalistic writing should not be mundane. Eloquence, force and spirit can be achieved through simplicity in word choice. In fact, concise writing usually improves force and increases understanding. Avoid using long words or any words your readers may have difficulty understanding.

Avoid Complex Sentences

As with individual words, short sentences are preferred over long sentences because they're easier to read and to understand. If a sentence begins to reach 40 or more words, it's a good idea to break it into two sentences. Actually, a 20-to-25-word sentence is probably the optimum length, but nobody is suggesting you count each word in your sentences. The point is to remember that the longer it is, the more burdensome the sentence will be for your audience.

Along with word count, consider your use of commas. Commas set off phrases, and too many phrases in a sentence denote complexity. The more commas there are, the more complex and difficult a sentence is to follow. One incomprehensible sentence can send the reader to a less demanding story. Watch those comma clauses, and if you're using too many in a single sentence, rephrase it or break it into two or more sentences.

But strings of short, simple sentences are boring. They sound like a first-grade primer on the order of "See Spot run. Run, Spot, run," and that also will be a reader turnoff. The objective is to alternate between shorter and some longer sentences, simple sentences and some more complex sentences. The change of pace should avoid boredom without interfering with reader understanding.

Active Voice

Editors and teachers share a disdain for sentences written in passive voice. In passive voice, the subject is acted upon: "Snodgrass was walked to the electric chair at 5 a.m." In active voice the subject does the action: "Snodgrass walked to the electric chair at 5 a.m." Although the difference seems easy to remember from this example, writers have trouble with voice in news stories, particularly in their leads:

Iowa's state lottery bill <u>has been approved</u> by the Senate in a close vote taken this morning.

Change this lead to active voice by focusing on the outcome rather than the vote:

A state lottery <u>is now legal</u> in Iowa following the Senate's narrow approval of the bill this morning.

You can check your lead voice, and indeed much of your entire article's voice, by rewriting verb forms that include giveaway words (used in conjunction with another verb) such as *were, has been* and *have been.* Admittedly, there are times when passive voice is appropriate, but the lead of a news article should not be one of them.

Use Strong Verbs

Verbs are a mainstay in journalistic writing. They add motion and life to a news story. A journalist should seek them out and use them when they are appropriate descriptions of what happened . . . a hint that strong verbs can be inaccurate. For instance, following the state lottery lead, to say that the bill "sailed through" rather than "cleared" the Senate would mislead the reader unless the Senate vote was close to unanimous. But, within these accuracy guidelines, you should replace weak verbs with strong ones:

A bystander hit the purse snatcher who was running through the crowd. The force of the blow swung the fleeing thief into the path of a truck.

That's an active enough passage due primarily to the story's circumstances, but it could be better:

A bystander slugged the purse snatcher who was racing through the crowd. The force of the blow whirled the fleeing thief into the path of an oncoming truck.

But avoid the obvious exaggeration and probable inaccuracies of the following passage:

A bystander hurled his fist into the purse snatcher's face as the robber darted and weaved through the crowd. The crushing force of the blow lifted the fleeing assailant off his feet and hurled him into the path of a speeding truck.

Dangling Modifiers

Dangling modifiers are a common error in any type of English writing, but they occur frequently for journalists who must write on deadline. A dangling participle is a phrase that often begins with a word ending in *-ing,* such as *fleeing, remembering,* etc. The phrase usually begins a sentence. The dangling element occurs when the phrase is not followed immediately by the noun that it modifies. Here are a few examples, which should sound confusing if not ridiculous:

Being of sound mind, the judge sent him to prison rather than committing him to an asylum.

Consisting of a mass of silicon chips and electronic boards, he said computers are the devil's toys.

Running naked through the park, a police officer grabbed her and took her to the station.

Following an endless chain of high tension and drinking that lead to alcoholism, a California beach house was the only escape he had from nightmares of his years in Vietnam.

The problem with each of these is that the participial phrase isn't followed immediately by what it modifies: the defendant, computers, a woman and (his only) escape. Being on a tight deadline, a journalist can make similar embarrassing errors without realizing it.

Collective Nouns, Their Pronouns and Verbs

Another irritant of teachers and editors is the collective noun. Common nouns used in news stories include: company, team, choir, group, committee, firm, organization, troop, administration, band, jury, squad, crowd and dozens of other words that mean collections of people acting as a cohesive unit. A collective noun is singular and its accompanying pronoun and verb are singular, regardless of what is heard on radio and television commercials: "Come on down to Jones Sporting Goods. They're having a sale. . . . " The proper form for collective nouns, their pronouns and verbs is:

The jury <u>was</u> given <u>its</u> instructions and retired to <u>its</u> chamber to deliberate.

Laser Products <u>claims it</u> was first to introduce the product to the marketplace.

The Grateful Dead still <u>sells</u> out <u>its</u> concerts.

The word *none* often presents problems. In most instances it stands for "no one" and takes a singular pronoun and verb: "None of the ships <u>has</u> returned to its dock." But when the reference means "no two," or "no amount," *none* becomes a plural: "None of the bills <u>were</u> paid."

More complicated is the rule for a noun such as *couple.* When *couple* refers to two individuals, use a plural verb: "The couple <u>have</u> a 10-year-old child." But when *couple* means a unit, use singular verbs: "Each couple <u>has</u> a private room."

The word *percent* is usually singular: "They said 40 percent <u>was</u> received"; but *percent* becomes plural if the word following an "of" construction is plural: "They said 40 percent of the tickets <u>were</u> received."

The word *whereabouts* always requires a singular verb: "His whereabouts <u>is</u> unknown."

Wordiness

In journalistic writing, wordiness is an error equal to using cumbersome words or writing long sentences. Edit your copy for wordiness as your last task before turning it in. If you edit your work critically, you'll discover dozens of unnecessary words. Remove them and rewrite to ensure that the remaining words still make sense. Long sentences may be a clue to wordiness, along with long phrases in sentences. Watch for multiple adjectives, unnecessary adverbs and any redundancies. Consider the following example:

Williams fought long and hard through rounds one, two and three. His fighter's stance became shaky and his knees became wobbly by the halfway point of what must have been a painful fourth round for him, but he valiantly managed to call upon his training to duck and weave the devastatingly forceful blows of his younger, stronger opponent. Finally, in the beginning moment of the dreaded fifth round, which was destined to be his last of the evening and the end of his long pugilistic career, he was caught off balance with an uppercut that sent him reeling back into the ring's ropes. He dropped with a loud thud to the cold canvas and lay there in a state of unconsciousness.

Some editing of the paragraph produces the following less flowery and more concise rendition of the same event:

> Williams fought hard through round three. His stance became shaky by the middle of the fourth round, but he managed to duck his younger and stronger opponent's blows. In the first minute of the fifth round, an uppercut sent him into the ropes. He dropped unconscious to the canvas.

Of course, reducing the original long-winded sequence was a relatively easy task. Much more difficult is honing a shorter sentence, such as a lead, for wordiness. For instance, the following seems readable enough:

> Fourteen elementary school children were injured early this morning on their way to school when the bus in which they were riding had a collision with a dump truck owned by the city.

But it can be honed to its essence of information with:

> Fourteen school children were injured this morning when their school bus collided with a city dump truck.

Here, the unnecessary words are removed and a few wordy passages are rephrased for simplicity. The clutter is gone; the information remains and in a much easier-to-grasp manner. Just as every lead should be honed to the bone, so should later paragraphs of the story.

Avoid Jargon

Journalists get their information from knowledgeable sources, and these sources frequently speak in terms unique to their profession or agency. For example, a statistician might use the term *median* in interpreting survey results. It means the halfway point: perhaps $30,000 was the median family income; half the survey respondents made less and half made more. But most news readers won't understand that the term means a special kind of "average" score. Avoid using words your general reading audience won't know. If you must use a jargon term, explain what it means.

Other forms of jargon are fad or superfluous phrases, often heard in government agencies, corporations or the professions ("decision-wise," "impinge upon") and disguised or grandiose phrases such as "negative cost containment," "employment reduction program" and "operationalization of quality enhancement programs."

Attention to Detail

The most effective way to write is through detail rather than generalities. A college student did a story about unwed mothers on welfare. She visited a young mother in a public housing unit in the Los Angeles barrio, and wrote all the customary descriptions of the poverty in which this family of three lived: garbage in the stairwell, graffiti on the hallway walls, peeling paint on the doors. But the student also wrote that when the young mother offered her coffee, it was served to her in a chipped cup. Readers will recognize instantly that when anyone serves a guest, the server takes the chipped cup. This single detail said more about poverty than all the common descriptors: The young welfare mother didn't have an unchipped cup.

Show, Don't Tell

Remember that your readers missed the scene of the action and didn't have a chance to talk with your sources. You must show your readers through your writing so they can see it as if they were there. For instance, if you want to tell your readers what it feels like to be in a mannequin manufacturing plant, don't say, "At first glance, the parts room is sickening." Instead write, "A rush of nausea grips visitors to the parts room where bins of unassembled arms, legs, heads and torsos trigger the ghoulish specter of a scrapyard of human bodies."

Readers may have trouble envisioning dimensions given in numbers. So instead of writing, "The building was 125 feet high," write, "The building was 10 stories high." Instead of writing that the warehouse was 150 feet by nearly 1,000 feet, say it was about the size of three football fields placed end to end.

Proper meanings and uses of words
Accept means to receive; except means to exclude.

Aid means help; aide is an assistant.

Use afterward, not afterwards.

It's all right, never alright.

Allude is suggesting without saying; refer is direct mention.

Allude means suggesting a reference; elude is to escape.

It's <u>after all</u> (two words), not afterall.

It's <u>a lot</u> (two words), not alot.

However, it can be either <u>a while</u> or <u>awhile</u>.

<u>Among</u> means there are three or more; <u>between</u> means only two.

Use <u>backward</u>, not backwards.

<u>Bazaar</u> is a fair; <u>bizarre</u> means strange or unusual.

<u>Beside</u> means next to; <u>besides</u> means in addition to.

Use <u>between</u>, not "in between."

Lowercase <u>black</u> in reference to a person's race.

She's a <u>blonde</u>, he's a <u>blond</u> but they both have <u>blond</u> hair.

<u>Compliment</u> is praise; <u>complement</u> is adding to or assisting.

Poets <u>compose</u> a sonnet; sonnets are <u>comprised</u> of words.

<u>Counsel</u> is to advise, or an attorney; <u>council</u> is a group.

Things are <u>different from</u> each other, not <u>different than</u>.

<u>Ensure</u> is to guarantee; <u>insure</u> refers to insurance.

<u>Entitled</u> is the right to something; books are <u>titled</u>.

<u>Farther</u> is a distance; <u>further</u> is an extension.

<u>Fiscal</u> refers to budgets; <u>physical</u> refers to material.

A <u>kid</u> is a goat; instead use <u>child</u> or children.

<u>Lady</u> is used for nobility; use <u>woman</u> instead.

<u>Lose</u> means not to win or to misplace; <u>loose</u> is the opposite of tight.

<u>Personnel</u> is a group of people; <u>personal</u> is private.

Pilots are <u>fliers</u>; posters are <u>flyers</u>.

Speakers <u>imply</u>; listeners <u>infer</u>.

It's <u>spokesman</u> or <u>spokeswoman</u>, not spokesperson; same for chairman and chairwoman; it's <u>representative</u> if the sex isn't known.

A synonym for "torn down" is <u>raze</u>; but <u>raise</u> means lift.

<u>Their</u> means it belongs to them; <u>there</u> is a location.

Use <u>toward</u>, not towards.

COMMONLY MISSPELLED WORDS IN NEWSWRITING

The journalist's most common spelling errors include the most frequently misspelled words in the English language. That suggests they are words a journalist uses frequently, and that these words present spelling difficulties even for people who are generally good spellers. Learning how to spell them now gives you a host of benefits:

1. Use these words instead of searching for synonyms that you know how to spell.
2. Save writing time by not having to refer to a dictionary as often.
3. Improve your grades by avoiding these misspellings.
4. Pass a job entrance examination that requires a spelling test.

Although most of the words aren't specific to journalism, the list does include many of the most frequently misspelled words in journalistic writing.

absence—"s" then "c"
accessible—two c's and two s's
accidentally—"tally" is the hard part
accommodate—two c's and two m's
accompanying
accumulate—two c's and two u's
acquaint—don't forget the "c"
acquisition
adjacent—it has a "d"
advantageous—"eous" is the hard part
advisable—no "e" in the middle
adviser—"e" not "o"; but it's "advisory"
allege—no "d"
analyze—"y" not "i"; "z" not "s"
athlete—no middle "a"
argument—no "e" after "u"
autumn—"n" on the end
auxiliary—one "l" and two i's
bankruptcy
benefitted—second "e" and two t's
bona fide—two words
bookkeeper—two k's
boundary—with an "a"
burglar—no second "u"
bureaucracy
business
calendar—one "e," in the middle
canceled—one "l"

Caribbean—two b's
cassette—two s's and two t's
catalog
changeable—retains the "e" in "change"
character—with an "h"
colleague
colonel—the military title
column—"n" on the end
commitment—one middle "t"; but it's "committed" with two t's
compatible—with an "i"
concede—no s's
conceivable
conscience—like "con" and "science"
conscious
consensus—single "c" at start
cooperate—no hyphen between o's
debtor—silent "b" and an "o"
defendant—not "ent"
dependent—not "ant"
desperate—with a middle "e," not an "a"
dilemma—two m's
doughnut—it's made of dough
embarrass—two r's and two s's
environment—it has a middle "n"
equipped—two p's
existence—no a's
expense—an "s," no "c"

faculty

familiar

February—first "r" is silent

foreign—an exception to the i-
before-e rule

foresee—middle "e"

forfeit—another i-before-e exception

fulfill

grammar—"ar" not "er"

gray—the color

government—it has a middle "n"

guarantee

guidance—with an "a"

homicide—an "i" in the middle,
not an "o"

indict—to bring legal charges
against; has silent "c"

initiative

innovation—two n's near start

insistence—no a's

intercede—no s's

irrelevant—two r's

itinerary

judgment—no middle "e"

knowledge—"know" plus "ledge"

legitimate

leisure

length

liable—silent "a"

liaison

library

license—"c" then "s"

lien

lieutenant

lightning—no middle "e"

likable—no middle "e"

likely

maintenance

manageable—"ea"

maneuver

marriage

mileage

miscellaneous

misdemeanor

monitor—two o's

mortgage—silent "t"

necessary

negotiate

ninth—no "e"

noticeable—"ea"

obsolete

occasionally—two c's, one "s,"
"ally"

occurrence—two c's, two r's and
"ence"

offense—no "c"

omission—one "m," two s's

opinion

overall—one word

pamphlet

parallel—one "r," two l's in the
middle

partial

peculiar—"liar" ending

phenomenal

physician

pompon—ends in an "n"

possession—two sets of double s's

practically—another "ally" word

precede—middle "c," no two e's
together

preferable

prerogative

privilege—no "d"

procedure

psychology

publicly

pursuing

questionnaire—two n's and an "e"
on the end

raze—good synonym for "tear
down"

receipt—silent "p"

receivable

recipient

recognize

recommend—one "c," two m's

recruit

recurrence—two r's, "ence"

regardless—there is no word "irre-
gardless"

reimbursement
relevant—"ant"
relieve
resistance—"ance"
restaurant—silent "a" in middle
salable—no "e" in the middle
salary
schedule
scissors
seize
separate—an "a" after "p"
sergeant
serviceable—retains the "e"
siege
similar
simultaneously
sizable—no middle "e"
specialty—has a middle "i"
sponsor—no "e"
sophomore—it has the middle "o"
subpoena—silent "b"
subtle—another silent "b"
sufficient
suing
summary
superintendent
supersede—no c's
surgeon—silent "e"

surprise—don't forget the first "r"
surveillance
technique
temperature
theater—not "re"
their
thoroughly
through
throughout
tomorrow—one "m"
totaled—one "l"
traveled; traveling—one "l"
unforeseen—"fore"
unnecessary—two n's and two s's
until—one "l"
unwieldy—not "ly"
usage—no middle "e"
vacuum—yes, it has one "c" and
   two u's
valuable—no middle "e"
vehicle
volume
Wednesday—silent "d"
weight
whether
whiskey—with an "h" and an "e,"
   but "Scotch whisky"
yield

Compound Forms

Correct use of compound forms is one of the most difficult aspects of spelling to be mastered in the English language. Should it be homeowner, homeowner or home owner? Compound forms are particularly challenging because few rules cover the array of possibilities. The Associated Press Stylebook offers a section on the use of hyphens with rules that cover compound modifiers, duplicated vowels, and avoiding ambiguity. Other entries in the stylebook deal with prefixes, suffixes and the use of anti-, but after that, you're on your own.

What you can do is be aware that there are compound problems with words such as candlelight; back stair; followup and knockout as nouns or adjectives, but follow up and knock out as verbs; yard lines; peacetime; insofar as; and officeholder. Remember that there is some doubt, and check the AP Stylebook or a comprehensive, recent dictionary.

STYLEBOOK

Appendix A of this textbook is a section on newswriting style. The Associated Press and the United Press International stylebooks are arranged alphabetically. The presentation in those primary reference books for journalists provides more detail and specificity than is offered in this textbook's appendix, and the primary references should be the first choice for accepted style usage. However, this textbook's appendix presents newswriting style by categories: capitalization, abbreviation, punctuation and numerals—the four most difficult and frequently referenced sections of the primary manuals.

Use the stylebook presentation in Appendix A to complete some of the exercises that follow this chapter.

Thinking it Through

EXERCISE 5.1

Capitalization

Indicate that a lowercase letter should be capitalized by placing three parallel lines under the letter.

A a conference on "housing the homeless" began today in new york city.

attending were: president george bush; the pope; pulitzer prize winner norman mailer; actress jane fonda; katherine graham, publisher of the washington post; henry kissinger, former secretary of state; and six nobel peace prize winners.

principal activities are expected in the committee on financing urban housing and its corporate donations subcommittee. a major announcement has been scheduled by a securities and exchange commission task force representing the fortune 500 companies.

cities in the united states targeted for action include new york and boston, and south down the eastern seaboard to philadelphia, washington and baltimore. Other major urban centers include atlanta, houston and miami in the south; the midwestern cities of chicago, detroit and minneapolis, and in the west, denver, san francisco and los angeles.

a report issued wednesday morning by the department of housing and urban development titled "poverty, crime and the plight of the homeless" sets the conference theme. ronald lehman, chief of the hud research division, said, "the homeless problem in our cities must be solved to effectively combat crime."

B   some 100,000 college students converged on a private florida beach and told officials they intend to remain on the property for the duration of spring break.

samuel g. sheridan, a senior at cornell university, told ocean ridge police he is acting president of students for open beaches, an organization formed at the ivy league schools, which now has a following of students from 200 universities who are vacationing in florida this week.

sheridan said: "we believe the beaches belong to everyone. million-dollar homes, eight-foot brick fences and city council restrictions hold no sway with mother nature."

ida wilcox, mayor of ocean ridge, a town of some 25,000 residents, said the students will be removed from the property by force if necessary. "we have no interest in the spring break crowd. we're a quiet, residential community, not a tourist spot." she said ocean ridge has no health or safety facilities.

police commissioner geraldine johnson said the students climbed fences and pitched tents during the night. several confrontations occurred with beachfront homeowners, but no injuries were reported, she said.

johnson said her eight-person police force has been reinforced with 60 state troopers who have been stationed on the beachfront property. Several first-aid stations were set up on the beach by the florida health and safety department.

mayor wilcox said she contacted governor gene ortega, who is sending his chief of staff to the site tuesday morning. "our city has a duty to protect private property," she said. "the ocean ridge homeowners association will receive the law enforcement it expects."

C   wingate gardens and museum opened thursday with more traffic than the old edmonds airport has seen in 30 years.

museum director norman hastings said more than 20,000 visitors were on hand to witness the first public showing of the new edifice since renovation began on the city's former air terminal nearly two years ago.

secretary cartwright dillon, who cut the ribbon to start wingate's public tour, said, "this is a finer museum than those i've seen in cities twice this size."

among exhibits drawing large crowds were photographs of lynchburg before the yellow fever epidemic of 1888, paintings of seattle harbor ships by pacific coast artists, an engine from the northwest railroad, an underground trip through a coal mine shaft and a display of 18th century pianos, spinets and church organs visitors were allowed to play.

however, visitors had to be satisfied with gazing at pewter plates and viennese crystal from italian immigrants to the region, two paintings by whistler and a remington sculpture, all of which were behind protective glass. additional security was provided for emerald-shaped diamond greek rosary beads dating from a.d. 1500.

crowds spent most of the visit in the botanic gardens, which have been a fenced secret since hampshire bros. of london began work some 18 months ago. known for its characteristic english tudor garden specialty, hampshire bros. provided more than 300 species of european and african flowers and plants, and nearly 100 varieties from america and canada. wingate gardens will be featured later this month in better homes and gardens.

exhibit curator glenda rose said wingate will be open weekdays from 9 a.m. to 4 p.m. saturday and sunday hours are 1 to 6 p.m.

D   the schedule of speakers for programs by the brookdale advertising federation inc. was announced this morning.

highlighting the list is an appearance by gertrude evans of los angeles, president of evans and hubble advertising agency, which handles the mcdonald's account worldwide. her presentation, set for oct. 5, will be open to the public and will feature "it's more than a meal," a film documenting the hamburger firm's unprecedented winning of seven cleos, the national advertising award.

"humor in advertising" is the topic of the nov. 2 ad federation meeting. herbert g. dolan, vice president for programming, said the presentation by dr. leonard lambert, associate professor of marketing at bowling green state university, will be an "amusing look at alka-seltzer and volkswagon award-winning ads lambert originally wrote for esquire."

january's program, set for the 20th, will be the winners of this year's cleo awards. "we can count on this one to bring members out," dolan said.

guest for march 9 is millionaire salesman william packer jr., champaign, ill., who made his fortune selling billboard space. packer's ad reputation includes space donated to the red cross, national seatbelt safety and the young men's christian association.

may 5 is the scheduled date for local federation award presentations. the event includes prizes for print and broadcast with the best-of-show recipient earning a $500 u.s. savings bond.

the final meeting on july 7 is the annual brookdale and greshman county political roast-off. on hand will be mayor alvin dowdelle, brookdale city council-woman alice winters, alderman g. henry robinson of clovedale and state sen. gina mccarthy of the 4th district, democratic majority leader of the legislature.

dolan said the roast-off drew a crowd of more than 500 last year and raised nearly $10,000 for city charitable causes the ad federation supports.

EXERCISE 5.2

Abbreviation

Draw a circle around words in the following exercises that should be abbreviated.

A   Deputy Secretary John T. Ridge of the United States Department of State, the youngest member of President Bush's administration, was released from the United States Embassy in Chile Friday.

Fifteen other Americans remain captives in the latest embassy hostage crisis incident.

Ridge, a former director of Amway Incorporated and assistant public defender in Orange County, California, said he "simply talked my way out and got them to take me to a plane bound for Miami, Florida."

After being debriefed by Central Intelligence Agency officials, Ridge was led to a press conference by Vice President Dan Quayle, who had flown to Miami on United States Air Force One.

The freed Ridge said there were only six captors holding the embassy, but they had 9 millimeter automatic weapons and threatened to explode grenades they carried. "They didn't start talking with us until February 23," he said.

Brigadier General Henry R. Smythe Senior, acting for the Department of Defense, prevented Ridge from going into more detail. Smythe, a former commander of the Third Armored Division, said, "The rest of the hostages will be out of there by Saint Patrick's Day."

Ridge will be flown to Fort Wayne, Indiana, later in the week to visit his wife, Doctor Lynda Ridge, at their home on Elmwood Street, and his father, Professor Oscar G. Ridge, 1244 East Lincoln Street.

Ridge came to national attention five years ago when it was reported he had begun his own firm, E&J Realtors Corporation, with a $1,000 graduation gift and turned it into a $5 million-a-year operation.

He earned a Bachelor of Science degree in marketing while running his business and reached a directorship level in Amway on his 25th birthday, August 15, 1987. He completed a law degree and served two years with the Third Ward Public Defender's Office in Orange County before being named a deputy secretary.

B Three city officials were indicted Wednesday on charges they had used insider information to make $1.5 million in the livestock commodity market.

City Treasurer T. William Slater, 1011 River Road Drive; Lieutenant Commander Alex Niles Junior, Second Ward commissioner, West Spruce Cove; and the Reverend Horace Abott, Fourth District city councilman, 555 East Thirty-seventh Street, were charged with violating Securities and Exchange Commission sanctions against using privileged information to profit on the securities exchanges.

The three were equal partners in Vetchem Limited, a firm that specialized in veterinary medicines. The Securities and Exchange Commission alleges the firm learned of an outbreak of anthrax—hoof and mouth disease—in Texas, Oklahoma and Kansas, and the owners used the information to buy beef futures.

Securities and Exchange Commission prosecutor Lillian Moreaux said, "These three men knew when the United States Department of Agriculture reported the disease, there would be a dramatic rise in the price of beef, so they bought thousands of contracts on the futures exchange."

Bill Wade, counsel for the accused trio, said records at the trial, set for February 2, will prove that Vetchem Limited bought and sold commodities frequently.

C Abbreviate properly if abbreviation is necessary; otherwise leave the space blank.

Senator Sims _____   100 East 85th St. _____

Private Jones _____   North Maple Boulevard _____

Number 1 son _____   202 Ninth St. West _____

Attorney Tom Lyle _____   Fort Wayne, Indiana _____

March 14, 1990 _____   Commander Edwards _____

Eighteenth Street _____   United States Marines _____

Mount McKinley _____   Sergeant Major Smith _____

First Amendment _____   The Revered Earl Taylor_____

Associate Professor Mark Milligan _____

Sergeant First Class Shirley White _____

Vice Admiral Henry Bettinghouse _____

Use proper abbreviations for the following:

cash on delivery _____   Sage Publishing Company _____

Grand Old Party _____   Central Intelligence Agency _____

before Christ _____   Interstate 20 _____

miles per hour _____   Masters of Fine Arts degree _____

RCA Corporation _____   National Broadcasting

Saint John _____   Company _____

                                   Central Standard Time _____

répondez s'il vous plaît (it means "please reply") _____

Equal Employment Oportunity Commission _____ Nevada _____

North Atlantic Treaty Organization _____ Virginia _____

National Education Association _____ Missouri _____

Trans World Airlines _____ Pennsylvania _____

EXERCISE 5.3

Punctuation

Use correct editing marks to show punctuation throughout the stories without changing the construction of the articles. When inserting punctuation using carets (ᴧ or ᵛ) be sure the point of the caret indicates exactly where the punctuation is to be placed.

A   Two women are dead and 13 other people injured following a freak accident at the Take Back the Night march in downtown Zenith Thursday

An 18 wheel tractor trailer jackknifed at a barricaded intersection and skidded into marchers leading a candle light antirape demonstration

Mrs Sally Kingston 43 of 114 E 42nd St a physician at St Marys Hospital and Stephanie W. Cline 22 Whitecastle Apartments No 17 a college student were killed instantly as the trailer overturned on them shortly after the 8 pm march began

Other marchers near the Front and Third streets intersection were hit by packing debris from the trailer The driver Thomas A Henderson 35 Tupelo Miss received head injuries and facial lacerations from broken glass

Witnesses said the truck driver may not have seen the barricade or the marchers until it was too late David M. Hartmann who was near the march leaders said It was so quick and so terrifying that I didnt realize what happened until it was all over He said marchers were too surprised to scream I heard screeching brakes and watched the truck It seemed to come out of thin air and turned over just in front of me

Mayor Ned Seagate also a march participant called the incident the citys worst tragedy of the decade We were trying to save lives with this demonstration instead we lost lives He said the city will begin an immediate investigation into why the truck driver didnt see the barricade in time

Listed in critical condition were Jerry McMann 51 2624 Courtside Drive Cherl R Franklin 28 157 W Victory St Amy B. Milsaps 24 Clinton Mo Terry L. Phipps 39 3160 Fair Oaks Ave and Andrew H Bond 63 Springfield Ill

B   I will never write another mystery thriller said Mrs. Jean Raddison Centervilles most noted author

Raddison told members of the Centerville Literary Society Monday that her last book Tender Love in Youth earned her a 10 week stint on the national best sellers list

Why should I write another mystery she asked when my first romance novel has made me a millionaire Ive written a dozen other books most of them mysteries in the last 20 years and those did little more than pay my grocery bills

Raddison has earned a regional following for her mysteries, according to society members Having mystery devotees has been wonderful she said but if youre writing for a living and thats what I do theres no substitute for a few hundred thousand romance fans

I signed a $100000 contract two weeks ago for the movie rights to the screenplay of Tender Love in Youth she said

Mysteries may be memorable they just arent as marketable as romances she said Her New York based agent had been urging me for years to try a love story because the mysteries often had a strong romantic sub plot she said Maybe thats why the mysteries had such a following

Raddison told the society I and my family will be leaving Centerville for a few months when the movie production begins but will return as soon as possible after that

Very few people know this but many of the characters Ive used in my books are based on people right here in Centerville she said She refused to name local residents who provided patterns for her hero and heroine in Tender Love in Youth

Several noted authors attended the Literary Society event including Paul Ashley a science fiction writer from Albany New York Dottie R. Davis Chicago a romance novelist whose new book Elegant in Lace also is on the best seller list Patricia Jenkins of San Jose California a Pulitzer Prize winning poet and Eugene Balkin St. Louis editor of the Post Dispatch

EXERCISE 5.4

Numerals

Use editing marks to correct numerals in the following stories. If a numeral should be spelled out, circle it. Circle also if the numeral is now spelled out but should be a figure. Remember that circling something is an editing mark meaning "do it the other way." If the number in the story is already in its correct form, don't circle it. Make other editing changes such as omission and inclusion marks to delete unnecessary numbers or to add proper numeral uses.

A

Harmony, a 30-person choir from Sixth Street High School, took first prize in the 5th annual city charity telethon Friday.

The choir, directed by 17-year-old Linda Damask, performed three selections including a 14th century ballad, a show tune from Forty-Second Street and Seventy-Six Trombones. Miss Damask accepted the three-foot-high trophy and a check for $1000.00 as the program ended at 11:00 p.m. in the evening.

The telethon earned more than one hundred thousand dollars in pledges during its 72-hour airing. Twelve celebrity judges voted on the two hundred acts entered in the 3-day event.

Earning the number two place and a $500 prize was a 5-piece rock band from the city's Third Ward. A $250 check went to 3rd place winner James West III, age twelve, for a ten-minute video.

B   Police squads from a five-county area cooperated in a drug raid Wednesday at 8:00 p.m. that ended in sixty-two arrests and netted more than $1,250,000 in crack cocaine.

The raid centered on Eighth District public housing units that have been the scene of twenty shootings resulting in nine deaths since August 5th.

With temperatures remaining near eighty degrees, most of the arrests were made on the streets and park areas outside the five-story housing units. However, a building on Thirty-Eighth Street was entered, and two crack manufacturing plants were found, police said.

Weapons confiscated during the night included twelve .22-caliber pistols, seven thirty-eights, three twelve-gauge shotguns and two submachine guns.

A crowd of some three hundred residents gathered by 9:30 p.m. to cheer as the officers loaded arrestees into twelve waiting police vans.

Interviewing, Quotes and Attribution

Virtually all news stories contain quotes. In fact, most stories are derived from interviews with people who become sources for news and who are named and quoted in the article. Because interviews are the primary basis of news-gathering, every journalist has to be adept at interviewing and using the information from interviews effectively in a news report. This chapter offers techniques for conducting successful interviews and for including the fruits of those interviews in a readable news story.

INTERVIEWS

One of the most frightening experiences a beginning journalist faces is his or her first one-on-one interview with a real news source. One challenge is just being able to hear your own questions above the pounding of your heart. Having that first interview behind you is a feat; having done it well is even more satisfying. The time to practice—and make your mistakes—is now. The entire interview process can be broken into discrete steps to be approached individually. The first may be deciding whom to interview.

Who Should Be Interviewed

Both by tradition and the logic of news values, the optimum interviewee for any news story is the person in highest authority among those who have information on the topic. If the topic is related to

help you learn about the topic before you speak to your chosen source.

- Getting a copy of the interviewee's resume and talking to the person's friends and colleagues.

Written Questions

Using your background information, prepare a list of questions you intend to ask your source during the interview. Always draft questions or topic headings, even if you have to jot them on the back of an envelope as you sit in the source's reception area. But it is better to have the questions typed neatly on a clean sheet of paper because you want your source to catch a glimpse of them.

There are no drawbacks to using written questions during the interview. Here are some advantages:

1. When you prepare questions, you are forced to think about the interview in advance.

2. Writing down what you need to ask keeps you from forgetting something important and helps focus the scope of the interview in your mind. It often gives a journalist an idea of the possible scope of the finished story.

3. Having the questions in front of you keeps you on track during the interview. Written questions help you control the interviewing situation, and you must be in control.

4. One of the best reasons for using written questions—and the rationale for letting the source glimpse at your page—is to massage the source's ego. "This journalist must think I'm important. That list of questions shows she's been preparing to talk to me . . . probably spent the last two days working on this interview. Of course I'm important." The source is now in a willing mood to talk and probably has a lot of respect for your professional abilities. That's the kind of impression you want to make with every source, particularly when you're going to be asking tough questions.

Don't let the source read the questions—if asked, decline pleasantly but firmly. But don't be afraid to let the source see you refer to the questions during the interview. You aren't hiding the fact that you've prepared them.

Finally, don't let your written questions dominate your interview. They're designed to keep you on track, but they aren't supposed to exclude useful deviations from the "script." If the source's answers open a potentially fruitful area of interest, harvest it and come back to your questions later . . . if at all.

Types of Questions

Journalists use the entire range of question types in their quest for news and information. Two basic categories of question are the close-ended and the open-ended.

Close-ended questions usually seek facts or confirmation/denial: How many homicides were committed in this county last year? Does this city need a payroll tax? The answers are expected to be short.

Because journalists usually want sources to provide as much information as possible, open-ended questions are used more frequently: Why was there such an increase in the number of homicides in the county last year? What do you think about this city's need for a payroll tax?

But journalists quickly learn that the breadth of answers depends more on the person answering than how the question was put. An intended close-ended question might elicit a 10-minute response. Generally, the longer the question, the longer the answer. A long question cues the interviewee that a long response is appropriate; shorter questions cue short answers. However, there is no guarantee that sources will respond to these cues. So journalists rely on non-verbal cues such as nodding agreement to keep the source talking and using the note-taking pen to cue that it's time to stop.

The Interview

Arrive at the interview on time. Have your note pad, pencil or pen, tape recorder and anything else you might need.

Do you really need a tape recorder? If you're in broadcast news, obviously you do need one. But if you're a print journalist, recording an interview can cause problems. Don't worry about the awkwardness of a tape recorder on the table near the source . . . the source will overcome taping nervousness quickly. The real problem is internal; your thoughts may drift during the interview. If you know you're taping, you may not listen as intently because you know you can always go back to the tape. However, if you are on a tight deadline, you probably will spend twice as much time trying to find needed passages on the tape as you would from glancing at your note pad.

The best recommendation for a print journalist is to tape an interview when you aren't on a tight writing deadline or when you are worried about possible later denials by the source. If these conditions don't exist, tape only as a backup safeguard. Don't rely on the tape recorder.

Worries about taking notes fast enough or well enough aren't justifiable reasons for relying on the tape. Just ask the source to repeat important passages or to speak more slowly. Don't be afraid of looking foolish; be afraid of being inaccurate. Sources will be happy to oblige rather than risk being misquoted.

What you should rely on is your pen. It can be used to guide the source through the interview. For instance, when the pen is in motion on your note pad, you're giving your source a cue that what's being said is worth writing. If you stop writing, you cue your source that you aren't really interested in the information being given. A good ploy is to keep your pen moving—keep taking notes—when the source is providing worthwhile information; stop moving the pen when the source wanders off track. If the source gets on a tangent that has no bearing on the story, put the pen down (listen politely, but don't write). Your source will learn quickly from these non-verbal cues, and your interview time will be spent more profitably on pertinent information. Obviously, the pen ploy only works when you hold your note pad at an angle so the source can't see what you're writing.

There is a logical pattern to what happens during interviews that should be incorporated into the order of your written questions:

1. The first few minutes of the interview should be reserved for building source-interviewer rapport. It is possible you won't use any of this information; it's intended only to make you and the source comfortable during the interview process. Your first few questions should be non-threatening, personal questions the source will want to answer: questions about the source's family, schools attended, the pictures on the walls or items on the source's desk. If you see something that suggests a hobby or interest, ask about it and engage in conversation. Your first goal is putting the source at ease in talking with you.

Another tactic to put sources at ease is to begin with non-threatening factual questions taken from your backgrounding information such as: "You've held this position six years, is that correct?" or factual questions that might go beyond your backgrounding such as: "About how many people do you now have on your staff?" This information is likely to be used in the story, and taking notes on such items at the beginning of the interview shows the source that your note taking is being done only for accuracy.

2. Next come the questions related to the news topic for which the interview was arranged. There may be half a dozen or more of these questions designed to elicit the information you need for your story. It's best if these are arranged in some logical manner (general to specific, chronological, etc.) so the source perceives them as a coherent unit.

Occasionally the source may help fine tune by interjecting, "You forgot about our purchase of Acme in 1987."

3. Near the end come the "bombs," those questions you know the source doesn't want to hear, and maybe you don't really want to ask. But you frequently will have to ask embarrassing questions such as, "What's your approximate annual income?"; "Why did you go back on your promises?" or "Have they told you yet that you're being fired?" Asking questions like those is part of the news job, so you ask them. But sources don't like hearing them, and they don't have to answer them.

Put the bomb questions near the bottom of your list in case the interview ends abruptly. Add one or two more congenial questions after the embarrassing ones to help your source save face and to end the interview on a positive note.

4. Remember to ask your source if there's anything you forgot to ask. Journalists who give their sources a prompt or an opening often uncover great news stories. When you control a relatively structured interview, your backgrounding may be flawed and you may be missing something important. Give your sources an opportunity to fill in the gaps or take you where you hadn't thought to go.

5. Finally, ask if you can call the source back if you need to clarify or check facts. When you're back at your desk writing the story, frequently you will notice an information gap that requires calling the source. If you've already suggested this may happen, your source won't mistake the call as a poor reflection on your journalistic capabilities. But more than one such call per story is likely to be unnerving.

Assuming the interview ends amicably, and most of them will, use the opportunity to get additional phone numbers: unlisted numbers, home phone, numbers that bypass secretaries. Explain to the source that you will be working on the story at odd hours and may need to call to verify some information.

Telephone Interviews

The primary difference between an in-person interview and a phone interview is that the journalist is usually on deadline. That may mean you haven't had time to do much backgrounding, prepare questions or think through the interview. Compared with the personal interview described in the preceding section, the phone interview forces you to wing it.

Some of the same principles still apply. Jot a few questions on a pad so you don't forget. Be certain to establish who you are and your purpose at the beginning of the conversation. Try to build rapport with good tele-

News reporters often rely on telephone interviews, taking notes and keyboarding quotes directly into their desktop computer terminal. When information gathering for the story is complete and the facts have been verified, the news article will be written on-screen.

phone manners. Ask if there's anything else the source wants to add. Ask if you can call back.

Common Interviewing Traps

You won't be in journalism long before you experience all of the following difficulties.

1. The source agrees to an interview but keeps postponing. It could be just a busy schedule, but if it continues you should recognize the source has no intention of holding the interview. Confront your source on using the tactic; be persistent without being obnoxious.

2. The source keeps wandering off the interview topic. Try putting your pen down. If that doesn't work, wait for a pause and ask another of your prepared questions. If the source is giving you non-pertinent information and doing so in a long-winded manner, you may have to interrupt (try not to be abrasive) and steer the interview back onto the topic. Recognize that some sources try to tell you what they want you to know, not what they know you want. Your backgrounding should alert you when this is happening.

3. In the middle of the interview the source says, "Now this is off the record. . . . " Immediately hold up your hand like a stop sign in the source's face and reply, "If it's off the record, don't tell me." If you allow a source to tell you something off the record, you can't publish that information. The source is probably relying on that. Giving a source off-the-record privileges compromises journalists and the free flow of news. Your first response should be to refuse. You may find that the source willingly tells you the information anyway, on the record. If not, at the end of the interview ask your source if he or she wants to tell you now, on the record.

4. After telling you something during the interview, the source then says, "Now, that was off the record." You say, "No, it wasn't." Then explain that when you set up interviews, all your sources are told pointedly that they are speaking for publication. Once an interview begins, you must give your permission before a source is allowed to go off the record, and you never give permission, you say.

5. After the interview, the source asks to see your story before you turn it in. This is a definite no. You don't have time to show stories to sources, and you don't need the hassle of being edited by a source. Simply explain that your editor doesn't allow you to do that (get your editor to make it a policy for you). However, if the story is highly technical or extremely complicated, you may ask the source to review your finished piece for accuracy before you turn it in. Now it's your decision and it's being done

at your convenience. This is the right approach when you aren't certain of the story's accuracy.

The interview is completed, and the note pad is full. What becomes of all those quotes when it's time to write the story?

QUOTES

Beginning writers forget the purpose of quotes in a story, so they often make poor choices in deciding what to quote. The purpose of quotes is twofold: (1) to tell your audience exactly what the source said and (2) to liven the written article.

A news story should include ample passages that tell readers or listeners exactly what the source said in his or her own words. Doing so lends authority to the article and sparkle to the written text. Quotes humanize the story and the quote marks themselves break up dense clumps of type. But using too many quotes or using them indiscriminately lessens their distinctiveness and counteracts their benefits. Journalists need to learn how to select quotes judiciously to make their stories effective. Here are some rules for deciding what to quote:

1. Quote the important statements made by central news sources in the story. A central source is someone integral to the article's news values. Important statements should be recognized easily, if not when the reporter heard and recorded them during the interview, then at least when the writer reviews notes to build the story.

How much important information should be used in direct quotes depends on several factors:

- story length—the longer the story, the more space is available for including worthwhile quotes;
- significance of the quotes—select quotes in their order of significance;
- length of the quotes themselves—avoid using long quotes regardless of story length;
- your restraint—don't overload the story with quotes, because that counteracts their impact in the story.

2. Consider the quotes themselves. Is something being said in an interesting or novel manner? Sometimes the source's turn of a phrase qualifies for a direct quote even if what is being said is not critical to the story. But be judicious in your selection of uniquely phrased quotes:

- consider the complexity of the quoted material—if you think a reader will have difficulty understanding the quote because of its complexity, don't quote that material directly;
- don't misconstrue a cliche for a unique phrase;
- avoid quoting material that contains jargon—you'll have to explain what the source was saying immediately after using the quote, so why waste a direct quote on jargon;
- avoid making a "you had to have been there" error—the quoted material may have made sense in context of the entire interview, but the quote by itself will leave readers wondering what the source meant.

3. Recognize dangers. Using direct quotes doesn't take the journalist off the hook of responsibility for what is published. Sources can be inaccurate, biased, angry and vindictive. The source may have said it, but if it's libelous and it gets published, you can be sued regardless of the quote marks. Watch out for these:

- slanderous statements—be wary of personal attacks on others;
- axes to grind—news sources frequently are embroiled in controversy and try to use the media as a weapon against their adversaries;
- statements the source probably can't verify—if you can't figure out how the source could know a piece of information, ask more questions;
- statements that contradict your backgrounding or that contradict information from your other sources—if the pieces of the puzzle don't seem to fit, keep probing until you find out how they do.

The general method of including quotes in a story will be: (1) primarily paraphrasing what sources say; (2) using relatively short single-sentence quotes; and (3) using partial quotes consisting of a single, relatively long phrase that is less than a full sentence in length. Avoid using short, partial quotes consisting of only a few words in a phrase. Fragmentary quotes detract from readability:

Smith said the group "must approve" a potent "package" of proposals.   (fragmentary)

Smith said the group "must approve a forceful package of proposals."   (longer phrase)

Quotes should be used throughout the story rather than being clumped together in one or two parts of the article.

Finally, quotes should be included in as organized a manner as possible. They generally will be presented in a way that supports the topic being addressed in the article, but they also might be presented in a manner that links them with a given source so the information that source provided is closely associated with the source's name. Readers have difficulty following who is being quoted when two or more sources are offering information throughout the article. Consider the following passage:

> Dr. Lester Morcrum, a local veterinarian, said the city's canine population has doubled in the last two years. "We have dogs that run wild and scavenge for food. Many run wild in suburban neighborhoods," he said.
>
> City Dogcatcher Nadine Holden denied Morcrum's estimate saying, "We get no more calls today than we did two years ago." She said her department keeps "the only reliable canine records in this county."
>
> Mayor Victor Yardly said: "There has been no increase in reported incidents of dog bitings. We have no reason to suspect a crisis exists."
>
> "By the time there is a crisis," Morcrum said, "we'll have an epidemic of rabies on our hands."
>
> Yardly said the city doesn't act on "speculation in matters such as this." He said, "First we need some evidence of a problem, then we'll deal with it."
>
> Holden said her office can handle any problem in the dog population within 48 hours of an incident meriting such action. "We simply do not have sufficient evidence at this time."

Quote organization in this passage is confusing because there is too much shifting from source to source. The difficulty could be solved by combining each source's quotes into single paragraphs containing all of that source's quotes: They are on the same theme. Also, the passage contains unnecessary quotes and could be simplified by omitting a few of the more redundant statements.

USING THE EXACT WORDS

Journalists are often faced with problems about using the exact words a source has used. There might be times when a reporter believes the notes taken during the interview aren't completely accurate. Assuming there was no tape recorder, or it didn't work, what if the quoted notes are smeared? What if the source spoke too rapidly for the journalist to capture the words accurately? In these instances, the obvious choice is to paraphrase what the source said rather than to use direct quotes that might be inaccurate.

But there are other instances that aren't so clear-cut. What if the source spoke in such broken sentences that there are no complete statements? Or perhaps the source used improper grammar—most of us don't use perfect grammar when we speak. What if the source used an inaccurate word such as "genetic" instead of "generic"? Or the source might have used profanity. Should the journalist change the quotes?

There are two approaches: that of the purist and that of the realist. A purist insists that anything between direct quote marks in a story will always be exactly the words that the source used, with no exceptions, ever. The purist may have fewer direct quotes in a story, but they will always be accurate. This journalist will never be fired for changing a direct quote.

A realist concedes that people frequently don't speak with perfect grammar, that sources occasionally use profanity they later regret, that sources can misuse words without even realizing it, and that spoken information can be confused or disjointed. People often say "er" and "uh" when they speak, and the realist points out that these stammers aren't included in the purist's quoted text. In short, the realist agrees with the Associated Press Stylebook that there is some room to change the actual words of a quote if the quoted material contains the essence of what was said and if the words that appear in quotes are very close to what was actually said. But the realist's professional life will include ethical dilemmas as this writer grapples with where to draw the line in "getting near" quotes. The realist always runs the risk of being confronted by sources who occasionally have tape recorders that do work.

QUOTE PUNCTUATION

Although a punctuation section is provided in Appendix A, so much of a journalist's trade consists of quoted material that specific rules for punctuating quotes deserve additional attention.

1. A comma is used before a direct quote containing a complete, single sentence:

Terrell said, "Crimes of this nature cannot be tolerated."

2. Omit the comma if the quote is shorter than a complete sentence:

Terrell said crimes "resulting in a death cannot be tolerated."

3. A colon introduces quotes of more than one sentence:

He said: "Let's not act in haste. We can build a new bridge when we know if there's enough traffic to justify it."

4. Punctuation almost always precedes (comes before, reading left to right) quote marks in written English:

"The first experiment," Adams said, "involved testing reading skills of third graders." He beamed at the audience and said, "Every student gained two grade levels in six months."

The ordering rule is that commas and periods always go inside quote marks; semicolons, question marks, dashes and exclamation points go inside the quote marks only when they're part of the quoted matter. Because journalists use commas and periods most frequently, the rule about punctuation going inside quotes works at least 95 percent of the time.

5. When the same person is being quoted across paragraphs, omit the end quote mark of the continuing paragraphs but start new paragraphs with a beginning quote mark:

Simmons said: "Toxic waste was never a problem for this rural county, but financing public services and public works projects was always a problem.

"Now that we've solved the latter predicament, we find ourselves at the forefront of the former," she said.

The last paragraph of quotes by the same speaker has an ending quote mark.

ATTRIBUTION

Effective attribution is an important aspect of journalistic writing and an integral part of using quotes. Attribution is how journalists tell readers where the information came from, and it's an essential element of all non-fiction. While its purpose may seem simple enough, effective attribution can be particularly difficult for beginners, who tend to first under-attribute and then to over-attribute their news stories.

The basic guideline for attribution is to be certain the reader always knows where the information is coming from. That means that a single attribution usually is insufficient; readers must be reminded throughout the story. An example of how it's done should provide further guidelines:

> John J. Millchamp, 22, was sentenced to life imprisonment this morning following his Friday conviction in the stabbing deaths of four Pine Grove waitresses.
>
> Millchamp, a student at State Votech, claimed he was innocent of all charges. His attorney, Adele Stoner, said the case would be appealed immediately.
>
> "We understand the jury believed it was doing its duty," Stoner said, "but an innocent man is wrongly paying the price of community outrage against these heinous crimes."
>
> Judge Richard Bearden denied Stoner's request to move the trial to another county or to delay the trial until news coverage of the murders waned. Stoner said the jury was reacting to media coverage of the slayings instead of the facts in the case.
>
> Millchamp told the judge that he had been mistakenly identified as the killer. "I was a frequent customer of the bars where those women worked, and I dated two of them," he said. "But I've dated a lot of women, and I never hurt anyone in my life."
>
> He said he was confident police would find the real murderer, and that his innocence would be confirmed.
>
> The families of the slain women were present at the sentencing. Cory G. Alton, father of Susan R. Alton, 21, the first victim found in June, said he believed justice had been done.
>
> "There is no doubt in my mind," Alton said, "that John killed my daughter. He was the last date she had before they found her body."

Here are some attribution principles shown in the article:

1. Each time a source is named, he or she is identified immediately. However, the first identification isn't belabored. For instance, Millchamp's full name and age begins the lead, but his identification as a State Votech student comes in the second paragraph. Stoner is identified by her full name and her title, as is Judge Richard Bearden. Every time a new source is introduced in the story, the full name, with middle initial and title or the person's relationship to the story, is given. Providing the full name and significant identification on first reference in the story is a basic principle in newswriting.

2. Throughout the article, in virtually every paragraph, the source of the information is given. It is not necessary to include attribution in every paragraph. The rule is to include enough attribution throughout the story so the reader never wonders who has provided that information. Because this article is based on information from three different sources (Millchamp, Stoner and Alton), frequent attribution is used so the reader has no difficulty following what information comes from which source.

3. Every direct quote is linked with attribution, called a "tag line," such as "Millchamp said," "Stoner said" and "Alton said." Notice that it's never "said Millchamp" or "said he." The only instance in which the tag is reversed is to avoid the confusion of splitting the two words when the source's identification is particularly long. Consider the following instance:

> "I never hurt anyone in my life," <u>Millchamp</u>, a part-time computer programmer at Southside Savings and Loan, <u>said</u>.

The right way is to reverse the tag to:

> "I never hurt anyone in my life," <u>said Millchamp</u>, a part-time computer programmer at Southside Savings and Loan.

4. "Said" should be the verb of choice in almost every tag line instance. The article example uses two other verbs, "told" and "claimed," but "said" is used seven times in this relatively short story. Novice writers worry about overusing "said," so they try to find synonyms such as "stated," "explained" or "admitted." But there are two problems with commandeering substitutes:

a. Only the writer is concerned about overusing "said"; readers hardly notice it because they're so accustomed to reading it that the word slips into the background. In fact, synonyms such as "stated" or "explained" draw the reader's attention. Since frequent use of "said" isn't a problem for readers, writers should feel free to use the word as often as needed.

b. The substitutes for "said" really aren't synonyms. Each has a different shade of meaning, which may or may not be appropriate. For instance, "stated" is a very formal way of saying something . . . the reader will wrongly assume you mean some sort of official pronouncement was made. "Admitted" is a synonym for "confessed," which is vastly different from "said."

5. "Said" should be the verb of choice in tag lines unless another word is more accurate. If you are describing a confession, use "admitted" or "confessed." If you are introducing a source's explanation, you may use "explained." Just be sure any time you choose a verb other than "said," that your selection is based on its being a more accurate verb than "said."

6. Should it ever be "says," in the present tense, instead of "said"? "Says" is often used in feature articles, but rarely in news stories. A possible reason for using the present tense is if the statement is something the source can always be expected to say:

> "We need more funds to provide quality education," Superintendent Jones says.

7. The article example uses attribution frequently enough so the reader is never confused about which source is providing the information or about whether the information is coming from a source rather than from the reporter. Using frequent attribution increases objectivity because the reader never confuses news with what might be considered the reporter's opinion. Consider the following passage from the example:

> Judge Richard Bearden denied Stoner's request to move the trial to another county or to delay the trial until news coverage of the murders waned. Stoner said the jury was reacting to media coverage of the slayings instead of the facts in the case.

If the reporter includes the underlined portion without first attributing it to Stoner, readers might assume the writer is making a judgment. Certain statements require direct attribution:

a. controversial statements;

b. predictions and forecasts;

c. direct quotes;

d. anything that the reporter could not possibly know unless the source said it.

This last part of the rule requires more explanation. It will be obvious to the reader that a reporter can know that a suicide victim fell from the 10th story of a building. If there were witnesses or police at the scene, the reader will recognize that one or more of them provided the information. However, if the reporter writes that the suicide victim had been suffering from depression, readers will expect some attribution with the statement.

Likewise, attribution is essential in reporting anything a person "thought," "believed," "recalled" or "expected." These key words, and many others, suggest the only way a reporter can know the information is if he or she has been told it. Instead of writing, "Mrs. Jennings wanted a promotion," write, "Mrs. Jennings said she wanted a promotion." The journalist can't know what people think or what they did when they were alone unless these sources divulge the information.

8. In case these many rules for using attribution suggest that every sentence or every paragraph in a news story requires attribution, that isn't correct. Attribution should be used where it is required, and used judiciously throughout the story, just enough so readers don't forget that the information comes from sources.

SUMMARY

Most news stories come from interviews, so every journalist must be adept at interviewing and using the information effectively in a news report. The first formal interview is usually tense, but the process is less intimidating when approached through its discrete steps.

The first step is selecting a source, usually the person in highest authority with information on the topic, preferably the one closest to the news event. Next, arrange the interview:

- get the person's full name, the proper spelling and the title; phone for the interview as soon as possible;
- tell the source your name and that of your news outlet; then the source knows the interview is for publication;
- tell the source the general topic; this allows the source to prepare or to suggest a more knowledgeable source;
- confirm the source's preferred name, spelling and title; set the interview time and place; call back to remind.

Before going to the interview, do your backgrounding homework. Prepare by checking "morgue" files, using the library, asking news room colleagues and contacting experts in the topic area. Write out a list of questions to ask during the interview to help you stay on track. Written questions indicate competence, and they make sources feel important. But don't let sources read your questions, and don't rely on them exclusively if the interview takes a more fertile turn.

Arrive at the interview on time with note pad, pencil or pen, and tape recorder. In broadcast news, the recorder is a must. However, a print journalist should rely on the tape only in verifying quotes, if there's no immediate deadline or if there is some concern about later source denial.

Interviews usually have a sequence you can incorporate into your prepared questions:

1. Spend the first few moments building source rapport; ask non-essential, sociable questions about hobbies or family.
2. Then ask the questions related to the news topic at hand; these should be arranged in some logical order.
3. Put the "bombs," those embarrassing questions, near the end; follow with a congenial question for a happy finish.
4. Give your source an opportunity to add anything you may have forgotten to ask.
5. Tell the source you may have to call to verify information or add missing elements.

Regardless of precautions, every journalist must deal with the entire range of common interviewing traps:

- source grants an interview, but keeps postponing—the source is avoiding the interview; confront and be persistent
- source wanders off the topic—it may be a ploy or just a personal quirk; take charge and steer back to the topic
- during the interview, source says, "Now this is off the record"—block that attempt immediately; you are likely to get the information on the record later
- after saying something in the interview, source adds, "Now, that was off the record"—explain that it wasn't; able journalists can neutralize this obstacle amicably
- source wants to see your story before you turn it in—say your editor doesn't permit you to do that.

When the interview is over and it's time to write, consider that quotes are used to tell what sources said in their own words and to liven the written article. Quote important statements by central sources, and interesting or novel statements. But remember that a journalist is liable even for material quoted directly.

Sprinkle quotes throughout the story in an organized manner relying chiefly on paraphrasing followed by single-sentence direct quotes and partial quotes. If deciding whether to use the source's exact words or very close equivalences, be prepared to defend any direct quote changes.

Quote punctuation and the use of attribution follow specific rules. For attribution: (1) identify each new source when named; (2) use enough attribution throughout the story so readers never get confused about the information source, but you do not need attribution in every paragraph; (3) place attribution next to all direct quotes; and (4) use "said" as the preferred verb choice, even if you think it's being overused.

Thinking it Through

EXERCISE 6.1

Selecting Sources

For the following events use the facts given to select sources from the list of possibilities for story information providers. Use the blanks provided to label each possible source as follows: "A" if you believe the source is indispensable; "B" for a secondary source; and "C" for a source you would contact only if time permits. The exercises may be done on a separate sheet of paper or on your VDT.

A Your city is named by Time magazine as one of the nation's five "up and comers" among cities in its population category. Reasons given included your university, the number of new businesses that have been started in the last five years and the decrease in reported crime during the same period.

———————— mayor of your city

———————— head of your city's Chamber of Commerce

———————— president of your university

———————— academic vice president of your university

———————— public relations director of your university

———————— chief of police

———————— head of crime statistics for your city

———————— your city's most notable business person

———————— one of the editors of Time magazine

———————— head of the independent survey company that provided the report on which Time magazine's story was based

———————— survey company's writer or evaluator who judged cities in your city's size category

B A two-passenger airplane crashes into a ditch at the end of your local airport's runway during a landing at 6 a.m. Pilot and George X. Rarick, owner of a local import firm, both killed in the crash. Drugs found in the wreckage.

_____ police lieutenant at scene of crash

_____ Rarick's wife

_____ the pilot's wife

_____ air controller who brought the flight in for the landing

_____ head of narcotics squad at the scene

_____ head of airport security

_____ a motorist who was an eyewitness to the crash

_____ official from the Federal Aviation Administration on the scene

_____ a local pilot who was a close friend of the dead pilot

_____ public relations director for the airport

For the following events, list five sources you would contact for your story. Number the sources first through fifth in your order of preference **after** making your list.

C A baby antelope crawled under a fence at your local zoo and made its way uninjured across a major highway. A counter clerk at a yogurt store in a nearby mall notified the zoo to capture the animal. The mother of a 5-year-old girl heard her daughter crying when the antelope ate the youngster's yogurt cone. The mother enlisted the clerk's help to hold the antelope in the store's supply room until a zoo truck arrived.

D "Boxcar" Tom Ringle, 64, a World War II hero who has been a resident of your city for at least 20 years, was found stabbed to death in his cardboard lean-to near the railroad tracks. Police said he may have been dead two days. A butcher shop owner reported the murder this morning. He was concerned when Ringle didn't show up yesterday to sweep the shop as he has been doing for nearly five years. There's a nearby Salvation Army post, a secondhand clothing store and a liquor store. Also, a group of local citizens called HAVEN has been engaged in a campaign to get the city government to fund a "halfway" housing project for the city's homeless.

EXERCISE 6.2

Selecting Quotes

The following numbered-line passage is all direct quotes. Based on the information contained in the passage, select the lines you would **not** use as direct quotes in your news story, and say why you wouldn't use these lines.

A

1. Ladies and gentlemen of the jury, I implore you to consider the facts in this case, both those presented by the prosecution and those by the defense.
2. Jackie Green was only following her maternal instincts when she shot her husband.
3. By any criterion of self-preservation she was defending her son who had been beaten into a coma by his stepfather.
4. Had she not gotten her husband's pistol and acted as she did, her little boy might have been killed before her very eyes.
5. Who can deny a mother's right to protect her child?
6. Who among us would deny the same sense of helplessness and panic if faced with the same choices?
7. This wasn't the first time his stepfather beat the boy, although it might have been the last.
8. Jackie's action prevented a lawless act, but can we call hers a lawless reaction?
9. I think mothers across the nation would be outraged with anything other than a finding of innocent.
10. I leave the decision in your hearts.

The following numbered-line passage is all direct quotes. Based on the information contained in the passage, select the lines you **would** use as direct quotes in your news story, and say why you would use these lines.

B

1. It was another example of criminal neglect by the County Highway Commission.
2. I was on patrol at the Bay Bridge ramp at about 3 p.m. when I saw the school bus stop and unload the children.
3. They walked across the bridge, because the weight of a loaded school bus is more than the bridge's safety limit.
4. Parents have complained about this problem for more than five years, but the Commission says it doesn't have the funds for bridge repairs.
5. Well, I guess they'll have to find the funds now.
6. When the schoolchildren were safely on the other side, they waited for the bus to come across.
7. The driver got about 50 feet when the bridge collapsed and sent the bus tumbling straight down into the water.
8. The driver didn't stand a chance. The bus sank instantly.
9. I called in for help and waited with the children who were crying and very frightened.
10. A dredging crew fished the driver's body out of the bay about an hour later.

From the following acceptance speech, select four sentences you believe **should** be used in a local paper's follow-up news story about the presentation.

C

I've been an actor for a quarter of a century, and have had the pleasure of being on stages all over the world. I've received many plaques and awards for my acting, including a recent Oscar for best supporting role. We actors are an immodest lot, so I will tell you that one wall of my study is filled with the tributes and mementos I've been given. But I must say that being honored by your high school for lifetime achievement is a most wonderful thing.

I remember my years in this building and the people who made me feel I could accomplish anything I set out to do. It is fair to say that my junior and senior plays on this very stage convinced me that acting should be my life's pursuit. My high school friends and teachers here in Appleton are responsible for any success I have had. They imbued me with a spark, a sense of worth de pied en cap. Others may recall their high school days with loathing, but my memories of those years are golden moments of strength and friendship.

What does this award mean to an old actor such as myself? It draws me closer to my hometown and its people. The plaque itself is not all that large, but it holds a special place in my heart. And I can assure you this plaque will become the centerpiece on my study wall. This tribute from Appleton High takes center stage, next to the right hand of Oscar.

_____ **Writing Practice** _____

EXERCISE 6.3

Attribution

Write news story segments—portions that will come **after** the lead of a news story (don't write a lead)—in which you use direct quotes, partial quotes and paraphrasing based on the following passages of direct quotes. Use the suggestions and rules from the chapter to determine which elements of the passages should be quotes. Use attribution frequently enough for reader understanding but not so frequently as to interfere with readability.

A   From police detective Gerald M. Valdez.

We were tipped off by an informant that a deal was going down at the Westgate Holiday Inn by the interstate. Sgt. Dedrie Hammond and I posed as newlyweds and checked into a room next to the one the informant said would be where the action was. We set up a listening device against the wall.

Two men showed up at the door and were let into the room where the deal was going down. We thought we heard them talking about crack, and we waited until we thought they had time to get the stuff out in the open.

Then Dedrie waited at the inside door adjoining the two rooms, and I went to their front door. I smashed in the door with my foot and shouted, "Police! You're under arrest!" When I saw what was going on, I ducked back quick. Two guys in the room had machine guns, and they opened fire almost as soon as the door broke in. The noise was deafening. I caught a slug in the side.

Sgt. Hammond broke her door in while they were shooting at me. They probably didn't hear her come through. She's the top marksman on the squad, and it really paid off. She took out both of the gunmen before they could spin around and get a shot at her. I think they would have killed me if she hadn't been so quick and so accurate.

The two other men were on the floor from the time the shooting began. Dedrie held her gun on them. Our backup squads came in and made the arrests.

B   From Valerie Brazden, head of the Kansas Farmers' Cooperative

Prices in the 1980s fell at such a steep rate—particularly in the first half of the decade—that the only farmers making a living were exotic fruit growers in California. Most of our land in Kansas is planted in wheat, so our people took a beating that nearly equalled what happened in the Great Depression. Families that had been on the land for six generations were going bankrupt and moving to the cities.

There's an old farmer's saying about how to survive in tough times: Get into cash crops. Our people got into cash crops with a vengeance. We went from corn and wheat, to soybeans and cotton. Those who could borrow enough tried growing fruits or vegetables. Beef can be a tricky business for farmers without any experience, but the Co-op brought in some expertise from Oklahoma and enticed them with land if they moved their cattle here.

All of this was working well until the weather changed. We blame it on the greenhouse effect, but nobody knows for sure if the extreme temperatures—burning summers and icy winters—are temporary or if they're here for good. We had a couple of bad years in 1980 and 1981, then a few good ones when we first got into cash crops and things looked like a silver lining. But the last four years have been terrible and we expect about the same number of failures as we had in the 1980s.

People then blamed the farmer's problems on too much borrowing. Some of our folks—even the small family farmers—owed the banks or the government more than $1 million. When they went under, the rest of the nation said they had been living too high on their borrowing power. But that wasn't it. They just thought they could make it work if they could keep farming.

Today there's less heavy financing in Kansas. We operate in a leaner and meaner environment. But we still can't beat the weather. If these weather extremes continue, the breadbasket of America is going to be empty by the year 2000.

C   From Sara Duncan

Sure I'd heard about pollution and toxic waste. I used to watch those stories on the evening news and say things like, "Why, those poor people!" It just never occurred to me that the same thing was happening right here at my house.

Our youngest, Lisa, was only 2 years old when she became ill. We kept taking her to the doctor, but it didn't matter what he prescribed. Lisa just got sicker and sicker. She was bedridden for nearly a year before she died. They said it was a virus.

Our youngest boy, Victor, was 5 when he began to break out in sores all over his body. He was in such pain that we'd put him in a tub of ice to try to cool the blisters. That's been going on for more than a year now. They have him down at the hospital. He's never been to school yet. But I have some hope he's getting better. We visit him every day.

Ginny, our 8-year-old, complains of headaches, and Bobby, our oldest, has backaches and is starting to limp.

The doctors say the two older ones might just be going through some genetic problems, but we don't have any stuff like that in our family. I keep telling them that it has to be the paint plant across the river.

I can't prove it, of course, but we hired a lawyer to find out if our land is poisoned. Between medical bills and legal fees, we're broke now. I'm convinced it's toxic waste or something else from the plant.

Now when I see one of those stories on the evening news, I see us instead of the people on television. I know the kind of misery they're feeling because we've been living it, too.

PART TWO

Frequent Article Types

Accidents, Fires and Disasters

News is often defined as "changes to the status quo" or disruptions to the normal routine. While these definitions are too simplistic to fully encompass everything that constitutes news, they do capture a significant amount of the day-to-day events journalists report. Accidents, fires and disasters are a staple for news coverage, and research shows that news media audiences pay close attention to these stories.

THE NEED TO KNOW

People are interested in dangerous storms, slayings, traffic fatalities and fires less from a sense of morbid curiosity (although that human frailty can't be discounted) than from of a sense of "surveillance." We need to know what is happening around us, to people who might be acquaintances, and to stay abreast of events that also might affect us. Obviously, an impending hurricane or a series of fires in our neighborhood pose a potential threat to our own security and that of our friends and family. But auto accidents, toxic waste contamination, robberies, homicides and airline hijackings also let us track the general state of our environment and serve as a warning system for our future safety and well-being. In short, news about these events serves a need-to-know purpose. Reporting them is not an excuse to titillate or sensationalize. The news media, and their audiences, regard these reports as a necessary public service.

This chapter's use of story types such as accidents, fires and disasters includes the entire scope of stories on news that disrupts the status quo and serves the audience's daily need to know. Most crime stories are part of this genre as are severe-weather stories, although the crimes aren't accidents and the storms usually aren't disasters.

Reporting Difficulties

One aspect of accident, fire and disaster-related news that makes coverage difficult is the deadline nature of these events. Invariably, they must be reported under deadline pressure to provide coverage as soon after the event as possible. Such stories often appear before all the facts are known, even to those in authority such as police or fire department officials. Another difficulty is the emotional nature of the event: tragedy, destruction, pestilence and death are emotion-packed news elements. In the midst of fear, panic and loss, sources become confused or antagonistic. These events are a challenge to accurate, comprehensive news coverage, yet they require as much accuracy and clarity as any other story.

Reporting Ease

Journalists' use of the inverted pyramid news structure provides a relatively simple formula for information gathering and article writing. Putting the most important elements first will usually result in an efficient presentation for both writer and reader. In fact, the inverted pyramid newswriting structure serves its intention best for accident, fire and disaster-type stories. The organizational format is so efficient that it allows discussion of the entire genre of this wide range of news events as a single unit.

NEWS VALUE CONSIDERATIONS

With some possible exceptions, accident, fire and disaster-type stories can be reduced to a model of news value selection based on the criteria shown in the model in Figure 7.1.

Consequence

Consequence is by far the most frequent decision point for accident, fire and disaster-type stories. How many people are affected by the event? Does it concern the entire community, a majority or a large segment of this media outlet's audience? If the story does, then it's likely to be a

Primary and interrelated values:

Consequence	Action	Proximity/Timeliness
• human life • injuries • property	• drama level • controversy • continuing	• concern of local audiences • how immediate is it • continuing

Secondary and more distinctive values:

Human Interest	Novelty	Prominence
• emotional response	• uniqueness	• importance of people involved

Figure 7.1 News value selection model for accident, fire and disaster-type stories

major news item, and consequence is likely to be the lead ingredient. Some of the considerations that constitute consequence are human life, injuries and property loss, in that order. For instance, 25 people killed in a commercial airline crash is more consequential than five people killed in a similar crash. One person's death in an automobile accident is more consequential than five people being injured. But human injury is generally considered more consequential than property loss, although a building destroyed by fire is more consequential than a firefighter being overcome by smoke inhalation during the blaze. Most of the consequence decisions can be placed in their proper order of descending news values by merely applying the reasonable ruling order of life, injury and property loss.

If the event is an impending disaster such as a storm or a drought, consequence can be assumed. Such news stories will interest virtually all members of the audience because each of them might be affected by the consequences of an impending disaster. In this case the potential severity of the event determines its consequence news value.

Action

Action provides the second-most-important consideration in the news value model. Remember that action refers to the visibility of the news event. Is it likely that the media audience has, or will, come in contact with the event? Again, an impending disaster assumes that all members of the audience might come in contact. A downtown fire during working hours suggests many people will have seen the event, but even the aftermath of a late night building fire will be seen by many the next morning.

Elements of an event's visibility include those placed with "action" in the model. Drama level is the relative interest level of the audience that the reporter might anticipate. A bank robbery is a dramatic event per se, but it becomes more dramatic if people are in the bank at the time, if weapons are used, if injuries occur or if hostages are held. A storm has a higher drama level if the wind velocity is unusually severe, if there's lightning or if it has swept across an adjacent state wreaking havoc en route to this locality.

While the element of controversy isn't normally associated with such stories, it can be. An earthquake always qualifies as a dramatic event, but the action interest level of the story increases if the earthquake occurs after local debate about the structural safety of buildings. A high-speed chase on a local freeway includes an added action dimension if the city is already embroiled in controversy over police policies following a recent pursuit that resulted in the death of pedestrians. Dozens of possible events qualify as dramatic action and become heightened in audience interest because they involve public controversy.

The last aspect of the model's action news value involves the event's span. An impending event such as a threatening storm increases concern because of its eminent destructive possibilities. More often the action is heightened because the event is of a continuing nature: bank robbers still at large; a block fire that continues to rage; a highway accident in which the lives of the critically injured hang in the balance. The action news value increases because the event is not complete.

Proximity/Timeliness

In the same way it affects action news value, the continuing nature of an event helps determine its proximity/timeliness news values. Proximity influences news value as explained in Chapter 1: the more a news event concerns the media's local audience, the more newsworthy. And the more an event is immediate, current and likely to continue, the greater its timeliness value. Certainly the audience interest in a news event is greater if that event occurs here and now.

While they can be viewed as separate elements, the model's upper set of news value considerations (consequence, action and proximity/timeliness) are really very much related. Still, the journalist should evaluate newsworthiness of an accident, fire or disaster-type story using the model's suggested order of news values in both the upper and lower sets.

Human Interest

The lower set of news value decisions in the model depend more on the particulars of the story itself. Human interest, the likelihood that a news story will evoke an emotional response among audience members, can be a compelling element even if the three major values in the model are not present. Journalists recognize, for instance, that an event involving only a single individual—a miner trapped underground or a young girl whose life depends on a vital operation—can be a powerful human interest story. The miner is trapped a thousand feet below ground. No others have died; the incident took place in Kentucky three days ago and only the single miner is at risk. Yet all of the major media are on hand as experts work around the clock to save the miner. Readers in Florida as well as viewers in Oregon will stay with the story.

The same sort of human interest emotion occurs when an infant is discovered abandoned in a dumpster behind a fast-food restaurant in Boise, Idaho. How is the baby doing? Has the culprit who abandoned the child been found? What will become of the baby? None of the three previous news values of consequence, action or proximity/timeliness is involved, but these stories are powerful because they evoke emotion.

Novelty

Like the broader category of human interest news value, the novelty value also depends on the facts of the story. Sometimes it's a humorous incident involving a burglar found in a locked safe full of money. More often it's a bizarre incident such as the busload of children and their driver who simply disappeared for almost a week in a Northern California farm community (they had been kidnapped for ransom and held, bus and all, in a huge covered pit their captors had dug . . . everyone was rescued unharmed). None of the other news values need be present if the story carries enough interest to merit coverage on novelty alone.

Prominence

The same as for novelty, prominence is a news value that demands none of the others. A relatively minor traffic accident involving a judge or a corporate executive officer rates coverage because of the person involved. An alleged arsonist, who is charged with using the same method of operation as one who has terrorized the city for six months, qualifies for coverage because of the notoriety associated with the previous arson cases. Even minor incidents that involve the judge, the heiress or the former football star merit coverage based on these people's prominence.

The model can serve journalists as a guide for weighing the relative merits of an accident, fire or disaster-type news story. Remember that consequence, action and proximity/timeliness, probably in that order, are often interrelated and are usually the chief decision points for these "disruptive" news stories. But the three other elements of human interest, novelty and prominence also play a role in decision making about disruptive news. These latter three values can certainly be part of the first set; they can interact among one another and they can also determine newsworthiness independently.

EXAMPLES BY STORY TYPES

Beginning journalists usually have to prove their competence by working their way up from successfully reporting routine accidents and fires to more important ones, and then to major events such as local disasters. By using the news values model to weigh the relative merit of a story's facts, reporters can improve their news gathering decisions and decrease the amount of time required to write an effective news article. The following examples show ways a reporter can actually apply the news values model throughout the news gathering and newswriting process.

Accidents

Here's a set of facts for a relatively routine accident story:

1. Chester D. Krigle, 33, was driving north on Winchester Road with daughter, Eileen, 6, this morning at 8 a.m. when brakes failed in front of Birchfield Elementary. Krigle was taking Eileen to her first day of school.
2. Krigle's car hits a car stopped in front of the school from which Coleen L. Nino, 29, is letting her two children, Nina, 9, and Mike, 7, out for school.
3. Krigle's car ricocheting off the Nino car, runs up a curb and knocks down a tree in the schoolyard. The tree falls into the glass front of the school and sprays pieces of glass across the interior lobby. Bobbie Lokoski, 7, is hit by some of the flying glass.
4. Police and ambulances arrive. Those taken to the hospital include Krigle and his daughter, Coleen and Nina Nino, and Bobbie Lokoski. Krigle's car is demolished. Nino's car is badly damaged.

As the reporter, you arrive on the scene at 8:30 a.m. What do you do? Applying the news values model for an accident story, go through the

Accident Do's and Don'ts

Accuracy in names and story facts are paramount in an accident news story. Spend the energy necessary to get them right.

Don't draw conclusions about who may have been at fault. Lawsuits and insurance claims usually follow accidents. Your story must be totally objective in providing information about the accident. Often the facts you gather on deadline change in hindsight, after the excitement of the event has passed.

Accident stories—the sequence of events that occurs, the people involved and their relationship to the events—can be deceptively complex. Be sure you know what happened; then work to get the information across clearly to your audience.

steps. According to the model shown in Figure 7.1, the story seems to be a top-set (consequence, action, proximity/timeliness) incident at this point. It involves some consequence of human life, injuries or property damage. There is a drama level, though mild, and it concerns local people in an "immediate" incident. There are possible continuing events related to the physical condition of those involved.

While there is a human interest and uniqueness level to the story, these don't supersede the top set of values in the model. At this point, the prominence level is unknown.

But first things first. Begin by talking to police at the scene to determine whether there's an official record of what happened. To which hospital were the accident victims taken? Did Krigle actually say his brakes failed? Are any eyewitnesses available? If there are, get quotes on what they saw. Then talk with the school principal or other official who can substantiate what happened, especially in the lobby. Find out if there's an estimate of damage to the school building. Do these things at the scene while police and witnesses are available. Then get to the hospital.

Your primary concern, and that of your readers, is the people who were injured. What is their condition? Is this a story with fatalities, with critical injuries or with minor injuries? So far, "consequence" appears to be the main news element. You might be able to ascertain injuries by a phone call, but hospital personnel are often reluctant to provide such information.

At the hospital you learn that Krigle is in surgery for a broken back. His daughter, Eileen, is in satisfactory condition following treatment for a head injury. Coleen Nino is undergoing tests for a possible broken neck but is in satisfactory condition. Her daughter, Nina, is being released now; she's fine. Robert [Bobbie] Lokoski is in satisfactory condition but is being held for observation. He lost a lot of blood from cuts on his back and legs.

Back in the news room at 9:30, your 11 a.m. deadline is nearing, but you have time for an important task. You need to find out if either the Krigle or Nino family are prominent community residents. If you've been a journalist in this city for any length of time, you probably already know if prominence is a factor, but regardless of what you may think, check the names in the morgue files and in your city directory. If prominence is not an issue, you're ready to write the story.

Line up the news values. The consequence is injury and property damage; the action has some drama; it's a proximate and timely story; it is somewhat unusual, but the novelty is not compelling.

In organizing the story, avoid any temptation to warn about safe driving on the first day of school or to overemphasize the uniqueness of a car hitting a tree that smashes into a school building. Drawing on the near-comedic sequence of these events would be in poor taste. This story should begin with a simple news lead focusing on the consequence and the action. Here's an example:

> Two children and two adults were injured as an automobile struck another, then toppled a tree into the glass front of Birchfield Elementary School at 8 this morning.
>
> Chester D. Krigle, 33, 919 W. Center St., suffered a broken back. His daughter, Eileen, 6, received head injuries in the accident as the two were arriving for Eileen's first day of school.
>
> Krigle's car hit Coleen L. Nino's parked vehicle as she was letting her two children out in front of the building. Mrs. Nino, 29, was undergoing tests at Methodist Hospital for a broken neck, but her daughter, Nina, 9, was uninjured and released.
>
> Glancing off Nino's car, Krigle's jumped the curb and smashed into a tree in the schoolyard. The tree fell into the glass front of the school and sprayed broken glass across the lobby.
>
> Seven-year-old Robert Lokoski was cut on his back and legs by the flying glass. He was reported in satisfactory condition but was being held at Methodist for observation.
>
> Linda G. Wilson, principal at Birchfield Elementary, estimated damages to the building at $25,000. She described a chaotic scene for the opening day at her school.
>
> "As we stood on the walkway greeting returning pupils and their parents we heard a crash and then saw a car hit the tree. People ran as the tree fell. . . .

The story would continue with eyewitness descriptions of the event, needed to complete the details and to capture the drama. Chronological presentation from witnesses is unnecessary because the sequence of events has already been presented in the first five paragraphs. Instead, quotes will be used in the remainder of the story to paint for readers a verbal picture of what it was like to be there when the accident happened. Should the story run longer than the allotted space, the scene setting can be cut at any point because all the necessary facts in this accident story have been presented in the first five grafs.

The key aspects of reporting this story are the news gathering procedures and story organization techniques. Both are made more efficient in this type of story by using the news values model that places consequence in human injury first and drama through action second.

Fires

The same basic principles that relate to accidents can be applied in news stories about fires through this fire story fact set:

1. Botkins' Hardware, 210 Front St., burned during the night in what appears to be a spontaneous combustion fire, according to Fire Chief E.W. Dillman.
2. Packing materials ignited in a storeroom, setting off paint and solvent cans, and the blaze engulfed the two-story brick structure within minutes. Time the fire started is estimated at 2 a.m. It was a three-alarm fire that brought half the city's firefighters to confine the fire to the store, keeping adjoining buildings in the downtown area safe. Other than blackened walls, connecting buildings were not damaged.
3. Two firefighters, Alvin D. Wales, 48, and Jane B. O'Shannesy, 31, were hospitalized. The department spent two hours ensuring that the fire was completely quelled. The entire Botkins store was destroyed along with all contents.
4. Owner Gregory Botkins, 85, was called to the scene at about 3:30 a.m. He watched the remainder of the incident and was taken home under sedation after giving his report to fire officials.

As the early morning reporter, you arrive at the scene about 5 a.m., as firefighters are mopping up and putting away equipment. Your deadline for the story is 8:30 a.m.

Similar to the accident story procedures, you begin by interviewing all the authorities available: the fire chief, police, a few firefighters and a few onlookers who watched the blaze. These sources give you the official

Fire Do's and Don'ts

Be sure your opening paragraph indicates that there was a fire.

Don't use phrases such as "burned to ashes" or "completely destroyed." There's a tendency to overdo the writing, especially when the reporter has been at the scene of a fire and witnessed the destruction firsthand.

For most fire stories, think in terms of human life first, property damage second, descriptions of the scene third and other relevant details last.

Don't get carried away by fire clichés such as "flames licking at the eaves," "oven-hot temperatures," "fiery inferno" or "charred remains." Someone already beat you to those phrases.

---

facts, and some provide quotes about the heat, the explosions they heard, and so forth.

But you realize soon enough that there's nothing very unusual about the fire itself, except that it could have destroyed much of the neighboring structures had it not been contained so promptly. Consequence to property is the value of the store and its contents, perhaps $200,000, according to police estimates. Insurance will probably cover the property damage. There's not much action here because the fire occurred during the night. Botkins, his family or store workers could probably offer some human interest aspects, but not in time for your deadline. It is a timely, proximate event, and there were two injuries to firefighters.

There are really only a few possibilities here, one of which occurred to you when you heard the fire was at Botkins' Hardware. That store is probably the oldest operating business in the city. It is still run as a 1930s-type hardware store and is a landmark stop for visitors who tour your city. Botkins' father founded the place in 1921, and Gregory Botkins had been the sole proprietor since his father died when Gregory was 19. There's a folder on Botkins' Hardware an inch thick in your morgue files; some writer does a local feature on the place nearly every year. So you return to the office to read the file, convinced that prominence of the store itself has to be the news value in this story.

Of course that doesn't mean you'll ignore other possible angles. A call to the hospital at 6:30 a.m. yields the following information: Jane O'Shannesy suffered mild smoke inhalation and was released at 6 a.m. Alvin Wales, 48, had a heart attack while fighting the fire and was dead on arrival at the hospital.

You suggest to your editor that another reporter be assigned to write the Wales death story as a sidebar (a secondary story associated with the Botkins fire story; sidebars are discussed in Chapter 14). A fireman's death while fighting a fire deserves special attention: You can't do justice to the Wales' death story on your tight deadline. Instead, you read the Botkins' Hardware file for background information, then return to the fire scene at 7:15 a.m. to talk with owners at neighboring businesses. Several owners arrive by 7:30, and you interview a couple of old-timers as well as a few more-recent business people.

You've had time to rough out some historical paragraphs about Botkins' Hardware that you can use in your article. You have several interviews with good quotes and dramatic reaction to the burned-out building. Now you're ready to write:

> Botkins' Hardware at 210 Front St., a city landmark and its longest continuously operating business, was destroyed by fire early this morning.
>
> Six hook-and-ladder crews consisting of about 40 firefighters worked from 2:30 a.m. to 4 a.m. to successfully keep the three-alarm blaze from spreading to other buildings.
>
> Firefighter Alvin Wales, 48, died of a heart attack he suffered while fighting the store fire. Jane B. O'Shannesy, 31, another firefighter, suffered smoke inhalation. She was treated and released at St. Joseph's Hospital.
>
> Adjacent buildings received smoke and heat damage, but the fire was confined to Botkins' Hardware. Police estimated a $200,000 property loss for the building and its contents.
>
> Fire Chief E.W. Dillman said the fire started at about 2 a.m. by spontaneous combustion in packing materials in a storeroom. The blaze set off cans of paint and solvent, engulfing the two-story brick structure in flames within minutes, Dillman said.
>
> Owner Gregory Botkins, 85, was called to the scene about 3:30 a.m. and watched while the fire destroyed the business he has run since he was 19. He was taken home under sedation after giving his report to police.
>
> Downtown business people coming to work this morning gaped sadly at the remaining blackened bricks of what was one of Pineville's most renowned memories of a bygone era. The store, founded by the late Benjamin Botkins in the same building in 1921, was a favorite draw for hundreds of visitors annually. Its shelves and bins were stocked with washboards, rolling pins and mallets, products reminiscent of 1920s America.

"I used to spend my lunch hour in Botkins'," said Donna Adler, a secretary at Hargrave Securities Co. in the next block. "You could wander those crowded aisles all day and not get bored just looking at the stuff."

From this point the story will continue with quotes from other business people while weaving in the history of Botkins' Hardware for as long as there is room to tell it. Throughout, the article will remind readers that a fire has ended that history, at least temporarily.

This fire story, with its attendant "prominence" feature of Botkins' Hardware, is more involved than the usual fire story, which normally focuses on the fire itself. However, it does contain the necessary elements of most such events, in approximately the same order.

Disasters

Here's a fact set for a limited disaster-type weather story:

1. You are the late-night reporter for the local morning daily, and you get a call at 10:30 p.m., about an hour before the presses are scheduled to roll for the next morning's edition.

San Francisco's 1989 earthquake was one of the decade's most violent natural disasters. Here a Marina district neighbor walks by the wreckage of a 4-story building.

2. The call is from Lt. Peter Anderson of the local police, who says his patrol officers are helping keep a crowd of about 50 people under control on Elmwood Drive as Civil Defense workers inspect the mess.
3. A tornado touched down in the city a little while ago, about 9:45, and hit three houses on Elmwood.
4. The tornado destroyed three houses, and the workers have found three bodies so far. Killed were Douglas and Hilda Raven of 825 Elmwood Drive and Jessie M. Cason, 823 Elmwood. The third house hit was 819 Elmwood, a vacant house that has been for sale two months. Damage was done to several nearby homes, but no one else has been reported injured. The three bodies have been sent to Larson-Walker Funeral Home . . . no further plans yet known.

Disaster Do's and Don'ts

If the disaster is pending, such as a hurricane en route to your locality, focus on warning your readers about the potential harm it may cause, the estimated time of arrival, its severity and what your audience should do immediately for protection, including evacuating the area.

If the disaster is in progress, such as a blizzard that began yesterday and is forecast to continue for another day or two, again focus on warnings. In this instance, tell readers how to protect themselves, give official bulletins and write about the aftermath of destruction so far, using consequence (lives, injuries, property damage) as your guide. However, a possible exception to emphasizing loss of life might be to lead with information necessary to protect lives. A story on the explosion of a tanker truck carrying a toxic chemical might lead with a police warning to avoid the site.

Disaster stories usually are after-the-fact, such as the tornado story example. These should be handled as consequence-type stories. Try to put the disaster in perspective in terms of controversy, drama, human interest or novelty, and seek eyewitnesses to provide action quotes.

Notice that in two out of the three disaster-story-timing possibilities (pending, in-progress or after-the-fact), a journalist's responsibility is to warn the audience about a dangerous situation that may affect their lives or property.

Avoid humor in a disaster story, even if the facts are novel enough to warrant some humorous treatment.

Remember that disasters involve panic, confusion and lack of sound judgment. Double-check your facts, even if they come from official sources.

Don't overdo the disaster. Effectively written, the story will accomplish its goal without phrases such as "mangled corpses were strewn," "the worst disaster this city has seen" or "panic reigned in this normally quiet suburban neighborhood."

5. Anderson says eyewitnesses reported hearing a loud, howling noise above the rain tonight and those who looked out of their windows or ran outside saw the twister as it touched down along the street. Large trees were uprooted and tossed into the street or up against houses. Then the twister struck the three houses.

6. Anderson turns the phone over to Bob Hornsby, who says he saw the whole thing. He says, "I never saw a tornado before, and I hope I never do again. It was just the very most terrible thing I ever saw. There was this black-looking funnel-shaped mass of whirling dirt and debris reaching up about 60 feet into the sky. It sounded like it would destroy everything on the street. I watched while it smashed my neighbor's house into boards and blew it up into the funnel. I prayed to God it wouldn't hit our house next, and it didn't. It just went on back out into the street past us, and then it landed on two other houses down the street. Some other folks were out in their yard watching it, but I couldn't even hear them yelling above the noise from that thing. It just knocked the other two houses flat, like they had exploded."

7. Anderson comes back on and tells you he's estimating property damage at about $250,000 to homes, yards and trees.

Because your deadline is extremely tight now, you have time only to check your paper's files and find out that the last tornado reported touching down in the city was in 1978. That one hit a warehouse on the edge of town and cut a 10-foot path through the building, but nobody was hurt. You check the city directory to confirm name spellings and residences. There's no time to go to the scene; there's barely enough time to write your story.

Consider that this story is somewhat novel in your locality, which obviously is not in one of the country's tornado corridors (it has been more than a dozen years since a tornado hit the city). While novelty will be a news angle for this story, the rarity of a tornado here should be secondary in a story that involves loss of life. In fact, the writer should stress consequence first and action second (based on the quotes given by Hornsby), saving the novelty aspect for last:

A tornado hit Elmwood Drive at 9:45 Tuesday night killing three local residents.

Dead are Douglas and Hilda Raven of 825 Elmwood Drive and Jessie M. Cason of 823 Elmwood Drive. Other possible injuries or fatalities were not yet determined by 11:30 p.m. as police and Civil Defense workers remained at the scene.

Robert R. Hornsby, 818 Elmwood Drive, a witness to the storm's

Covering the Police/Fire Beat

Every newspaper and many television stations have a police/fire beat. The two usually are combined as a single reporting topic area, although the larger outlets may assign more than one journalist to the beat.

The two major considerations in working the police/fire beat are: (1) developing sources' trust and (2) staying alert to potentially libelous writing.

Police departments are notoriously clannish. Law enforcement officers and clerks often distrust outsiders, including journalists. Like that of the military, the police system includes semi-autonomous units at the county and city levels with a chain of command from captains to patrolmen. A reporter must learn the system first, especially to know the political entities to which police owe their allegiance. Then the reporter must develop sources at all levels, especially the desk people who control the official record of police activities. Breaking in can be slow and tricky, and once you've established sources, a wrong move can freeze the flow of information. Reporters don't have to cultivate as many sources on the fire beat because it generates news less frequently and fires are public news events.

Much of what occurs on the police beat is of news value, and almost all of it appears in the police records, usually on computer. Once the police beat reporter knows which records to use and gains access to them, most of the routine coverage of crime becomes mechanical. Stories usually are listings of the day's more newsworthy police activities, although longer and more interesting crime stories require multiple interviews and other sophisticated fact-gathering techniques.

Accuracy is paramount in police beat reporting and writing because libel (discussed in Chapter 17) is a constant danger when a person's reputation is at stake in a crime story. Libel suits can result from misspelling an arrestee's name or transposing an address.

Additionally, the police reporter must be on guard against the pressure-valve chatter heard in the precinct. Cops can sound off like football players in a locker room at half time, but neither's diatribes and boasts are ready for publication without careful verification.

One last warning about the beat: police and firefighters are notorious pranksters. A journalist new to the beat should expect to be the victim of a practical joke or embarrassing escapade. Watch for it, but take it in stride—it may be the first indication that you've been accepted.

havoc on his block, said, "There was this black-looking funnel-shaped mass of whirling dirt and debris reaching up about 60 feet into the sky.

"I watched while it smashed my neighbor's house into boards and blew it up into the funnel," Hornsby said. "I prayed to God it wouldn't hit our house next, and it didn't."

Hornsby said the tornado went past his house, into the street and hit two more houses. "It just knocked the other two houses flat, like they had exploded."

The third house destroyed was a vacant house at 819 Elmwood Drive that had been for sale two months.

Police Lt. Peter Anderson said residents on Elmwood Drive reported hearing a loud, howling noise above last night's rain. He said people who watched from their windows or ran outside saw the funnel as it touched down along the street.

Anderson said witnesses reported several large trees were uprooted and tossed into the street or against houses. Then the twister struck the three houses. He estimated property damage at about $250,000 to the homes and the street.

A crowd of about 50 people was held in check by police as Civil Defense workers inspected the damage.

The tornado was the first reported to hit the city since 1978. That tornado hit a warehouse on the edge of town, but no one was hurt.

The bodies of Cason and the Ravens were taken to Harrison-Parker Funeral Home.

The lead sets the tone and tempo for a disaster story. Because this story is an important news item, simplicity in the lead will carry greater weight than a long, melodramatic rendition of the event. In fact, the story's news impact is improved by using a brief, simple lead. It begins with the tornado, but includes the three deaths.

The consequence news value demands including the names of the victims early in the story. Immediately after the victims are named, the story paints the scene of the tornado disaster through the words of Hornsby, the eyewitness. Judicious selection of his most informative and powerful quotes provides the necessary scene setting. However, many of the Hornsby quotes are wordy and grammatically flawed. These should be omitted.

Next, the additional property damage to the vacant house, with no loss of life, merits a short paragraph that needs to be included for accuracy and comprehensiveness.

A chronological presentation of what happened, through Lt. Anderson's statements, follows. This portion of the article is the "official" story, attributed to Anderson, including an estimate of property damage.

The next-to-last paragraph adds perspective, in this case the rarity of a tornado hitting the town. The final paragraph, which an editor might delete, is a detail about the bodies. Because no funeral arrangements are known, the last paragraph reiterates that the story is the latest news as of the paper's 11:30 p.m. deadline.

In this disaster story, as in many others, the journalist must remind readers that there may be more to come. The example carries such a suggestion in its second paragraph:

> Other possible injuries or fatalities were not yet determined by 11:30 p.m. as police and Civil Defense workers remained at the scene.

If the Civil Defense workers find another body among the debris on Elmwood, a follow-up story will be printed in the next edition. A second-day story on this disaster will be likely in any event because its newsworthiness suggests an aftermath story of the scene in the light of the next day. Writers should indicate in disaster-type articles that a continuation of events may follow.

SUMMARY

Audiences pay close attention to stories about accidents, fires and disasters because these events can affect their lives. People maintain a surveillance over their environment to stay abreast of the conditions that pose a potential threat to their safety and security. Reporting such events serves a public need to know.

One difficulty reporters and writers face is the deadline pressure of covering accident, fire and disaster-type stories where the objective is to provide coverage as soon after the event as possible. Another difficulty is the attendant emotional strain sources experience in the midst of fear and loss, which often results in confusion.

Coming to the journalist's aid is the inverted pyramid structure that is the most efficient procedure for writing accident, fire and disaster stories. A model of newsworthiness considerations offers writers a series of news values against which facts may be weighed:

1. consequence, with the elements of human life, injury and property damage in descending order;
2. action, including drama level, controversy and whether the story is a continuing event; and
3. proximity/timeliness, dealing with where and when the story happens.

These first three are the chief considerations for most accident, fire and disaster-type stories, but three lesser considerations also must be assessed:

4. human interest, the emotional responses readers are likely to experience with the story;

5. novelty, the unusualness of story circumstances; and

6. prominence, whether well-known people are involved.

Journalists should weigh the story facts against each of these six dimensions. If the news values are applied properly, the writer can easily identify the story lead and the descending order of facts throughout the article. However, the model's list of news value considerations serves only as a writer's guide for organizing story facts. The model's worth depends totally on the reporter's ability to gather appropriate and sufficient facts for the story.

———————— **Thinking it Through** ————————————————

EXERCISE 7.1

Information Gathering

For each of the story situations, list the information gathering procedures you would attempt to make your news story as complete as possible. Pretend that you have a **two-hour deadline** from the time you begin this information gathering process.

A Fifty mph winds, lightning and hail were reported at 10 tonight in your city. Extensive damage includes: a 12-story building toppled creating fires and a dozen fatalities; gas leak in the downtown area; broken windows in stores; some flooding of neighborhoods; power outages; major streets blocked.

Official sources to contact by phone (try to list at least five sources by their probable order of importance to your story):

B An 82-car freight train hit two vehicles at a railroad crossing on the outskirts of town at 7:15 this morning. Dead are John C. Wells, 36, driver of one vehicle; Gloria Sims, 27, and her daughter, Mary, 5, in the other vehicle. Police investigating the accident say the warning barriers at the railroad crossing failed, and the train hit both cars at about 50 mph. Deputy Elliot Warner of the State Police says he thinks all the victims were killed instantly. Statements are being taken from the freight train engineer. Bart N. Halstrom, the local representative for Great Northern Railways, is at the scene.

List at least three official sources for quotes:

List three other information gathering tactics:

C The fourth rape victim in the Edgemont district of your city killed her assailant by shooting him with his .32-caliber pistol. She shot him three times in the back at close range following an attack in her home at 6:30 p.m. today, according to local police. The man, Gilbert R. Smith, 23, matches the description given by three other rape victims in the neighborhood. Police say his city utility company uniform also matches the description given by previous victims, although Smith is not employed by the utility company. Police say the killing ends their manhunt for the Edgemont rapist. The fourth victim is being treated at St. Michaels Infirmary. No charges are anticipated in the shooting.

List at least three official sources for quotes:

List three other information gathering tactics:

_____ **Writing Practice** _____

EXERCISE 7.2

Applying the News Value Decision Making Model

In the following story situations, use the chapter's news value decision making model to list three elements of the story you would use in an inverted pyramid story structure. List them in the order of their news importance. Use the city directory to verify any applicable story facts, then write a lead for the story.

A Two houses on Lincoln Avenue burned late this afternoon when live coals from the fireplace of one home set fire to a Persian rug. Dead is Mrs. Daniel C. Marshall, 51, wife of the city attorney, who was asleep in her home at 1158

Lincoln where the fire started. Her son, Thomas, 12, was taken to the hospital after rushing into the home to try to save his mother. He is in critical condition with third-degree burns. The Marshall home is destroyed. The next-door home received extensive damage from the fire. Officials estimate damage to the two homes at more than $400,000.

Order of three Decision Making Model news values:

Lead:

B A local couple, Terrance Arthur, 39, and Julie Arthur, 40, were killed on takeoff at 8:30 this morning when their single-engine Comanche left a private airport near Interstate 25. The plane hit the top floor of the Holiday Inn and caught fire. Julie, the pilot, reported engine trouble to the tower controller before the plane hit the building. No one inside the hotel was injured, although two people in the parking lot were hit by burning metal from the plane and were taken to the hospital. The plane's fuselage is wedged into an 11th floor hotel room window and will remain there—visible to the interstate—until authorities decide how to remove it safely. Police have roped off the area around the hotel.

Order of three Decision Making Model news values:

Lead:

C Snow falling in Panama City, Fla., is a rare occurrence indeed. It happened at 11 p.m. when temperatures dropped to 24 degrees. The city is crippled. Schools are closed; power is lost in parts of the city; a frozen water main has cut water supplies to several neighborhoods. Three inches of snow is on the ground. Mayor Joan Billings has asked residents to stay indoors. She says water lines will be repaired before noon, and the utility company is working to restore power. She urges people to leave their homes only for emergencies because of the slick roads. Automobile accidents claimed three lives during the night, and one couple was found frozen to death in a car near the beach. The forecast is for even lower temperatures through tonight with no improvement in conditions. In fact, there's a 50 percent chance of two more inches of snow by nightfall.

Order of three Decision Making Model news values:

Lead:

D Two armed robbers are holding patrons and employees hostage in a local jewelry store as police have surrounded the building. Shots have been fired and a SWAT unit is waiting to rush the store at the first sign of more shooting from the building. One of the hostages is the store's owner, Julius Kramer, this city's leading philanthropist and the most recent winner of the Man of the Year award. A store customer, Evellyn Falstaff, 58, was shot in the head during a gunfire exchange at 7 p.m. The robbers allowed an ambulance to take her to the hospital. However, there's a standoff between police and the robbers, who have asked for a helicopter in exchange for all of the hostages except Kramer. Police have refused and have set a deadline of midnight for the men to leave the store unarmed. (No further information is available for tomorrow morning's edition.)

Order of three Decision Making Model news values:

Lead:

E After nearly four hours of fighting it, city officials simply gave up at 10 p.m. and let the blaze consume what was left of Northside Mall. "It was like a half mile of fire," Chief Ralph Bailey said. "I don't think I've ever seen a fire that big, and I've been a fireman for 40 years." Bailey says there's no way to know how the fire started until his team can get close enough, maybe by daylight. Northside has been closed for about six weeks for renovations. The mall is believed to have been vacant at 5:30 p.m. when the fire began; no one is reported injured, although Bailey estimates damage at more than $20 million. He says he's sure this is the city's most expensive fire. Some 50 local police were on hand to keep onlookers away from the burning buildings. "We had as much trouble with the crowd as with the fire," Bailey says. About 25,000 people from the northern suburbs were on hand to watch as their primary shopping center lit the evening sky during the after-work rush hour. Stopped cars were blocking traffic on the main arteries and side streets—any of the many vantage points from which the blaze could be seen. Suburban residents even left their homes and drove to the site, attracted by the awesome sheets of flame reaching as high as 100 feet into the night sky and stretching half a mile. Outbound traffic didn't clear until nearly 9 p.m.

Order of three Decision Making Model news values:

Lead:

Death Stories and Obits

Regardless of the circumstances, a person's death is worthy of news coverage. Newspapers traditionally report births, marriages and deaths as the landmarks in a person's life. These are the stories families clip out of the newspaper, photocopy and send to relatives. These are the stories found between the pages of the family Bible as a permanent record of the person's life.

If the person has achieved some prominence in the community, the local media's coverage of that person's death will be more extensive. A death story will be done in addition to an obituary. If the person achieved little community prominence, an obituary will be the only notice of death.

DEATH STORIES VERSUS OBITUARIES

An individual's prominence determines whether a death story will be written, though every death in the community merits an obituary. Death stories are separate news stories in the newspaper. A journalist writing a death story should think of it as having front-page potential, though few will merit that treatment. Still, each death story has its own headline and usually contains a picture of the deceased. Obituaries, on the other hand, appear in a column of obituary notices: a grouping of all deaths recorded in the community that day or the previous day.

How prominent must a person have been to deserve a separate death story? This depends primarily on the size of the community. The smaller the community, the more likely any given individual in it will receive a death story. The rationale is that smaller communities have fewer deaths each day, so the death of a 75-year-old piano teacher might rate a death story. She will have touched the lives of many community residents through her years of teaching piano, and her death will be worthy of news coverage because so many newspaper readers will have known her. In a large city, which might have several dozen deaths each day, the piano teacher's death rates an obituary, but probably not a death story. Still, if one of the teacher's pupils had become an internationally acclaimed pianist, a death story might be warranted.

Newspaper editors in larger communities make their decisions about doing death stories based at least in part on whether the deceased has a file in the newspaper's morgue. If there is a file, the chances are that the person has gained enough prominence to merit a death story. In fact, metropolitan newspapers assign updates on possible death stories to reporters who are between assignments, or to cub reporters as worthwhile newswriting practice. These assignments involve revising the background information on older living news makers in anticipation of the story that will be done when the person dies. But the usual death story is a news piece about the person's death, written on deadline after the person dies.

At most newspapers, an obituary is one notice in a column of obituary notices, all of which follow a rigid, prescribed structure. Most newspapers provide a standardized obituary check-sheet or form that the reporter fills out when taking information over the telephone from funeral home personnel: name spellings, age, circumstances and time of death, survivors and funeral arrangements. The information from this completed form becomes the basis for writing the obituary. Many newspapers charge a small fee, perhaps a few dollars, to defray the costs of information gathering and publishing an obituary. Most newspapers charge the family the regular classified ad rate for a "death notice," or a paid ad about a person's death. But despite these seemingly routine procedures in writing obituaries, newspapers take them very seriously. Often beginning reporters are assigned obituaries during their first few months on the job. Success at obituary writing can determine whether the cub reporter continues as a permanent newspaper staff member.

DEATH STORIES

Because it is a news story emphasizing a person's death, a death story is almost always a "who" story that usually begins with the person's name, age and identification. An exception to beginning with the deceased's name is when the person's position or other distinguishing characteristic is more notable than the person's name.

There might be cases where the circumstances of the death have more news value than the person's prominence. Examples include deaths from freak accidents, the victims of crime, or death by an unusual or dread disease. In such instances, the death story is likely to be a "what" rather than a "who," but the person's name, age and identification should follow in the second paragraph of the story.

Key Elements

Most death stories will be written with the following kind of "who" lead:

> Marylou L. Quincy, 58, whose line of sequined wedding gowns launched a multimillion-dollar company, died at 7 p.m. Monday of cancer.

In death stories where an accomplishment is more recognizable than the person's name, use this kind of "who" lead:

> A local seamstress whose line of sequined wedding gowns launched Sparkling Brides Inc., died of cancer at 7 p.m. Monday.
> Marylou L. Quincy, 58, founded the multimillion-dollar firm after her wedding gown creations became the hit of fashionable European ceremonies in the early 1960s.

Death stories stressing "what" leads will be similar to the following:

> A blasting cap exploding in a Timberville teenager's pocket claimed the boy's life early Sunday.
> Daryl Wayne Pilar, 16, of 1470 Sycamore View died at 2:50 a.m., six hours after undergoing emergency abdominal surgery, a Medical Center representative said.

Because of the person's prominence, death stories will stress the major accomplishments the person achieved in life. The death story should focus primarily on those elements, and they should be featured in the first several paragraphs. Sometimes it's difficult to determine what the person's major accomplishment is. Try to identify the achievement that most readers will remember or will want to know about this individual. For instance, when screen actor and dancer Ray Bolger died, the lead of his death story had to identify him as the scarecrow, the last survivor of the cast in the *Wizard of Oz*. Though Bolger had a long and successful career on stage and screen, most of the reading public would remember him best as the scarecrow in that acclaimed film. Likewise, if the person was a business leader, mayor of the city and a municipal court judge, most readers will remember that the person was mayor. Use that as the identifying focus of the story.

However, these other death story requirements must be included early:

1. full name, with middle initial
2. age
3. the fact that the person died—don't forget this one
4. when the person died—include time of day
5. circumstances of death.

Including five elements in addition to the most notable achievement may seem to crowd the lead, but all of the elements can fit into the 30-word guideline if the lead is written concisely:

> Ansel P. Ritter, 66, former head of the award-winning architectural firm that designed Madison's City Hall in 1975, died at 8:15 a.m. today of a heart attack.   (28 words)

Careful editing can shorten the lead and add emphasis without sacrificing any critical information:

> Ansel P. Ritter, 66, former head of the architectural firm that designed City Hall, died at 8:15 a.m. today of a heart attack.   (23 words)

Instances do occur in which not all of the elements designated for a death story lead (name, age, etc.) may fit into the first paragraph; for example, when a person's achievements include several equally important accomplishments. More often, however, long leads stem from unusual circumstances of death:

> An elderly woman who was taken to University Hospital Sunday died this morning of yellow fever, the first local case of the disease in 30 years, doctors said.
>
> Leann K. Alexander, 81, died at 5:30 a.m. from the disease associated with being bitten by mosquitoes in swampy terrains of equatorial countries. Local doctors brought in federal disease control experts to make the diagnosis, according to University Hospital officials.

Notice that when death story leads are long, necessary information that can't fit in the lead sentence is used early in the second paragraph. This is the usual method to avoid crowding any lead. And, as in any other news article, death stories contain needed attribution.

Following the lead, death stories provide readers as complete a picture of the person's life and achievements as space will allow. An inverted pyramid structure is usually the preferred format for the first few paragraphs after the death story's lead, with information about the person's life arranged in descending order of importance. The remaining paragraphs form a chronological presentation.

Substance and Perspective

Superior death stories include both substance and perspective. The journalist should find out as much about the person as time and circumstances permit, including quotes from family and associates. Additionally, these facts and character insights should be placed in perspective with events in history, to give readers greater appreciation of their significance. In the Ray Bolger example, today's readers should have been given a paragraph about the *Wizard of Oz,* who the other leading actors were, the roles they played, and why the film was a classic motion picture. If the person was a local politician, include something about the political climate of the city during the era in which the person achieved prominence. If the person was a local civil rights activist in the 1950s, write about the civil rights movement in your city during that decade.

When the person's major achievements have been documented, three other elements remain for the rest of the death story: (1) a brief chronology of the person's life, (2) survivors and (3) funeral arrangements.

While chronological highlights constitute the bulk of information in the usual obituary, these elements take a less prominent place in the death story because of the attention paid to the person's achievements. Highlights include date and place of birth, schools attended, military service and marriage, among other possibilities. The survivors paragraph should follow the chronology, and the last paragraph of the death story should be funeral and burial arrangements. More information on how to write these last segments of the article is given in the explanation of obituary writing.

OBITUARIES

While it may seem that obituaries are nothing more than fill-in-the-blanks writing exercises, they are extremely important stories to survivors and to the newspaper that publishes them. Family members con-

Reporters, copy editors and news interns usually write several obituaries per day after phoning funeral homes, police and family members to verify facts. Successful journalists take pride in every obituary they write, regardless of how routine these stories may seem.

sider the obituary a permanent record of their loved one's life, and they expect it to be complete and flawless. Newspaper editors know they will hear complaints about errors in obituaries, and some of the errors may require a published apology and correction. Editors rightly believe that a journalist who can't handle an obituary shouldn't be trusted to do other news stories.

And yet obituaries should be the easiest type of news story to write because they follow very specific formulas. Most newspapers provide their own obit forms to local funeral homes, and some papers even allow clerical assistants to write the obit. Virtually all newspapers insist that each obituary follow the same format, prescribed by that paper's policy. Because each paper's obituary format differs, it isn't possible to learn one format and expect it to apply at every newspaper. However, a journalist can be assured that the formula given in Figure 8.1 will correspond generally to those used by most of the nation's newspapers.

LEAD: Person's full name, age, identification, at least one outstanding or unique aspect of person's life; (might contain circumstances of death, exact time of death and current address)

DEATH CIRCUMSTANCES: If not in lead, include here

HIGHLIGHTS OF CAREER: More complete presentation of person's contribution in lead

LIFE CHRONOLOGY: Birthdate and place, then milestones from earliest to most recent, including school, military, marriage, memberships

SURVIVORS: Immediate family, then other relatives in descending kinship order; include local residents

FUNERAL ARRANGEMENTS: Visitation, services and burial

Figure 8.1 Obituary story format

Although you may be asked to follow the format used by your local newspaper or to adhere to a certain stylistic procedure (such as the use of courtesy titles throughout the obituary), the following presentation is based on strict conformity to the Figure 8.1 obituary format. But these instructions emphasize complete sentences, separate paragraphs rather than a single paragraph block and the same journalistic style of writing required in any other news story. And, as in any other news story, accuracy in an obituary is imperative.

OBITUARY LEADS

Begin the obit lead with the full name, including middle initial. Be certain that the name is spelled accurately. Don't rely on funeral home personnel to get the right spelling. Cross-check the name in the city directory, in your newspaper's morgue files or with the deceased's next of kin. In fact, you should call the next of kin to confirm all facts in the obituary. You will find that in most cases, even the bereaved family members of an accident victim welcome the opportunity to ensure that the obituary is a factual record of the person's life.

The person's age should follow the name, and many newspapers include the person's address at this point in the lead. Again, be sure you have the accurate age and correct address.

Wording Care in Obituaries and Death Stories

Beginning reporters who are dealing with real deaths for the first time have two types of writing problems. One is over-writing: the use of unnecessarily flowery phrases. The other problem is word accuracy. Here are a few do's and don'ts about writing obituaries and death stories:

- The first reference to the deceased is by full name, but subsequent references include courtesy titles such as Mr. Smith or Mrs. Jones. For a woman who has never been married, check with a close relative or friend the preference of the deceased to have "Miss" or "Ms." or no title. For most newspapers, an obituary or death story is the only article in which courtesy titles are used in subsequent references.
- People die "after" operations. If you write that a person died "from" an oper-ation, be prepared to prove it in court.
- Although attribution isn't needed in most obituaries, if the source is remote—the person died on a cruise or in another city—attribute the story to the ship's doctor or to hospital authorities.
- Keep the obituary simple. People "die"; they don't "pass away," "go to the great beyond" or get "called to their Maker."
- Be very careful about reporting that a person died from a contagious disease such as leprosy or tuberculosis, or from a social disease such as syphilis or AIDS.
- Injuries are "received," not "sustained." People don't always "suffer" under a physician's care, nor do they "entertain" an illness.
- Everyone dies of "heart failure." Be more specific by writing "heart attack" or "heart disease."

Next, identify the most notable aspect of the person's life, such as his or her career position title: a secretary at Johnson's Realty, vice president of Acme Glass Co. or the mother of three Williamsburg residents. Obituaries of more prominent individuals should contain additional identifying information, such as: "an unsuccessful candidate for sheriff in 1974," "author of the best-selling novel 'Hail to Freedom' " or "who donated the land on which the public library now stands." Items of this sort are often unobtainable from the funeral home. You can learn them from the newspaper morgue or from family members, employers or friends.

Finally, the lead should contain the circumstances and time of death. Be as specific as possible about the cause of death and try to pinpoint the exact time. Some newspapers require that all of these elements be placed in the lead; other newspapers permit elements to be placed in the second paragraph.

Following are a few examples of leads written according to the obituary pattern given:

Florence J. Ballard, 72, of 121 Waverly St., a World War II nurse and the mother of five children, died at 3 p.m. Thursday following an operation for kidney failure.

William H. Silano, 39, of 3749 Eagle Road, a certified public accountant with McIntyre Corp., died at 5:03 a.m. Sunday of a non-smoker's lung cancer.

Justine Tyra Reynolds, 15, of 405 Cooper Apartments, a Ridgeway High School student, died at 7:15 this morning after being struck by a hit-and-run driver on Vincent Avenue.

Shane B. McDonald, 84, a resident of Harris Nursing Home and former aide to a Kentucky governor, died at the home at 9:55 p.m. Monday of pneumonia.

Notice that an obituary differs from other news stories in its attribution requirements. Because obituaries are part of an obituary column, readers will assume that most of the information comes from the funeral home or the family. You don't need to write, "according to Parker and Sons Funeral Home." However, if the journalist suspects readers might wonder about the source of some obituary information, it is appropriate to add attribution to the coroner, the newspaper's files, an attending physician or even a spouse.

CIRCUMSTANCES OF DEATH

If the death circumstances are not included in the lead, perhaps because of their length, these details belong in the second paragraph. For example:

Oscar C.L. Rhoades, 27, of 227504 Washington Place, a bartender and musician, died at 2:40 a.m. Saturday after falling from his fourth-floor apartment window.
Mr. Rhoades' wife, Marian, told paramedics her husband was repairing a television set when an electrical shock threw him backwards through the window. He was pronounced dead on arrival at City Hospital.

This obituary might appear to be a suicide or a drug-related incident without the explanation from Rhoades' wife. The example raises a separate issue about writing obituaries, that of honesty and propriety.

The information included in obituaries, just like that in all other news articles, must be true. But some circumstances of death can be as painful for the survivors as for the deceased. Should suicides, drug overdoses, or sexually related diseases be included in the obituary?

Journalists must tell the truth in obituaries, but they should use judgment and restraint. Suicides should be reported as "an apparent suicide," "an apparent self-inflicted wound," or the suicide should be attributed in the obituary to a doctor or coroner. If there are extenuating circumstances, such as a suicide following a diagnosis of cancer or a suicide in conjunction with psychological treatment, these should be reported. Drug-related deaths, and those stemming from diseases such as AIDS, also should be reported and attributed to a medical authority.

But there are circumstances that, as a matter of propriety, need not appear in an obituary. For instance, it isn't necessary to report that the deceased was a member of Alcoholics Anonymous, spent time in jail, flunked out of school or was homosexual, unless these incidents have special news value in the obituary. Use some common sense in deciding what is appropriate to include in the permanent record of a person's life.

HIGHLIGHTS OF CAREER

Assuming that the obit's lead paragraph contains all of the required information, the writer next describes highlights of the person's career. In a pattern similar to the normal inverted pyramid structure, the main element of the story, the single outstanding or unique aspect about the person, receives additional emphasis in the second paragraph. Changing some facts in the preceding Rhoades obituary, the first two paragraphs might be written as follows:

> Oscar C.L. Rhoades, 47, of 227504 Washington Place, a guitarist and leader of "Blue Notes," a six-piece jazz ensemble, died at 2:40 a.m. Saturday of leukemia.
>
> Mr. Rhoades gave a solo performance at the White House in 1979 and played concerts in Carnegie Hall and Lincoln Center in New York City. Music critics in the mid-1970s called him one of the nation's masters of blues guitar technique.

The second paragraph of this obituary provides specific highlights of Rhoades' musical career. The reader learns that his performance at the White House was the apex of his professional life, as it might be for many musicians, and that he played at two internationally known concert halls.

Another highlight was the flattering critical reviews of his performances. If there was more worthy information, depending on Rhoades' musical renown, it might be placed in a third paragraph on career highlights:

> His "Blue Notes" ensemble began performing in Houston in 1986 at the Foundation House and was a frequent attraction at city country clubs and charity events. Before his illness, Mr. Rhoades' group performed at a Women's League Charity Ball that raised more than $50,000 for the Library Association.

While the use of two paragraphs of career highlights is more common in death stories than in obituaries, the point is that these milestones in a person's life should precede lesser elements in the story. They should also be arranged in descending order of their importance, as called for in inverted pyramid newswriting structure.

One other example of career highlights is the second paragraph in this more typical story:

> Elise Hilary Crews, 57, of 422 W. 14th St., vice president of marketing at Union Mfg., died at 4:15 p.m. Thursday of a brain tumor.
>
> Mrs. Crews owned an advertising agency before joining Union Mfg. as director of the Products Marketing Division. She became a vice president in 1980 and served on the firm's corporate board of directors.

If there are no career highlights worthy of inclusion in the obituary, begin the chronology segment of the story immediately after the lead.

CHRONOLOGY

The chronology section of the obituary is a point-by-point presentation of the person's life from birth to death. It includes the following types of information when available:

1. birth date and place of birth
2. schooling, usually from high school through college
3. military service, including rank and branch
4. work history, including firms and job titles
5. marriage, including date and place

6. other major chronological elements such as residences in different cities, awards, church membership, civic memberships and offices held.

This may seem like a lot of detail, but most obituaries have only a few lines of chronology. Journalists should try to obtain as much of this information as possible for the permanent record of a person's life, although many of these details won't be available in time to write the obituary.

Here are a few examples of the chronology section of an obituary:

She was born July 10, 1938, in Chicago and graduated from St. Ann's Academy. Mrs. Harding earned a B.A. in English from Loyola University in 1960 and her teaching credential from Chicago Teachers College in 1961. She began her teaching career at Lauderdale High School in St. Louis, Mo., the same year.

Mrs. Harding moved to Lincoln in 1965 to teach English and serve as assistant principal at St. Agnes High School. She married Dr. Jonathan E. Harding in 1967, and the couple moved to San Antonio, where Capt. Harding served three years as an Army physician at Brooke General Hospital.

In 1970, the couple returned to Lincoln, where Mrs. Harding opened a Montessori school. She was an unsuccessful candidate for the Lincoln School Board in 1978 but was elected to a two-year term in 1980. She continued as principal of the Lincoln City Montessori School until becoming ill last year.

Mr. Lang was born Oct. 8, 1934, and graduated from Kirby High School in 1952. He served two years in Korea as an Air Force staff sergeant and returned to Clayton where he married Emma May Beecher in 1956.

Mr. Lang was a butcher at Safeway. He became head of the meat department at Kroger in 1967.

He was an elder at First Presbyterian Church, a Mason and the former secretary of the Clayton Lions Club.

Mrs. Epperson was born in Concord, Jan. 3, 1923, and attended Simpson School.

She married Herbert L. Epperson in 1941, and the couple lived in Detroit, where they had five children. They returned to Concord in 1955 to take over her family's dry cleaning business.

Mrs. Epperson was a member of the Church of Christ choir and the Concord Ladies Auxiliary.

A Disclaimer about Standardized Obituaries

As the chapter says, each newspaper has its own policies about how to write an obituary. A few of the **exceptions** newspapers may make to the model the chapter uses are:

- length—many newspapers limit the total number of words in an obituary, or they expect a far more truncated writing style than is suggested here
- content—some limit the entire obituary to include only name, age, address, day of death, funeral home in charge and im-

mediate family survivors
- suicide—some papers won't publish that suicide was the cause of death
- time of day—some newspapers just give day of week
- cause of death—some papers give only a vague cause of death such as "after an illness"; some include these circumstances only in the more detailed death stories
- paragraphs—many newspapers run the entire obituary in a single block of type with no new paragraphs

SURVIVORS

This section of an obituary is one of the most important and the most highly structured. It is a listing of the deceased's living relatives, in descending order of family relationships. Getting the order right is easy enough. Figure 8.2 presents the usual sequence of relationships, with the top listing order for a decedent with children and the bottom listing order for one without children. In either case, the spouse is named first. Both sequences are similar, except that the top includes children and grandchildren.

Each newspaper's policy determines how many levels of relatives to include in an obituary, but the policy is likely to stress local residents. Hence, a newspaper that limits survivor listings might include spouse and children, skipping all other non-local residents but including the deceased's local cousins. The purpose is to include the names of the closest relatives and of all local survivors who will read and perhaps save the obituary notice. Newspapers in smaller communities are more likely to include all known living relatives as a courtesy to readers.

Because obituaries are expected to receive close scrutiny by family members, the survivors listing must have accurate name spellings and addresses. Errors in the obituary survivors paragraph result in reader complaints.

With Children:

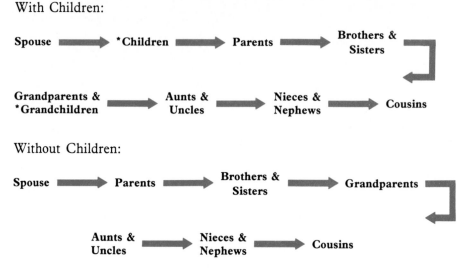

Without Children:

Figure 8.2   Survivors paragraph order of relations

Punctuation in the survivors paragraph follows standard news style. It may seem difficult at first, but correct punctuation becomes routine once the basic pattern for a semicolon paragraph is learned. Here is an example:

> Survivors include her husband, James A. Sipes; two sons, Harvey S. of 2283 Wayward Place and James Jr. of St. Paul, Minn.; three daughters, Elaine M. Parsons of Denver, Alice L. Beck of 407 Cedar St. and Virginia S., at home; her father, Edward H. Leeke of Oak Manor Home; and two cousins, William L. Hamstead of 1454 Avery Ave. and Jessie R. Garrison of 349 Verde Drive.

A few observations about the paragraph:

1. It introduces the listing of names in a simple manner, although without a colon.
2. A semicolon separates each set of relatives: after the spouse, the two sons, the three daughters, the father and before "and" introducing the two cousins.
3. Either there are no living grandparents-grandchildren, aunts-uncles, nieces-nephews, or (more likely) they aren't local.
4. The address of each local relative is given after the name. Omit

the addresses for survivors with the same address as the deceased. Last names of survivors with the same last name as the deceased are not used.

5. Non-local survivors are identified by their city and state (when the state isn't obvious: for instance, Denver doesn't require "Colo.," but Lincoln could be "Neb." or dozens of other states).

Here is another example:

> Mr. Jones is survived by his wife, Gladys Lilly, nee Westheimer; his mother, Harriet M. of Jackson, Miss.; two brothers, Henry T. of 1277 E. Logan St. and Paul E. of Chicago; a sister, Rosemarie H. Reed of 344 Sutton Lane and her daughters, Linda and Claudia; and an uncle, Barry Wingate of 578 W. Cherry St.

Close scrutiny of the second example shows that Barry Wingate, an uncle, is out of order. According to the order of relationships given, an uncle should precede the deceased's nieces, Linda and Claudia. However, concise writing and clarity of meaning take precedence over the pre- scribed survivors order. Placing Linda and Claudia with their mother, at the same address, creates efficiency and reduces confusion. When clear writing conflicts with ordering "rules," go with the former every time.

Many newspapers that don't provide the names of out-of-town rela- tives do give the number. This listing usually ends the survivors para- graph with phrases such as "four grandchildren and six great-grand- children."

FUNERAL ARRANGEMENTS

The last part of an obituary—although this, too, is an ordering "rule"— is the funeral arrangements paragraph. Actually, news values suggest putting funeral arrangements high in an obituary because readers who learn of a death may want to pay their respects to the family, attend services or be at the grave site. Still, most newspapers place funeral arrangements last in the obituary.

Each of the major religions has its own customs relating to death. Certain denominations hold wakes, ranging from solemn vigils over the corpse to festive parties. In other sects, mourners tear their clothing, and friends visit the deceased's family daily for a week after the burial.

Individual families' funeral observances may differ, regardless of religious affiliation. In all, there are no easy guidelines for the multitude of possible funeral arrangements an obituary writer might face, but the general considerations can be described.

There can be at least four aspects related to funeral arrangements: (1) visitation; (2) funeral service; (3) burial; and (4) memorials.

Visitation includes preliminary rituals, usually viewing the body as it lies in state in the funeral home. Visitors pay their respects to the family at designated hours that are given in the obituary. Included under this heading are a wide variety of pre-service activities, including a wake or other ceremonies.

The funeral service is the ceremony itself. Services are held at funeral homes, at the deceased's residence or in places of worship. The time the service begins, the religious leader officiating and the ceremony's location are published in the obituary.

Burial usually follows the funeral service. Often there is a procession of vehicles to the cemetery burial site, unless the body is to be cremated. Burial frequently includes another short service at the graveside.

Memorials include flowers and donations. Some families designate a favorite charity to which donations can be made in lieu of sending flowers to the funeral home. The obituary should include such a request.

Here are two obituary funeral arrangements paragraphs:

> Visitation will be from 3 to 6 p.m. Thursday at Peabody Funeral Home. Funeral services will be at 10 a.m. Friday at Grace Episcopal Church, the Rev. Albert G. Perry officiating. Burial will follow at Edgelawn Park. The family requests donations to the National Cancer Society in lieu of flowers.

> Services will be at 9:30 a.m. Tuesday at Hope and Hartwell Funeral Parlor, Rabbi David L. Simon officiating. Burial will follow at Drexell Cemetery.

SUMMARY

A person's death is worthy of news coverage. Surviving relatives certainly think this is true, and journalists should remember that death stories and obituaries will get very close scrutiny from family members of the deceased.

Death stories, or separate news articles, are written about prominent people. The death of less prominent citizens is marked only in obituary columns. However, the community population size and circulation of the newspaper partially determine whether a separate death story will be written. In larger communities, editors assign death stories if there is a morgue file on the deceased. Otherwise, the death will be marked only by an obituary notice in a column of obituaries, all of which are written according to a highly structured format prescribed by each newspaper. Many newspapers also run "death notices," or classified ads purchased by the family.

Death stories almost always are "who" stories beginning with the person's name, age and identification. In special cases where the circumstances of the death supersede the person's prominence, the story may have a "what" lead. Leads should include: (1) the person's full name, (2) age, (3) the fact that the person died, (4) day and time the person died and (5) circumstances of death. After the lead, death stories emphasize highlights of the person's life and achievements. The last three elements to include are: (1) a brief chronology of the person's life, (2) survivors and (3) funeral arrangements.

Obituaries are written from information contained on forms the newspaper provides to funeral homes. Although they may seem little more than transcribing exercises (because they must conform to each newspaper's format policy) obituaries must be complete and flawless. The general format for an obituary is:

1. lead—full name, age, identification and one outstanding aspect of the person's life. The lead also might contain the circumstances of death, the exact time of death and the current address.
2. death circumstances—if not contained in the lead;
3. highlights of career—more details about the person's achievements;
4. life chronology—birthdate and place, milestones from earliest to most recent, including schooling, military, marriage, memberships, etc.;
5. survivors—immediate family, then other relatives in descending kinship order, including local residents;
6. funeral arrangements—visitation, service and burial.

Accuracy in name spellings, dates and all other details of the obituary is essential. Editors rightly believe that a journalist who can't do a good job on an obituary shouldn't be trusted to do stories requiring more skill and enterprise.

_____ **Thinking it Through** _____

EXERCISE 8.1

Obituary Forms

For each of the next exercises:
1. Use the City Directory and other guides at the back of this text to verify the facts.
2. Use the verified set of facts to fill in the provided example of a newspaper's obituary form (page 183). The form may be copied for use with exercises A, B or C. Print the information onto the form.

A Melvin Edward Masters died of pneumonia while under a doctor's care at Lakeside Nursing Home. He was 84 and had broken his hip in a fall at the home last month. He died at 10:20 p.m. Monday, Lakeside authorities said. Masters was a retired carpenter who had owned his own shop here for 40 years. His former carpentry shop is now The Woodworks, 1576 Hoover St. downtown, a firm that employs 300 people, owned and operated by two of his sons, Bernard H., 108 Old Farm Road, and Melvin Jr., 675 Northwood. Another son, James R., lives in San Francisco. Masters has a married daughter, Julia Bonnie Lasker of Virginia City, Va. Masters was a deacon of the First Presbyterian Church. He donated the funds for its Masters Recreation Building in 1978. He was born Dec. 3, 1909 in Baton Rouge, La., and graduated Istruma High School in 1928. He attended Louisiana State University for two years and dropped out after the stock market crash in 1929. He served in the Coast Guard for three years as an ensign. After his honorable discharge, he earned an associates degree from County Technical College in St. Louis, Mo., in 1934. He worked as a carpenter's apprentice in St. Louis before opening Masters' Carpentry here in 1936. He married Elizabeth L. Linstrom in 1937. Masters retired when his wife died in 1980. He was a member of the City School Board from 1957 to 1969, a Mason, a past president of the Lions Club and a member of the Rotary Club. He was named to the City Hall of Fame in 1975. Other survivors include six grandchildren, a brother, Lionel K. Masters of 208 Estate St., and a sister, Mrs. Dixie Lynn Beaudreaux of Baton Rouge. Claremont Mortuary will have visitation Wednesday from 9 a.m. to noon. Funeral Services will be at First Presbyterian Church Thursday at 11 a.m., the Rev. Hiram Hancock presiding. The body will be cremated. The family requests donations to the First Presbyterian Church Recreation Fund in lieu of flowers.

B A lightning bolt struck and killed Blair Kelly Thomason when she was golfing at the Fairway Country Club at 8:45 a.m. Wednesday. Mrs. Thomason was on the second green when lightning struck her. A threesome waiting at the second tee witnessed the incident and said the lightning began several minutes before yesterday morning's rainstorm which was predicted for the afternoon. Funeral arrangements are incomplete at this time, according to Martin and Young

Obituary Fact Form (please print)

Deceased:_____ Age:_____ Address:_____
Day:_____ Time:_____ Funeral Home:_____
Cause/Circumstances of Death:_____
_____
Source (if needed):_____
Employer:_____ Job Title:_____
Career Highlights:_____
_____
_____

Birth Date:_____ City:_____
High School:_____ Date:_____
College:_____ City:_____ Degree:_____ Year:_____
College:_____ City:_____ Degree:_____ Year:_____
Military:_____ Rank:_____ Years:_____
Marriage Date:_____ City:_____
Places Lived & Dates:_____
Church Affiliation:_____
Offices/Honors:_____
Civic Affiliations:_____
Offices/Honors:_____
Other Memberships/Recognition:_____

Survivors:
Spouse:_____ Address:_____
Children and Addresses:_____
_____
_____
Parents and Addresses:_____
_____

Other Local Relatives:
Relation, Name and Address:_____
_____

Funeral Arrangements:
Visitation Place:_____ Times:_____
Service Place:_____ Time:_____
Officiating:_____
Burial Place:_____
Memorials:_____

Additional Information:
_____
_____
_____

Figure 8.3

Funeral home, although a wake is scheduled from 8 tonight. Mrs. Thomason, nee Kirkpatrick, was born June 19, 1964. She was graduated from St. Mary's Academy for Women in 1982 and received her bachelor's degree in health education from the University of Michigan in 1986. She spent two years on the Womens Professional Golf Association circuit, winning two national tournaments in 1987. She married Dr. Rudolph Thomason of 3105 Greenvalley later that year. The couple had one child, Barbara Ann, 2. Survivors include her parents, Mr. and Mrs. Eugene B. Kirkpatrick of 578 Hightower; a brother, William R.; three sisters, Emma Babette of Louisville, Ky., Mrs. Nicolle Cox of 1493 Easthaven St. and Juliet S., who lives with her parents; and a grandmother, Alicia K. Gibson of 2240 Glen Place, Apt. 15. Mrs. Thomason was a member of the Ladies Auxiliary and the Parent-Teacher Association of St. John's Catholic Church.

C Frank Swensen, who has resided here most of his life, was found dead in his apartment Friday at 11 a.m. from an overdose of crack cocaine, according to the county coroner. He was an engineer with the firm of Haley and Associates, 2711 Adams St., and an activist with the American Civil Liberties Union during the McCarthy era of the early 1950s. He was an agnostic. Mr. Swensen was born here on March 27, 1931. He was graduated from Central High in 1948 and refused military service as a conscientious objector. He earned his B.S. degree in engineering from Boston University in 1952 and began work with Nelson Manufacturing here in 1953. He served as a local representative of the ACLU from 1953 to 1955 and was a spokesman for the Machinists Union during a strike here in 1957. He was responsible for a peaceful settlement to the strike, which might otherwise have resulted in violence, according to newspaper accounts quoting then-Mayor Jimmy Dillard. Mr. Swensen married Lottie M., nee Greer, in 1958 and the couple had three children: Benjamin J. of 854 Lexington, Mrs. Lorine A. Hadley of 2111 Oakmont Grove and Joseph H. of St. Petersburg, Fla. He was divorced from his first wife in 1972 and married Christie M., nee Pierotti, in 1973. He was divorced again in 1977. Mr. Swensen is survived by both former wives, his three children, seven grandchildren and two sisters. Visitation is from 1 p.m. to 7 p.m. tomorrow. Funeral services are scheduled noon Sunday at Martin and Young Funeral parlor with a graveside service at 1 p.m. at Shadyview Memorial Park. The family requests donations to the ACLU in lieu of flowers.

Writing Practice

EXERCISE 8.2

Death Story Leads

Write a first-paragraph lead of less than 30 words for each of the following death notices. If circumstances merit using a second paragraph, write it also.

A Kathy Parnell Jerman, 67, of 885 Lester Road, the state's grandmother of the year in 1990, died Tuesday at 4 a.m. from food poisoning after eating at Victor's Steak House Monday night, according to doctors at City General. The six other restaurant patrons who were hospitalized were released by 11 p.m. Monday.

B Charley W. Deloach died of a heart attack Monday at 3:20 p.m. He was 71 years old and resided at 21 Oak Manor Circle. Mr. Deloach was a prominent farmer in the 1950s who developed the Ashcroft Center with a $2 million loan on his 80-acre farm. Ashcroft was this city's largest shopping center before malls came into vogue in the late 1970s. At one time the center had 100 retail outlets and still has more than 60 operating stores.

C The Rev. Dr. Linda L. Uhlhorn of Preston Apartments, No. 1905, passed away after being diagnosed with terminal leukemia two years ago. She died at 8:45 p.m. Thursday at age 55. Mrs. Uhlhorn was the first female to head a major church in the city, Good Shepherd Methodist. She was named pastor at age 40.

D George Hector Garcia, 21, of 4100 Talbert Drive, Apt. 219, died at 5:30 p.m. Sunday of injuries he received when a car struck his motorcycle at Parkview and Willow Saturday afternoon. Mr. Garcia, a junior in the honors program at State College, was the valedictorian at Fairfield High School here three years ago. He had turned down a Princeton scholarship to remain in town and help support his family through his job as an organ donor courier between local hospitals. He was en route to Children's Hospital when the accident occurred.

EXERCISE 8.3

Obituary Paragraphs

Use the obituary form fact sets in Exercise 8.1 A, B or C to write selected paragraphs of an obituary. From one or more of the three fact sets, write

1. a career highlights paragraph
2. a life chronology paragraph
3. a survivors paragraph and
4. a funeral arrangements paragraph.

EXERCISE 8.4

Obituary Forms

Use the obituary forms on pages 186 and 187 to write an obituary story.

Obituary Fact Form (please print)

Deceased: Weller, David Gene **Age:** 59 **Address:** 404 Valley Drive
Day: Tue. **Time:** 8:10 a.m. **Funeral Home:** Patton Bros.
Cause/Circumstances of Death: hit by motorist at corner of Valley Drive
    Madison Avenue
Source (if needed): Patrolman Lisa R. Quick
Employer: retired **Job Title:**
Career Highlights: vice president of graphics, Smith-Lawson Advertising
    Agency, New York City

Birth Date: 11/14/1932 **City:** Brooklyn, N.Y.
High School: Kingspoint High **Date:** 1950
College: Boston Univ. **City:** Boston **Degree:** B.A. **Year:** 1956
College: NYU **City:** New York **Degree:** M.B.A. **Year:** 1965
Military: U.S. Navy **Rank:** seaman **Years:** 1950-52
Marriage Date: 1955 **City:** New York City
Places Lived & Dates: New York City, 1957-86; (this town), 1986-91
Church Affiliation: First Presbyterian Church (this town)
Offices/Honors: president, New York Advertising Club, 1978
Civic Affiliations: Troup 15, Boy Scouts, scoutmaster; Optimists Club
Offices/Honors: choir leader, First Presbyterian Church
Other Memberships/Recognition: Optimists Speaker of the Year, 1989
Survivors:
Spouse: Alicia R. (Lovejoy) **Address:** 404 Valley Drive
Children and Addresses: sons: Wayne G., 2027 Hartway, Scott L., Erie,
    Pa.; daughter: Elaine C., Cleveland, Ohio
Parents and Addresses: deceased

Other Local Relatives:

Relation, Name and Address: grandchildren: Becky Lynn, 8, Wayne Jr., 5,
    both of 2027 Hartway; daughter-in-law: Stella Jean Weller,
    2027 Hartway
Funeral Arrangements:
Visitation Place: First Presbyterian Church **Times:** 10-3 Friday
Service Place: First Presbyterian **Time:** 10 a.m. Saturday
Officiating: the Rev. Sandra O. Stanley
Burial Place: Memorial Park, following services
Memorials: First Presbyterian Church, 1018 E. Jefferson St.
Additional Information:
    Mr. Weller kept a 7:30 to 8:30 a.m. vigil at the corner of
Valley Drive and Madison Avenue weekday mornings for the past three
years. He waved to passing motorists on their way to work.

Figure 8.4

Obituary Fact Form (please print)

Deceased: Craig, Catherine M. **Age:** 80 **Address:** Builtmore Hotel
Day: Mon. **Time:** 11:15 p.m. **Funeral Home:** Brighton Mortuary
Cause/Circumstances of Death: heart attack
Source (if needed): Dr. John B. Bursin
Employer: **Job Title:**
Career Highlights: owner, Craig Plantation; chairman United Way, 1962;
    homecoming queen, State College, 1932; queen of Charity Cotillion,
    1949; first female head of Farmer's Co-op, 1957-60
Birth Date: 3/27/1911 **City:** (this town)
High School: Central High School **Date:** 1928
College: State College **City:** (here) **Degree:** B.A. **Year:** 1932
College: **City:** **Degree:** **Year:**
Military: Womens Army Corps **Rank:** captain **Years:** 1941-44
Marriage Date: 1945 **City:** here
Places Lived & Dates: London, 1941-44; Paris, 1980-83
Church Affiliation: Episcopalian
Offices/Honors: Who's Who; state's Outstanding Farmer, 1958
Civic Affiliations: Performing Arts Center; State College Alumni Club
Offices/Honors: president State College Alumni Club 1966
Other Memberships/Recognition: Outstanding Women of America, 1960
Survivors:
Spouse: **Address:**
Children and Addresses: son: Calvin S. Jr., Craig Plantation; daughter:
    Constance N.Lacy, Miami; daughter-in-law: Melanie P.; son-in-
    law: George H. Lacy, Miami; grandchildren: Barton C. and Donna
    E., Miami
Parents and Addresses: deceased

Other Local Relatives:

Relation, Name and Address: grandchildren: Betty A. and Calvin III,
    Craig Plantation
Funeral Arrangements:
Visitation Place: Brighton Mortuary **Times:** 9-8 p.m. Thursday
Service Place: Central Episcopal Church **Time:** 11 a.m. Friday
Officiating: the Rev. Phillip C. Vincent
Burial Place: Craig Plantation
Memorials: Performing Arts Center in lieu of flowers
Additional Information:
married Col. Calvin S. Craig Sr., owner Craig Plantation, when
both returned from Europe after WWII; she was WAC nurse; he was
injured (lost lower legs stepping on a mine in infantry attack;
confined to wheelchair); two met in Army hosp.; Craig died 1955.

Figure 8.5

EXERCISE 8.5

Obituaries

From each of the following fact sets, write a complete obituary after verifying the information in the directory and guides at the back of the text.

A A 47-year-old man died at his home of heart disease at 5:10 Monday morning. Richard E. Beckwell of 1641 American Ave. left the hospital 10 days ago to die with his family: his wife, Judy A., nee Holstead; two sons, Harold J. and Calvin S.; and a daughter, Jacqueline L.. Other survivors are: his mother, Mrs. Louis M. Beckwell of 22505 Elm Parkway; two sisters who live in Indianapolis, Ind.; a brother, Rex W. of 712 Ninth St. W.; two aunts, one uncle; and seven nieces and nephews.

Funeral arrangements are being handled by Niles Funeral Home, where visitation will be held from 9 a.m. to noon and 3 p.m. to 7 p.m. Tuesday. The family has asked that, in lieu of flowers, donations be made to the local chapter of the Heart Association. Services will be at Gates of Prayer Temple beginning at 9 a.m. Wednesday, Rabbi Marshall N. Golden presiding, with burial afterwards at Reform Memorial Cemetery.

Beckwell was born here Nov. 2, 1945, and was graduated from Holston High in 1963. He received an appointment to the Air Force Academy, but was asked to leave a year later. He earned his bachelor's degree in business administration in 1967 from the University of Minnesota and his law degree in 1970 from the University of Kentucky at Lexington. He served as a second lieutenant in the Army's judicial branch. He moved back to town in 1972 and was married that year. He worked in the law offices of Kemper and Hart. He became an assistant district attorney in 1976 and deputy district attorney in 1984. Beckwell was treasurer of Gates of Prayer Temple in 1982. He was a Boy Scout Troop leader and a member of the Optimists Club. He served as vice president of the State District Attorney's Association in 1986.

B Marjorie Aretha Evans of the Lyons Apartments, No. 330, died Thursday at 2 p.m. of kidney failure. She was born Marjorie Aretha Jones in New York City, Aug. 22, 1925, and moved here in 1942, when she married Grover Nathan Evans. She worked in the Prestige Dry Cleaning plant and was promoted to plant superintendent in 1965. Her husband died in 1982. She retired in 1988.

Mrs. Evans was a member of the Second Street Church of Christ and was president of its Ladies Auxiliary in 1972. She sang in the church choir and was a member of the Gospel Touring Chorus, associated with the church. She belonged to Battered Wives.

Visitation is scheduled at the church's chapel Saturday from 10 a.m. to 4 p.m. A funeral service will follow Second Street Church of Christ Sunday morning services at 11, the Rev. Jack Y. Cobbins, officiating. Burial will be at 1 p.m. at the Hill Street Cemetery.

Mrs. Evans is survived by her three sons, Jacob A. of 2229 Bayside, W. Doyle of 941 Dunlap and Clyde E. of Los Angeles; two daughters, Mrs. Bernice K. Trent of 385 Washburn Drive and Mrs. Violet L. Bowles of Kansas City, Mo.; a sister, Erma Jean Jones, who lived with her here; three cousins; 12 grandchildren and two great-grandchildren.

C Jerry "Cotton" Fitzgerald, 57, died in his home at 3954 Flag Road from an apparent self-inflicted gunshot wound, sheriffs deputies said. Mr. Fitzgerald was suffering from depression after being fired from a 30-year job with A-Plus Advertising. He had been unable to secure gainful employment for the last three years, his wife, Deborah, said. She found the body at 11:15 a.m. Saturday.

In addition to his wife he is survived by his daughters, Mrs. Helen A. Hodges of 414 Roundtree and Mrs. Amelia G. Weems of Syracuse, N.Y.; his son, Donald B. of Applegate Apts., No. 7; his father, Walter H. of Longview Retirement Home; a brother, Vernon L. of New Orleans, La., and a sister, Mrs. Katie P. Johnston of Charlotte, N.C.; two grandsons and two granddaughters.

Mr. Fitzgerald was born here on May 4, 1933, and was graduated from Holsten High School in 1950. He attended City Junior College and served in the Air Force in Korea as an airman first class from 1952 to 1954. He received his bachelor's degree in 1958 from Northern Illinois University and returned here as a copy writer with what was then Ace Advertising. He was married in 1960. Mr. Fitzgerald worked as a writer, production chief and account executive with the same firm, which became A-Plus Advertising.

Funeral services are at St. James Episcopal Church at 9:30 a.m. Monday, Deacon Chauncey Lipscomb presiding. Burial to follow the services at Southside Memorial Park.

Mr. Fitzgerald was the local president of the Junior Chamber of Commerce in 1963. He received awards from the state Advertising Federation in 1968 and 1970 for his commercials. He won a National Award of Merit for public service announcements for seat belts in 1978. His sandy-white hair brought him the nickname "Cotton." He was known locally as an aggressive businessman and as a practical joker among his advertising associates. He was a member of St. James Episcopal Church and served as chairman of its annual fund raising drive in 1980 and 1981. He was on the local board of the United Way and the Veterans of Foreign Wars.

Speeches

A speech, as the term will be used here, means a relatively formal address by one person to a group. As recently as 50 years ago, speeches were among the primary ways to communicate information. Politicians, educators, scientists, theologians—those who had a new idea or a persuasive message— shared their views with audiences through public speaking. In early 1940, on any given evening in Eureka, Kan., an orator from France seeking grass-roots support for the United States to enter World War II, might have been the only live entertainment in town. The mass media dutifully covered these speech events and reported them in newspapers, on radio and in magazines.

Today, especially at the smaller daily newspapers, the weekly luncheon of the Kiwanis, Rotary Club, Lions Club, etc., is still an assigned news story. The article appearing in the next day's paper is likely to be a report about the guest speaker's presentation. So, even if the formal speech was a more essential news source in the past than it is today, speeches remain an important aspect of news coverage.

Two types of stories about speeches are carried by the news media, the speech "advance" or "advancer" and the speech story. The speech advance is a news article that might appear in the media to let the public know the speech will take place. Many organizations have publicity committees or public relations personnel who regularly send news releases to the media before their organizations meet. Well-organized publicists furnish photographs and background material on scheduled speakers, including the time, place and topic of the presentation. If the speech is open to the public, or if editors believe the organization is large enough to merit media coverage, a journalist will be assigned to rewrite the release into a news story for publication. Although rewrites are discussed in Chapter 15, speech "advances" have special implications for how the speech coverage story, the second type of speech story, will be written.

An advance story on a speech usually contains some information about the sponsoring organization, and the speech topic is mentioned prominently, but the advance always focuses on the speaker. The story begins with a "who" lead that includes the topic, time, place and sponsoring organization:

> A 25-year-old law clerk for the United States chief justice will speak on "Youth and Ambition" at City College's commencement May 15 at 10 a.m. in Jones Auditorium.

The rest of the advance deals with the speaker, including as many relevant facts about the speaker's expertise on the topic as space permits. Obviously, the more prominent the speaker, the longer the story, but other news values also should be considered.

> Patti G. Ellenburg, a 1987 graduate of City College, is the youngest person ever invited to deliver the college's commencement address. She received her law degree at Stanford last year and won a job with the Supreme Court's chief justice against more than 300 applicants for the position.
>
> Some 600 graduating seniors, their families and friends are expected to . . .

Advance stories influence the content of later speech stories because journalists assume that readers who are interested in the speech already will have learned about the speaker from the advance story. The result is that the story after the speech will contain less speaker background information than the advance had. In fact, the speech story should include only enough background on the speaker to establish that the person is qualified to talk on the topic. While advance stories focus almost entirely on the person who will be speaking, speech stories focus on what the speaker said.

WHAT CONSTITUTES A SPEECH

By considering what is taking place when a speech is made, we can reduce the process to its component parts and analyze how a journalist can use them to advantage.

There are some similarities between a speech and the usual method of news gathering: the interview. For instance, both forms include:

- a source assumed to be knowledgeable about the subject matter;
- who provides information to the public;
- from the source's perspective;
- to be interpreted and organized by the journalist;
- for presentation in the mass media.

Of course an interview offers the journalist an opportunity for a lot of information exchange, or questions and answers, and control of the interview format. But a speech gives the speaker control of the speech environment. The interview is usually informal in that the source probably has not prepared an extensive presentation for the journalist in a one-on-one exchange. But a speech is a relatively formal offering designed to be given in a public forum.

Some components of the speech environment are:

1. an audience will be present when the speech is given;
2. this primary listening audience, not the journalist or the general public, is the speaker's first concern;
3. speakers are usually invited or contracted to make their presentations to the primary listening audience; hence the speaker is presumed to have a willing group of listeners;
4. the speech usually is a persuasive message (few speakers merely entertain or give lessons);
5. usually the speaker's presentation has been prepared to appeal to that audience's interests, and the speaker will offer information reasonably in accordance with the audience's existing viewpoint;
6. the speaker usually has a vested interest in presenting information in line with his or her own views or at least those of the organization the speaker represents.

In all, then, a speech usually contains a persuasive message, either overt or concealed, delivered in a friendly environment compatible to both speaker and listeners. This speaker-audience rapport frequently raises problems for the journalist because the information presented in the speech may be one-sided, and the opportunities for questions may be limited or nonexistent. Journalists must remind themselves that speakers normally present only one point of view.

INTERPRETING THE SPEECH

The journalist's job in covering a speech is to provide an organized news story for a mass media audience. Doing so requires much more than merely transcribing what was said during the speech . . . a tape recorder can do that. Most American journalists don't use shorthand, but even if they could transcribe the speech verbatim, that isn't what covering a speech is all about. Instead, reporters must listen to what is being said and, at the same time, they must decide what is worthy of being disseminated to their readers. You need to be able to listen, think critically and take notes simultaneously. Covering a speech well is a demanding undertaking, and being alert in your thinking during the speech is the most difficult part.

For instance, only a small part of the speech can become the news story. A 20-minute speech may run to 12 double-spaced pages of text, or 3,000 words. The entire news story on the speech event may contain only 800 words, and many of these will be extraneous to the speech itself. The process is one of distilling the entire speech to its essential points, then organizing them so readers can understand the gist of what was said. Consider the following speech segment:

> We are not in the movie-making business. We are in the entertainment business, and in the business of providing a return on our stockholders' investment. Therefore, our board has decided to sell the studio that has been the cornerstone of our enterprise for more than 60 years. We will use the proceeds from this sale to purchase the majority of stock in CablePlex, a conglomerate that operates, among other ventures, five metropolitan television cable franchises. Our studio's library of feature films will catapult CablePlex into an enviable position as a leader in the cable television industry, which we believe is the entertainment industry of the future.

The segment is packed with newsworthy business dealings, but it is far too long and involved to merit being transcribed as a full quote in a speech story. Instead, the reporter might write:

> Smith said Star Industries will sell its Family Films Studio and purchase controlling interest in CablePlex, a conglomerate that includes cable franchises in five major cities. The studio's current film library will make CablePlex a cable industry leader, he said.

Journalists must interpret speeches for their media audiences. The interpreted speech story probably will not read or sound like the speech

Speech events, even the mundane dedication of a new fire station, can prompt headlines. After the politician praises local firefighters, he may use the speaking occasion to announce that a civic center will be built on the old fire station site, that fire protection funding is being cut—perhaps his own retirement plans.

that was given, but the story should capture what was said and the tone of the event. A superior news story on a speech will:

- supply the essential information in an organized context;
- relate the remarks to current events, if relevant;
- balance biased views from the speech with appropriate counterpoints that were not given in the speech;
- capture the speaker's presentation style;
- capture the tone of the event.

A reader who was in the primary listening audience during the speech should be able to read the speech news story and consider it a truncated but accurate rendition of what was said at the event itself. The Family Films speech might be placed in context with the following additions:

Smith said Star Industries will sell its Family Films Studio and purchase controlling interest in CablePlex, a conglomerate that includes cable franchises in Los Angeles, Minneapolis, Dallas, Cleveland and Tampa.

The transaction conforms to a practice by other movie studios to use their film library holdings as programming content for cable television. Smith said his studio's feature films will make CablePlex a cable industry leader.

"We are not in the movie-making business; we are in the entertainment business," he said, calling cable television the entertainment industry of the future.

While the Family Films example offers some insight about writing speech stories, it involves only a single paragraph of a speech. Converting an entire speech into a news story is much more involved. Fortunately for journalists writing on deadlines, converting the whole speech usually isn't necessary. The essence of the information provided in a speech is often contained in only a few portions of the presentation, and there are some guideposts for the journalist who can think while listening and writing.

ASPECTS OF A SPEECH EVENT

Figure 9.1 offers a model of what occurs at a speech event, including the discrete portions of the speech itself, assuming it is organized in one of the more standard patterns.

Mood Setters

The event usually begins with an introduction of the speaker that might be only a few sentences or might last 10 minutes. Journalists might learn more about the speaker's background, expertise and personality through the introduction, but remember that a speaker often sends a short biography or resume to the person who will be doing the introduction, and you can ask for a copy.

The best approach is to search morgue files for pertinent facts about the speaker before the event. At the event, try to talk with the speaker directly if that is possible. Introducing yourself to the speaker before the event serves a dual purpose:

1. The speaker is warned that the remarks are "for the record," in case there is any doubt about the public nature of the presentation, particularly the less formal question and answer session.

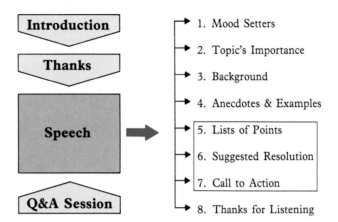

Figure 9.1   Diagram of a speech event

2. You identify yourself as a journalist, which may prompt the speaker to spend a few moments with you to clarify some points after the presentation.

However, what is said about the speaker during the introduction usually isn't much help to the reporter. Another rather meaningless part of the event is the speaker's "thank you" for the introduction and to the audience for the opportunity to speak. "Thank you" remarks may last a couple of minutes, and after they're given, the speaker launches into the prepared speech, which we will estimate here at 30 minutes' speaking time.

You should pay attention to the beginning of the speech, remembering that organized speeches follow patterns that can make your work easier. Listen to the beginning to determine if the speaker is a seasoned presenter. Generally, the more experienced the speaker, the more likely the speech will be well-organized. If the speaker doesn't seem well-versed, begin listening intently right from the beginning. The chances are that the speech won't follow a pattern, and important information might be forthcoming immediately.

But an accomplished speaker probably uses one of the more established patterns, and that means you can relax a little at the beginning. The first thing you'll hear is a "mood setter" consisting of a few jokes or a story. Mood setters are designed to put the audience at ease and to win them over. Speakers usually devote the first few minutes of the speech to establishing rapport with the audience. An expert speaker's mood setters might actually relate to the topic, but most of these warm-up remarks don't. Even if they do relate, it's unlikely that you will be able to include them in your story.

Topic's Importance

During the mood setting stage, you should listen for the speaker's transition to why the topic should be important to the audience. This material relates to how listeners can use the information they will receive or why it is a necessary topic today. This portion of the speech may last a minute or two, and it just might contain some worthwhile information for your readers, but probably not. Putting it in the story will require too much explanation. You should listen so you know why the speaker thinks the topic is important, but you aren't likely to need many notes on this material.

Background

Next, the speaker's presentation of topic background is likely to be a major segment of the speech in the amount of time devoted to it: possibly five to 10 minutes. It is designed to inform the uninformed audience members, and to remind those who already are familiar with the topic.

Let's say the topic is airline deregulation, when the government loosened its control over carriers in the early 1980s. This portion of the speech reviews the conditions before deregulation, the decisions leading to deregulation and the outcomes after deregulation. If the speaker is talking to a general audience, this may be the first time listeners have heard the information. If the speaker is talking to a flight attendants' association, this background information is common knowledge. In either event, there isn't much worth reporting from this material.

If you, the journalist, aren't familiar with the topic, you should listen to background material as context, but be cautious about reporting what the speaker says as definitive. There's a lot of room for bias when the past is being reviewed for the speaker's objectives. If your article is going to contain any of this background material, be sure you check its validity before you include it.

Anecdotes and Examples

Either in conjunction with the background information or immediately following it, expect some anecdotes and examples. An effective speaker presents some compelling stories as the speech moves from background material to the next topic element. One or two of the incidents mentioned in this five-minute segment might be worth including in the news article. However, an anecdote that sounds compelling in a speech is not always as effective in print. More frequently, the journalist realizes while writing it that the anecdote is too long to include. Furthermore, anecdotes and examples need to be verified for authenticity. A speaker may embellish the facts to increase listener involvement.

At this point we're nearly 17 minutes into the 30-minute speech, and the journalist may not have written a single line that will appear in the final speech story. It was necessary to listen to much of the information to understand the theme and tone of the speech. And there might be a few jotted quotes, facts and examples that will make their way to the final story. But now, at about the midpoint of the speech, the demand for critical thinking increases.

Lists of Points

A well-organized speech usually includes a list of points, assertions that form the body of concepts the speaker intends to get across. Often the speaker will number these ideas in the speech, a tactic used to improve listener understanding and increase retention. For example, the speaker might say, "There are four reasons why . . . "; "Five lessons are learned . . . "; "These three steps . . . " When you hear numbers of this type, take them as a signal for you to begin taking notes. In fact, the list of points will probably appear in your speech story, although not necessarily the complete list or in the same order given in the speech. Still, you will probably take most of your notes during this five-to-10-minute segment of the speech.

Remember that when you're taking notes, you must concentrate on what the speaker continues to say as much as on the words you are writing. Every reporter develops a personal "shorthand" for note taking, such as using "w/o" for the word *without,* or abbreviating *important* to "imp," and these strategies help. But there is no substitute for critical thinking when you're making notes. Instead of wasting your energies writing notes you will never use, make judgments about what you're hearing before you write: Is it important and useful to your readers; will they understand it? If not, listen but don't write. Critical thinking during a speech is a journalistic skill that requires some practice, but you can achieve that level of expertise. Fortunately, according to the diagram, you will be under the most intense pressure only about a third of the time it takes for the entire speech.

Suggested Resolution

The next aspect of the speech is the speaker's suggested resolution to the problems presented. This is the outcome aspect of a speech, perhaps three minutes in length, and virtually all speeches contain an outcome so listeners aren't left hanging. The suggested resolution is a good possibility for your speech article's lead, so take copious notes during this part of the presentation. Remember that the advance story focuses on the speaker; the speech story focuses on what the speaker said. Thus, you may want to use the speaker's suggested resolution as a summary statement about the speech for your story's lead. But the "call to action" offers another possible lead.

Call to Action

A call to action is part of every persuasive speech and usually is present in most non-persuasive speeches. After the speaker suggests a resolution, the audience is called upon to do something, even if it is only to consider what the speaker has said. Frequently, the call to action is much more specific: write your congressman, vote for a certain candidate, use your local library, make a donation—depending on the speaker's purpose. An explicit call to action might prompt this story lead:

> Centerville Four-H'ers were urged to campaign for more beef on the dinner table, in a speech here Thursday.

The call to action is often a more compelling summary lead for the speech story than the suggested resolution, although these parts of the speech may blend. Calls to action, which might last one to three minutes, invite careful note taking because they are likely to be loaded with forceful appeals, worthy of direct quotes in your story.

Thanks for Listening

The last element in the speech is the "thank you for listening." This may be as quick as a word or two, or as long as a minute, but in either case it won't contain anything worthy of reporting in your news story. Instead, use this wrap-up time to get ready for questions.

With any luck, when the speech is over and the applause has died down, the speaker or moderator will ask for questions. If no such suggestion is made, you should buttonhole the speaker after the event. If you introduced yourself to the speaker earlier, you'll have a better chance of having your questions answered. But many speakers do open the event to a question-and-answer session. This often is the most noteworthy part of the event.

Valuable information can be gained through the Q&A because some listeners may be as informed on the topic as the speaker. Recall that most speaking environments involve speeches on topics related to the audience's interests. Listeners may challenge what the speaker said, or they may draw the speaker out by asking for clarifications and, most important, updates. Seasoned speakers use a prepared text that they may have delivered dozens of times. They adapt it to their expectations of each speaking occasion, and they update it, but not always as frequently as they should. A listener's question may prompt a response that's on the cutting edge of the topic area, and the speaker's answer may be news.

Occasionally a Q&A session evokes some tension in viewpoints between the speaker and individuals in the audience. Don't expect this to happen, but when it does you should consider leading your story with the contested points of view. The Q&A might also develop a localization angle when someone in the audience says, "That's fine, but what should we do about it here in Clinton?"

If you know something about the topic and nobody else asks these kinds of questions, you may have to ask them yourself. Your inquiry might initiate an exchange between the more knowledgeable listeners and the speaker. However, remember that you're there to report the news, not to make it.

Are you allowed to include comments from the question and answer session as part of your speech story? Of course you are, but be careful not to attribute an audience member's comments to the speaker. Your story might even lead with the speaker's response to a question at the end of the session. And, while your story need not separate all the Q&A answers from information given directly in the speech, clarity requires that you indicate if the speaker's comment was a response to a question. Write, "When asked about costs, Smith said . . . "

WARNING

This discussion offers some suggestions about how to cover speeches more easily by recognizing the segments that comprise an organized speech. However, this presentation would be incomplete—and might lead to disaster—if it didn't emphasize that some speeches are poorly organized. Unfortunately for the reporter, some speakers aren't very adept at their assignments, and journalists faced with covering an unorganized speech must engage their critical thinking from beginning to end.

Converting an organized speech to an effective speech story is difficult enough. Writing an effective speech story from a disjointed presentation can be pure agony. The journalist must bring order from chaos, and the only way to succeed is to remain alert throughout the entire speech. Virtually every sentence must be evaluated with the same critical judgment that is called upon only briefly during the kind of speech that follows a logical pattern.

However, the reporter should listen for the same phrases that indicate key segments of an organized presentation. Use the same procedure of listening critically before writing, and rely on your news value judgment. When you review your notes after the speech, you may find that your note pad now contains the outline of a relatively organized speech, one that can be converted into an effective story.

SPEECH STORY STRUCTURE

The structure of a speech story often has an inverse relationship to the structure of a speech. Your story should not be in chronological order as the speech was given because, as the diagram in Figure 9.1 shows, relevant information usually isn't heard until more than halfway through the speech. Often, the story's lead is taken from the final moments of the speech.

Remember that, like most news stories, a speech story is usually an inverted pyramid news article. It focuses on the main points in the speech: what was said, organized in the descending order of its importance to readers. A brief example is offered in Figure 9.2.

While this is a hypothetical speech that is far shorter than most, it serves as an example of how to write an inverted pyramid speech story for a newspaper audience.

The writer begins by ignoring the sequence in which the speech itself was structured. We already know that sequence isn't designed for the news reading public. Instead, the writer should extract or report from the speech what the news audience will be most interested in knowing.

Generally, the most important information in the speech is presented in a summary-type lead similar to that used in the example. An exception might be using a quote lead, but only if the quote has all three of these advantages:

1. It is succinct enough to fit in the lead and still leave enough room to include attribution to the speaker and the place and time of the speech.
2. It is theme-setting. A quote lead for a speech story should serve as an overview of the speech story. In other words, the quote should act as the summary element of the lead.
3. Readers can understand the quote.

Double-check the importance of the third rule: Too often writers select a cute or compelling line from the speech they just heard, believing that it encompasses the theme of the speech. In fact, the quote lead is likely to confuse the reader. It's one of those you-had-to-be-there-to-understand-

I appreciate the kind remarks Dr. Jones just made, and I thank you for attending in spite of the weather. They say winter is "the season when we try to keep the house as warm as it was in the summer, when we complained about the heat."

But this winter weather is a perfect backdrop for what I have to say this morning. We have an opportunity to save enough money in one year alone to enable this university to hire 20 additional faculty, and 20 more the next year.

You see, not so long ago the cost of running a school's physical plant was only about 5 percent of its annual budget. But in the past decade, those costs have doubled. Nothing has changed except the weather and the cost of heating, which is up again this year. Part of the increase is fuel prices, which have doubled since 1980, and the other problem is the extreme temperatures the nation has faced for the past five years running. No one suggests these trends will change.

Schools near the Canadian border have suffered the most. For instance, last year Central Michigan began its second semester a week late to ensure having enough funds to keep classrooms heated during the term. Another school is reported to have converted a $1 million endowed chair into an automated furnace control system. And a North Dakota university deferred faculty raises in response to fuel costs. If a university's purpose centers on what happens in classrooms—and I think we all believe that is the purpose—such responses to increased fuel expenses are contrary to our mission.

I want to suggest a three-point plan that will save heating costs while it continues the university's mission. In fact, my plan will actually further this university's mission.

The first suggestion is to shorten the daily class schedule by two hours. Classes that now begin at 8 a.m. should start instead at 9. Rather than running classes until 10 p.m., stop them at 9 p.m. Those two hours of heating savings—at the coldest parts of the school day—will result in a decrease of 20 percent in fuel costs every year.

Step two is to adjust the terms to start one week earlier in the fall and one week later in the spring. December and January are the coldest times of the year, and the two weeks adjustment will save an additional 10 percent in costs.

The last point is to shut down three campus buildings...the three oldest buildings that are seldom used for classes and which are already earmarked for removal by the end of the century. These buildings have 1930s heating technology. This university can no longer afford to operate them. The savings will equal another 20 percent of annual fuel costs.

In all, heating costs will drop 50 percent. That's nearly $1.25 million per year. My suggestion is to adopt this plan as soon as possible and use the savings to increase the number of faculty by 40 positions in the first two years. By doing so we will be putting our resources where they belong—into the educational program—without sacrificing anything.

I urge you to discuss this with your colleagues and to draft a proposal at the next faculty senate. You are the only ones who will be inconvenienced by these changes, and if you support this plan, I know this university will support you.

I appreciate your attention on this frigid winter morning, and I'll try to answer any of your questions.

Forecasting annual savings of $1.25 million in heating costs at State University, a consultant urged faculty representatives to support changing the class schedule and closing three campus buildings.

Shirley A. Ramsey, chief engineer at Detroit's Hastings Utilities, a consulting firm hired by State's Faculty Senate, presented recommendations from her company's findings to faculty members this morning at Walton Hall.

Hastings' plan includes cutting two hours of daily class offerings, adjusting the semester calendar to move two weeks of winter classes to the summer, and permanently closing the three oldest buildings on campus.

Ramsey predicted heating costs will drop 50 percent if the plan is adopted. "That's equivalent to nearly $1.25 million per year." She urged the faculty to "adopt this plan as soon as possible and use the savings to increase the number of faculty by 40 positions in the first two years."

According to Ramsey, morning classes should begin at 9 instead of 8, and evening classes should end at 9 instead of 10. "Those two hours of heating savings—at the coldest parts of the school day—will result in a decrease of 20 percent in fuel costs every year," she said.

Another 10 percent of current fuel costs would be saved, Ramsey said, by starting the fall term one week earlier and starting the spring term one week later, saving two weeks of heating costs during December and January.

The three oldest campus buildings, already scheduled for removal by the year 2000, should be closed now, Ramsey said. These include Flint, Watson and Taylor halls which, according to Ramsey, have 1930s heating technology and are seldom used for classes.

"This university can no longer afford to operate them," she said. "The savings will equal another 20 percent of annual fuel costs."

She urged the faculty to draft her firm's proposals, saying that while faculty would lose two weeks of summer vacation, they would regain the vacation time during the winter break.

"If you support this plan, I know this university will support you," she said.

★ ★ ★

Figure 9.2 Speech text (left) and story example

it quotes that really requires more context than a lead can provide. But if a quote meets all three of these rules, it can be an effective speech story lead.

In the school heating story example, the lead focuses on the consequence aspect of saving $1.25 million, and it includes the suggestions the speaker gave for the savings. However, there is only enough room in the lead to offer a cursory overview of the three suggestions. Still, the savings and the suggestions do summarize the news elements in the speech to be detailed later. The lead even provides a "who" and hints at the audience.

The second paragraph names the speaker immediately and gives the speaker's identification, which includes establishing Ramsey as a credible speaker on the topic. The graf tells what organization or group of listeners heard the talk, and it tells when and where the speech was given. These elements normally go in the lead paragraph, but in this example the "what" elements require more space in the lead.

The third graf, in classic inverted pyramid story structure, provides more details on the lead elements, the suggestions Ramsey gave for saving fuel costs. The fourth graf provides more details on the funds saved and what they should be used for. Notice that every paragraph of this speech story includes some attributive reference to Ramsey or to Hastings Utilities, for readers to know who supplied the information and whose views were being expressed. Remember that attribution is not required in every paragraph, but enough attribution is needed so the reader never has to guess the source of the information.

After providing details on the consultant's three suggestions for changes, in paragraph seven the writer adds information not given in the speech itself. The three campus buildings to be closed are identified. Also in graf seven, the writer is careful to attribute the statement that these buildings "are seldom used for classes" to Ramsey. A journalist should verify such statements independently, but if deadlines make that impossible, the statement should be attributed directly to the speaker.

Throughout the speech story, quotes are used to remind readers about the source of this article. Using the speaker's actual words also gives readers some flavor of the presentation itself. The example story might be improved if the writer had included some direct quotes before the fourth paragraph. But the story does contain enough quotes to achieve the intended result, though it only includes six direct quotes. As suggested earlier, it isn't necessary to transcribe a lot of the speaker's actual words. Let your critical thinking help you select quotes you can use in your story. Recalling rules in Chapter 6 about selecting appropriate quotes, consider whether the quote choices from the speech meet the standards for what is worth quoting.

The last three paragraphs of the story contain some interesting points about speech articles. First, the information in these last grafs isn't essential. The only necessary fact here is that the building closings should save 20 percent of costs, and this could be added to graf No. 7. Yet the last three paragraphs do round out the story. Let the editor decide if they should remain.

Second, the call to action seems to be buried in the ninth graf. Calls to action are potential lead elements in speech stories, and, on closer inspection, we see that the lead actually does include the call to action: "a consultant urged faculty representatives to support changing . . . " The ninth paragraph merely offers further details on the action sought.

Finally, the last paragraph is a likely "throwaway" contender. The speaker probably has gone beyond the boundaries of her firm's authority in telling faculty that the university administration will support this plan.

Hints for Covering Speech Stories

- Before attending, check the morgue to read background about the speaker and the topic. Definitely read the advance story.
- If you aren't familiar with the sponsoring organization, try to find out about the group: its officers, membership demographics, its purpose and what happened at the last few meetings. This speech may have been scheduled to help members decide a current issue.
- Bring a tape recorder if you feel more comfortable having one, but definitely bring two sharpened pencils or a pen and a note pad. As Chapter 6 suggests, deadline reporters should use tape recorders only for backup.
- Arrive early enough to meet the organization's leader or event moderator. Introduce yourself to this person and to the speaker.
- Ask for a copy of the speech. A seasoned speaker usually carries a second copy of the speech text to ensure against transportation difficulties or merely misplacing the original. If the speaker has a second copy, you might get it. But stay alert during the presentation. Reporters frequently get burned when speakers deviate from the printed text.
- Should you pay an admission price to the speech? Should you eat a meal at a luncheon meeting presentation or accept any refreshments? Check with your editor to determine your organization's policy on these ethical matters.
- Keep your wits about you during the speech. Listening, exercising good journalistic judgment and using your common sense are the essence of effective speech coverage.
- Position yourself in the room so you can attend effectively both to the speaker and the audience, to assess audience reaction.

However, Ramsey may be saying she has discussed the possibility with the university administration and has a guarantee that it will support the faculty's decision. If the reporter is unable to verify precisely what Ramsey meant, her quote might be included near the end of the story if it is attributed clearly to her.

The following are three other lessons contained in the example.

1. The news story on the speech focuses primarily on content that begins halfway into the speech, just as the Figure 9.1 diagram suggests. In fact, the news story contains only the material after Ramsey's guidepost remark: "I want to suggest a three-point plan. . . . "

2. Journalists must interpret speeches for their mass media audiences. Hence the reporter states that Ramsey is speaking on behalf of Hastings Utilities, a consulting firm hired by the school's faculty. Readers need to know what allegiances the speaker may have. The writer also includes the fact that Ramsey's remarks stem "from her company's findings," indicating an analysis has been done, which is another important piece of information readers need.

3. Context of the remarks is maintained in the story in one other way. The writer reminds readers throughout the piece that Ramsey's firm is making forecasts and predictions that may not be realized over time. For instance, if there is another big jump in fuel prices next year, the school won't be able to afford as many new faculty as Ramsey predicts. The writer's speech story clearly indicates the speculative nature of forecasts by attributing each of them to the speaker.

While the Figure 9.2 example includes all of the essential information readers need, if this story is considered highly newsworthy (perhaps the community is a college town), then a more complete rendition of the speech is justified. Figure 9.3 presents the rest of the story.

She explained that the cost of running a school's physical plant used to be only about 5 percent of its annual budget, but costs have doubled in the past decade through fuel price increases and extreme temperatures.

"No one suggests these trends will change," she said.

Drawing on examples of schools near the Canadian border, she said Central Michigan delayed winter classes one week to have enough money to heat classrooms, another school converted an endowed faculty position to buy an automated furnace control system, and a North Dakota university deferred faculty raises in response to fuel costs.

"If the purpose of a university centers on what happens in the classroom, and I think we all believe that should be the purpose," Ramsey said, "then these responses to increased fuel expenses are contrary to our mission."

She told faculty that Hastings' plan will put "resources where they belong—into the educational program—without sacrificing anything."

Figure 9.3   Speech story example continued

Here readers learn the background reasons for the suggestions Ramsey made in her speech. These aspects include the budgetary effects of a university's rising fuel costs, which may be national rather than local figures, and one of the key themes of the speech: the contrast between combating fuel costs and a university's educational mission. This theme is certainly a worthwhile aspect of the story, but it isn't essential. Readers can understand the news story without reading the last three paragraphs that contain this theme.

Notice that most of the background material in these last five paragraphs comes from the first half of the speech. This is a reminder that the journalist who postpones tuning in until the midpoint of a speech may walk away without a complete speech story.

SUMMARY

Although perhaps less so than 50 years ago, speech articles still command a significant portion of news space. One such story is a speech "advance" that focuses on the coming speech event and emphasizes the speaker. The other type of speech story is coverage of the presentation itself, appearing after the speech is given and emphasizing what was said.

Some of the components of the speech environment are:

- An audience is present when the speech is given, and this audience, rather than the general public, is the speaker's primary concern.
- The audience is a willing group of listeners to whom speakers usually present a persuasive message.
- The speech has been prepared for this audience and is likely to be in accordance with listeners' existing viewpoint. Speakers usually have a vested interest in the information they present.
- Rapport between speaker and audience may cause problems for a journalist who forgets that speeches can be biased.

The journalist's job in covering a speech goes beyond transcribing what is said. The goal is to provide an organized news story for a mass media audience. You need to be able to listen, think critically and take notes simultaneously. The speech story will not read like the speech that was given, but the story should: (1) supply the essential information in an organized context; (2) relate the remarks to current, relevant events; (3) balance biased views in the speech with appropriate counterpoints not given; and (4) capture the speaker's style and the tone of the event.

Formal speeches by seasoned speakers often have a distinct format: (1) mood setters; (2) why the topic is important; (3) topic background; (4) anecdotes and examples; (5) lists of points; (6) suggested resolution; (7) call to action; and (8) thanks for listening. Aspects five through seven usually are the essential elements of a speech, worthy of the journalist's closest attention, as is the question and answer period following the speech itself. However, many speeches are not organized well enough to fit a pattern; important information could occur at any point in the speech.

The usual speech story structure is an inverted pyramid news article beginning with a summary lead on the main aspects of what the speaker said. If not in the first paragraph, the second graf should include: (1) the speaker's name and identification; (2) when and where the speech was given; and (3) to what group of listeners. A speech story should be laced with quotes and with attribution.

Writing Practice

EXERCISE 9.1

Advance Information

For each of the following speeches, write an advance article based on the information about the speaker and the coming speaking event. Do not use any information from the speech itself.

EXERCISE 9.2

Speech

For each of the following speeches, write a speech story covering what the speaker said. Be sure to include pertinent information readers will need to know about the speaker and the event.

A Advance Information

Richard T. Ellison, legal economist with the Federal Bureau of Consumer Affairs, will speak at the noon meeting of the (your town) Products Pricing and Safety Council, a 150-member group that meets monthly at the Grand Hotel Ballroom.

The group is composed primarily of women who are activists for fair pricing of consumer products, including food and children's toys. Members of PPSC serve on the local Better Business Bureau Inc., the Chamber of Commerce, the Mayor's Action Council and several other city and state commerce boards.

Ellison has practiced law for 20 years with the Chicago Legal Aid Society and worked with Ralph Nader, consumer advocate, before joining the bureau.

Speech

Write for tomorrow morning's paper.

Ladies and gentlemen of (your town's) Products Pricing and Safety Council, let me thank you for allowing me this opportunity to address you today. Your program chairman, Mrs. Marina Langford, was a little bit surprised when she picked up the phone three months ago and found it was a call from my office in Washington offering my services as a program speaker for the PPSC. She was quite happy when she was told I would speak free of charge and would pay my own expenses. And she was delighted that I had not called collect. It was yet another example of a federal government that puts you, the public, first at any cost. You know that when it comes to spending tax dollars, your federal government does it better than anyone.

But, I confess, I have not come here today to talk with you about your federal government's spending program. I am here to speak with you about a problem the federal government cannot solve for you; a problem of such magnitude that even the Supreme Court is powerless to settle the issue. I am talking about a devilish scheme perpetrated by state politicians during the 1930s that has created a situation so preposterous that it would be comical if it was not so malicious.

I am referring to the state-level practice of price fixing, a legacy of corrupt politicians and Northern industrialists who cooperated in a mutual effort to fleece sovereign states of their raw resources. Put simply, the federal government has defined price fixing as any attempt by a state agency to predetermine a wholesale and retail price and to fix that price through state law. Obviously, this price fixing is more far-reaching than just setting a price the public must pay for a product. State agencies have, in most cases, stipulated the cost to the retailer, the cost to the wholesaler, the cost to the manufacturer and the cost to the grower or producer. In many cases, fixing the cost to these major handlers is a perfectly justifiable practice if conditions warrant.

Let me give you an example. We will pretend that Florida orange juice and California orange juice are basically equal products in quality, but are in bitter competition to capture the national market. We will say that California and Florida are the best climates suited for orange groves and that hundreds of thousands of acres in both states are planted in orange trees. We will pretend that California uses illegal aliens as laborers to grow the oranges and to crate them out of the fields while Florida has to depend on its own citizens to do the work. Let's assume that California's canning facilities are better; they are fully automated and can produce 10 times as many barrels of orange juice a day as Florida can produce with its less automated canning facilities.

By the time the two products are on the open market, California's orange juice costs only $1 a quart while Florida's costs $2 a quart for the same quality juice. Obviously, the California juice is the one the public will buy because it is a competitively superior product: It's cheaper.

But what is Florida to do? Are all of its orchards to be plowed under? Should all of its orange growers go bankrupt? Let us pretend that the Florida politicians say no. How can they protect their state's growers? First, they can pass a law making it illegal to import orange juice from outside the state of Florida. This is a prohibition akin to the alcoholic beverage prohibition dry counties have established in spotted areas across the United States. It means simply that no similar product produced outside the state's border may be brought in at any price. Secondly, the state can put a tariff on the incoming goods. Using our example with the California juice selling $1 lower than the Florida juice, the state can pass a tariff, or other import tax, on juice at $1 a quart, making the state's product again competitive within its borders.

Now, before going on, let me pause here while you consider why the federal government has sent me into your state to speak against price fixing. Is the government so interested in free enterprise in an open market that it doesn't care what happens to the little growers? Would the government send me here to tell you the Florida orange grower has to go bankrupt? You know better than that.

For years Uncle Sam has been supporting the farmer with crop subsidies. We have given aid to small businesses. We have guaranteed the American worker a minimum wage and given huge bailouts to industries where thousands of jobs were on the line. Remember that the U.S. government has high tariffs and high taxes on many imported products today. So I assure you, the federal government is not here to hurt small businesses, be they farmers or merchants. The government would go along with the import prohibition on orange juice and allow the $1 tariff. What the government is against, and what you should be against, is the third option left to the state: the kind of price fixing that guarantees a set price to everyone. This, unfortunately, is the kind of option most states have taken, and it is this price fixing that is most corrupting, both to the politician and to the American public.

Let me describe it to you using another example. Let's go back about half a century when the oil industry in Texas was beginning to blossom. On the windswept Texas plains, one derrick after another was built until the land looked like a pincushion. But at the time vast oil fields were discovered in Texas, there were no transportation facilities, no refineries, no storage tanks and no distributors. When the enormity of the oil find became apparent, instead of making an investment in Texas and boosting the economy there, the giant gas companies of the East sent crews into Texas to build pipelines. They built the pipes not to serve the people of Texas or the rest of the South and Southwest, but to pipe the oil quickly and cheaply to the eastern refineries. Texas established an oil regulation agency that was supposed to ensure that Texans reaped the benefits of their oil. But the Eastern refineries got control of that agency and the oil flowed out of Texas through the pipelines, most of which were paid for within 10 years.

Ladies and gentlemen, let's look at the situation in Texas today. The oil still flows through the pipelines to the Eastern companies that get paid for transporting the fuel through the pipeline. They get paid for refining the oil and for making gasoline and a thousand other products. The Eastern companies get paid to transport the fuel by truck and train across this nation and get paid, by the cargo gallon, to take the oil back into Texas. The producer gets a fixed low price for his crude oil; the pipeline owners get a fixed price; the refineries get a fixed price; and the transport firms get a fixed price. By the time the gasoline gets back to Texas, the distributor has taken a cut, the wholesaler has made a profit and the poor filling station owner barely makes ends meet. The Texas motorist—the very person who should save money on gasoline—pays as much for a gallon of gas as a motorist in Vermont or Wisconsin or Utah. Sometimes the Texas motorist pays more, and it's all because a state price fixing agency in the 1930s sold out to the Eastern refineries. And that same corrupt Texas agency fixes the price of gas and oil in Texas today.

But Texas is not the only state that has succumbed to corrupt price fixing. Everybody knows that Kansas City beef is the best in America. Did you know Kansas City beef is slaughtered and prepared in Chicago, that it is sold in New York and that it is sent by rail down the Mississippi Valley? Did you know people in Kentucky pay less for Kansas City steak than do people in Kansas City? And if that makes you wonder, did you know that most of the Kansas City beef is really raised on ranches in Oklahoma and New Mexico!

The kind of price fixing that the federal government would like to end is not the kind that guarantees a fixed price to the grower, the processor, the wholesaler and the retailer. All of these people perform a service by changing the nature of the product, by improving the merchandise the consumer actually buys. The government believes each of these people is entitled to a profit, and if price fixing is the only way to ensure that profit, then that kind of price fixing is a good thing. What the government does want to end is the kind of price fixing that promises unnecessary profit to handlers and big merchandisers who don't improve the product in any way. There are middlemen who drive up the price you have to pay when you shop every week at the grocery store. Corrupt price fixing agencies guarantee profits to these middlemen at the expense of the buying public. And, ladies and gentlemen, the buying public today can ill afford an increase in the cost of living.

I have come here today to build public sentiment against corrupt price fixing practices. You are the representatives of consumers in this area, and I need your support to launch a public action program. I don't pretend to know your state's business, but if you believe that a corrupt price fixing agency is raising retail prices, I think you should fight back both as consumers and consumer advocates. I recommend four positive steps. First, find out how your state agency works. Ask questions; make inquiries; do everything in your power to become fully informed on your agency's operations. Second, when you are convinced there is corruption, spread the information to others in your area. Talk with community leaders; take the proof to civic and service organizations; contact clubs that promote good government. Third, take legal action by hiring counsels and taking your case to the courts. Seek injunctions or grand jury indictments if you suspect criminal mischief. Fourth, and last, take legislative action by talking with your state representatives and senators. Send your legislators to the state capital with a clear mandate to end corrupt price fixing practices in this state.

Ladies and gentlemen, it is time to drive those who practice graft and payoff politics out of the statehouses of this nation. Price fixing—the kind that puts profits in the hands of needless middlemen—is making a mockery of sound economic policy. The little person on one end of the scale, the farmer or grower; and the little person on the other end of the scale, the individual retail consumer, both are being squeezed by corrupt state agencies.

It should be obvious to everyone that people in Wisconsin should pay less for cheese; that people in Georgia should pay less for peaches; and that potatoes should be cheapest in Idaho. Corrupt price fixing is a threat to the people of every state who allow it to continue.

Now I realize that you members of the Products Pricing and Safety Council are far ahead of most citizens in your concern about corrupt practices in your state. I urge you to keep up the good fight and bring the facts to your friends and neighbors. Thank you for allowing me to bring my message to you today.

B   ### Advance Information

Carol R. Payne, national president, Retired Americans Association, will speak at the dedication of a 500-bed county senior citizen's home at 2000 Summer Drive. On hand will be the governor, the mayor and representatives from all county senior citizen's groups. The dedication ceremonies for the $18 million Summer Home facility will begin at 9:30 a.m. Wednesday in the lobby of the home. Her talk is titled, "Older Americans: The Undeniable Choice." The dedication is open to the public.

Payne, 65, who lived in (your town) from 1965 to 1970, is a graduate of Arizona State University with a B.S. and M.S. in social work. Her husband, Cecil, now deceased, was administrator of (your town's) City Employees Union from 1965–70. Carol worked as a counselor in Charity Hospital's Gerontology Ward during that time. She served on President Reagan's Policy Commission on the Elderly from 1981 to 1984. In 1987 she was elected national president of the RAA, a 6-million-member political action committee. RAA has been in the news for the past two years because of its stand on socialized medicine. The PAC has pledged a $20 million campaign beginning later this year to pass legislation for socialized medicine.

Speech

Write for Wednesday's p.m. paper.

Good morning ladies and gentlemen. It's wonderful to be back in your city where I have fond memories and many good friends. I thank those of you who are here this morning. It's very good to see you again. And I want to thank your new mayor and the governor who have shown, through their cooperation on this city-state project, that government really does care about our senior citizens.

We dedicate an impressive facility today, one that epitomizes the words of Dr. Albert Schweitzer, who left his comfortable home in France to build a hospital in West Africa. A physician, clergyman and humanitarian, Dr. Schweitzer wrote: "Whatever you have received more than others—in health, in talents, in ability, in success, in a pleasant childhood, in harmonious conditions of home life—in all this you must not take to yourself as a matter of course. In gratitude for your good fortune, you must render some sacrifice of your own life for another life." The Summer Home is one example of this city's and this state's dedication to that principle.

In 500 B.C., the Greek philosopher Heraclitus alluded to change. He said, "You cannot step twice in the same river, for other waters are continually flowing in." Looking back 2,500 years, we might marvel that the ancient Greeks noticed change at all, because we are today on the threshold of the greatest changes humanity has ever seen. They are changes in the course of lives, accentuated by our aging population. I am reminded of Thornton Wilder's play "Our Town," written in the first half of the 20th century. In the play, characters visit their relatives regularly—not for Sunday dinner, but in the town's cemetery. Today, as the 20th century ends, most of us have family members in their 80s who are still very much alive and contributing to society. We are on the threshold of what the great anthropologist Margaret Mead called our chance to value the individual worth of every human being. She said, "For the future, our one sustaining strength will be the sense of our common humanity."

If we consider the demographic changes that are taking place today, we must recognize that by the year 2025 nearly one-third of all Americans will be 60 years old or older. Those over age 80 will be the single fastest increasing population segment. The Retired Americans Association is charting the implications of these population trends and comes up with two clear decisions that must be met now. The first is health care and the second is education.

Let's look at what's happening in health care. The average cost of nursing home care in the United States is $25,000 a year. Private, in-home care costs about $36,000 a year, or just about $75 a day. It is evident that most families cannot afford these costs, and it should be just as evident that government is the only sector of society that can prevent the family financial disasters associated with such health care costs. The RAA is launching a $20 million campaign next week to support legislation for a long-term health care plan similar to social insurance. Our program will be like Social Security or Medicare, and we believe it's the only way to tame the health care hyena that preys on the aged. But our RAA plan goes beyond care for the elderly. If we spread the costs of health care throughout the working life of individuals, we can insure adequate health care to all people, regardless of their age. Anything less, in these times of American affluence, is simply unacceptable.

Let's look at the figures. The United States now spends more on health care than any other nation in the world. Yet nearly one-fourth of our population under retirement age still has either no health insurance or inadequate health insurance. Minorities are particularly at risk, as are children under age 18. Many people in low-paying jobs or part-time jobs have no health care insurance whatsoever. We read nearly every day about people who were refused medical treatment at hospitals because they could show no proof of insurance. Hospitals that do treat the uninsured and indigent never recoup the losses of their compassionate gesture. A recent Louis Harris and Associates poll was taken in the United States, Great Britain and Canada. People were asked if they were satisfied with the current health care system of their country. Nearly 90 percent of Americans said our system needs fundamental change. That compares with 69 percent of the British and 42 percent of the Canadians. In the Harris poll, 61 percent of Americans said they would favor Canada's health care system to the one we have in the United States. That system is a government-funded insurance program that sets fees charged by doctors and hospitals. Additionally, in Canada people are free to choose their own doctors and their own hospitals. With a government insurance program, there is no need for commercial health insurance plans, no high premiums for policies that cover only 80 percent of health costs, after an annual deductible, that exclude dental insurance and limit psychological and drug abuse treatment programs. With commercial insurance programs, we all pay commissions for salespeople, and doctors pay exorbitant malpractice insurance fees. Is it socialized medicine? I guess the answer is yes, if we see socialized medicine as government involvement in health care. But we already have extensive government involvement in health care, without any of the effective controls that would prevent medical costs from being the single greatest inflationary aspect of our society.

The plan the RAA is offering will not cost Americans a penny more than they pay today—in fact it should cost only 60 percent of what health insurance costs today—and it would guarantee that every American would get the finest health care in the world, regardless of their current income level or the circumstances of their birth. It is true that people over age 60 will require the majority of health care expenses. But that is also the case today. In the near future, this population segment will be nearly one-third of the entire U.S. population, and, according to our projections, without a national health insurance plan many of your families will face the choice of having your savings wiped out or settling for less than adequate health care for your parents and grandparents.

The other clear decision I want to mention is education. Fortunately, this is the bright side of the population aging trend. By the year 2000, the working-age population will be moving for the first time toward more reliance on older Americans. The pool of workers between the ages of 24 and 50 will be shrinking, while the pool of capable workers between 50 and 80 will be growing. Employers will find they need to offer incentives to keep people 65 and older in the work force. It will be a time when capable people who would normally retire will be highly sought after for their skills and knowledge. But the jobs they will hold will require greater skills and knowledge. We must double our efforts now to ensure that all Americans know how to read, to operate computers, to understand mathematics and science. Businesses must create non-traditional methods of teaching new skills to workers in industry-supported continuing education programs so capable employees have the knowledge to remain effective in the technological workforce. We must remember the advice I heard from a gerontologist when I worked at this city's Charity Hospital more than 20 years ago. He said, "Older Americans will likely be not so much the problem as the solution." We must make that happen.

I think Summer Home is a beautiful beginning of a national solution to the problem of dealing with the elderly. A government-supported facility to provide a dignified setting for older Americans is a good start on the road to recognizing our commitment to our senior citizens. Thank you for inviting me to be here at its dedication ceremonies. I hope other communities will work as cooperatively as you have done to accomplish the goal this facility achieves.

C **Advance Information**

Dr. Jason L. Moody, research professor, Department of Chemistry, University of Alaska at Anchorage. Moody is 64, married to Beatrice Moody; the couple have two children and four grandchildren.

A native of St. Paul, Minn., Moody received his bachelor's from the University of Minnesota in 1947, and his master's from the University of Illinois in 1950, both in chemistry. He served as an Army artillery captain in Korea. He completed his doctorate in biochemistry at California Technical Institute in 1957 and joined the faculty at Cal Tech that year.

Moody worked for the U.S. Food and Drug Administration during the summers from 1960 through 1968. He became a professor of biochemistry at the University of Wisconsin in 1970. From 1975 to 1980, he headed a research laboratory at Greenfield Genetics in San Jose, Calif., where his work included development of a gene-grafting technique now used in agriculture to increase the yield of grains. That discovery earned him the Nobel Prize for chemistry in 1979. He was named research professor at the University of Alaska in 1981.

He is the author of *Future Fright,* a 1989 book about dangers to the environment. Moody has been praised by environmentalists for focusing attention on pollution and birth control. He has been criticized by business for his accusations against the chemical byproducts of industry.

Moody will be the luncheon speaker at a special joint meeting of the Chamber of Commerce (your town) and the local chapter of Greenpeace, an environmental group with some 200 area members. His speech is titled, "From Future Fright to Future Faith." The CofC and Greenpeace have been at odds during the past year about what kinds of restrictions should be placed on businesses receiving tax incentives for locating in the city's new 1,000-acre industrial park. The mayor called this one-day conference for Tuesday to bring the groups together to work out a compromise on their differences.

Speech

Write for Wednesday a.m. paper.

I want to thank you, Mr. Mayor, for inviting me here today, and for making this conference of concerned citizens possible. I think the idea of business people and environmentalists meeting face to face is as encouraging as it is novel. Frankly, the experience we're too familiar with is confrontational settings in the midst of a crisis, and I don't think that's any sensible way to plan for our future. In fact, this conference of business people and environmentalists is one of the best signs I've seen in a long time for the theme of my address today, "From Future Fright to Future Faith."

For the audience, I want to thank you for your applause when I was introduced. I don't know how many of you have heard me talk previously, but you're bound to be aware that I'm less than the ideal business luncheon speaker. In fact, I rarely get invitations to speak at business conferences because my theme has been construed to be anti-business. Actually, I'm not anti-business at all . . . I'm anti-irresponsible business. And my barbs aren't intended solely for industry leaders. You environmentalists are going to hear some pointed barbs too. I've been jeered at and scoffed, insulted and dismissed as a crank. So I want to thank you for your applause in advance of my remarks, in the likelihood there is a deafening silence at their conclusion.

I come before you today, speaking for myself alone, but also as a biochemist who sees pollution potentially as the holocaust described in the Bible. I see this planet's pollution problem as far more real and far more disastrous than a thermonuclear war. In the case of nuclear war, many will be spared and it will end quickly. Pollution, at the rate it is progressing now, is likely to lead to worldwide slavery, genocide and extinction for life as we know it on the planet.

Much of the blame goes to American business that has thrived for more than 90 years in an environment of almost unbridled recklessness supported by laws that promote greed and waste at the expense of our natural resources and our good sense. For instance, by the 1930s, at the start of the Depression, industrialized farming, lumberjacking and mining had eroded our topsoil and left hundreds of thousands of Americans starving. You don't remember it, but your parents do, and it made them reactionary and afraid that the same thing might happen again. Only when it was evident that some of the richest farmland in the country had been washed into rivers and streams did the government demand that crops be rotated, that trees be replanted and that strip mining be curbed. But it took an international depression to wake up the federal authorities to the greed of American industry. I think the federal government is asleep again today.

Dishonest scoundrels who care only about themselves and their profits are evading even the weak environmental regulations on the books today. These industrialists dream up products that aren't needed, use advertising to create a need, produce products designed to serve temporary conveniences and encourage quick disposal so a replacement product can be purchased. Think about paper plates, plastic utensils and now Styrofoam cups and containers. The market for these products is $6 billion per year in the United States, which is one of the few countries that even has such products. The waste tonnage is tremendous, and scientists now know that the man-made chemicals produced do not decompose. That is the first myth we can deal with today. The evidence shows that "biodegradability" in landfills is one of this country's great scientific lies. Dr. Barbara Packard, an archaeologist at Texas A & M University, has had her students sifting through landfills since 1980. She reports that the bacteria that destroy trash on the ground fail to destroy trash that's buried and deprived of oxygen. Dr. Packard's students found newspapers from 1950 that were still easily readable after nearly 40 years, and ears of corn buried at the same time that were still edible if cooked. This garbage will be our legacy to our children and grandchildren.

The second myth is that the air we breathe is limitless. Actually, all scientists realize this is a myth. Ninety-five percent of all of the earth's air is in a layer only 12 miles from the surface of this planet. After the 12-mile zone, the air's density decreases out to 900 miles, and then it disappears into space. Each week, we emit billions of tons of polluted filth into the 12-mile zone. One example that is excusable is the rubber and leather that is emitted from the friction of our shoes when we walk. That amounts to one ton of pollutants per million American walkers per day. But one example that is inexcusable is women's perfume. Perfumes are made from organics that add half a ton of pollutants per day for every million American women . . . just so they can smell better. But these uses are far overshadowed by the 300,000 tons of carbon monoxide, oxides of nitrogen and sulfur, asbestos, hydrocarbons and other metals and particles that automobiles send into the 12-mile zone. How many thousands of tons per day, then, might result from the waste products of industry? Perhaps 3 million tons or more from the United States alone. First the pollutants block out the sun's rays, they wither agricultural products, corrode buildings and highways, and cause damage to our bodies. Winds blow the chemicals across the world, and then they fall onto our cities, fields and streams in the form of acid rain. We as Americans, with less than 2 percent of the world's population, contribute more than 33 percent of the pollutants to the atmosphere.

The last myth is that we've controlled our population explosion. Actually, the United States has made considerable gains in population control, but in the four decades that scientists have raised our consciousness about the population explosion, virtually no dent has been made in the increase worldwide. In 10,000 B.C., the world's population was about 4 million. In the year A.D. 1, there were 170 million people in the world. In 1930, the estimate was 2 billion, and in 1975, the figure had doubled to 4 billion. In projections for the year 2015, less than 25 years from today, the world's population is expected to have doubled again to 8 billion. If the "doubling rate" remains at about 40 years, then 150 years from today the world will have 125 billion people. However, this cannot happen because there's only enough fresh water for about 18 billion people. To support life, a family of four requires a plot of land with grass and trees of about 50 square feet. Otherwise, not enough oxygen is produced to replenish the supply to sustain life for the family.

Is there anything that can be done to prevent the disaster these figures clearly predict? I'm a scientist, and I believe science offers solutions to most of these problems, if given proper research support and a willing government and industrial concern that has never been evidenced in this century.

The first problem of garbage could have been solved beginning in the 1940s with more research and government concern about plastics and other man-made chemical containers. It is possible to make satisfactory containers out of food products such as wheat, corn, oats and soybeans. There was really no need to produce glass bottles for soda pop or plastic containers for foods and drinks. In fact, a team of scientists had produced prototypes for such containers in the early 1950s, but the food and drink lobbyists prevented the government from giving the team adequate funding for complete development of the products. Had these funds been available, we would now be heating our containers, adding gravy and feeding them to our cats and dogs. Perhaps the non-edible bottles and Styrofoam containers that now fill our garbage dumps would instead have been edible containers sent to the African countries in time to prevent the millions of needless deaths from starvation.

The second solution, which also relates to all three myths, is a genetic approach to growth. In the past, through hybrid seed research, scientists have tried to increase crop yields. The idea was to produce more food on the same acreage. With the advent of genetics, there is hope for producing larger food animals. Imagine a cow that stands 8 feet high and is as long and as heavy as a 1964 Cadillac, or a chicken that weighs 75 pounds and lays 1-pound eggs. We're actually well on our way to developing such breeds, just as we've done with some pond-raised fish. But now imagine just the reverse of this concept. Imagine genetic alterations in the sperm and embryos of humans that would reduce the average size of an adult male to 3 feet tall with women somewhat shorter, all proportionately built to that size. If we were smaller, our food supply would last far longer. We would also require less of the 12-mile air zone and less of our diminishing supply of water. But beyond that, everything we now use—automobiles, paper products, bottles, trains, airplanes, houses, buildings, clothing—could be made smaller. The pollution from industry and from our own waste would decrease to less than half of what it is today.

I know it sounds silly at first, but the more you think about it, the more reasonable it actually is. What do we have to lose? The scientific literature on short people clearly shows that they are generally more healthy, more attractive and more intelligent than tall people. All we would lose is watching giants drop a ball through a hoop on the basketball court, and we could lower the rim to 6 feet and still have a great game. If we make people smaller, then all of our natural resources last longer. That solves the population problem, the pollution problem and the air, water and waste problem at the same time. As I see it, and as any thinking person should see it, shrinking people is the best solution to keeping the planet intact for a long time to come.

That's my message to you today. Thirty years ago it would be science fiction, but it could be science fact by the year 2000, and that's just around the corner. What it will take is more permissive legislation in genetic research. I am sure you are all concerned about altering humans by altering genes. I admit it's a scary proposition, but the alternative, by anyone's standards, is far more frightening. We should encourage our legislators to support the research. When science finds the means to solve our problems, we should all be eager to use the discoveries to save this planet earth.

You've been more than kind to listen to my faith in the future. If you don't applaud now, that's all right with me. You have every right to disagree with what you've heard, but I'm confident that the ideas I've offered will be the outcomes this nation will use to solve the world's resource problems. Thank you for your attention, and don't ask for any Styrofoam doggie bags for the leftovers of your lunch.

D Advance Information

Mrs. Holly Hickman, 57, president of Mathis Corporation, this city's largest employer, will address an open forum of business leaders and concerned citizens at the Bergin Center Board Room Sunday at 8 p.m. Mrs. Hickman, widow of James R. Hickman who founded Mathis in 1960, has been a resident of this city since she married Wayne G. Langley in 1955. They were divorced in 1966, and Holly married James Hickman at that time. She had served as vice president of personnel for Mathis from 1960 to her husband's death in 1982.

She holds a master's degree in counseling from the University of Illinois and a bachelor's in social work from Iowa State University.

Mrs. Hickman began the local Crimestoppers organization in 1980 and served as its chairwoman for the first three years of its operation. She now heads a coalition of local business leaders in a group called Stampout, an organization formed earlier this year to rid the community of drug abuse.

Her speech is sponsored by Stampout and is titled: "Say No to Drug Apathy." Tickets for the event are $100. Proceeds will go to the sponsoring organization for its efforts against drug abuse. The Civic Center Board Room holds 150. Fewer than 50 tickets are still available.

Speech

Write for Monday a.m. paper

It was a steaming August night last year when Olivia Mayfield and her boyfriend Clarence Fain sat on the swings in Winderwood Park and talked about getting married. She was 17; he was 20 and a student at State Tech. They had decided the next June would be the perfect time for the wedding. She'd have her high school degree and he'd be a draftsman at Mathis Corporation. That would be their ticket out of the project and into a new life as newlyweds in their own apartment on the east side of town. But neither of them made it. Both were gunned down by machine gun fire. Olivia died on the concrete below the swings in Winderwood Park. Clarence died in Charity Hospital 10 days later.

Police are still investigating the crime, believed to be part of a turf war among local drug dealers who mistook Olivia and Clarence as their targets in the park that night. Neither Olivia nor Clarence were part of this city's drug scene. They just happened to live nearby, and they just happened to be in Winderwood Park at the wrong time.

Most of us here tonight have difficulty imagining what it must be like to live in the project. We take some comfort in having put a 9 p.m. curfew on Winderwood

Park after the shootings, as if that might stop the drug traffic in this city. But we were shocked again two months ago when Doreen McGuire, a 35-year-old homemaker from one of this city's most affluent suburban neighborhoods, was stabbed and robbed in the parking lot of Eastgate Shopping Center in broad daylight. Her assailant, who police say was high on heroin during the attack, will stand trial next month.

Olivia Mayfield, Clarence Fain, Doreen McGuire. Those are the local names and faces of some frightening statistics. According to the Federal Department of Justice's figures for 1987, 76 percent of all suspects arrested for violent crimes in a dozen major cities were tested positive for illegal drugs. In this state, two-thirds of the inmates of our prisons were convicted of drug-related crimes, and four-fifths of all burglaries are drug related. Drug abuse is the single common link for the increase in crime locally, nationally and worldwide.

As citizens, we find the statistics forbidding because they threaten our safety and that of our families. But we should be nearly as concerned about how drug abuse affects the economic structure of our communities. It undermines productivity and the quality of our goods and services. Drug and alcohol abuse costs this state more than $2 billion a year in medical expenses, insurance, accidents and theft. At the national level, the drug price tag is $60 billion annually with another $120 billion for alcohol abuse.

But there is no need for me to dwell on the numbers that constitute the problem. The real question is how to stop drug abuse. Some say that nothing works. Not education, not law enforcement and not social services. They say the only answer is legalization of drug use. I say those people are quitters. They're willing to give up before the battle for a drug-free America really gets underway. They're wrong about law enforcement, wrong about education and wrong about rehabilitation. But unless we in the private sector are ready to become dedicated to the battle, these quitters will be right about the war on drugs.

We need to help by funding educational programs and rehabilitation centers that are long on tenderness while they are tough on enforcement. All of us can contribute our fair share to a centralized organization such as Stampout. The larger firms should be underwriting their own in-house drug programs for educating employees and providing remedies for those already in need.

Here's an example of an educational program that works, although this community hasn't tried it yet. It was begun a few years ago in Connecticut with the support of several Fortune 500 companies headquartered there. Called the Freedom Program, it involves theater, comedians and even puppet shows to help teach youngsters how to say no to peer pressure when they're approached to try drugs and alcohol. The Freedom Program is aimed at students in the third grade—that's right, 9-year-olds—because studies show that by the time a child is 12, most have already been approached to try drugs. The program got almost instant support from the Connecticut school system, which saw the effort as crucial to reversing the growing problem of junior high students who spend their school days stoned on crack cocaine. Two weeks from today, Stampout will put $50,000 into the Freedom Program here. We've got the support of the school system and of the Boy Scouts and Girl Scouts. We think this educational program is the right way to begin an effective drug prevention program locally.

But prevention can't work unless we do something to stop the flow of drugs. Dealers think law enforcement and the criminal justice system are a joke. A dealer can be arrested in the morning and be back on the streets the same afternoon. That has to stop, and we're beginning to see some legislative action toward that end. For instance, Congress has been decommissioning unneeded military bases. Recently, instead of being shut down, a few of these facilities have been turned over to local authorities as jails for drug dealers. The records show that it works. In communities where military posts have become county holding pens for narcotics criminals, the flow of illegal drugs has decreased to a trickle. When a dealer is put behind bars, or when an addict is caught in a felony while on drugs and put into these special facilities to await trial, it sends a message to the element that needs to hear it most. Drug enforcement is no longer a joke. It becomes a reality, and it stops the spread of this menace at its source.

But perhaps the best way for business to deal with the drug problem is drug testing. Now I know that's a sensitive issue. Mandatory drug testing is seen as an infringement on individual civil rights. Courts have even prevented mandatory testing of pilots, bus drivers, 18-wheel truck drivers and railroad engineers who have been involved in fatal accidents. Still, the courts have generally supported mandatory testing of industrial employees. We at Mathis have studied the problem on a volunteer basis for the past six months. We found that it works. We can identify high-risk cases and refer them to a treatment program. A good treatment center is effective nearly 90 percent of the time. At the very least, when we identify a Mathis drug user, we can move the person to a job that prevents him from endangering the safety of other workers or the public. We can get the person off the assembly line, out from behind the wheel of a transport vehicle and away from handling potentially dangerous equipment.

Beginning tomorrow morning, the Mathis drug testing program will be mandatory for all employees, regardless of their position in the firm. Here are the points of our program:

First, we will conduct pre-employment tests. From now on, getting a job at Mathis will indicate a person is free of drugs at the time he or she is hired. We're this community's largest employer, and our wages are among the best in our industry nationally. We think that demonstrating freedom from drug addiction is a small price to pay for the rewards of a good job. People with a drug problem who want to work at Mathis can stop abusing illegal substances now, and they'll test negative in less than 90 days.

Second, we are instituting random drug tests of all employees, regardless of the sensitivity of their jobs. If a driver is going to be referred to our treatment center, then a clerk or secretary should face the same risk of discovery. If Mathis has 100 resignations on my desk tomorrow morning, we're prepared to suffer that temporary employment setback. But I really don't expect any resignations. We've made no secret about being committed to a drug-free work environment for the past six months. We believe our employees have expected these measures for some time now.

Third, and we think this is the right humanitarian approach, Mathis will not terminate an employee who tests positive in the random testing. Instead, we have put half a million dollars into our own on-premises treatment program with a licensed medical staff. Employees who test positive will be given release time during working hours and what amounts to nearly $25,000 in drug therapy and psychological counseling. Only after a three-month treatment will subsequent positive drug testing result in possible termination of employment.

Fourth, to protect a person's career, good standing and personal liberties, our testing program includes several backup procedures to prevent errors and to protect against an abuser's identity being known to others.

Finally, our attorneys are prepared to fight any lawsuits filed by Mathis employees or their unions. We hope there won't be any suits, but we have a special fund in place to ensure a long legal battle—a national test case if necessary—to make mandatory drug testing a reality for American business.

What works for American business can also work in the community. Along with drug education and rehabilitation, business people need to support tougher law enforcement in drug-related crimes. Stampout is asking for your support of legislation that allows police to test felony offenders for drugs when arrests are made at the scene of a crime. We're not talking about drivers who exceed the speed limit or embezzlers who are caught with their hands in the till, but burglars, holdup men, hit-and-run drivers, and car thieves all should be subject to mandatory drug testing in approved labs when arrested at the scene of the crime. When a crime is deemed drug-related, the offender should be placed in the alternate criminal justice system I mentioned earlier: one streamlined so that dealers and criminal addicts get swift justice and end up in jail for a long time. Stampout will offer such a proposition in the coming special election. We intend to finance a major campaign for its passage.

I appreciate your support in attending this presentation tonight and for your willingness to hear about the education, rehabilitation and testing measures I've outlined. If we at Mathis can offer guidance for programs you may be considering at your own business, I have appointed a special drug-abuse liaison from Mathis who will consult with you at no charge. Her name is Brenda K. Thurman, our vice president of personnel. Again, thank you for your decision to say no to drug apathy in this community.

Meetings and Press Conferences

This chapter deals primarily with news coverage of formal, scheduled meetings. However, it is appropriate to discuss press conferences first because the format of those events falls in the narrow gap between speeches and meetings. Actually, all three of these events require the same kinds of reporting skills, including critical thinking and some fast-paced note taking, and they generally result in the same type of news article: an inverted pyramid story laced with quotes.

PRESS CONFERENCES

Press conferences range in formality from a hastily called gathering of a few reporters responding to a corporate official's invitation, to a presidential press conference in the White House. We've all seen the pomp and ceremony of a nationally televised presidential press conference, and while there's more happening in the room than meets the untrained observer's eye, you'll have time to read more advanced reporting books before you need to prepare for such a formal press conference. As a beginning reporter, you're more likely to find a lower level of formality.

What you will probably experience is a conference organized at the local, state or regional level. The most likely sources will be those from government or large business firms. Both institutions have learned that a press conference is an efficient way to disseminate information to the public quickly. The media have learned that press conferences range from one of the most important sources of news to a complete waste of time.

Generally speaking, a press conference is called when a news maker or an institution's representative has something important to say and seeks to say it to all the media simultaneously. In such instances, the news maker wants to get the widest possible dissemination for the information and wants not to show favoritism by giving an "exclusive" to one news outlet or one medium. The most practical method is the press conference. Accordingly, the press conference is almost always arranged by the news maker, at that person's convenience and to that person's advantage. True enough, press conferences are often called to announce or explain something the source would probably prefer not to talk about: a factory explosion, response to an audit showing an agency has overspent its budget or an indictment for influence peddling by a public official. But even in these cases the press conference has the advantage of putting the source in the driver's seat and reducing rumored speculation through a speedy, public statement. It's important for journalists to remember that news makers schedule press conferences at their discretion and for their advantage.

The news maker instructs aides, public relations staff or secretaries to contact known reporters at all media outlets—probably journalists the news maker has worked with previously—to invite them to a press conference. The news maker has set the day, time and place, usually in a room of suitable size in the organization's building.

While the details of time and place are often extremely important to the news maker, journalists are usually satisfied if the conference room has sufficient facilities such as electrical plugs, and if the event is slated quickly. No journalist wants to wait for a news story or worry that a competitor will get the story first. But news makers seek to maximize the advantage of time and place through scheduling ploys that increase the likelihood of coverage.

Even knowing that the press conference is an ideal format for the news maker, journalists usually attend it, but they base their coverage decisions on their judgment about the event's probable newsworthiness. Sources have called news conferences to get media attention when they know what they will say is of dubious news value. Editors once burned by sending reporters and camera crews to a no-news conference view requests from the same sources with skepticism. Depending on the news maker's position and past performance, editors may "qualify" the press conference by asking about the topic when the invitation is made, or through a follow-up phone call directly to the source.

When the arrangements have been accepted, a journalist assigned to cover a press conference should prepare for it by finding out as much as possible about the topic. As a journalist you may need to check the morgue files on the organization and the news maker, but usually it will be enough to have kept up with current events. You should, as much as possible, follow the specific suggestions made later in the section on meetings. However, unlike a meeting, which is usually scheduled periodically, a press conference is often an "irregular" event. Hence, background information on the topic may be scant.

What Happens at the Conference

You can assume the press conference will begin with a statement by the news maker. Because the conference is called by the source to disseminate some information, it's normal that the source will have the floor first and will use the opportunity to tell, without interruption, as much as he or she intends to divulge. Expect these remarks to be formal in that they constitute a prepared and possibly carefully orchestrated rendition of what the source wants the media and the public to hear.

In many instances, a speech will be read from a prepared text. Copies of the text will be distributed to the news media at, or immediately after, the event. The text, or the presentation, is shared with journalists in hopes that it will become the crux of the news story. However, this material may be worthy only of inclusion for some direct quotes and background facts, or lower elements in the news story. A reporter knows the presentation is slanted in the source's behalf; it is often a one-sided view of reality, the side that makes the source look as good as possible. The news activity really begins after the presentation.

In almost every press conference (the term implies an opportunity for two-way communication) a question and answer session follows the prepared statements. Journalists should always take advantage of this opportunity to dig for what may be hidden news value. Even in non-confrontational press conferences, much can be gained for public understanding by quick and perhaps intense questioning. However, journalists often find themselves presented with unexpected information and with little time to digest it or to react when the floor is opened to questions. Remember, the press conference format favors the source. A news maker's major advantage may be the journalist's inability to effectively question what was given in the presentation.

One advantage the media have is the benefit of numbers. If 12 reporters are present at the conference, several are likely to begin questioning the news maker as soon as the opportunity is presented. Others can gain more information from the early interplay and direct follow-up questions. Perhaps some of the journalists in attendance had more background information when they arrived at the press conference. In any event, sources usually don't get away with much at a press conference where half a dozen journalists or more are in attendance.

Conversely, the number of journalists attending presents some obstacles. You may not be able to get a question in during the allotted time. News makers are prone to call first on reporters who represent the major media: the wire services, the biggest television station, and so on. So, if you aren't one of the higher status hot shots, you may have to be more aggressive. But there are few journalistic conventions that govern a press conference question and answer session, few rules to abide by.

Your job is to ask meaningful questions that will help you write an effective story for your media audience. Sometimes that means following up on the source's answer to a colleague's question; sometimes it means initiating a new line of questioning directed toward your readers' specific interests.

The quality of journalists' questions after the opening statement is the main weapon the media have in a press conference format. In fact, the news maker even holds the drawstrings to the press conference curtain. If the questioning becomes too uncomfortable, the source can say "Thank you for attending," and end the conference. Journalists may try to prolong the session, or may call the news maker and associated sources for more information, but the chances are that the majority of news stories written about press conferences will be based entirely on the information obtained during the event.

As in the speech or meeting story, a news writer should ignore the sequence of press conference events. Treat the news maker's response to questions as part of the presentation. Write an inverted pyramid story that focuses on what was said, arranged in its news value order.

MEETINGS

The Trouble with Meetings

The only journalists who approach meeting coverage with any degree of calm are those who cover the organization's meetings consistently. Such reporters have a significant edge in two respects: (1) they know the people and (2) they know the issues.

Of these two, knowing the people and possibly the political dynamics involved is the most crucial. If you don't know the meeting participants, you spend much of your time trying to find out who is speaking. Even if

The press covers a hearing of the Joint Economic Committee on Capitol Hill. Print and broadcast writers, photojournalists and television video photographers record the committee's deliberations in a setting that approximates a meeting or press conference.

you can keep up with what is being said and who is saying it, the underlying implications may go unnoticed. That's because every organization has factions, groups of people with divergent views about how best to define and achieve the organization's goals. The organization pulls together, but members often pull teeth first. It doesn't take too many meetings to discover which factions represent which philosophies, such as saver or spender, liberal or conservative, status quo or change, talk or act. And it's pretty obvious who the group leaders are and which personalities clash. But many of these group dynamics occur discreetly. Emotional flare-ups are rare, so the uninitiated observer may sit through an entire meeting without realizing that underlying subtleties are taking place.

Reporters who are new to the organization (and don't know the people) can compensate somewhat by learning the issues. Two methods are to read the last several stories on the organization and to talk with the veteran reporter. Additionally, the reporter assigned to cover an organization's meeting for the first time can make some phone calls to officers and secure background on the organization's current issues. Try to avoid being at a meeting without knowing some background on issues likely to be discussed.

In all, then, the more you can do to learn about the people and the issues before the meeting starts, the easier time you will have covering the meeting and the better your story is likely to be. As suggested in the chapter on speeches, you should introduce yourself to officers of the organization and ask questions before the meeting begins as a way to bring yourself up to date on possible meeting activities.

Meeting Patterns

Similar to the speech, if not the press conference, the bulk of most meetings follow a highly structured sequence of events. Journalists should be familiar with *Robert's Rules of Order,* the parliamentary handbook for conducting a meeting. Organizations with large groups of members attending and voting usually do follow parliamentary procedures to keep order. However, most meetings consist of small groups of voting members or small groups of members who speak during the meeting. Such groups may follow some of the parliamentary procedures, but they often conduct their business in a less formal manner. Figure 10.1 shows a meeting agenda outline many organizations use.

Of the nine elements listed, three can be eliminated immediately as possible news items: call to order, next meeting set and adjournment. That leaves six aspects of a meeting, two of which may only be perfunctory: the minutes of the previous meeting and the treasurer's report.

Many organizations quickly dispense with reading the last meeting's

> I. **Call to Order**
> II. **Minutes of Previous Meeting**
> III. **Treasurer's Report**
> IV. **Announcements**
> V. **Committee Reports**
> VI. **Old Business**
> VII. **New Business**
> VIII. **Next Meeting Set**
> IX. **Adjournment**

Figure 10.1   Meeting agenda outline

minutes by voting their approval as written. More formal organizations often distribute copies of the last meeting's minutes. While these reports usually are either too cryptic or too verbose to be much help, a reporter might scan the minutes to learn some background from the previous meeting. In many instances the minutes will foreshadow topics to be debated and voted upon at this meeting. But the most beneficial way to use the minutes is by securing a copy from the organization's secretary well in advance of the coming meeting.

The other perfunctory element is the treasurer's report, which is usually read because doing so takes almost no time. This report consists of the balance in the organization's accounts, recent income and expenditures, and miscellaneous transactions that might be of interest to the group. The reporter might learn about the success or failure of recent fund-raising programs, and the general state of the organization's finances. But most treasurer's reports aren't newsworthy. In fact, the only instances in which minutes of the last meeting or treasurer's reports may be newsworthy is when the organization's members question these reports.

Announcements may or may not be newsworthy. Often the announcements are of interest only to members of the organization: a member is ill, a congratulatory letter was received, a committee meeting will be canceled. But some of the announcements might be newsworthy: a noted speaker has agreed to address the group, the telethon will be March 5, the consultant's report has arrived.

Receiving a consultant's report might initiate discussion of the report, debate, motions and voting during the announcement segment of the meeting. This would be unusual, because most organizations follow rules that allow debate only after the announcement portion of the meeting. However, depending on the organization's meeting procedures, everything after the call to order is open to debate and a possible vote. Votes are probably worth reporting in line with their action news value . . . a definitive decision is more newsworthy than a discussion that leads to no definite outcome. However, the substantial aspects of a meeting usually take place during committee reports and old and new business.

Most organizations find that they cannot accomplish their goals without dividing the work responsibilities among committees. Groups usually have standing committees that perform ongoing organizational activities such as membership, and special committees formed to oversee topical problems such as a fund-raising event. Most of the organization's business is actually conducted by committees and task forces that have some autonomy over their activity but that report to the entire organization on their progress and any impasses they encounter. Larger organizations may have dozens of committees that perform the bulk of the newsworthy work the organization does. In any case, regardless of the organization's size, a journalist should listen attentively to committee reports and take notes on any reports that spur debate by the organization as a whole. Some meetings consist primarily of these committee reports; old and new business are minimal.

Yet in other meetings, old business is the key news element because many organizations debate issues at one or at several meetings before voting at the next. If the journalist doesn't know the background of business the group has been discussing, putting "old business" votes in context for readers will be difficult. The main thing to remember in covering old business activities is that what you hear at one meeting may not be the entire issue. Worse yet, members of the organization and the general public who follow this organization's activities—those most likely to read your story—will find it superficial or inaccurate. Be sure you ask about the background debate on any old business item you intend to report.

New business is supposed to be just that: issues that haven't been discussed previously. This portion of the meeting is a likely candidate for coverage in line with the news value of timeliness: something new is more newsworthy than something old. New business may be the only aspect of a meeting for which a first-time meeting reporter has nearly as much of an edge as the reporter who usually covers the meeting. Of course the new reporter still doesn't know the people well enough to place their actions in proper context.

While few meetings can be expected to follow the agenda example completely, the list is an excellent tool for keeping up with the activities that take place at most meetings. Memorizing the list is a good hedge against those times when a meeting agenda won't be available.

Writing the Meeting Story

Several philosophies exist about what constitutes news for meeting stories. These decisions depend primarily on the news value of what takes place. A secondary consideration is the newsworthiness of the organization: perhaps a city council deserves more complete coverage than the Kiwanis. But size of the community makes a difference, too.

Larger newspapers and broadcast media may report only the major activities of a meeting. Television newscasts may carry the single most important aspect of a meeting without reporting any of the other activities. Newspapers in smaller communities may expect reporters to write a story that includes as many of the meeting activities as possible, with extensive quotes and the nuances of each major decision.

A sensible guideline for newspaper reporters is to include all of the issues on which votes are taken during the meeting, especially for meetings of public bodies. The principle here is that any vote by a public body should be recorded for the record. Obviously, newsworthy debate that doesn't lead to a vote also should be in the story. If a meeting story writer includes all the issues on which votes are taken, the article is likely to contain more than will be published, but editors will have everything of potential value from which to choose. Deleting the more trivial meeting elements can be an editor's decision.

Organizing a Meeting Story

Although most meeting stories follow the inverted pyramid structure, the variety of activities during a meeting may confuse the journalist when it is time to write the story. For instance, a school board may meet for two hours and make decisions concerning a dozen or more issues. A journalist may see similarities between some of the separate items. But the most difficult task for the writer is to compress the lengthy proceedings into a manageable news story.

Let's suppose, for example, that the school board acts on or hears the following items:

1. set the dates for the next two calendar years
2. hire half a dozen new teachers
3. officially close a junior high school
4. appoint two new administrators
5. approve building repairs at two elementary schools
6. hear a report from a state evaluation team
7. approve the purchase of land for a new high school
8. increase prices for school lunches
9. hear list of early applicants for school superintendent
10. slate Dr. Martin Luther King's birthday as an official school holiday
11. double the hours of actual road driving required in drivers' education courses
12. finalize merging two elementary schools in adjacent neighborhoods.

The writer may have little difficulty deciding what the meeting story's lead should be: perhaps the need for a new high school has been a hotly debated public issue; maybe one of the new administrators is a controversial political figure. Aligning the meeting activities in descending order of news value should be simple enough for any journalist who stays abreast of current events. But how can a news writer cover a dozen meeting decisions, and probably some of the rationale for several of them, without writing a very long article that is likely to confuse readers?

There are 12 items in all, and while we don't have enough information to determine which are the most newsworthy, it's evident that just lining them up in their proper news value order will befuddle readers. The secret to increasing reader understanding is using a slightly more sophisticated organizational procedure in the inverted pyramid news story structure. Figure 10.2 presents that procedure.

The first step in organizing a meeting story is to decide which elements will be your lead. In the school board story example, the new high school and school lunch price increases are deemed the most newsworthy elements. We can assume that building a new high school is an important decision for this community; lunch prices affect all students and parents, a matter of consequence even if the increase is small.

Now the next step is a new wrinkle to the inverted pyramid story structure. Because there are so many meeting activities to be included in the story, it's necessary to combine them into groups of related content.

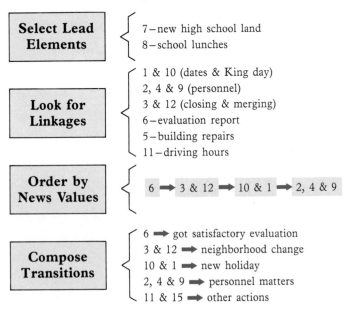

Figure 10.2   Meeting story organization procedures

Some of this assembling may be forced. For instance, combining the school dates for the next two calendar years with observance of Dr. King's birthday as a new school holiday meshes a more newsworthy event (the holiday) with a much lesser news element (the school calendar). Deciding to combine the two under the heading of changes in the school calendar is logical only if the new holiday has been previously reported and is non-controversial. However, if the holiday was news or controversial, it would have qualified for the story lead. Since it didn't, in this case, combining the two elements makes sense.

Other elements can be consolidated more easily. For instance, the personnel matters go together if all the changes are "business as usual" for the school board. If controversy surrounds any of the appointments, a separate category would be required for the disputed appointment. One of the elements in this group does seem to qualify as a separate category: the applicants for school superintendent. But, again, if an appointment was imminent, this topic would be a lead contender. Because the board is just at the stage of reviewing the list of early applications, no separate treatment is required.

Officially closing a junior high and finalizing the consolidation of two elementary schools appear to be closely related. Both of these votes seem to be the culmination of previous school board actions. If they were controversial, these decisions would be logically grouped with the new high school land purchase as part of the story's lead.

The grouping process leaves three items that can't be coerced into combinations with any other story elements. The building repairs might go with the school closing and merging group, but repairing buildings isn't comparable to closing or merging schools. The repairs should be a separate element. Doubling the required hours of road driving deals with a school schedule change, true enough, but readers will be hard-pressed to see any connection between driving and the King holiday. Driving hours should be a separate element. When combinations of similar story elements don't facilitate reader comprehension, leave the outlying topics for separate treatment. For example, the state evaluation team's report is certainly an educational matter, yet it seems to have little association with any of the other actions taken at the meeting. The evaluation report is a perfect candidate for separate treatment.

Through a process of looking for linkages among elements not selected for the meeting story's lead, the writer groups 10 individual meeting actions into six groups: one 3-item group; two 2-item groups and three 1-item "groups." Although some of the items have been forced into a collective, readers will have far less difficulty coping with six groups of items than with 10 separate items from the meeting.

The next step in the process is to put the news values in inverted pyramid descending order. Earlier chapters said that ordering news values was the first step in story organization, but with so many story elements, ordering should be delayed. There's no need to try to order 10 separate elements if you can reduce the list to six groups and then order the groups.

We decided earlier that the evaluation report wasn't worthy of being part of the lead, but we might now say it is more important than the rest of the elements. So, after the lead items, the No. 1 news value is the evaluation report. Next comes the closing and merging group, the No. 2 news value. The school calendar might be suitable for ending the story, but because it has been grouped with the new Dr. King holiday, we'll rate that group as the No. 3 news value. The group of three personnel changes becomes this story's No. 4 news value. That leaves two separate items, driving hours and building repairs, both considered rather trivial aspects of the meeting.

At this point we can create another grouping by putting the last two topics into a catch-all category worthy of nothing more than a brief

What if You Miss Something During the Meeting?

No doubt you *will* miss something during the meeting. Here are ways to compensate:

- Listen for the main points being made during the meeting. There will be some verbal cues about what is important, just as there are in a speech. Meetings frequently get bogged down in minutiae; you need to keep a broad perspective.
- Meeting stories usually contain fewer direct quotes than speech or press conference stories. That suggests being even more discriminating in your note taking for quotes. Spend more time noting the main gist of arguments during debate, facts and figures (dollar amounts and dates), and matching what was said with who said it.

- It would be very unusual for a reporter to interrupt a meeting to ask for a clarification, so you should ask speakers for clarifications after the meeting.
- If you need some interpretation, remember that group factions may offer their own impressions of what occurred. Be sure to get balanced views from both sides of an issue.
- Get speakers' names and titles right. You can't be responsible for matching names with faces when you arrive, but you certainly are responsible for complete accuracy before you leave. Ask meeting participants their full names and name spellings, their titles and group office.

listing. In so doing, the original 10 non-lead meeting items are reduced to five groups with the last group being "in other action," a facile method of including meeting decisions that are newsworthy only as a matter of public record. Actually, most meeting stories have several items that can be handled in this manner, often reducing a dozen meeting votes to no more than three or four outcomes worth writing about in the body of the news story.

The final step in the process is an organizational aspect the writer has already thought about while forming topic combinations. The content categories suggest headings for the groups of similar meeting elements. The new teachers, new administrators and superintendent applicants were combined under a heading of personnel matters. A transition to the paragraph that deals with these three elements should focus on personnel changes. Likewise, the King holiday and calendar changes might be introduced by a transition on dates or next year's school calendar. The catch-all group at the end will be introduced by a simple line like "in other action."

However, "groups" of only one news item, such as the evaluation report, may require more obtrusive transitions because elements too unique to be grouped usually can't be worked smoothly into the story. A writer will just have to try harder to find good transitions.

THE MEETING STORY

We can now look at how the writer might bring the organized elements of this meeting story together:

> Purchase of a $1.5 million tract for a new high school and higher prices for school lunches were approved by the Erie County School Board Wednesday.
>
> The board voted 7-2 to buy a 25-acre tract in the Summerville District. The decision ended three months of debate about whether the city needs a new high school. Voting against the purchase were board members Thomas L. Irving and Mrs. Patricia Jennings who said this year's budget projections make the land purchase premature.
>
> But the board unanimously voted to raise the price of school lunches from 60 to 80 cents. "We've put this one off as long as we could," said J. Lane Peterson. He said the higher price is only one-third the actual cost of feeding students. Board member Bea Gaddy said, "Five years ago the 60-cent price was half the actual cost."

In its final meeting of the school year, the board also heard a state evaluation report, changed the commission of three schools, approved a new school holiday and handled personnel matters for the coming year.

The county's educational system received a satisfactory rating from the State Department of Education. Deputy Secretary Lillian Miller of Timberlake told board members that Erie schools scored 85 on the state's five-year evaluation, an improvement of four points during the period. "You were ahead of nearly 75 percent of the county systems, according to student achievement tests," Miller said.

School Board head Brian H. Scotton asked Miller if the state was satisfied with the county's progress. She said most systems' scores had remained the same, but at least a dozen others did exceed Erie's four-point improvement.

Scotton reminded board members that funding for the system's program improvements has come from school consolidations. The board then unanimously voted to officially close Graham Junior High, which was inoperative this year, and to finalize merging Eastway and Ketchings Elementary schools.

The expected new school holiday also was approved unanimously as the board voted to close schools in honor of civil rights leader Dr. Martin Luther King Jr. Approving the next two school years' calendar, the board set the new holiday for the Monday in January closest to King's birthday.

The board approved hiring six new teachers and appointing two new administrators. Lee Junior High acting Principal Mrs. Rita C. Gaylord will become principal in the fall, and Dr. Wilson W. Black will head the system's Guidance Center beginning in July. Board members also heard the names of four applicants received so far in the search for a new school superintendent. The closing date for applying is next month.

In other action, the board:

—Doubled the hours of road driving time required in drivers' education courses and

—Approved a total of $10,000 in building repairs to Coldwell and Tibbs Elementary schools.

This meeting story example is an acceptable outcome of the procedures suggested in Figure 10.2. In fact, it closely follows the inverted pyramid organizational pattern of selecting lead elements, seeking linkages, ordering news values and composing transitions. The procedures reduce what seemed to be an unmanageable number of meeting activities to a concise and easily understood news story.

The first three paragraphs of the story form the normal inverted pyramid, focusing here on two major news elements: the land purchase and the lunch prices. Then, in the fourth paragraph of the story, there is an element that wasn't included in the procedures. That paragraph reads:

> In its final meeting of the school year, the board also heard a <u>state evaluation report</u>, <u>changed the commission of three schools</u>, approved a <u>new school holiday</u> and handled <u>personnel matters</u> for the coming year.

This can be called an organizing paragraph, a theme paragraph or a foreshadowing paragraph. It's a writer's device to increase reader understanding, and using an organizing paragraph is a particularly good idea in a complicated news article or one that contains several rather diverse events. The meeting story isn't complicated, but it does have a lot of different elements.

The organizing graf adds coherence early in the story to keep readers on track as the article bounces from one news element to the next. But it's really nothing more than a foreshadowing of the elements that will be covered in the rest of the story. It says to the reader, "If you read the rest of this meeting story, you're going to learn about: (1) the state evaluation report, (2) school building assignments, (3) a new school holiday and (4) personnel matters . . . in that order. Like a good road map, this paragraph charts the reader's way through the story. It is particularly helpful where the terrain is rugged: in meeting stories that contain lots of twists and turns.

The organizing paragraph in the example may look like an afterthought, something the writer included when it became evident that the meeting story might confuse readers. Actually, it will be a forethought in most instances, part of the writer's decision making that occurs during the last two steps of the story organization process. Realizing there are four groups of loosely related news elements to include, the writer will decide to include this paragraph while ordering the group news values and composing transitions.

Of course, the writer tries to give readers additional guidance through the article by using transitions. But because meeting stories usually deal with diverse news elements, using smooth transitions is difficult. For instance, the example uses an effective transition from the state evaluation report to the school closing/merger:

> Scotton reminded board members that funding for the system's program improvements has come from school consolidations. The board then unanimously voted to officially close Graham Junior High. . . .

This is a rather long transition, but it does tie ideas related to the state evaluation with another meeting activity, the closing/merger. The other transitions don't do as good a job of guiding readers. They are:

> The expected new school <u>holiday also was approved</u> unanimously. . . .

> The <u>board approved hiring</u> six new teachers. . . .

> <u>In other action</u> . . .

While these transitions fail to tie preceding elements with those that follow, they at least do return readers' attention to the scene of the school board meeting to introduce the next group of decisions.

Effective transitions are easier to write in chronological story structures because the time element can serve as a transitional device: then, next, afterwards, and so on. The inverted pyramid structure, and meeting stories in particular, shuns chronology because usually it is meaningless: The order in which meeting events occur has little to do with their news value. The only time-related transition used in the meeting story was the word "then," used after Scotton's school consolidation reminder.

In all, the school board story is a legitimate example of news coverage for a meeting. Many meetings won't be as involved as the example suggests; others will be more involved. The organization process given in this chapter will help a journalist during the reporting stage and story writing stage of coverage. Most important, the process will result in greater reader understanding of what happened at a meeting.

SUMMARY

As a news story type, press conferences fit somewhere between speeches and meetings. Government and business sources use the press conference as an efficient way to disseminate information quickly. Moreover, the press conference is arranged by the news maker, at that person's convenience and to that person's advantage. Journalists need to remember that the source is in the driver's seat. Still, if journalists expect a press conference to be newsworthy, they attend.

For a press conference: (1) news makers invite reporters from all the media; (2) journalists prepare as best they can, finding out as much as possible about the topic; (3) at the conference, the news maker begins with prepared remarks; and (4) a question-and-answer session follows. Reporters should be aware that:

- the news maker's formal remarks may be orchestrated so the media hear what the source wants to share;
- formal statements can be one-sided, the side that is best for the source;
- news makers hope these remarks will become the crux of the story, even if journalists rate them low in news value;
- the reporters' only press conference advantage is in the number of interrogators at the question-and-answer session, where the news activity really begins.

Meetings are a difficult assignment for reporters who don't cover the organization regularly, because they know neither the people nor the issues. Backgrounding can compensate for not knowing the issues, but a newcomer has little hope of tapping the underlying group dynamics.

Still, most meetings follow a formal pattern of nine agenda items, six of which may qualify for news coverage. The minutes of the last meeting and the treasurer's report aren't likely to be of interest unless members question them. Announcements may have some news value, but the substantial aspects of a meeting usually take place during committee reports and old and new business. The action news value suggests meeting votes are probably worth recording, and all issues on which an official body votes should be included for the public record.

Because the number of meeting activities may be confusing, the chapter presents a procedure for organizing meeting elements for the story. This procedure includes: (1) selecting lead elements, (2) looking for linkages, (3) ordering by news value and (4) composing transitions.

Thinking it Through

EXERCISE 10.1

Press Conference Questions

For each of the next exercises, list five questions you would ask the press conference source during the question-and-answer session following the remarks. List your questions in order so the most critical piece of information you need, if you got the chance to ask only one question, is first.

A Jancie Wilcox, a publicist for rock star Fatal Grace, calls a press conference this morning and makes these remarks:

We regret that Saturday's concert will be postponed indefinitely due to Miss Grace's illness. She has been admitted to a Los Angeles area hospital for recuperation following her six-month tour of Eastern Bloc countries. No plans for rescheduling this concert have been made, although this city will definitely be among those on her next tour schedule.

Full refunds will be made for all tickets sold, although fans wishing to hold their tickets until Miss Grace performs here will be awarded an additional ticket for every ticket they decide to keep. Her hope is that her loyal fans will understand that health is the only reason for this cancellation.

Miss Grace asked me to relay her deepest regrets for giving such short notice to those who have showed their loyalty to her. She asks for their understanding and prayers for a speedy recovery.

B Bill Dobson, commissioner of the State Department of Environmental Protection, calls a press conference and makes this opening statement:

Our department is issuing a revised form that new businesses must file before being issued a state business license. Since 1980 a new business has been required to complete a 30-page document containing more than 250 questions dealing with environmental safety. Those documents were required of everyone, including retail florists and accounting offices. The state has been tracking the number of business licenses issued in the past three years and determined we were way below projections. The governor authorized a survey this year that showed business people categorically resented having to complete the 30-page document and having to pay attorneys huge fees for helping them do it properly. Additionally, the forms contained several pages constituting an environmental impact report. The governor's survey seemed to confirm that a host of anticipated businesses either decided not to open in this state, or did so without a business license. We estimate perhaps 2,000 such cases occurred this year alone, and we believe the lengthy document was the reason.

When this department began requiring the report, we were responding to tougher standards the federal government set as a prerequisite to offering state matching funds for public works. We believed the battery of questions was required. However, we now believe we were overzealous in demanding that all businesses complete the lengthy document. In the future, all business applicants will file a much shorter form. Only those businesses that fall into certain predetermined categories of operation integrally involved in hazardous materials will be required to complete the more extensive 30-page document.

We believe the state's decision in this matter will result in putting us back on target for new business applications and the tax revenues those businesses produce for the state. We intend to strictly enforce the new, shorter form filing. Those who ignore it will be prosecuted to the fullest extent of the law. And those applicants who are identified from the short form as being required to complete the longer document will not do business in this state without complying.

Are there any questions?

C Mrs. Tilda Fox, vice president of communication for the local Westwheels Mfg. Co., calls a press conference at the end of the company's fiscal year and makes these opening remarks:

Westwheels is very happy you were able to be here today to hear our company's good news. We have experienced our best year ever by posting a record 20 percent profit before taxes on sales of $140 million. We want to thank our employees, their families and this community generally for helping to make us the city's premier manufacturing company. Part of showing our appreciation is to announce a plant expansion. We will be increasing Westwheels' operations here by half again as much. That means another 200,000 square feet of factory area and another 250 jobs for local citizens. Our plant addition will get underway in two months, with an estimated completion date of next April.

Now I'm sure you members of the press have some questions to ask, so go ahead.

D Police Chief Taylor Malone Jr. calls an emergency press conference at 9 a.m. and makes these opening remarks:

We have a serious situation here today. A drug bust we've been working on for a long time sort of exploded in our faces. The narcotics squad located a warehouse by the railroad yard that has been used for storing tons of drugs. We had a special team of police officers ready to raid the place at sunrise today, but we didn't expect there would be a delivery at that time. When our men converged on the place, they met resistance by heavy gunfire, including automatic weapons. We lost two officers.

That puts us in a tense position. We don't negotiate with killers, but we're afraid there might be some innocent people in the warehouse with them. More than 50 policemen arrived on the scene by about 7:30 a.m., and we have the place surrounded so nobody's getting out of there. We've got enough firepower out there to level the place, but we're holding off now until we get orders from the mayor. We'd like to see this thing resolved with no more injuries, but we're prepared to do what we have to do. We've given the people in there until noon to come out.

I guess you folks have been listening to all this on your radio monitors for the last hour, and we've turned a few news people away from the scene, so I wanted you to know what's going on firsthand. I'll answer a few questions now.

EXERCISE 10.2

Looking for Linkages

The following numbered activities occurred at a meeting you covered. Group as many of the activities as you can by putting their activity number in the same vertical column. For instance, if you believe activity Nos. 2, 6 and 7 are similar enough to be grouped, put those in one of the lettered vertical columns. Don't try to order the columns at this point (Group A is no more newsworthy than Group C). If there are activities you believe should not be grouped, list those numbers in the "Non-Grouped" column. After completing this grouping process, write the relationship or general rationale you used to group each set of activities as you did. These assignments may be done on a separate sheet of paper approximating the grouping format shown.

A At a philanthropic civic group's luncheon meeting, the following events take place:

1. Oscar Davis is appointed to succeed Vanessa Coleman as vice president of the organization . . . Coleman is moving to Tampa
2. the annual 10-K run raised $8,350, the committee chair said
3. the group votes to donate $1,000 to the Children's Home
4. a masked ball will be held at the Bates Museum in three months; attendance is $100 per couple
5. the group votes to end its annual 10-K run because similar events by other organizations cut proceeds by a third this year
6. the group votes to forbid smoking at all future meetings
7. the annual Founders Dinner will be held at Bergin Civic Hall in six months; tickets are $100 each
8. the group votes to donate $2,000 to the zoo
9. the group discusses sponsoring a three-day cruise as a fund-raising event to replace the 10-K run

10. the group votes to sponsor a Volunteers Picnic this summer to honor all local citizens who donate time to a registered charity

11. the group names Murray Industries as the year's corporate giver; Murray executives will be recognized at the Founders Dinner

12. the group votes to provide dinner one day a week at the Homeless Care Center

13. the annual Grand Masters Art Auction Committee announces the event will be in nine months; tickets are $25 per person in advance, $35 at the door.

Group A	Group B	Group C	Group D	Group E	Non-Grouped
_____	_____	_____	_____	_____	_____
_____	_____	_____	_____	_____	_____
_____	_____	_____	_____	_____	_____
_____	_____	_____	_____	_____	_____

Rationale for each grouping:

Group A _____

Group B _____

Group C _____

Group D _____

Group E _____

B The local chapter of the American Medical Association holds its quarterly meeting and takes the following actions:

1. votes to form a committee to meet with statewide insurance companies to lower the cost of malpractice insurance locally

2. goes into a closed-door session (bars the press) to discuss an ethics case

3. approves a motion to accept Lakewood Hospital's offer to provide clinical services for local physicians suffering from alcohol and drug abuse

4. hears a report from a fact-finding committee showing that local malpractice insurance premiums are 15 percent above the national average

5. votes to empower the malpractice insurance committee to tell statewide firms that local physicians have a $50 million fund ready to form their own malpractice insurance cooperative

6. debates whether the group should form a local ethics committee to work with the current AMA statewide Ethics Board

7. debates current trends in "minor emergency" clinics, then votes to rescind

the group's 1985 decision that barred local members from operating more than one such clinic

8. defeats a motion to rescind an earlier decision that prevents local members from advertising fees for services

9. defeats a motion to rescind an earlier decision that prevents members who operate a "minor emergency" clinic from advertising that the clinic's services are equal to those of a hospital's emergency room

10. discusses the number of cases of local physicians who had their licenses revoked or who voluntarily left the profession after facing ethics violation charges by the state Ethics Board.

Group A	Group B	Group C	Group D	Group E	Non-Grouped
___	___	___	___	___	___
___	___	___	___	___	___
___	___	___	___	___	___
___	___	___	___	___	___

Rationale for each grouping:

Group A _____

Group B _____

Group C _____

Group D _____

Group E _____

C The State College Student Government Association holds its weekly meeting and completes the following business:

1. appoints two students to fill vacant senatorial posts from the College of Arts and Sciences; one student to a senator post in the College of Business

2. recognizes Mrs. Deborah Rutherford, faculty adviser to the SGA for 20 years, on her retirement at this, her last meeting; presents a plaque and a corsage

3. passes a resolution urging the university president to spend whatever amount is necessary to make all campus classrooms accessible to students in wheelchairs; administration has been saying the school can't afford to begin these projects this year

4. votes $7,500 to have Dr. Joyce Brothers as a speaker for the Student Forum in February

5. votes against paying $5,000 for three graduate students' trip to London to

attend a conference and present a research paper . . . agrees such funds should come from academic sources

6. after discussion, votes to reaffirm SGA decision that all members be full-time students with 2.5 or higher grade point averages . . . most of the senatorial vacancies result from grade deficiencies

7. votes $8,500 to have former President Jimmy Carter as a speaker for the Student Forum in March

8. agrees to sponsor a university-wide talent show with prizes instead of continuing a beauty pageant . . . some women's rights groups picketed at last year's pageant

9. votes against spending $9,000 for comedian Steve Martin as a Student Forum speaker in April

10. elects Sen. Brenda Jones of the College of Education to fill the unexpired term of SGA treasurer

11. approves the charter for the Gay Coalition to become an officially recognized student organization . . . ending some controversy about this charter.

Group A	Group B	Group C	Group D	Group E	Non-Grouped
_____	_____	_____	_____	_____	_____
_____	_____	_____	_____	_____	_____
_____	_____	_____	_____	_____	_____
_____	_____	_____	_____	_____	_____

Rationale for each grouping:

Group A _____

Group B _____

Group C _____

Group D _____

Group E _____

EXERCISE 10.3

Ordering News Values

Return to Exercise 10.2 and put the group sets and the individual news elements in descending order of news values. Remember that some of the non-grouped items may be lead elements, and some may be rather trivial items. While the information provided is too sketchy to assure your order is correct, you should be able to make a case for each ordering decision based on probable news value for the meeting story events.

A   The philanthropic civic group's luncheon meeting story:

**News
Order**   **Rationale for Order Decision**

_____ Group A   _____

_____ Group B   _____

_____ Group C   _____

_____ Group D   _____

_____ Group E   _____

Non-Group Items	Story Event Number	
_____	_____	_____
_____	_____	_____
_____	_____	_____
_____	_____	_____

B   Local American Medical Association chapter quarterly meeting:

**News
Order**   **Rationale for Order Decision**

_____ Group A   _____

_____ Group B   _____

_____ Group C   _____

_____ Group D   _____

_____ Group E   _____

Non-Group Items	Story Event Number	
_____	_____	_____
_____	_____	_____
_____	_____	_____
_____	_____	_____

C University Student Government Association weekly meeting:

News Order		Rationale for Order Decision
_____	Group A	_____
_____	Group B	_____
_____	Group C	_____
_____	Group D	_____
_____	Group E	_____

Non-Group Items	Story Event Number	
_____	_____	_____
_____	_____	_____
_____	_____	_____
_____	_____	_____

Writing Practice

EXERCISE 10.4

Transitions

Write an effective transition to take readers smoothly from one news element paragraph of a meeting story to the next. Write a phrase or a one-sentence transition that would help introduce each *following* paragraph so your reader has less difficulty understanding the story's flow.

A Two candidates, Judy C. Johnson and Edgewater Judge Mickey Rico, were offered to run for attorney general. Members voted overwhelmingly to place Rico's name on the ballot, citing his recent success against a popular Democratic candidate for the Edgewater judgeship.

Transition: _____

_____

Although Jewell Lacey has never run for an elected office, her experience in the state's executive branch spans nearly 20 years. Gov. May called her the most knowledgeable financial officer in the state. Members voted unanimously to place her name on the Republican ballot as comptroller.

Transition: _____

_____

Republican candidates for reelection include: Secretary of State Michael G. Vales, State Treasurer Rusty Waits and Lt. Gov. Carla Aycock. Each received unanimous votes at the meeting.

B Following heated debate on the costs involved the City Council postponed a decision about building a high-speed subway system from the northern suburbs to the central business district. Cost estimates ranged from a low of $60 million to more than $100 million.

Transition: _____

_____

The proposal to raze the Commerce Building at 200 Main St. and replace it with a six-story parking garage won narrow approval with a 6–5 Council vote. City planners estimated the facility will pay for itself within 10 years of operation.

Transition: _____

_____

There was no debate or dissenting votes in a decision to renovate the Department of Public Safety Building. The work is scheduled to begin next month with $5 million in state matching funds. A group of city policemen at the meeting applauded the uncontested action.

Transition: _____

_____

Mayor Quinn was recognized in the audience and Council members gave her a standing ovation for her work during four years in office. This was the last Council meeting of her administration.

EXERCISE 10.5

Press Conference Story

This is a rough-note fact set. **Use the City Directory to check all facts before writing the article.** Direct quotes you may use are included in quotation marks. Check spelling and AP/UPI style before turning in your story.

As a science reporter for your paper, you are called to a 9 a.m. press conference at Barnham Research Lab, a subsidiary of Modern Medical Center. The following statement is read by Dr. Winston H. Vinson, director of research for Barnham:

"Today we are ready to announce what we believe is a major breakthrough in the fight against AIDS. Our Barnham staff has been working on this project following a discovery made more than three years ago in our Medical Technology Instruments Division. We found that one of our diagnostic machines made a body tissue scan that correctly identified cells affected by the AIDS virus. The detection occurred earlier than any previous procedure for diagnosing the disease. It was at least six months ahead of the next best diagnosis procedure.

"As you know, AIDS is considered the most threatening plague facing the world today. While there still is no cure for the disease, early diagnosis followed by pathological treatment can be an effective method of delaying the advent of debilitating body functions brought on by the disease. In short, if AIDS can be diagnosed early enough, treatment can greatly extend normal body functioning and delay the deterioration brought on by the disease.

"Additionally, our medical researchers working with the new diagnostic system have combined known pharmaceutical treatments for AIDS and have developed a new serum that appears to be more effective than previous pharmacological therapy for the disease. Again, the Barnham Research Lab is not claiming a cure, but we believe early diagnosis in cooperation with this new serum therapy should extend the average survival rate of an AIDS patient no less than five years beyond the current rate of survival."

Modern Medical Center Board President Dr. Catherine Ellis adds these comments: "We at Modern Medical Center are proud of this work by Barnham Research Lab personnel. It is unusual to announce a medical breakthrough such as this at such an early stage of experimental testing, but the nature of the AIDS crisis demands swift action on any diagnostic or treatment discoveries. Modern Medical Center is aware that its reputation is on the line with today's news. We are confident in Barnham Research Lab's people and the accuracy of their statements here today."

Here is some more information from the press conference:

1. The diagnostic instrument is called an EAS, an Early AIDS Scanning device. In tests with a random sample of high-risk AIDS candidates, the instrument correctly diagnosed the virus 10 months earlier than any other known diagnostic procedure. It was accurate in 95 percent of the cases.

2. Further tests with the serum produced better results than other treatments. None of the patients receiving the drug is showing any symptoms of the disease. However, this test began only one year ago, so the long-term effects of the serum are unknown. Still, most patients diagnosed with AIDS experience extensive symptoms within a year that result in requiring hospitalization. None of the patients given the experimental serum has required hospitalization. Half of those patients who were diagnosed with the EAS but were treated with currently accepted procedures other than the new serum have been hospitalized. The

remaining half in the non-serum treatment experiment have shown symptoms of the disease but have not required hospitalization.

3. Vinson says the Food and Drug Administration is reviewing the lab's evidence. If the FDA is satisfied, the serum, called BRL605, will be approved within 90 days.

4. The diagnostic procedure will be available at Modern Medical Center Monday at 8 a.m. The EAS instrument is being sold to hospitals across the country; areas with high-risk demographics will have priority. Vinson says the machine requires only a week's training for technicians and is a relatively inexpensive medical instrument at $150,000 per unit. BRL605, on the other hand, is expected to cost $50 per dose, although the medicine is taken only once a week. It will be available only through a physician's prescription.

You ask Vinson if the diagnostic procedure combined with the BRL605 serum has prevented test patient symptoms from appearing for nearly a year, hasn't Barnham Research Lab in fact found a cure for AIDS? Vinson says no, the AIDS virus is still present in the test subjects, so "our discoveries aren't a cure, they merely retard the degenerative effects of the virus. No one knows how long BRL605 will delay the symptoms from appearing, but it may be long enough to keep some patients alive until a cure is found." He reminds you, "The serum is not effective in treating the AIDS virus if it is diagnosed too late. Tests show that if symptoms have begun, the serum has no effect in retarding or halting the normal degenerative effects of the disease."

Write the story for this afternoon's newspaper.

Good News and Brights

Contrary to a popular misconception that all news is bad news, journalists quickly discover that an equal number of the events they cover actually fall under the heading of good news.

Research studies show that even the front pages of daily newspapers, the choice spot to herald alarming changes in the status quo, present a balance of good news and bad news stories. Each of the two categories accounts for about one-third of total content throughout a newspaper, with the remaining third of the stories defying classification as either good or bad news.[1]

Network television news has a 2-to-1 bad news dominance, but local television news is more balanced on the good news-bad news spectrum, with stories near the end of the newscast twice as likely to be good news.[2]

Journalists report murders, suicides, vice, fatalities, corruption in government, family cruelties and a host of similar bad news events. Covering these incidents can be interesting and exciting; it's also necessary. But a steady diet of bad news would be emotionally debilitating without some balancing good news.[3]

[1] Jack B. Haskins, "What We Know About Bad News," in Joseph P. McKerns, ed., *Communications Research Symposium: A Proceedings*, vol. 3 (Knoxville: University of Tennessee College of Communications, 1980), pp. 149–173. See also: Barbara W. Hartung and Gerald Stone, "Time to Stop Singing the 'Bad News' Blues," *Newspaper Research Journal* (February 1980), p. 21.

[2] Gerald C. Stone and Elinor Grusin, "Network TV as the Bad News Bearer," *Journalism Quarterly* 61:517 (Autumn 1984); Gerald Stone, Barbara Hartung and Dwight Jensen, "Local TV News and the Good-Bad Dyad," *Journalism Quarterly* 64:37 (Spring 1987).

[3] Ben J. Wattenberg, *The Good News Is the Bad News Is Wrong* (New York: Simon and Schuster, 1984).

News media managers recognize that their audiences also seek this emotional balance. Recent print and broadcast news media trends indicate that editors now put more emphasis on a balance between good and bad news. The success of ventures such as *USA Today* and the many prime time television news "magazine" shows confirm the value of combining solid hard-news reporting with features and color stories, or soft news. Using the two content types adds balance without weakening either one's intrinsic worth, and together they contribute to a more complete news mix.

Although news value decisions aren't based on whether the story is pleasant or disturbing, journalists know that an interesting good-news story will be among the most popular and memorable articles of the day. Beyond the potential audience impact such stories might have, they're also fun to report and write. This chapter offers suggestions on how to write one of the more basic forms of good news: the bright.

BRIGHTS DEFINED

The form is a short, pithy news article designed to maximize reader impact. Often it is less than half a dozen paragraphs in length, yet it conveys all of the necessary information in as compact a manner as possible. The subject of a bright is not always good news, but nine times out of 10 it is. Therefore the term *bright* is synonymous with a humorous or entertaining article: one that brightens the page by making readers smile.

But brights aren't jokes, and they aren't intended to evoke belly laughs. They are written to make the most of unusual news quirks or offbeat human interest incidents. Frequently they contain a believe-it-or-not element, but they must be as accurate as the day's most serious news story.

If the definition seems to waffle, that's done by design. There is no single quality that discriminates a bright from other types of news stories, except perhaps its length. However, there are several distinctions in writing style that are associated primarily with brights:

- brevity in writing . . . every word counts;
- a trade-off of details for quick reader comprehension;
- gentle teasing through a tongue-in-cheek writing style.

A long and painful ordeal ended when American hostages arrived at the U.S. military base in Frankfort, West Germany, after their release from Tehran, Iran, in 1981. News audiences viewing this scene breathed a sigh of relief that the crisis was finally over.

BRIGHT STORY STRUCTURE

Two types of story structures typify a bright. One is the familiar inverted pyramid story organization using descending order of news values. The other is a "manufactured" bright structure. Let's use the following set of facts to compare the two types of bright story structures.

1. Dr. Mason T. Burke, 52, an associate professor at State University, has begun his Zoology 101 lab the same way every term. He brings a brown paper bag into class and challenges any female student to reach into the bag without looking and take out the live animal inside. The prize is not having to take the first test. In 18 years, no one has taken the challenge.

2. Yesterday, Laura McKinney, a 19-year-old sophomore accounting major from Dallas, agreed to do it. She took a harmless king snake out of the bag. McKinney said: "I was scared to death. I

just knew it was going to be a snake, and I've never touched a snake before. We could all see the bag moving, so we knew there really was something alive inside. But he said it wasn't harmful, and since nobody else was going to do it, I thought I'd go ahead and try. It really wasn't so bad. I was surprised that it didn't feel slimy at all."

3. She said she didn't do it to avoid taking the first test. "I did it to see if I could. I'll probably take the test anyway. I think the class is just great, and that first exercise really made everyone want to learn about zoology," she said.

4. Burke said the exercise is designed to help students overcome their fear of touching animals. "It may be chauvinistic, but the reason I only offer the bag to females is that I've always found them to be more squeamish during the first term. All students in the class have to touch the snake during the first class period."

The story isn't exactly front-page news, but a reporter should recognize that it's interesting enough to draw reader attention. It can be made more interesting if it's written as a bright rather than a straight news story.

INVERTED PYRAMID BRIGHTS

Because a bright is still a news story, the inverted pyramid succeeds as an efficient way to structure news values for readers. In most instances, an inverted pyramid bright begins with a "featurized" lead intended to grab the reader's attention, instead of a straight summary lead. Consider a 5W and H lead for the snake story:

A sophomore at State University accepted her zoology teacher's challenge and, without first looking, took a live king snake from a brown paper bag Tuesday.

This summary lead has two major drawbacks: It's more confusing than informative, and it's dull. In fact, the summary lead here virtually destroys any hope that the story will reach the reader interest level it should have. Since the summary lead doesn't capture the tone or richness of story events, a more effective article beginning is suggested. Here are some featurized leads that beginning newswriting students composed for the story:

Zoology 101.

Sounds dull for most of us, but Dr. Mason T. Burke, associate professor of zoology, has a way to "liven" things up.

*   *   *

For one student this semester, that funny feeling on the first day of class paid off.

*   *   *

After 18 years, a young woman was finally tempted by the serpent.

While these featurized beginnings only suggest what kind of article may follow, they do capture the tone of a bright, and they are anything but dull. A summary lead can work effectively, but both of the bright structures discussed here rely frequently on the featurized type of lead.

The diagram in Figure 11.1 depicts a featurized lead as the first story element in an inverted pyramid-type bright. After catching the reader's attention and setting the article's tone in the lead, the writer makes a transition to the 5 W's and H of the news story. Sometimes the "bridge" is minimal; sometimes it is a separate paragraph. Using the snake leads, here are examples of bridges to the story:

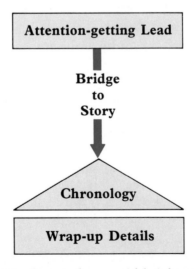

Figure 11.1   Inverted pyramid bright structure

Zoology 101.

Sounds dull for most of us, but Dr. Mason T. Burke, associate professor of zoology, has a way to "liven" things up.

His first lab class of the term can be a lively experience for any female student who will blindly stick her hand into a wiggling paper bag and extract the live animal inside.

*   *   *

For one student this semester, that funny feeling on the first day of class paid off.

Dr. Mason T. Burke's first lab session of Zoology 101 begins with an eerie contest for female students, and Laura McKinney bagged the prize Tuesday.

*   *   *

After 18 years of refusals, a young woman was finally tempted by the serpent.

Her lure was the subject of Dr. Mason T. Burke's object lesson in zoology lab classes.

A bridge isn't essential in either type of bright. For instance, the first two lead examples can be followed immediately by the chronology, or how it all began:

Dr. Mason T. Burke, associate professor of zoology at State University, walks into class on the first lab day holding a wiggling brown paper bag. He's been doing that for 18 years.

But without the bridge, there's no transition between the featurized lead and the factual news elements of the story. The tone change in the article will sound too abrupt, and the reader will wonder what the featurized lead meant or even why it was used. The bridge's more subtle change in tone and added story information are needed to make a smooth transition between the lead and the coming chronology.

Chronological story telling forms the body of most brights. After the bridge, the writer in effect tells readers: "It all began when . . . " However, using that line to introduce the chronology section would be rather trite. If the bridge is effective, the writer can just tell readers what happened, from beginning to end, without fanfare.

Most brights do rely on chronology in the body of the story, but that method of presentation isn't a requirement. Sometimes the body of the bright is a mixture of chronology and inverted pyramid structure; sometimes it's only inverted pyramid. Because the subject matter in a bright usually requires a lot of explanation in a very short space, chronological presentation aids readers in following the sequence of events. The writer begins at the start of the incident and takes the reader through what happened to its conclusion.

But the body of a bright should be one of the most exacting exercises in tight writing a journalist faces. Each paragraph and each line of the story should prompt the writer to decide if the reader needs to know this piece of information. For instance, the snake story contains unnecessary verbiage in the quotes and several facts that are peripheral to the essence of the story. The writer needs to sift through this material to select only what is essential for reader understanding. Including more than is necessary pads the story and defeats the purpose of a bright, which should be a quick, easy read. Details that are extraneous to the bright's central theme should not be in the body of the article.

Inclusion Decisions

Here are some considerations about what to include from the snake story example:

Include:
- Burke's name and title; McKinney's name and identification—these are necessary in a bright as in any other news story . . . they authenticate;
- State University, a zoology lab, it happened Tuesday, Burke's been doing the exercise 18 years;
- details of the challenge, the brown paper bag, reaching without looking, the harmless king snake, avoidance of the first test, McKinney took the challenge;
- purpose of the exercise, all students touch the snake.

Possibly include:
- only females are asked; this isn't critical, but it does help readers understand the story;
- some of McKinney's quotes, although much of what she says can be paraphrased to keep the story concise;
- McKinney will take the test; again, not essential, but it rounds out the story.

Delete:
- all of Burke's quotes; they should be paraphrased;
- most of McKinney's quotes; select those that reflect the tone of the event; definitely omit the chatter.

The last section of an inverted pyramid bright, usually a single paragraph, is the place where further details may be added. A news article, even a short one such as a bright, must contain the necessary facts that form a complete story. Writing the body of a bright as concisely as possible often results in omitting some details the reader may need to know. These facts would interfere with the earlier story narration, but they can be placed at the end of the piece without disrupting story flow. As always, if the editor decides they aren't needed, these wrap-up details can be deleted.

MANUFACTURED BRIGHTS

A single difference—use of a punch line—distinguishes the manufactured bright from the inverted pyramid bright structure. And by using a punch line, journalists take a small step away from straight, non-fiction newswriting. Let's consider the rationale for invoking a writer's license in crafting an effective bright.

A bright is not exactly a joke. It reports a real event of at least some news interest to readers. Yet a bright is often about a quirk of human nature or an odd occurrence, such as the snake story, that is interesting reading at least partially because of the way it is written. In straight news story form, it's dull, but with a little flare in the writing, it can sparkle. One of the best methods to add sparkle is for the journalist to enter into a tacit agreement with readers through story presentation. Like a joke teller, the writer saves the punch line until the end of the story.

In fact, before writing this type of bright, the journalist decides that the article will be much more interesting if an element of the story is withheld from the reader until later in the article. The delayed element becomes the punch line. Readers are being told, in effect, "Trust me on this one. If you read the whole story, you'll find out everything you want to know, and the wait will be worth your effort." Readers enjoy a good story, too, so they will go along with the writer. Of course, if you enter into this tacit agreement with your reader, your story must deliver. The punch line has be worth the reader's wait.

Several potential pitfalls exist with the manufactured bright. Here are some decisions you should make before electing to use this form:

1. Be sure the element you save for the punch line is not critical to the story's meaning. The reader must be able to follow the story without the missing element. Any tacit agreement is broken the

instant the reader becomes confused. If there's any doubt about reader understanding because of the missing fact, write an inverted pyramid-type bright instead.

2. Be sure the punch line is worth their wait; if not, readers will be disappointed rather than entertained by the story.

3. Don't use a punch line that requires a lot of explanation. Like that of a joke, the manufactured bright's punch line should be able to stand on its own, without a lot of clarification.

4. Don't add a lot of wrap-up details after the punch line. Doing so will read like a weak joke that ends with, "Oh, I forgot to tell you that . . . "

If you think a manufactured bright can succeed on all these points, then by all means write it. This form, done effectively, can make one of the day's most memorable news stories.

Figure 11.2 shows the structure for a manufactured bright with a punch line.

The punch line usually follows the chronological presentation, but it may be the last lines of the story instead. Sometimes wrap-up details precede the punch line; often the wrap-up details are omitted.

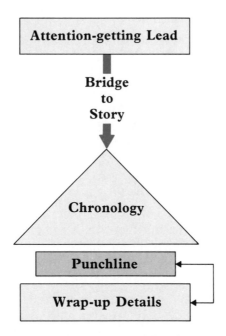

Figure 11.2 Manufactured bright structure

Let's look at an example of the same snake story as a manufactured bright:

> Here's a brown paper bag with a live animal in it. Will you stick your hand in without looking and take out the animal?
>
> That's the challenge Dr. Mason T. Burke, 52, associate professor of zoology at State University, gives women in his first lab class. The exercise is designed to help beginning zoology students overcome their fear of touching animals, Burke said.
>
> Any female student who agrees to extract the contents of the grab bag can avoid the semester's first test. Burke said he offers women the option because he has found them more squeamish than their male classmates. But in 18 years, no female student has met the challenge.
>
> Tuesday, Laura McKinney, a 19-year-old sophomore accounting major, took the plunge.
>
> "I was scared to death," Miss McKinney said. "We could all see the bag moving, so we knew there was something inside." But "since nobody else was going to do it, I thought I'd go ahead and try." She said she will probably still take the first test.
>
> What did Miss McKinney pull from the bag?
>
> A wriggling but harmless king snake.

The manufactured punch line is that the animal in the bag was a snake. Readers probably guessed that from the beginning of the story, but they kept reading to find out, or to be sure they were right. The article is an example of setting up the tacit agreement in a non-threatening manner. Writer and reader join in the playful game.

This bright begins with an unusual, featurized "you" lead in which the writer uses direct address to draw readers into the story. "You" leads are gimmicks that journalists should try to avoid, but in this case the lead is effective because it places the reader in the same situation the class faced: "Will you stick your hand in without looking . . . ?" Now the reader experiences the sensation of being there for the challenge. It's a ploy, of course, but the "you" lead is also part of the game.

Remembering that a bright must be succinct, we can assess how concisely the snake story is conveyed. Miss McKinney's quotes are cut to the bone, and both of Dr. Burke's quotes are paraphrased. Three of the paragraphs are one-liners, and some severe omissions have been made to include only essential information. Sentences are kept short, and the wording is crisp. Yet, even with its brevity, the story is a smooth, easy read. However, there are two bothersome elements related to the succinctness of this manufactured bright.

One factual element stressed in the story might be omitted altogether. Arguably, too much emphasis is placed on females being the target of Dr. Burke's challenge. Most of the third paragraph is devoted to that story fact, and a case can be made that a streamlined bright would not even mention it. However, skeptical readers might question why no student reached into the bag in 18 years, and chauvinistic skeptics might wonder why a female accounting major was the first to do so. The advantage of including the females-only fact is to allay these concerns, thereby diminishing the possibility that readers will be confused. The disadvantage is the amount of space required to include the fact in this bright.

One factual element omitted from the manufactured bright is that all students in the class must touch the snake by the end of the first lab session. From a news value perspective, that fact should be worthy of inclusion. But this element of the story is sacrificed to achieve two goals: (1) to avoid ruining the punch line by revealing the snake's presence too soon; and (2) to avoid interfering with the punch line's effect by adding the explanation afterward. So, in this manufactured bright, the journalist decides that everyone's having to touch the snake is not an essential element of the story.

You may have some reservations about using writer's license this way in a news story, and you may be right. If a journalist has to rationalize a departure from accuracy (even by omission), the decision probably was inappropriate in the first place. However, the journalist might decide defensibly that all students touching the snake is no more newsworthy than some of Miss McKinney's quotes, the fact she's from Dallas, Dr. Burke's age or the fact that the snake wasn't slimy. An honest news value decision should present little concern about abridging personal ethics in using writer's license this way.

MORE ON HONESTY

Beginning journalists have a more consequential honesty consideration than whether they include all of the story's news values. Given some latitude with writer's license and featurized leads, there's a tendency to go overboard in story telling. Embellishing the writing style is one thing; embellishing the truth is a totally different and prohibited excess. Readers can take a joke, but they won't condone inaccuracy. Under no circumstances should a journalist lie to readers.

Writing an effective bright, even the manufactured variety with a punch line, doesn't impel journalists to lie. However, the added freedom in writing presentation often yields the same results. In their attempt to write an interesting story, beginners find they have strayed too far from the facts. For instance, in the snake story, one of the following leads is inaccurate:

> A State University zoology teacher has a way of slithering into his students' hearts on the first day of lab class.

> Dr. Mason T. Burke of State University "has it in" for his zoology students.

> Ask State University zoology teacher Dr. Mason T. Burke how he gets students to enjoy his labs, and he'd probably say, "It's in the bag!"

All three leads use the writer's license effectively, but one exceeds the bounds of accuracy. To say "slithering" in the first example is okay because readers can't presume that the teacher actually slithers into his students' hearts.

The third lead example seems to border on inaccuracy because Burke never said, "It's in the bag!" But this lead unquestionably is worded to suggest that the quote is something Burke *might* say, not something he did say.

The second lead example is a lie. In stating that Burke "has it in" for his students, the lead inaccurately says that Burke purposely tries to hamper his students. That suggestion will not be validated in the bright story. Quite the opposite. Because of the inaccurate lead, the writer will have to stress later in the article that Burke had no intention whatsoever of persecuting his students or impeding their progress in the class. This effort to grab readers' attention results instead in misleading them, and it forces the writer to include elements completely unrelated to any of the story's news values.

Perhaps the line being drawn between writer's license and accuracy is too narrow to be helpful. A better way to stay on the safe side of the accuracy dilemma is simply to ask yourself if what you are about to write is the truth. Teasing readers with a mutually acceptable writing style can be effective only when the journalist maintains complete accuracy throughout the story.

SUMMARY

Journalists find that an equal number of the events they cover can be classified as either bad or good news, an outcome confirmed by studies of media content. Most modern news media offer some balance between good and bad news stories, recognizing that both types have intrinsic value. Together they contribute to a more complete mix in news presentation. Journalists know that an interesting good-news story will be among the most popular and memorable events of the day. They're also fun to report and write.

One type of good news story is a bright, defined as a short, pithy news article designed to maximize reader impact. They are written to make the most of unusual news quirks or off-beat human interest incidents and are typified by:

- brevity in writing;
- use of fewer details to hasten reader comprehension;
- gentle teasing through tongue-in-cheek writing style.

Two types of bright story structure are the inverted pyramid and the manufactured bright. A format for the inverted pyramid-type bright is: (1) attention-getting lead, (2) bridge to story, (3) chronology and (4) wrap-up details. The format for a manufactured bright includes a punch line, a concept that leads journalists into using their writer's license to make an otherwise dull news story sparkle. Here the writer enters into a tacit agreement with the reader to withhold a fact until later in the story. Dangers do exist, including:

- the possibility of confusing readers;
- using a punch line that isn't worth the reader's wait;
- using a punch line that requires a lot of explanation.

Beginning journalists, who are experiencing their first taste of latitude with writer's license and featurized leads in brights, must remember to be honest with their readers. To embellish writing style does not mean to embellish the truth.

—————— **Thinking it Through** ——————————————

EXERCISE 11.1

What to Include

The following sets are notes of story facts for a bright you are writing. In the blank next to each line of information, write whether you would **include (I)** this information, would **omit (O)** it or are **not sure (NS)** which you would do. The exercises may be done on a separate sheet of paper following the format example in Exercise 11.1A.

A _____ 1. freeway accident at 7:30 a.m. rush hour

_____ 2. 18-wheel truck brushes pillar on overpass

_____ 3. no injuries

_____ 4. truck has tire blow out

_____ 5. rear doors jarred open

_____ 6. part of cargo falls onto shoulder of interstate

_____ 7. cargo is plastic-covered 2-foot squares of money

_____ 8. old bills going to federal compound for burning

_____ 9. denominations $1s, $5s, $10s and $20s

_____ 10. drivers screech to halt and begin taking money squares back to their cars

_____ 11. two kids bicycling to school witness entire event

_____ 12. Deputy Vincent T. Lane, State Highway Patrol, halts scavenging

_____ 13. Lane tickets six motorists for stopping on freeway

_____ 14. Lane arrests truck driver J. Perry Albright, who was participating in money scavenging

_____ 15. Albright says he put money in truck cab to protect it from motorists

_____ 16. local Treasury workers guard truck until repaired

Explain your rationale for marking each "not sure" item you identified:

No. _____ —

No. _____ —

No. _____ —

B _____ 1. Army Sgt. Wayne Hale and squad of 10 soldiers missing for 30 hours after a field exercise

_____ 2. several units from base searching by air and ground

_____ 3. state police and rescue units called in

_____ 4. national media already on scene

_____ 5. Hale calls in from Waffle Shop three counties away

_____ 6. all okay except one sprained ankle and sunburns

_____ 7. squad got lost in woods and wandered off course

_____ 8. lost for a day

_____ 9. ended up at State Route 17, a closed road

_____ 10. farmer gave squad ride to town in a soybean truck

_____ 11. Army van finds "closed" sign on Waffle Shop door

_____ 12. owner Mrs. Sue Ky says men ate everything in sight

_____ 13. Hale presents Army a bill for $363

_____ 14. field maneuver was a map reading exercise

_____ 15. Hale says compass wasn't working

_____ 16. compass stamped "U.S. Army—1941"

Explain your rationale for marking each "not sure" item you identified:

No. _____ —

No. _____ —

No. _____ —

C _____ 1. five teenage girls hold seance with Ouija board

_____ 2. happens at 9 p.m. Saturday in Dade family home

_____ 3. board an old wooden one found in Diane Dade's attic

_____ 4. written on Ouija is "To Rebecca from Grandma"; Rebecca was Diane's grandmother's name

_____ 5. at 10 p.m. Kristi Kerr, 15, 361 Elm, goes into trance

_____ 6. others follow Kristi to field behind Dade's house

_____ 7. parents having card party in den don't see exit

_____ 8. Kristi points to spot in field

_____ 9. Diane speaks in man's voice with Irish accent

_____ 10. male voice tells them to dig at spot

_____ 11. two other girls return with shovels

_____ 12. trances end for Diane and Kristi

_____ 13. all begin digging

_____ 14. after an hour they uncover a small, locked coffin

_____ 15. they run back to house, disturb card party

_____ 16. parents inspect field

_____ 17. parents call police

_____ 18. police come and open "coffin" . . . really a wooden box

_____ 19. find a leather bag

_____ 20. inside are five gold coins

_____ 21. coins are dated before Civil War

_____ 22. gold in coins valued today at about $1,000 each

_____ 23. worth of old coins probably $20,000 each

_____ 24. inside top of box carved: "To Rebecca from Grandpa"

_____ 25. hasn't been determined who should get coins

Explain your rationale for marking each "not sure" item you identified:

No. _____ —

No. _____ —

No. _____ —

_____ **Writing Practice** _____

EXERCISE 11.2

Bright Leads

Write bright story leads for the three fact sets in Exercise 11.1. Leads should grab
a reader's attention, be in tone with the subject matter of the story and be written
as concisely as possible.

_____ **Thinking it Through** _____

EXERCISE 11.3

Manufactured Bright Punch Lines

For each of the three fact sets above, identify which element you would withhold to use as a punch line for a manufactured bright. For each selection, briefly explain your choice. As part of your explanation, use three of the decision points given in the chapter to help avoid pitfalls in manufactured brights.

A freeway

Punch line element: _____

critical to story?

worth waiting?

need to clarify?

B soldiers

Punch line element: _____

critical to story?

worth waiting?

need to clarify?

C Ouija

Punch line element: _____

critical to story?

worth waiting?

need to clarify?

_____ **Writing Practice** _____

EXERCISE 11.4

Write a news bright for each of the following fact sets. Decide if the bright should be an inverted pyramid-type or a manufactured bright.

A You notice this ad in the classifieds: "Boy for sale, cheap. Call 472-4653."

You call on Mrs. Gail Applegate for an appointment. When you arrive, she tells you it was supposed to be an object lesson, but it backfired.

She's the mother of seven, and her 8-year-old boy, Timothy, had gotten into an argument with her after being punished. "He's really a good kid," she says, "but when he gave me that old line, 'I wish I wasn't your little boy anymore,' I thought I'd do something about it this time. All of his older brothers and sisters have used that line on me before, and so I thought I'd teach them a lesson by placing the ad and then showing it to them all."

What happened, you ask, and she tells you she got four calls from people seeking an adopted son, two calls from adoption agencies, a personal visit from the Child Abuse Prevention Center and a visit from Detective Paul Henderson of the local vice squad. "Thank goodness he didn't arrest me," she says, adding, "I thought it would just be a little family joke, but I learned my lesson fast."

Mrs. Applegate is 45 and a resident of 274 Quincy Ave. Her husband is Dr. Jack P. Applegate, head psychologist at Oakhill Clinic.

B Engineers at Tubular Products Inc., a local exercise and health products plant, have teamed up with two doctors at the Cardiovascular Research Lab here to produce a machine they say is a breakthrough for people who have given up on stressful exercise programs.

Drs. Kenneth B. Tankersley and Judy N. Akers announced today at a CRL press conference that CRL's joint patent with Tubular will bring a new industry to the city.

The two doctors, now husband and wife, were former Olympic cyclists and have continued their interest in bicycle races. Tankersley purchased a recumbent bicycle a few years ago, the three- or four-wheel bicycle a rider pedals and steers while lying on his or her back. Last year, Judy received a spinal injury in a car accident. She was unable to continue her usual exercise routine, but found she could do a non-strenuous half-hour riding program on the recumbent. The two doctors worked with Tubular's engineers to develop an indoor model of the recumbent bicycle, one without wheels, that can be pedaled in a stationary semicircular frame.

"You just lie on the sling 'seat' and pedal," Tankersley said. "Instead of going around the block, you propel your body from a horizontal position to a vertical position and back down by working the pedals."

"I was able to get the same workout in 15 minutes on the new device as I got in half an hour of riding," Akers said.

Tankersley added that the product looks more like an orthopedic hospital rehabilitation device than an exercise machine. "It isn't streamlined. In fact, a person using it looks like a gerbil on a running wheel. But I think it will be a breakthrough for medical therapy rooms, too."

Tubular will manufacture the machine, to be called "RollerToner," beginning in June. It will sell for $300 for the standard model, $450 with a built-in color television set and $600 for the deluxe model with leather body sling and weight pulls for arm muscles.

"I gained 25 pounds after I hurt my back," Akers said. "The weight came off in six weeks with the RollerToner, and it stays off if I spend 15 minutes on the machine every other day."

Tankersley said the product is still under testing at CRL, but, "Our early results show some impressive gains in circulatory rehabilitation and in stabilizing blood pressure problem cases. It's too early to speculate on the possibilities now, but we're very confident."

Akers said: "We think the real advantage of the RollerToner is that it will be enjoyable. People who don't jog, walk, ride bicycles, go to aerobics or to a gym, will be delighted to have this non-strenuous program to come home to."

The couple suggested other possible enhancements to the device, including: tanning lamps, vibrating body sling, motorized pedals, blood pressure and heart rate monitors, and stereo earphones.

C Brady G. Simpkins, director of the city's Tax Collection Division, and Nina O. Wenzel, head of City Utilities, are opponents in next month's race for city manager. The two have been embroiled in a local controversy about dress codes for city workers, but they ended the war today.

Three months ago Wenzel fired an information clerk for wearing jeans at work. "Her job was greeting the public and directing them to the right Utilities office. She had been warned that wearing the proper uniform was a job requirement," Wenzel said.

Simpkins hired the information clerk in his Collection Division, saying her job performance rating was superior. "I think visitors to our office care more about the person's efficiency than what the person wears."

In a campaign appearance last month, Wenzel wore a curly blond Dolly Parton look-alike wig loaded with sequins. Removing the wig, she demonstrated that her audience couldn't remember the proposals she had just made for improving city government.

Simpkins countered by wearing a stovepipe hat in a television commercial that said "Lincoln is remembered more for his deeds than for his tweeds." Simpkins revoked the dress code in the Tax Collection Division.

Wenzel purchased new uniforms for her Utilities workers. Employees held a rally after work hours to show support for her stand on dress codes. They were joined by city police and firemen.

But this morning Simpkins and Wenzel told reporters in a meeting at city hall that they were ending the dress code feud.

"We agreed it was interfering with public attention to the real issues of city management," Simpkins said.

"Besides," Wenzel added, "I was afraid he was going to dress like Lady Godiva and ride down Main Street on a white horse. I didn't think anybody would benefit from an antic like that."

The candidates told reporters that the remainder of the campaign would focus on important issues. However, after the election is over, regardless of who wins, the two will co-sponsor a charity event to raise money for a public pavilion in the city park. The event will be a fashion show.

D Local canine club officials were flustered yesterday afternoon when their dress rehearsal for the annual Northwest Regional Dog Show turned into a near riot. The rehearsal included some 100 dogs and their trainer-owners, who do a walk-through of the regional event to be sure everything goes smoothly before nearly 1,000 entries take to the arena this weekend. Halfway through the rehearsal, held at the Bayside Auditorium, two alley cats got into the arena during the obedience judging event.

"Pandemonium broke out," said Mrs. Blance Overbeck, chair of the club's event planning committee. "When the dogs spotted those two cats, it was mayhem."

"I saw it from the outset," said Rudolph Cannon, a professional trainer from Pullman, Wash. "One of those cats was chasing the other, and the two were running fast when all of a sudden they realized there were dogs all around them. At first the dogs were as startled as the cats, but you should have seen the look on those cats' faces . . . just like a cartoon double take.

"After that, the uproar was deafening. The obedience dogs were already loose, and none of the rest of us could hold on to our leashes," Cannon said.

Stephanie Overbeck, 7, the chairwoman's daughter, said, "You shoulda been there! All the dogs were chasing those two cats and running into each other. The big dogs were stepping on the little dogs. They knocked over chairs and tables and even people."

Cannon said, "Just when it looked like those cats would be goners, they jumped out of a half-opened window, probably the one they came in through. The little dogs couldn't jump that high and the big dogs couldn't get through the opening. They just stood there barking and howling."

The commotion brought security officials to the arena to find out what had happened. Canvassing the parking lot outside the area, the guards found two teenaged boys who said they were watching the dogs for a while, but denied seeing the cat incident. The boys were not held.

"It took us half an hour to get things back to normal," Mrs. Overbeck said, "but we were able to finish the program without any further difficulties.

"I'm not saying I'm glad it happened, but I am glad it happened tonight instead of this weekend," she said. "I think the security guards will be more alert after tonight's brouhaha."

E A grandfather, Daniel U. Hooker, 73, of 4675 Hillsboro Lane, was playing golf in his usual foursome at Mulberry Park Golf Course yesterday, and he got another hole-in-one.

"I Rodney-Dangerfield-em," Hooker said with a chuckle as he explained how he made the shot that stunned his buddies.

"On the par-3 No. 15 hole, I got up to the tee with a 5-iron, but since I don't hit 'em as hard as I used to, I went back and got a 4-iron," he said.

Hooker said he hadn't played well all day, scoring a 90 for 18 holes. "I'd been doing everything wrong, and the trajectory on that hole wasn't the greatest either." But on the 160-yard 15th hole, he hit a shot similar to the boomerang one comedian Rodney Dangerfield did on a television beer commercial.

Playing partner William T. Garvin, 60, said, "He hit a stinking tree. The ball caromed off that thing and rolled onto the green and 'ker-plunk' . . . right into the hole."

It was Hooker's fourth ace and the second he has made on the No. 15 hole at the course.

Rewrites

A rewrite may be loosely defined as a news story produced by revising one that has already been written or published. When cities commonly had both morning and evening newspapers, there was a far greater need to know how to do effective rewrites. A writer reporting to work at a morning daily (the work hours might have been 2 p.m to 10 or 11 p.m.) would find several stories clipped from that day's afternoon paper (off the presses between 11 a.m. and 1 p.m.). The writer knew the clippings meant that these stories should be rewritten for the morning paper. The same procedure occurred at afternoon papers, where writers found clippings from that morning's paper (off the presses between midnight and 2 a.m.) on their desks at 5 a.m. when they reported for work.

Rewriting articles from competing papers served two purposes: (1) every paper's readers deserved to know the important news, even if it appeared first in another publication—readers couldn't be expected to read the other publication; and (2) readers deserved to know the latest developments in any important event. If, for example, a house was destroyed by fire at 9 p.m. and the story was in the morning newspaper, the afternoon paper's news staff couldn't ignore the event. Reporters had to tell their readers about the fire, including the latest details about its cause, damage and victims.

Today we have fewer competing dailies, but the reasons for doing rewrites remain. If a daily paper writes about a drowning in Pleasantville on Sunday, the *Pleasantville Weekly News* must cover the event again, and in more depth, for its Thursday edition. The reduction in the number of major dailies also has meant an increase in the number of editions each publishes as these newspapers try to serve subscribers in distant areas. Important stories must be rewritten and updated for each edition. And while there are fewer big-city dailies, the number of media voices has multiplied to include suburban dailies, inner city and county weekly newspapers, news magazines, newsletters, more specialized publications, and radio, cable and local television news. Any of these competitors might report a story that another media outlet needs to rewrite for its readers.

Stories in the newspaper morgue files and those stories that appear in computer data bases also suggest a rationale for doing rewrites. A journalist who doesn't examine previously published articles on a subject is guilty of providing less than adequate coverage. Background information taken from such sources may be crucial to a reader's understanding of today's news. As electronic data bases proliferate, more editors will require writers to scan these published articles to incorporate the important information into their current stories.

If these reasons aren't enough to underscore the need for rewrites, consider the thousands of news releases that bombard the press every day. These articles are written, but not yet published. Many releases contain important information media audiences need to know. In fact, evidence shows that news releases do form the basis of later media coverage, and may prompt a significant number of news stories.[1] Still, no self-respecting journalist would publish a news release without first doing a rewrite.

There are only two approaches to rewriting news articles. The best approach by far is to add new information to the original story. The other approach is through rearrangement.

NEW INFORMATION

A case can be made that adding new information to a story is less a rewrite and more the creation of a new story, because the added information does make the new story an original. However, the part of the new article that reiterates the original is a rewrite. An example will clarify the distinction.

Updating

Assume you are a city government reporter for a metropolitan paper that competes against two suburban weeklies. No one from your paper was assigned to cover this week's council meeting in one of the suburbs

[1]Judy VanSlyke Turk, "Public Relations' Influence on the News," *Newspaper Research Journal* (Summer 1986), pp. 15–27.

because your editor believed that nothing of significant news value was on the agenda for that meeting. However, the following story about the council meeting appeared in the suburban paper this morning:

> Angry homeowners shouted down last night's proposed City Council ordinance to ban parking recreational vehicles on Clayton driveways.
>
> A well-organized group of some 40 residents refused to give up the floor microphones in Clayton City Hall until a dozen of their representatives were heard. Following the half-hour presentation, the council voted unanimously against the proposed vehicle ban.
>
> "If we can't keep government out of our pocketbooks, we should at least keep government out of our yards," said Nancy Jernigan, 2203 Warring St., chief spokeswoman for the group.
>
> Jernigan said she polled her friends in the local See Scenic America club, and all agreed they should protest the ban at the council meeting.
>
> "We gave up parking our motor home on the street," said Richard G. McClary of 319 Minor St., "but this ordinance would force us to rent huge storage facilities to park our vehicles or buy a fenced community lot and pay for a 24-hour guard patrol."
>
> Mayor Inez U. Gann said, "The city receives several letters and phone calls each year complaining that motor homes parked in driveways are 'unsightly.'" She added that, "The council was unaware of the problems this ordinance would cause recreational vehicle owners."
>
> Mayor Gann said she would appoint a committee to talk with the owners. "Perhaps we can work out a compromise that will satisfy everyone."
>
> *(story will continue with other Council meeting news)*

Several consequences are evident from the story. The first is that your editor should have sent a reporter to the meeting because this is a newsworthy story. Another result of the story's appearance is that your paper should carry an article on this news event, even if your paper was beaten on the story's debut, because your readers need to know this news. Area radio and television stations are likely to cover the "citizen's motor home rebellion" in Clayton, and the story is likely to be a local topic of conversation. Finally, and a lucky circumstance for rewriters, it's evident that the original story is not very complete. There's plenty of room for updating and additional reporting.

Your reporting task this morning is to call Mayor Inez Gann to ask:

1. Does she have further comment on last night's City Council meeting?
2. Who will she appoint to the committee?
3. Does she have some compromise plan in mind?
4. Did the Council expect the organized protest—had Jernigan or anyone else notified the council in advance?
5. Was there any attempt to keep the citizens from speaking or to silence the floor microphones?
6. What did McClary mean when he said, "We gave up parking our motor home on the street"?
7. What kind of letters and phone calls does the city receive complaining about motor homes parked in driveways?
8. How many complaints so far this year?
9. Who on the council drafted the proposal?
10. How soon might the council discuss the issue again?

Of course, other questions also should be asked, and some might ensue from Mayor Gann's answers to these.

Next, call Nancy Jernigan and Richard McClary. Each should be asked for comments and for the names of others who spoke at the meeting. Find out why the group decided to take its stand, if there is a compromise that might satisfy the group and any other facts relevant to the story or its aftermath.

Finally, consider if there are other sources who might add perspective to the story. For instance, perhaps there is a recreational vehicle dealer in Clayton who had a vested interest in defeating the proposal (such an ordinance could have put the dealer out of business). Another tactic might be to investigate the circumstances under which Clayton recreational vehicle owners gave up parking on the street. These last avenues of inquiry constitute a first line of reporter exploration for most rewrites: those for which the original story is more thorough than the portion given in the example. When the original story seems to possess all the necessary facts, a rewrite journalist must dig deeper to come up with additional newsworthy information.

Let's assume you did some additional reporting to update the recreational vehicle story. Your article's beginning paragraphs might read as follows:

> Clayton Mayor Inez U. Gann said she wants recreational vehicle owners to use a city motor pool lot instead of parking motor homes on their driveway.

"We can solve the 'eyesore' complaints by letting owners use a patrolled city lot free of charge," Mayor Gann said today.

"That's not the point," said Nancy Jernigan, 2203 Warring St., chief spokeswoman for a group of some 40 residents who protested Wednesday night against a Clayton City Council proposal to ban driveway parking of recreational vehicles.

Jernigan said her group is committed to "our right as homeowners to keep our possessions on our property."

She said: "A recreational vehicle is neither an eyesore nor a hazard. People who own one are proud to have it on display."

Although the Clayton City Council voted against the proposal, Mayor Gann said she would appoint a committee to talk with the vehicle owners about a compromise plan.

She said she thinks using a secured city lot is the ideal solution. "We have four lots with ample room for all of Clayton's motor homes."

Obviously, the rewrite is no longer the same story as the original because it contains new information. Also, the new information is newsworthy enough to become the new lead for the story. But just as evident is the fact that some information from the original story—the sources, when the event occurred and that the council defeated the proposal— remains high in the rewrite. The repeated information is necessary for your readers to understand this story. After all, they didn't read the original story, or at least not in your newspaper.

These few paragraphs of the rewrite constitute the updated information. If you were able to gather this much additional information, you probably have enough other facts to write an entirely new story as your rewrite. But let's assume that the two new pieces of information—the offer to use a city motor pool lot and Jernigan's quote—are the *only* two new elements you had time to get. How do you complete your rewrite? You should use the remaining pertinent information from the original story, but in your own words:

The mayor's offer to let vehicle owners use a city motor pool lot counters an argument voiced by one resident at the meeting.

Richard G. McClary of 319 Minor St. said the proposed ordinance would force owners to park their vehicles in rented storage facilities or to purchase a fenced community lot and pay to have it patrolled around the clock.

But Jernigan's stand on the issue during the meeting was a more fundamental protest against government encroachment. "If we can't keep government out of our pocketbooks, we should at least keep government out of our yards," she told the council.

Mayor Gann said the council offered the proposal because several residents had complained that motor homes parked in driveways were unsightly. But she said, "The council was unaware of the problems this ordinance would cause recreational vehicle owners."

Jernigan said her friends who belong to Clayton's See Scenic America club all agreed to fight the council's proposal at the meeting.

Her group refused to relinquish floor microphones in Clayton City Hall until their representatives had been heard. When speakers completed a half-hour presentation, the council voted unanimously against the proposed vehicle ban.

Notice that the rest of the story retains enough of the original story's information so readers can understand the context of what happened at the council meeting. However, actual words from the original story are contained only in direct quotes, and the rewrite does not follow the original story's order of presentation. The rewrite is a new inverted pyramid structure that relegates the least important news values, and the oldest events, to the bottom of the story.

Localizing

Your medium has a duty to inform its audience. National, regional and statewide stories that affect your readers must be reported, even though these stories may have appeared in other media first. A common practice is to localize such stories through the same rewriting procedures outlined above. Updating, or providing more recent information, is one possibility. Localizing is another. Instead of merely seeking more-current information, look for relationships between the more distant news event and your readers' interests (as discussed in Chapter 16).

Several localizing strategies may be used.

1. Link the distant news event with a recent local event. For instance, if a federal transportation panel decides that more-sophisticated computer technology should be required to prevent motorist fatalities at railroad crossings, search your morgue files for recent articles on local accidents at railroad crossings.

2. Contact local authorities to find out how distant news events might influence local policy. For the railroad crossing story, call local rail officials for their reaction to the federal panel's decision. Ask if there are plans to implement the new ruling locally, and when new technology systems might be installed.

A student intern reads stories sent over the Associated Press news wire. Virtually all news outlets subscribe to one or more wire services and use the articles either in their entirety, in an edited form or as information for localizing stories.

3. Contact local sources for reaction to the distant story. Your city manager may tell you this community has been asking the rail companies for better protection at crossings for years; that this federal ruling is a landmark decision that might prevent the deaths of an average of six local residents annually.

4. Remember the human interest aspect. People in your community often are affected by distant news events. The national rail crossing decision should prompt your call or visit to a local resident who was recently injured in a train-car accident. Localizing distant stories should include the reaction of local residents.

All of these procedures for localizing will result in the same sort of rewrite described in the section on updating. The difference is that these new story leads will focus on changes in proximity rather than timeliness: moving the emphasis of the distant news event to this locality's concerns.

REWRITING WITHOUT NEW INFORMATION

There is no doubt that doing a rewrite without providing new information is the lazy approach. Some editors may forbid doing this kind of rewrite because it too closely resembles the original article. At best, the "rehash" rewrite is only a minimum journalistic effort: a last-minute maneuver to provide information this medium's audience needs to know. But the duty to inform readers is fundamental in journalism, so if the pressure of deadlines permits nothing more than a "rehash" rewrite, then do it . . . and do it well. The way to achieve this objective is to make the rewrite as dissimilar to the original story as possible. Two approaches are possible, although the first is by far the preferred.

Find a New Lead Buried in the Original Story

From the rewriter's standpoint, a bungled original story is a lucky find. The more poorly the original story is written, the easier it is to do a successful rehash rewrite. Of course, you should anticipate that the original story will be a good piece of journalism, but read it critically to look for flaws you can correct in the rewrite. For instance, does the original story bury the real lead? Consider the following unlikely original story candidate:

The "St. Lukes Saint" retired from the city police force this morning after 20 years on the job.

Patrolman Henry L. Watkins, who earned his "Saint" nickname because of his special concern for his district's homeless population, said he could contribute more as a full-time volunteer.

Watkins had received his third reprimand from precinct headquarters for failure to respond to radio dispatcher calls.

"I think they were telling me that I was spending too much time assisting the street people," Watkins said. "They began making me answer calls from the precinct every hour."

A group of about 50 homeless began a vigil in front of the 5th Precinct Headquarters on Vine Street this morning to protest Watkins' resignation. Police Lt. Charles Levy met with the protesters at noon. . . .

While it would be unusual for a news article to miss the lead as in this example, such errors do occur. A rewriter should recognize that the real news story here is the protest in front of police headquarters by the district's homeless. The rewrite can lead with the most significant news element, missed in the original story:

Fifty homeless people began a vigil in front of the 5th Precinct Police Station today to protest the resignation of a patrolman known as the "St. Lukes Saint."

A similar and more frequent occurrence than a missed lead can also be used to advantage in a rewrite. This technique involves selecting an acceptable lead element that was not used as the lead in the original story. An article frequently includes two or more major news elements, any of which might suffice as the lead. The original story's writer may have selected among elements that narrowly competed for the most important news value. Recognizing that there are additional lead possibilities, the rewriter selects one of the other elements for a lead.

Consider the following original story:

Sadie A. Freemont, 53, of 277 Whitcomb died Tuesday in a two-car crash resulting from a high-speed chase by police seeking to apprehend a suspected robber.

Freemont's vehicle was hit by a car driven by Clifton V. Hunter, 28, who was fleeing the scene of a convenience store robbery when two city squad cars began chasing his car at speeds approaching 90 mph.

Hunter is reported in critical condition at Charity Hospital.

Two events occurred: a high-speed police chase on city streets and the death of a local resident. Can the journalist rewriting this story lead with the high-speed chase and hold the Freemont death for a later paragraph? The answer is no. Doing a rewrite offers no justification for breaking the rules of news values. We know that the loss of life is paramount to virtually all other possible news values, so Freemont's death must be in the lead. However, it need not begin the lead nor does the lead have to use her name. After all, this story will focus on the speed chase, not the innocent victim:

> A high-speed chase by police trying to capture a suspected robber ended in the death of a local resident Tuesday.
> Sadie A. Freemont, 53, of 277 Whitcomb died when her car was hit by . . .

The point of this subterfuge example is to emphasize that a new lead can be selected for the rewrite only when that substitute lead is equal in news value to the original story lead. Here's a better example of such an instance:

> A passing grade in every subject is the new requirement for high school sports eligibility.
> The ruling came with yesterday's 6–5 vote of the Adams County School Board, which also passed a controversial 10 percent across-the-board pay raise for teachers and a 25-cent increase in the cost of school lunches.
> The passing grade ruling requires students who participate in varsity sports to maintain a D or better grade in all subjects. Debate on the measure focused on whether the ruling should apply to required course work or to elective and required subjects.
> Three of the School Board members voted against the measure because they said it discriminates against high school athletes. Dennis Cotton, 2nd District board member, said: "No such grade requirement is demanded of band members or cheerleaders. Even student council members are allowed to fail a class and keep their office as long as they maintain a passing average overall."
> In approving the 10 percent pay raise for teachers, the Board said the increase was needed to stem the rash of teacher transfers to adjacent counties. Dr. Joyce Early, 6th District board member, said the county has lost nearly 60 teachers in the past two years, and the county still has more than 100 applications for transfer.

Early said county teachers' pay has not kept pace with salaries in any of the four touching counties. "We've put this off too long already," she said. "We will simply have to divert the necessary funds from other school improvement projects to put the money where the need is greatest right now."

School lunch costs in the county will increase from 50 to 75 cents beginning next fall. The Board debated a two-step increase of 10 cents for the coming year and another 15 cents in the second year. However, Board President Elaine Wakefield called the two-step plan "a gutless attempt to avoid public criticism" on the 50 percent increase. "We've held school lunch costs for nearly 10 years now, and parents are well aware that the price of groceries is twice what it was in 1980."

The news value of this story suggests that all county media would have sent reporters to the school board meeting. However, timing or logistics might have prevented attendance, and today's deadline may demand a rewrite as the only way to provide this news to your media audience. Also, the newsworthiness of the board's decisions would result in a longer original story than the one shown. However, this example is sufficient to demonstrate alternate lead choices.

The journalist writing the original story determined that passing grades for sports eligibility was the most newsworthy outcome of the meeting. But that writer also recognized there were two other possibilities by including them in the second graf of the story:

> . . . which also passed a controversial 10 percent across-the-board <u>pay raise for teachers</u> and a 25-cent increase in the <u>cost of school lunches</u>.

We may assume that sports eligibility was selected for the lead because the issue had been in the news before this school board meeting. In fact, if the measure had not been a topic of public controversy, selecting it for the lead would have been an error in journalistic judgment. After all, the teacher pay raise and the cost of school lunches affect more members of the audience than does the sports eligibility topic. Even if the sports issue was a matter of current public controversy, either of the other two measures would qualify as a lead for this news story.

When several equally worthy news values in the story can qualify as the lead, the rehash rewriter's assignment (to make the new story as dissimilar to the original story as possible) is greatly simplified: Lead with one of the other news values. In the example, the choice should be the cost of school lunches. There are two reasons for this choice:

1. More members of the audience will be affected, in this case all school-age children and their parents.
2. School lunch prices was the third item discussed in the original story. Information on that school board decision was at the bottom of the original story, so it is least likely to be recognized as repetitive in the rewrite.

The rewritten story might begin:

School lunch costs next fall will increase from 50 cents to 75 cents per day, the Adams County School Board decided at yesterday's meeting.

The Board also voted teachers a 10 percent across-the-board pay increase and ruled that students participating in varsity sports must pass in all subjects to remain eligible.

Notice that the rewrite cannot ignore the other two news values. They must be included high in the rewrite, just as they were in the original story, because all three represent the major news values of the school board meeting. However, if the three topics are deemed of equal weight, any sequence of presentation will suffice, so the story can lead with lunch costs, move to teacher pay raises and then include the sports issue.

Inverted pyramid structure requires that details of the lead element follow all necessary news values:

In voting for the 75-cent lunches, Board President Elaine Wakefield said, "We've held school lunch costs for nearly 10 years now, and parents are well aware that the price of groceries is twice what it was in 1980."

The Board discussed a two-step lunch cost increase of 10 cents the first year and 15 cents the second year, but Wakefield called the two-step plan "a gutless attempt to avoid public criticism" on the 50 percent increase.

After all details of the lunch increase are given, the story should provide information about the teacher pay raises and should end with the sports eligibility information. The rehash rewrite is complete: a properly sequenced inverted pyramid news story that hardly resembles the original news article from which it was taken.

Reorder and Reword

Actually, as indicated in all the preceding examples, the wording for a rewrite always should be changed. But this final method of doing a no-new-information rewrite is the most difficult kind of assignment. Here, there is no new information, the original story is written properly and there are no acceptable substitute leads. In this most desperate form of rewriting, no major organizational changes are available. The rehash rewriter can only change the words, the sentences and the paragraphs.

As the rewriter strives to make the new story dissimilar to the original story, the finished rewrite still must follow all of the principles of a well-written news story. That means there can be no changes that conflict with the proper presentation of news values. No important information can be discarded and no trivial information can be given undue emphasis. Figure 12.1 offers an example of a weather story and its reworded rewrite.

Several observations can be made about the rewrite. Obviously, it is shorter than the original story, and it should be. A no-new-information rewrite longer than or of equal length to the original should alert an editor that there is a problem in the rewrite. If there is no new information, and if the wording is changed, the rewrite should be a tighter rendition of the original.

The rewrite's lead retains the vital information from the lead of the original story, but every effort has been made to use different words. The only repeated key words are "ski" and "resort." Additionally, there is a slight change in focus for the new lead. We might assume that the original story is a wire service report from a bureau in Denver, and that the rewrite is a deadline effort by a non-Colorado media outlet to report the news to its readers. The rewrite lead is localized for its intended audience, those readers who might be planning a visit to the ski area. And the rest of the rewrite also reflects this shift in primary audience focus.

Tighter, more concise wording is evident in every paragraph of the rewrite. Facts from separate sentences in the original article are combined into one sentence of the rewrite, and the wording is reordered to shorten sentences wherever possible.

But the most striking change in the rewrite comes from the omission of unnecessary facts and phrases in the original story. For instance, "80 percent of the most popular ski resorts" becomes merely "most popular ski resorts" because out-of-state readers don't need the specific figure. Also, much of the directly quoted material in the original story is paraphrased in the rewrite, and two of the original story's direct quotes are omitted. Deleting unnecessary quotes is a convenient method of making the rewrite dissimilar to the original story; however, removing all direct quotes might weaken the rewrite's readability.

A storm centered on Leadville, Colo., will close most of the state's ski resorts through the busiest vacation week of the season.

Weather bureau reports issued continued warnings for sleet and hail with possible 2-foot-high snowfalls each of the next 10 days.

The Colorado Highway Patrol has closed all roads except interstate and major U.S. highways in a 100-mile radius of Leadville. The area includes 80 percent of the most popular ski resorts in Colorado.

Colorado Gov. Martin Cochran said, "Forecasted weather conditions leave little room for optimism. We urge Colorado residents and all out-of-state tourists who planned visits to the impacted areas to cancel their trips immediately."

Gov. Cochran said, "Severe storms in the ski resort areas demand every precaution to protect people's health and safety." He said the state will notify travelers immediately if conditions improve.

Ginger Weems, director of tourism for the state, said weather conditions will cost the state almost $10 million in tax revenues on anticipated tourist income of more than $100 million. "It's our largest weekly source of revenues from an estimated 200,000 visitors to the Colorado ski country."

She added that storm-forced changes in visitor travel plans this year will have "a serious impact on the state's tourist industry for the next five years. People who booked lodges and put deposits on vacation rentals and air flights this year may think twice about planning winter trips to Colorado in the near future," she said.

Visitors to the Colorado ski resort region are warned to cancel their trips due to severe weather conditions.

Two-foot snowfalls with sleet and hail are forecast for the next 10 days, the weather bureau said.

All but the interstate and major U.S. highways in a 100-mile radius of Leadville, Colo., were closed by the state's Highway Patrol, cutting access to Colorado's most popular ski resorts.

Out-of-state tourists who planned visits to the impacted areas were urged by Colorado Gov. Martin Cochran to cancel their trips. He said travelers will be notified if conditions improve, but, "Forecasted weather conditions leave little room for optimism."

Director of Tourism Ginger Weems predicted the storms will cost Colorado more than $100 million in tourist spending. She said the 200,000 visitors who vacation in the ski country bring the state's largest weekly source of revenues.

Weems said the state's tourist industry might be affected for the next five years. "People who booked lodges and put deposits on vacation rentals and air flights this year may think twice about planning trips to Colorado in the near future."

Figure 12.1   Original story (left) and reworded rewrite

If an editor determines that this rewrite is still too long, the final paragraph can be chopped, as it would be in editing any inverted pyramid story.

One final point. Would it be possible to place the two Weems' comment paragraphs, or even the first one, above the governor's comments? Doing so would help the dissimilarity aspect; the rewrite would look less like the original story. But news value considerations prohibit such a tactic because the governor's warning to out-of-state tourists and his pessimism about improved weather conditions are far more important to the rewrite's audience than the information about Colorado's internal tourism revenue losses. Again, a rewrite must follow all the rules of a well-written news story.

SUMMARY

A rewrite is a news story created by revising an existing story. In the heyday of morning-evening competitive papers, the rewrite was a daily news room staple. Today the skills needed to do a rewrite remain indispensable because each news outlet's audience must be informed and because of the deluge of press releases that flow into news rooms.

Adding new information to the original story and rearranging the original story's contents are the two procedures for rewriting news articles. New information can be in the form of an update, in which more-current information is added to the original, or through localizing. The chapter describes methods for gathering additional information on deadline, to add the latest developments, reactions or local significance to the original story. Examples are given to demonstrate how to incorporate new information into the early portions of the rewrite.

A "rehash" rewrite—one that contains no new information—is the other rewriting method. Editors disdain the approach as lazy journalism, but under deadline pressure they assign these rewrites because the duty to inform readers is fundamental. If the original story is poorly done, the rewriter's task is simple: take the bungled story and rewrite it as it should have been written originally. Even if the original story is well-written, there might be competing lead news values that afford an opportunity to use one of the originally rejected leads for the rewrite. But the most difficult assignment is to rewrite a story simply by resequencing and reworking the wording. The chapter provides suggestions and examples of these rewriting approaches.

Thinking it Through

EXERCISE 12.1

New Information Sources

For each of the following original stories, decide sources you would use to update or localize for a rewrite. Fill in the blanks that follow each story to indicate the sources you would contact, in the order in which you would make such contacts on deadline. Give yourself one hour from the time you are assigned the rewrite to the time you must complete it. That leaves you only half an hour to gather new information. After each source blank you complete, briefly explain what information you would be seeking from the source. These exercises may be done on a separate sheet of paper or on-screen.

A The city's public school system was rated second in a 10-state region by the U.S. Department of Education in a report released in Washington, D.C., today.

Dr. Lillie Chung, superintendent of schools, said, "We thought we were doing an exceptional job, but we never anticipated this level of recognition. It came as a complete surprise."

The report placed city schools first in the nation in science achievement, percentage of faculty with post-graduate degrees and in classroom student-teacher ratio.

At a rating of 96, city schools finished only slightly behind the 97 score achieved by a rural county school district in Indiana. All of the regional first-place school systems were in rural districts.

Charles G. Brown, U.S. secretary of education, praised Dr. Chung and the city school district in a personal letter accompanying the report. He wrote, "Your teachers and administrators have every reason to be proud of the accomplishments you have achieved. The problems of metropolitan school districts have never been more acute, yet your city schools outscored the entire nation in three of the 100 quality categories judged."

Dr. Monica G. Hoover, author of the Education Department's national school rating report, announced she will send a staff team to the city to study the system's science achievement success. "We hope to determine how the rest of the nation can emulate outstanding performance in each of the academic subject areas," she said.

Superintendent Chung said the Washington team will be welcomed in the city schools. "We believe our approach to teaching science is innovative. At least one teacher at every class level has won a national award in the past two years for student achievement in the sciences."

SOURCES IN YOUR ORDER OF SELECTION (provide a name or position identification for your source):

1. _____

Information sought:

2. _____

Information sought:

3. _____

Information sought:

4. _____

Information sought:

5. _____

Information sought:

B   A 2,000-employee International Paper Co. plant for recycled paper products will be the anchor industry at the new Hilltop Industrial Park, Mayor Christy Quinn announced from New York City today.

Two other major industries, a General Electric home satellite reception manufacturing plant and an AT&T computer assembly plant, also signed contracts to build facilities at Hilltop Park, the mayor said.

International Paper officials said they anticipate being in production at their firm's new 200-acre park site within a year. Hiring for the plant will start in six months, officials said.

The GE home satellite plant at Hilltop will be that firm's only United States production facility for high-tech television reception dishes. Designed for rooftop or window installation, the aluminum dishes are less than 2 feet in diameter and weigh only 20 pounds.

GE officials at this morning's announcement said they hope to have architectural plans completed next month for the company's 300-acre site plant, with construction to begin in about three months. The plant will employ 3,500 people.

Representatives for the AT&T computer assembly plant said groundbreaking at their 150-acre Hilltop site will begin immediately. The plant's assembly line will be highly automated and will use the latest robotic manufacturing technology.

Although officials declined to discuss the models of AT&T computers that will be assembled here, Pat Sinclair, vice president of AT&T Research and Development Division, said, "We expect this product to dominate the international intelligent computer industry for the next five years."

Sinclair said the plant will hire only about 500 area residents, but another 500 AT&T engineers and technicians will be relocated from California and New Jersey to work at the Hilltop site.

SOURCES IN YOUR ORDER OF SELECTION (provide a name or position identification for your source):

1. _____

Information sought:

2. _____

Information sought:

3. _____

Information sought:

4. _____

Information sought:

5. _____

Information sought:

C   The state Legislature will be able to retain its proposal to remove the sales tax on groceries only if the Senate approves a substantial tax increase, Gov. Bobbie R. May said Monday.

Although a projected budget surplus for the year estimated at $65 million is enough to remove the sales tax on food for the state's poor, it is insufficient to cover the cost of eliminating food taxes for all state residents, May said.

The state House has approved the governor's plan to eliminate the 7 percent sales tax on food in four phases beginning July 1. The first stage will cost taxpayers $90 million this year. When the plan is fully implemented, the cost will be $300 million annually, according to the bill.

At the time the House passed the measure, the budget surplus was projected to be $100 million. However, a downturn in the national economy has reduced that estimate by nearly one-third.

Gov. May said she hopes the Senate will follow the House lead in increasing income taxes by 1 percent, enough to eliminate the food sales tax.

She said, "Those income earners who make more than an annual $15,000 family income will not miss the additional 1 percent they pay in state taxes, but everyone, especially the poor, will appreciate the difference in the check-out line when the food tax is eliminated."

Gov. May's remarks came at a luncheon with Statehouse reporters who asked her if she is considering running for reelection in the coming gubernatorial race.

"I've given that some thought," she said, "and I probably will be in the race."

May had campaigned four years ago on a platform to limit the governor to one consecutive term in office. She helped initiate the necessary legislation during her first year, but the bill was overwhelmingly defeated in the House.

She told reporters that although she had opposed consecutive gubernatorial terms, "the House debate convinced me I was being naive. I've also learned that an administration cannot accomplish its objectives in four short years," she said.

SOURCES IN YOUR ORDER OF SELECTION (provide a name or position identification for your source):

1. _____
   Information sought:

2. _____
   Information sought:

3. _____
   Information sought:

4. _____
   Information sought:

5. _____
   Information sought:

D A measure to bar the local chapter of a parent-teen crisis organization from meeting without a license was defeated at last night's Westpark City Council meeting.

The group, Tough Love, is part of a national association of local chapters composed of volunteers. Members advise parents on how to deal with teen problems such as drugs, crime and sex.

Two councilmen, E. Walter Lemmon and Lawrence H. Gibson, had to be physically restrained by fellow Council members when debate on the Tough Love proposal became heated.

Lemmon and Gibson, leaders of the Council's conservative and liberal factions respectively, were standing face-to-face shouting threats at one another when other councilmen pulled them apart.

Gibson told Lemmon, who offered the proposal to bar Tough Love meetings without a license, that volunteer organizations aren't accountable to the city.

"I've got two teenage daughters," Gibson said, "and my wife and I have gone to those meetings dozens of times. They probably saved one of my children's lives."

Lemmon's motion to ban Tough Love meetings was based on requiring city licenses for family counseling clinics. "Any group that lets armchair psychologists tell people to kick their kids out into the street should expect public scrutiny," he said.

The Tough Love organization's approach to family crises is for parents to set strict requirements by which their children must abide in order to remain in the family unit. Family crises frequently take the form of teenage alcohol and drug abuse, sexual promiscuity and run-ins with the law.

Lemmon told the Council these matters should be the purview of licensed practitioners including doctors, psychiatrists, clergymen and board-certified clinics. "If they (Tough Love) want to practice family counseling, they should submit their credentials just like any legitimate counselors," Lemmon said.

Gibson said a volunteer organization that charges no fees "is as free to meet as a bridge club.

"We should applaud Tough Love for solving family problems before they reach the courts," he said.

The shouting match began when Lemmon told Gibson that parents who can't control their own children "ought to go to jail instead of the children."

Gibson leaped from his council chair, and the two faced off in a shouting match that ended when other councilmen pulled them apart.

The vote against the motion to ban Tough Love meetings was 6 to 4.

SOURCES IN YOUR ORDER OF SELECTION (provide a name or position identification for your source):

1. _____

Information sought:

2. _____

Information sought:

3. _____

Information sought:

4. _____

Information sought:

5. _____

Information sought:

E (assume you are writing for a Benton news medium)

Claude S. Pace, 35, escaped from the maximum security prison at Riverport early Sunday morning after killing a guard, prison officials reported.

Pace, a 5-foot-10 Hispanic with a pronounced left-leg limp, is the subject of a statewide police manhunt. He is suspected of being armed with an automatic shotgun, Riverport Police Capt. Willie M. Crain said.

State Highway Patrol vehicles and local police in a 10-county area are searching rural areas for Pace, who was serving a life term for murdering two Benton women. The suspect was reported seen Sunday afternoon at a gas station on Route 42, 25 miles south of Benton.

Melvin H. Jones, 38, the guard at Riverport Prison, was found strangled at 4 a.m. Sunday. His weapon was missing and his security keys were found on a dirt road half a mile from Riverport.

Capt. Crain said Pace had been asking fellow prisoners from this state about their hometowns. "He may have enough information about the local terrain to evade capture for several more days if he has enough food and water," Crain said.

But Crain warned citizens to report any suspect resembling Pace to police. "Don't attempt to confront him," Crain said. "He's armed, extremely dangerous and he's already serving a life term."

At his courtroom conviction two years ago, Pace swore he would kill the district attorney and a witness who testified against him during the trial. Benton police now have the witness in protective custody.

Pace has been behind bars much of his life. He served five years for manslaughter when he was 17 and an 8-year sentence for armed robbery when he was 23. He was 32 when he returned to Riverport Prison for the murder convictions.

SOURCES IN YOUR ORDER OF SELECTION (provide a name or position identification for your source):

1. _____

Information sought:

2. _____

Information sought:

3. _____

Information sought:

4. _____

Information sought:

5. _____

Information sought:

_____ **Writing Practice** _____

EXERCISE 12.2

No-New-Information Rewrites

Rewrite the five stories in Exercise 12.1 as no-new-information rewrites—as if each had appeared in its current form in a competing media outlet or as a wire service story. Some may be reorganized effectively without violating tenets of news values. Others may be rewritten effectively only through the rewording process.

PART THREE

Advanced Article Types

Continuing Stories

News rarely is a static occurrence. The ebb and flow of events usually extends beyond a single reporting period, although many news stories must be single representations of those events, tendered at the time of the report.

Consider the single news story about a local grandmother who makes violins. Her craft began as a hobby 20 years ago. As the quality of her work progressed, friends purchased a few of her violins, but that was 10 years ago. For the last five years, fiddlers from neighboring states came to town to buy her instruments. This week, the first violinist of the New York Philharmonic Symphony paid $5,000 for a made-to-order Granny violin. A news article on this event is appropriate, possibly a feature with pictures chronicling the purchase and telling the story of the violin-making grandmother.

This is an example of a single representation of an event at one point in time: the $5,000 purchase. The story should contain the history of the grandmother's success, including events of the last 20 years, but it will focus primarily on this week's purchase, the news event that prompted coverage. She's been making the violins for 20 years and could continue making them another 20, but this one article may be the only news report about her work. The event is certainly not static; the news report is. The same might be true for stories of a farmer's election to head a co-op, the bankruptcy of a savings and loan, the first sweepstakes win by a local breeder's horse and many similar incidents.

However, most news events suggest at least two stories:

1. the advance notice and the event itself, such as a concert, fund-raising event or speech; or

    2. the event and its aftermath, such as a sudden storm and its toll.

Some events contain all three news aspects, such as a plant strike or a political convention.

    Countless events are fluid enough to suggest a series of news stories. For instance, important legislation at any level of government should suggest:

    1. a preliminary story on discussions for the needed legislation;
    2. the bill or proposal itself;
    3. debate on the measure as it progresses through committees and legislative bodies;
    4. a story on the outcome of the measure; and
    5. a follow-up story on the effect of the legislation.

Crime stories run the gamut from commission of the act through arrest, charges and trials. Stories about human courage in combating illness, about business, scientific discoveries, public policy concerns such as the environment and energy, and dozens of other major issues deserve continuing news coverage.

    Much of this text has already noted that timeliness is one of the primary news elements; that the recency of an event directly affects its newsworthiness. Similarly, deadlines demand publication of the most recently available information, even though the writer may not have all the information needed to tell the complete story. Sometimes, the story won't be complete until later in the day, the next day or the next week. So journalists make their deadlines while acknowledging that events are still unfolding. These are the kinds of continuing stories this chapter emphasizes.

    The unique aspect of a continuing story is that readers must be reminded of what already transpired. To understand the importance of today's news—sometimes to be able to understand it at all—readers often need to know about earlier events that spawned the most recent developments. Thus, the journalist often needs to identify these background events in a complex tie-back lead.

TIE-BACK LEADS

Perhaps the simplest way to relate current events to previous ones in a lead is demonstrated by a single-incident crime story. Consider the following example of a previous story lead:

A gunman escaped with $280 in cash and a waitress's diamond engagement ring in a robbery at the Highland Cafe at 11 p.m. Thursday.

Now the follow-up lead:

Rickey C. Waldrop, 24, 1675 Adams Lane, was arrested at Bailey's Pawn Shop today as the suspect in <u>Thursday night's Highland Cafe holdup.</u>

Police said the shop's owner notified them when Waldrop tried to pawn <u>a diamond engagement ring matching the description of one taken from a waitress at the cafe during a robbery.</u>

If we assume that the two events (robbery and arrest) occurred over a relatively short span of time, such as a week, then the continuing story's lead paragraphs are fine. There are enough explanations in the first and second paragraph to let readers know this arrest is related to a recent robbery.

The preceding example isn't very complex because most arrest stories must include tie-back elements to the original crime. We're used to reading this kind of story format. But continuing stories often are more complex than the robbery example, as is the following story about a public policy measure:

Proposition 8, in which voters will decide if businesses must provide day care services, will be the most controversial measure on November's ballot, Gov. Cissy Coleman said Monday.

Coleman said she will "fight for its passage like a street fighter."

If voters approve the proposition, every state-licensed business with more than 50 employees would be required to provide on-site day care services or pay qualifying employees up to $1,000 annually to obtain necessary day care for their children.

The measure represents more than a year of partisan legislative jousting since Coleman made day care the primary plank in her re-election platform.

Emphasizing that her party has fought heavily financed opposition from Republican legislators, Coleman said, "It is a tribute to Democratic strength in this state that the proposal even made it to a general election ballot."

Speaking against the bill last week, Senate Minority Leader Bill Lyon called it "an emasculated version of a day care bill that has been sliced and diced to pieces in committee." The Senate narrowly defeated the bill, after which Coleman announced she had enough signatures to put the original measure on the November ballot.

Coleman said Monday that more than $2 million has already been spent by foes of the day care plan. "We're talking about a law that might cost big businesses $200 million a year," she said, "and I predict their public campaign to defeat Proposition 8 will make their recent legislative lobbying seem like child's play."

She said she is confident that the measure will pass. "There are 400,000 workers who will be in the voting booths Nov. 5 to ensure its success," she said. "Our two-worker family employment system demands it."

Here the news event that prompts the continuing story is an interview with Gov. Coleman. This is simply the latest of many stories published on the topic since Coleman's re-election campaign more than a year ago. But the story's writer cannot assume readers will know about the day care measure, its significance or the developments that have taken place during the past 18 months.

As in the preceding example, the writer of any continuing story needs not to assume that readers are ignorant, but rather to consider them inconsistent followers of the news. Audiences are limited in their ability to select and retain messages from the vast media barrage. A reporter can very easily forget that the audience isn't as devoted to the mass media as are journalists. But to overlook this audience frailty is a major error in writing the continuing story: The journalist must give adequate background information quickly, or the audience may not read past the second paragraph.

Writing the continuing story requires a presentation that deftly tells today's news interspersed with necessary background events. Figure 13.1

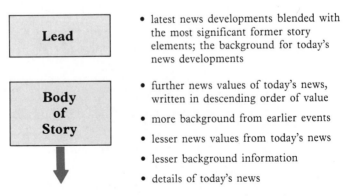

Figure 13.1   Blending today's news with previous events

shows how today's and yesterday's news elements should be blended in constructing a continuing story. In overview, the continuing story's organization is similar to that of any other inverted pyramid news article: It begins with the most important news values and presents lesser news values in descending order through the story. But in the lead and possibly through two or three paragraphs, the continuing story writer uses every necessary piece of background information to give the reader perspective on today's events. In fact, two inverted pyramid presentations are taking place simultaneously in the continuing story: today's news and previous events. Each is included with the most noteworthy elements first, followed by lesser news values. Obviously, today's news precedes more dated information in the story's lead, but some significant elements from previous events also appear in the lead.

Often, after the opening paragraph, a continuing story contains a terse review of past events in the second paragraph. The writer then returns to today's next-most-significant news elements. Current events are melded with previous events in succeeding sentences and paragraphs throughout

Presidential contender Jesse Jackson draws attention to the pesticide poisoning issue in California by breakfasting in the home of Tina Bravo, whose son died of cancer. Stories by journalists, who follow Jackson's early campaign trail, will blend this breakfast event with the pesticide issue.

the body of the story until all the necessary background information is provided. The remainder of the article contains only the lesser current news elements.

Because the continuing story's blending structure is so different from previous approaches, a graphic presentation can help reveal how this blending occurs, as shown in Figure 13.2. The inverted pyramid is divided into sections representing the lead paragraphs, the central body of the story and the concluding paragraphs. Current news elements begin the lead, with previous events or perspective included. The central body contains almost equal amounts of today's news and previous events. The last third of the story does have some previous news elements, but it is composed primarily of today's news.

Previous elements are concentrated early in the story so the reader will have a secure grounding about how today's events relate to past events, but the need for such background information decreases as the necessary past elements are depleted. The audience learns what happened today, is told how it came about and then receives the details of today's events.

Previous information does not come out of the writer's memory. For many stories, as in the first example of the violin-making grandmother, the background comes from reporter interviews: all freshly gathered information, although the information itself may date back 20 years. But the Granny violin story isn't a continuing story. In the two examples of continuing stories—the gunman arrested when he pawned a diamond ring, and the child care proposition—the background comes from previously published stories. We should imagine that the journalist preparing to write the continuing story has pulled the previous stories from the

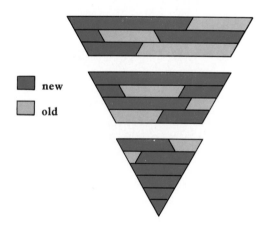

Figure 13.2 Mixing new and old in continuing stories

morgue files or computer bank. Those previous stories are in front of the writer as the continuing story is being composed.

Never rely on your memory, even if you were the reporter who wrote the original articles. Check your original notes and use the morgue files for correct name spellings, dates, ages, addresses . . . all of the information you might include in the continuing story. Doing so is the minimum accuracy level a writer should reach. If the original stories were not your own, use your journalist's healthy skepticism to verify facts from the original story that you might use in your continuing story. Verification is compulsory, particularly if the original stories were produced by a competing news outlet. You don't know the competency level of the original writers, and your editor won't be satisfied that you "just used what was already written," especially if your story perpetuates errors. For all you know, the original stories might be a hoax.

MORE COMPLEX CONTINUING STORIES

When the scope of previous developments requires more extensive backgrounding in the new story, writing the continuing story becomes even more challenging. The Proposition 8 story required telling the reader about several developments in the day care proposal during more than a year of its progression. However, providing readers sufficient grounding in that continuing story was relatively easy. Consider these previous events in writing a more difficult continuing story:

> First story: An 8-year-old girl was badly injured in a car crash in which her parents were killed. She is in the hospital and needs a kidney transplant.
>
> Second story: The community starts a campaign to raise $150,000 for the operation. Several fund-raising activities are slated.
>
> Third story: After two months $50,000 is raised for the girl's operation, but the girl goes into a coma and is given only weeks to live.
>
> Fourth story: The girl recovers from the coma, and doctors say if she doesn't have the operation within 10 days, it is unlikely she will survive.
>
> Fifth story: An anonymous benefactor donates the additional $100,000 needed for the girl's operation. Medical authorities begin the search for a kidney.

> Sixth story: A suitable kidney is found and the operation is set for the next day.

Now, for the continuing story:

> Doctors announce the girl's operation was a success. She was taken from the post-op recovery room back to her hospital room at 2 p.m. Her condition is "good" and there is every reason to believe she will recover fully.

Before writing the continuing story, recognize that much of the information in the five previous articles will serve the normal function of chronological presentation in the new story. The trick, then, is to decide what information from the earlier stories a reader will need to know early in the continuing story.

> A successful kidney transplant was performed today on Mary S. Guffey, the 8-year-old <u>who lost her parents in a car accident earlier this year</u>.
>
> Doctors at Surgical Hospital reported Miss Guffey was in good condition following the five-hour operation that <u>residents of this community helped make possible through their donations</u>.
>
> "We have every reason to believe she will recover fully," a smiling Chief Surgeon Stanley Parker told reporters at noon. He said the transplant team was "pleased with every aspect of the procedure."
>
> Miss Guffey was injured in an automobile accident in which her parents were killed. The child has been under hospital care awaiting the kidney transplant since that November accident.
>
> Miss Guffey's life was in danger 10 weeks ago when she went into a coma while waiting for a kidney donor. She recovered, but doctors gave her little chance for survival unless the operation was performed quickly.
>
> A $100,000 gift from an anonymous benefactor was added to the $50,000 raised through community charity events, and a suitable kidney was obtained Monday for the child's operation.

The underlined portion of the first two paragraphs indicates necessary background information that belongs early in the continuing story. Because there is little news related to today's successful operation, more than half of the story is recapitulation of the background events: the accident, Guffey's coma setback, community involvement and locating the transplant kidney.

Perhaps the most complex type of continuing story is one that requires combining several loosely related news stories into a single coherent article:

> City police evacuated the year-old Regency Office complex downtown today in the latest incident involving Gil Robinson Concrete work.
>
> More than 800 people filed out of the Regency building at 10:30 a.m. and were sent home after police received telephone complaints about groaning noises heard on the building's fifth floor.
>
> Police Capt. Keith Honeycutt said of today's Regency evacuation, "We don't know if these were prank calls, but with recent Robinson Concrete developments, we couldn't take any chances."

Pausing at this point in the story, we can see that some readers will be lost. Today's events are included early enough, but necessary background explanation is missing. Here is the paragraph that should be the story's third graf:

> Three other construction projects, all of which had Gil Robinson Concrete as the structural subcontractor, have collapsed during the past year.

And the fifth graf might read as follows:

> Robinson is facing a grand jury investigation into quality violations in public works projects. The Hanover Street Bridge, a city water tower and a pavilion in Turner Park collapsed during September's record rains. All were Robinson Concrete jobs.

With two of the first five paragraphs providing extensive perspective on today's event, the story will return to the scene of the Regency Office complex evacuation:

1. eyewitness accounts of the building being emptied;
2. quotes from Regency tenant employers about continuation of business in the next few days;
3. quotes from city building inspectors; and
4. any further background available on the Robinson Concrete investigation.

If Gil Robinson is indicted later by the grand jury, another continuing story will be written. It will lead with the indictment, the triggering news event, and will include all of the previous incidents reported to date. These are other events that would trigger a continuing story:

1. the Regency Office building is condemned;
2. another Robinson Concrete structure falls;
3. the Regency building is deemed safe and tenants return;
4. Robinson is not indicted by the grand jury;
5. former Regency tenants announce substitute quarters for returning workers; and
6. any developments that support Gil Robinson's guilt or innocence in the construction quality violations.

In short, there is a great likelihood that the article example given will be only one of several continuing news stories on Robinson Concrete's problems.

UPDATE OR OUTCOME STORIES

Several news stories in every newspaper edition will fall into the category of updates or outcome stories. These are the continuing stories of an incident reported earlier, usually the previous day. For instance, a "manhunt" story following a crime is certain to have an update as the manhunt continues and an outcome story when the suspect is caught. Here's another original story example:

> Some 200 workers at Wilson Mfg. Co. assembly line stood idle at noon today when their union contract expired without renewal.
> Wilson management and union leaders reported yesterday that they were "hopelessly deadlocked" on a new three-year contract in which workers are seeking a $1-an-hour raise.

And the next day's outcome story:

> Triumphant plant workers at Wilson Mfg. Co. were back on the job this morning after their union secured a $1-an-hour raise at midnight.
> Plant employees successfully pressured Wilson management negotiators by engaging in a work stoppage that began at noon

yesterday when their union contract expired without being renewed.

More than half the workers attended a union meeting at 7:30 p.m. yesterday to show solidarity for the across-the-board raise.

This outcome article leads with today's news event and moves quickly into a recap of yesterday's story in the second graf. Then the story returns to more immediate news (the attendance at last night's union meeting). The remainder of the story is likely to contain quotes from management and union officials about how the settlement was reached.

Here's an update example beginning with the original news story:

About 40 patrons of the Bunny Go-Go Club at 1645 Granger Road were arrested in a police raid at 9 p.m.

Vice squad Detective Henri Poston said police got a warrant for the raid based on information that illegal drugs were being sold on the premises.

Now, the next morning's update story:

City Council member Lester Andrews was among some 15 patrons booked today for possession of cocaine following Tuesday night's drug raid at the Bunny Go-Go Club.

Andrews and eight other local residents who were booked on possession charges were released on $5,000 bond to await a trial date. Twenty-six other patrons of the club were released without being charged.

Notice that this update lead easily blends the new information of Andrews' booking with the recap on the previous night's raid. The second paragraph contains some additional reader clues that this story emanates from yesterday's article on the police raid. This story is an update rather than an outcome story because it might be assumed further developments will occur between this second-day story's publication and the trial.

CONTINUING STORIES WITH CORRECTIONS

Deadline pressures force journalists to publish stories-in-the-making: portions of news events that are certain to be less than the whole story. It happens all the time. A nearing deadline means it's time to publish the latest information obtained. Sometimes this results in a story that contains inaccuracies.

There are no excuses for failure to verify information or for carelessness. But consider the following example of a story that breaks an hour before an 11 a.m. deadline:

> Police surrounded First City Bank where an armed robber was reported holding at least five people hostage this morning.

This story may be the best a reporter could obtain by phone on a tight deadline. But notice how the event is reported on the 6 o'clock evening news:

> A SWAT team burst into First City Bank at 3 p.m. today, killing one man and capturing two others who held more than a dozen bank employees hostage.

The next edition of the paper that carried the original article must now report the continuing story and correct its mistakes from yesterday's hurried rendition.

> A police SWAT unit killed one armed robber and captured two others who held 14 First City Bank employees hostage for six hours yesterday.
>
> Two bank employees were injured during the brief shootout in the bank's lobby at 3 p.m.
>
> Police initially reported a single robber was holding half a dozen employees in the bank, but further details of the incident led to bringing in the SWAT team to free the hostages.
>
> Killed in the shootout was Chester L. Graham, 28, who was on parole from a 10-year prison term for a previous bank robbery conviction. . . .

Although the original story was accurate, at least from what was known at deadline, later information revealed several errors requiring correction in the continuing story the next day. There are two reasons for including the corrections: (1) to set the record straight and (2) to tell readers that today's story is the same incident, with some changes, as was reported originally.

It is not being suggested here that journalists should go to press with stories that might contain inaccuracies. Part of a news reporter's professional judgment is deciding when a story is ready for publication. But no news medium can provide the information its readers need to know if it delays publication unreasonably. Often the solution is to indicate in the original story that further news developments probably will follow: "Police surrounded . . . at 11 a.m. today," " . . . at press time" or some similar statement. Another writing tactic is to use heavy attribution in the story: "according to Lt. Carl Brooks at the scene of the incident."

In those circumstances where the deadline story turns out to be riddled with errors (again, it shouldn't have been published), the best method of righting the inaccuracies is to run a full correction, perhaps as a sidebar to the continuing story (sidebars are discussed in Chapter 14). Including all the corrections in the continuing story would interfere with that day's news.

SUMMARY

Although news rarely is a static occurrence, many stories must be written on deadline, before events are completed. Some news events suggest three stories: advance notice of the coming event, the coverage of the event itself and a story on its aftermath. Other events are fluid enough to suggest a number of articles over time. Continuing stories require that readers be reminded of previous related events. Often journalists include these events in complex, tie-back leads.

The chapter discusses several types of continuing stories, their structure and their complex leads. Included are tie-back stories that combine two inverted pyramid presentations simultaneously in the continuing story: today's news and previous events. Information on which the writer draws for previous events comes from carefully verified, previously published stories, never from the journalist's memory.

When the scope of previous developments demands more extensive reader backgrounding in the new story, writing the continuing story becomes more challenging. Most difficult is a continuing story that requires combining several loosely related news stories into a single coherent article.

Updates or outcome stories are the continuing stories of an incident reported earlier, usually the previous day. Such stories are a news media staple. Another media staple occurs when deadline pressures force journalists into an unfortunate form of continuing story that includes a correction of a previous day's error.

The chapter offers examples of each continuing story type with suggestions about how to write them effectively.

_____ **Thinking it Through** _____

EXERCISE 13.1

Selecting from Previous Stories

For each of the following fact sets, select three lines of information from the previous stories that will be essential in your continuing story. Write in the blanks the number of each line you select and the information you would use. List the items in their order of importance to your continuing story. The exercises may be done on a separate sheet of paper or on-screen.

A   Two years ago:

1. Sharon V. Reedy, 16, wins citywide high school science project with computer simulation of a whale's body motion.
2. Her mother is Dr. Norma Reedy, vice president of academic affairs at City Junior College here.
3. Judges marvel at the realism of Reedy's computer graphics program.
4. She wins $1,000 scholarship to the college of her choice.

Last year:

5. Sharon V. Reedy, 17, earns full tuition scholarship to Massachusetts Institute of Technology on early scholars program.
6. Reedy is the first local student to attend MIT.
7. She will take a dual major in biology and computer science.

Today's story:

Sharon V. Reedy, 18, will accept a paid summer internship with the Defense Department's Submarine Technology Center.
    Her computer simulations of whales and dolphins will be studied by the Center's scientists for possible use in structural designs for atomic submarines.

Number	Item
_____	_____
_____	_____
_____	_____

B   Last week's story:

1. Some 50 residents stage an environmental demonstration at a local tire manufacturing plant.

2. The firm's president invites three of the environmental leaders into the plant to discuss their concerns about pollution from the plant's chimneys.

3. Half a dozen of the protesters are arrested for throwing rocks through plant windows.

Yesterday's story:

4. Hattie S. Littlejohn of 805 Benton St., Apt. 10, spokeswoman for the environmentalists, holds a press conference.

5. She says the firm is "this city's worst offender of the federal Clean Air Act."

6. Littlejohn says her group intends to picket the plant "from dawn 'til dusk unless the plant installs modern equipment to reduce the pollution hazards to residents of this town."

Today's story:

Jessie D. London, president of Hardgrip Tires, says the local plant will be closed.

"We had been planning this plant closing for the past year. Meeting the United States' environmental regulations is simply not cost effective in the tire manufacturing industry," he says. "We have purchased a plant site in Mexico and will import Hardgrip Tires in the future."

Number	Item
_____	_____
_____	_____
_____	_____

C **Four years ago:**

1. Calvin B. Murray, 16, was killed when his three-wheel trail bike overturned on an incline during a supervised race here Saturday.

2. Several injuries involving the trikes were reported this spring, but this was the first local death.

3. Parents groups banded together to outlaw the sport in this county.

4. The county's single sales outlet for these three-wheel vehicles voluntarily ceased handling the trikes.

Three years ago:

5. The incidence of accidents involving three-wheel trail bikes, and charges of design instability forced the manufacturer to stop production of the vehicles.

6. More than 150 teenage deaths nationwide have been attributed to the trikes during the five years in which they've been sold.

7. Countless lawsuits claiming unsafe designs have been settled by the manufacturer for an estimated $100 million.

Today's story:

Robert C. Beale, 15, died yesterday from injuries he received when his three-wheeled trail bike overturned in a meadow near Route 7.

Beale purchased the vehicle from a used motorcycle shop in town that has been advertising the trikes for $200.

Number	Item
_____	_____
_____	_____
_____	_____

D **First day of trial:**

1. Bonnie Gentry, 26, testifies she dated Samuel Porterfield, 34, and drove a car for him when he burglarized a house in Glen Cove in August. Christine Nicks, 30, said Porterfield gave her a necklace police later identified as one stolen from the home of Mrs. Kimberly Haines, 210 Oak Haven Court.

2. Medical examiner testifies that Mrs. Haines was killed by shots fired from an automatic pistol.

3. A ballistics expert testifies that the bullets that killed Mrs. Haines were fired from Porterfield's pistol police found in his nightstand.

4. A neighbor of the Haineses testifies to seeing a car matching the description of Porterfield's parked in front of his house on the night of the murder.

Second day of trial:

5. Two witnesses testify that Porterfield was at a party with them on the night Mrs. Haines was killed.

6. Porterfield says he was at the party, became intoxicated and someone at the party took him home. He believes the man at the party stole his gun and his car, robbed the Haineses' home and killed Mrs. Haines, then brought the gun and car back to his apartment while he was asleep.

7. Porterfield cross-examination scheduled for next day.

Story for third day of trial:

Porterfield's attorney changes plea to guilty of murder in the second degree. Judge excuses jury and sets date for sentencing in two days. Guilty plea calls for minimum 15 years to life prison sentence.

Number	Item
_____	_____
_____	_____
_____	_____

E One year ago:

1. Dr. Louise Moseley, a former University of California mechanical engineering professor, opens Moseley Motors Corp., a five-person engine design firm, here with federal grants amounting to $1 million; one-third from the Small Business Administration, one-third from a minority entrepreneur grant and one-third from an alternative energy research grant.

2. Moseley says her firm holds patents on a new fuel injection system for passenger automobile engines.

3. She hopes to design a more efficient combustion system that will retain engine firing power while reducing fuel consumption levels.

Six months ago:

4. Moseley Motors Corp. announces it will manufacture a prototype engine for a full-size American automobile.

5. The firm has secured a patent for miniaturization of cylinders in an engine approximately half the size of a standard eight-cylinder automobile engine.

6. The engine functions in the usual manner, but its cylinders operate at maximum efficiency on half the gasoline flow required by a conventional gas engine.

7. Moseley's breakthrough is based on spraying gasoline vapors into the cylinders through miniaturized openings in the fuel injectors.

8. The U.S. Department of Energy has advanced Moseley Motors Corp. $100 million in plant start-up costs for the new engine.

9. Moseley Motors will expand its operation to a 350,000-square-foot manufacturing plant in the Northwood suburb.

Today's story:

The first prototype Moseley Motors Corp. engine was tested at Jensen Speedway yesterday. The vehicle, a modified Lincoln Continental, reached speeds of 100 mph and averaged 42 mpg on regular unleaded gasoline during the three-hour track test.

Two Detroit auto manufacturers placed orders for the engines amounting to more than $500 million together.

Number	Item
_____	_____
_____	_____
_____	_____

_____ **Writing Practice** _____

EXERCISE 13.2

Continuing Leads

Write a two-paragraph lead for the continuing (today's) story in each of the exercises in 13.1.

EXERCISE 13.3

Continuing Stories

Write the entire continuing story for each of the following sets. Some sets contain a single previous story; others contain more than one.

A   Yesterday's story:

"Buttons and Bows," an old-time gospel group composed of women age 65 and older, had clergymen clapping for encores on opening day of the Interfaith Convention here.

The group's 15 women, who arrived from Little Rock, Ark., in their own tour bus, played washboards, gourds and spoons in a gospel show reminiscent of a 1900s tent revival.

Rounds of applause from the 600 Interfaith delegates kept the ladies on stage nearly an hour beyond their luncheon performance and delayed the day's convention program.

Mrs. Harriett Hollister, 72, the group's leader, said, "We always get a warm welcome, but today's audience was the best yet."

She said "Buttons and Bows" is in its fifth year of touring. "Our church in Little Rock sponsored us at events in the city 10 years ago, and we began getting invitations to perform across Arkansas."

Five years ago, the demand was so great that the women used some of the church donations they received at performances to purchase a used touring bus and pay a driver, said Floree Callaway, 88, the group's oldest member.

Songs the group performs range from "When the Roll is Called Up Yonder" to spirited renditions of "Won't You Come Home, Bill Bailey."

The Rev. William N. Ames of Chicago, Interfaith president, said he heard the group perform at a retreat in Springfield, Mo. "I knew our delegates would be delighted with these ladies and their gospel music," he said. "Some of the younger clergymen had never heard church music performed on handmade instruments."

Today's story:

1. "Buttons and Bows" tour bus is hit by a truck at 8 a.m. on interstate highway two miles south of town.
2. Three women are injured; Mrs. Lottie Pickens, 78, of Little Rock, Ark., was killed in the crash.
3. The entire group of women was brought back to Lincoln Medical Clinic here for treatment or observation. No other information available about their condition at this time.
4. Group was returning to Little Rock following yesterday's performance at the Interstate Convention underway here.
5. Interstate Convention delegates observed a moment of silent prayer for Mrs. Pickens and the other injured women.

B   **Three weeks ago:**

Immigration officials arrested 22 illegal aliens at the Hutzell Pants Mfg. plant at 502 Front St. early this morning.

A dozen women, some under age 15, and 10 men were held at the Navy Reserve armory pending deportation.

R. B. Thurmond, 52, 218 Cherry Ave., owner of Hutzell Pants, was charged with violations of the child and alien worker acts. He posted $25,000 bond and was released pending a trial date.

This morning's arrests marked the fourth incident of alleged immigration violations this year.

In an 11 a.m. press conference, Mayor Christy Quinn said her administration will no longer intercede on behalf of local business owners who violate the alien employment laws.

"This administration thought federal authorities moved too swiftly in penalizing business owners under the law that went into effect Jan. 1," Quinn said. "We believed the new law didn't give owners sufficient warning, but this is the fourth local infraction." The mayor said she will not intercede in Thurmond's case or in any future violations.

Immigration officials said records confiscated at Hutzell Pants Mfg. indicated those arrested were receiving hourly wages of from $1.50 to $2, less than half of the required minimum wage.

Officer James P. Goodwin said, "The new law is designed to protect illegal aliens from corrupt employers just as it is designed to protect American workers from losing jobs to people who are forced to work for less than minimum wage."

Last week:

Gary T. Mullikin, 37, plant foreman at Hutzell Pants Mfg., was arrested and charged with violations of the child labor and alien worker laws.

Mullikin, 915 W. Cannon St., Apt. 3, is being held in County Jail pending a hearing on bail.

County Immigration Bureau Director Helen V. Durdem said a further investigation at the Hutzell plant revealed that Mullikin was responsible for hiring 22 illegal aliens who were deported two weeks ago.

"Testimony by informants at Hutzell implicated the foreman," Durdem said.

She said her Bureau is investigating allegations that Mullikin arranged transportation into the United States for the 22 workers.

"Our information suggests Mullikin may have paid as much as $20,000 in Hutzell funds to a steamship company suspected of bringing illegal workers into the country," Durdem said.

Today's story:

1. The owner and the plant foreman of Hutzell Pants Mfg. were indicted yesterday by a federal grand jury in connection with violations of the illegal alien law.

2. Thurmond and Mullikin will stand trial next month.

3. The two men are charged with conspiracy to bring more than 50 illegal aliens into the United States.

4. The charges include immigration violations connected with workers arrested at Hutzell and three previous illegal worker arrests in the city—all four local incidents involving illegal workers since the new law went into effect Jan. 1.

C Three days ago:

The majority of the student body at Centennial College held an unauthorized noon rally to protest a philosophy professor's dismissal.

At least 600 of Centennial's 1,000-member student body met in the Greek Theater on campus to hear protest speeches by 20 students in Dr. Barry Alexander's Philosophy 101 class.

Alexander, who has taught at Centennial for six years, was denied tenure three weeks ago. A termination letter to Alexander from Centennial President Nancy D. Estes was read at the rally. No reason for the tenure denial was given in Estes' letter.

Alexander, who addressed the rally, said he had been given a conference with Estes, but the president told him the college doesn't discuss reasons for tenure denial out of court.

He said he was conferring with his own lawyer about bringing suit against the college.

Alexander thanked the students for their support, but asked them not to jeopardize their own college careers by engaging in an unauthorized rally.

Gilbert S. Mason, 19, a sophomore philosophy major and one of the rally's organizers from Alexander's class, said he believed Alexander "is the best teacher at Centennial. One of his strengths is his unorthodox teaching methods designed to provoke thought about religious dogma," Mason said.

Jerilyn Holmes, 20, a junior English major and another member of Alexander's philosophy class, said Centennial College "has a long history of curbing classroom innovation." She said, "We have one of these cases every couple of years, and it's time for students to speak out against Centennial's stifling, traditional policies."

Holmes said she and Alexander's other students intend to "take a risky stand on his behalf, whether he wants our help or not."

Two days ago:

Twenty Centennial College students spent the night in the Greek Theater on campus as part of a continuing protest against the termination of a popular faculty member.

The students were all members of Dr. Barry Alexander's Philosophy 101 class at Centennial. Alexander was denied tenure, the equivalent of termination of his teaching position.

Mary W. Cutler, 18, a freshman philosophy major and class member, said the group intends to remain in the outdoor theater until Centennial authorities explain why Alexander was fired.

Centennial President Nancy D. Estes said the college "has no intention of discussing the matter with student protesters.

"We are more concerned with these students' health and safety," she said. "Security officers remained on guard duty at the Greek Theater last night to ensure the students' protection, but this unauthorized campus demonstration must end today," Estes said.

She said she has invited the 20 protesters to meet in her office this afternoon "to try to settle this misunderstanding before it ends in severe penalties to all participants."

Several hundred Centennial students joined the protesters during parts of the morning, bringing them food, drinks, blankets and books.

Yesterday's story:

Centennial College President Nancy D. Estes met with some 200 students yesterday afternoon at the Greek Theater where 20 students are engaged in a two-day protest.

The unauthorized sit-in is a protest against the dismissal of Dr. Barry Alexander, a Centennial assistant professor of philosophy.

Estes told the students they would be forcibly removed from the outdoor theater and expelled from the college if they did not return to their dormitories by nightfall.

Her remarks were drowned by shouts and jeers from the crowd when she refused to explain why Alexander was not given tenure at Centennial College.

"Our position is not to discuss tenure decisions out of court," Estes told the crowd. "This protest is not in your interests, those of the college or even Dr. Alexander's," she said.

Gilbert S. Mason, a 19-year-old sophomore philosophy major and one of the protest organizers, told Estes that "a college campus is the last place to deny explanations. We will not leave this spot until we have your reasons for firing Dr. Alexander."

Today's story:

1. President Estes reads a statement to a gathering of some 300 Centennial students in the Greek Theater on campus.

2. The statement says, in part: "Acting in their capacity as the College's Tenure and Promotion Committee, a majority of the six elected members of the Centennial faculty voted to deny Dr. Barry Alexander's tenure application on the grounds that he failed to engage in sufficient documented research and scholarship to earn tenure at this College."

3. She said attorneys for the college advised her not to reveal committee votes in tenure denials, but "This situation was getting out of hand. We don't believe in force, although you were leaving us very little choice," she tells students.

4. She said the protesting students will suffer no penalties from the College if they leave the Greek Theater before nightfall.

5. "We have met your request for an explanation in Dr. Alexander's case," Estes says. "Now we ask you to abide by the rules of this institution, to disperse peacefully and let this case be settled in a lawful manner rather than by a confrontation that no one wants to see happen."

6. At noon, all students left the Greek Theater without incident.

D   **This morning's story:**

Municipal Airport was closed late last night as a man identified as a suspended pilot threatened to explode a hijacked Federal Express 727 jet into the airport tower.

Police marksmen lined passenger concourse rooftops at midnight with orders to take any "kill shot" opportunity at the man in the cockpit of the captive taxiing jet.

The airport tower and most of the passenger facilities were evacuated by 11 p.m. No flights were scheduled before 7 a.m. today.

The man who seized the cargo jet was demanding he be reinstated as a Federal

Express pilot. He was suspended indefinitely for psychological counseling after suffering a breakdown when his wife died in July, company officials said.

According to police Capt. Frank N. DeWitt, Scott J. Barnes, 56, a 20-year pilot with the overnight parcel carrier company, gained access to the airplane at 8 p.m. by showing his former identification card to security guards at the freight terminal.

Barnes followed the usual procedure for assigned pilots to board a scheduled flight, DeWitt said, and the guards probably recognized him without realizing he had been suspended.

Police termed the situation "extremely tense" at midnight:

—Barnes had stationed the 727 jet on a runway out of rifle range of the terminal area;

—the airplane's engines were on, and the plane's nose was pointed at the airport tower;

—Barnes was negotiating with police and a Federal Express representative by radio, but police said Barnes' demands for assurances had changed several times as had his deadline for exploding the plane into the tower;

—police said it appeared Barnes was willing to kill himself in the threatened crash and had been talked out of doing so twice during the four-hour standoff;

—federal tactical units in military vehicles were brought to the scene but kept hidden from sight of the jet.

Today's story:

(You are writing for an afternoon newspaper with an 11 a.m. deadline for the first edition; street delivery at 2:30 p.m. Consider that radio and television will have carried much of the "headline" news on this major breaking story during the morning hours.)

1. After setting several deadlines, Barnes radioed that he was done talking. At 2 a.m. he throttled the jet's engines and the plane rolled toward the Municipal Airport tower, gaining speed as it approached.

2. Two tactical squads of federal agents moved into position, forming a "V" with the tower. They waited until the plane came within range of the sharpshooters.

3. Several rifle shots burst the jet's cabin windows, possibly killing Barnes, but the plane retained its course toward the tower.

4. The tactical units fired bazookas at the cockpit of the plane, exploding the nose and the pilots' cabin, but the jet had attained a speed that took it past the agents and into the tower.

5. One of the jet's wings hit the tower, and the jet burst into flames. Portions of the wing exploded, sending shards of burning metal across the tarmac and showering one of the groups of federal agents.

6. Firefighting teams stationed near the tower doused the plane and tower with spray and had the fire under control within 10 minutes.

7. The tower was blackened by smoke from the burning plane but remained standing. Airport officials said it would be inspected for structural integrity before it is reopened.

8. One federal agent in the tactical unit was killed by portions of the jet's wing; two others were injured and taken to St. Michael's Hospital, where both were listed in critical condition at 10 a.m. today.

9. Barnes' body was found in the plane's fuselage.

10. Airport authorities said Municipal Airport was operating as usual beginning with its earliest flights this morning. Air traffic controllers were working temporarily out of the old tower, which is suitable as a backup, authorities said. They estimated $500,000 in damage to the tarmac and tower, assuming the tower was not damaged structurally.

11. Barnes' picture had been posted in the overnight carrier's office, and security guards had been warned about Barnes' suspension, Federal Express representatives said. However, in his pilot's uniform and with his identification card, it was understandable that he gained easy access to the waiting airplane, they said. They reported Barnes had been given a pension and was under psychiatric care paid for by the company. The 727 jet was worth $2.5 million.

Sidebars, Color Stories and Profiles

Newspapers, television, radio, newsletters, magazines and brochures . . . in fact all mass communication media use forms of sidebars, color stories and profiles to give audiences the complete story. When a news event is multi-dimensional, and when one of those dimensions qualifies as a separate news story in its own right, a sidebar, color story or profile is written to accompany the main news story.

Consider a major corporation in your city holding its annual shareholders' meeting. The company's president, in a surprise statement, announces his retirement effective today. Joan R. Haley, the firm's comptroller, will become the new president. Several rumored plant and product development changes are announced by Haley before the shareholders' meeting ends. A local news story on these events will contain three major elements: (1) a focus on Haley's being named the new corporation president, (2) information about the retiring president and (3) the plant/product changes. However, two of these elements suggest separate news stories: one profiling the former president, his career and successes with the company; the other profiling Haley, her career and future plans. Newspaper readers might expect a picture of each person to accompany the profile article, which would also contain some quotes and information on family and community involvement. The two profile stories might be combined in a single sidebar with the theme "president retires, new president takes reins."

The point here is that this major local news event deserves more depth than a single long story can successfully provide. Many readers, especially corporation employees, will want to know as much as possible about the two people in the news. Perhaps Joan Haley was known to local residents only as a name on this corporation's organizational chart. News audiences will be drawn to information about her. Although the retiring president is likely to be a prominent community member, audiences will be interested in reviewing his career with the firm, learning why he decided to retire at this time and knowing his personal plans for the future. That story serves as a tribute to a notable local citizen, and readers will be drawn to it with nearly equal interest.

Could a single story do justice to this multidimensional news event? The answer is yes, but not with as much impact as these several dimensions can be given through a main news story and one or two profile sidebars. We know that the first three paragraphs of a single story would provide highlights of all three news elements (both presidents and the plant/product changes). But the personal profile information on the story's two main characters would begin late in the story, perhaps a dozen or more paragraphs down. Multiple stories placed in close proximity to one another would offer more details and would do so beginning earlier in each story. Figure 14.1 suggests how such stories might increase reader attention to the news event.

The increased effect on audience attention seen in Figure 14.1 would be true for any of the print media. Although perhaps not as obvious as in this visual depiction, multiple story treatment in the electronic media provides similarly increased impact for broadcast news audiences. A television newscast would lead with the main story followed by separate interviews with Haley and the retiring president as part of the report package.

Many news stories have enough angles to suggest separate treatment for one of the story aspects. *Sidebar* is the generic term for a separate-but-related story; color stories and profiles are two distinctive sidebar subcategories.

SIDEBARS

Some points that distinguish sidebars are that they:

1. relate to a main news story; this means the news event must be
   a. significant enough to justify more than one story,
   b. multidimensional enough to require separate coverage of at least one main story aspect and

Columbia Corp. names new president

Joan R. Haley, former comptroller at Columbia Corp., became the firm's third president as John D. Anthony took early retirement at the stockholders' annual meeting here Friday.

Columbia announced plans for a major plant expansion expected to add 250 more local jobs within a year. A $3.5 million factory addition is expected to make Columbia a leader in the cellular telephone industry nationally, Haley said after she accepted the firm's presidency.

Anthony managed to keep his retirement plans secret from all but the nine Columbia board of . . .

Haley gets Columbia leader role

After 21 years of work, night school and an MBA degree, Joan R. Haley, 53, of 2119 Ridgeway Place took the reins of

Anthony has 'dream of sun, sailing'

"CEO's ought to sail away when their ship is riding at high tide," John D. Anthony said Friday.

At 62, the 12-year

Figure 14.1 Main news story with two profiles

    c. clearly more newsworthy than the subject of the sidebar (otherwise the sidebar would have been the main news story);

2. accompany the main news story; sidebars are
   a. published at the same time,
   b. adjacent or in close proximity to the main story and
   c. have enough content overlap so the audience recognizes a relationship;

3. embellish the main news story:
   a. add force or focus,
   b. provide additional facts or
   c. offer perspective to help audiences grasp the context of today's news in relation to other news events.

Obviously there are too many rules here to serve as practical guidelines. Thus, rather than focusing on individual points, the following discussion highlights several types of sidebar story examples.

Fires are everyday events in most cities, but a fire worthy of headline attention might occur once or twice a year. Let's say it's a fire outside of town that destroys a home on the National Register. Fortunately, no one was injured because the current owners purchased the house recently and were having it restored before living there. The main news story would relate to the fire itself: how much damage was done; its cause; firefighters, neighbors and the owners called to the scene; and owner plans for rebuilding.

Additional information in the main news story would include some description of the house, its historical significance to the community and its current value; and some mention of any comparable homes in the area. A chronological presentation of noteworthy historic developments associated with the house would begin deep into the fire story.

But a better treatment of the historic highlights would be as a sidebar to the fire story. News audiences, even lifelong local residents, will want to canvass such facts as who built the house, when and why; what prominent citizens owned it; when it was last restored; and so on. This information deserves more attention than it could receive buried at the bottom of the fire story. Figure 14.2 shows how the story might be

Lightning bolt destroys Oakshadow

Oakshadow, the area's oldest home, was destroyed by a single lightning bolt in Tuesday night's electrical storm, county fire officials said.

The house, which was listed on the National Register as it marked its 150th birthday in 1990, collapsed at 10:30 p.m. County firefighters were called to the blaze at 9 p.m. and spent an hour drenching water on the house to no avail.

No injuries were reported as the house has been vacant pending renovation by the new owners who purchased . . .

Long journey to list of historic sites

Fire ended 150 years of events at Oakshadow that paralleled the history of Winn County.

• 1840 – Henry Winn Claybrook, territorial magistrate, completed the home for $8,500.

• 1863 – Confederate soldiers occupied . . .

Figure 14.2   Sidebar listing of historic events

handled to emphasize these significant developments in the destroyed home's history.

Because this sidebar is a listing rather than a complete news story, it doesn't demonstrate all of the subtler points about sidebars mentioned earlier. Yet it does show how readers can be better served when an important aspect of a main story becomes a separate story. The following example covers more sidebar elements.

In your community, social service agencies have been working with local women's interest groups to help solve the problem of temporary shelter and security for victims of family abuse. Camp Buttress, a 10-acre preserve in a pine forest not far from the city, was built with $500,000 in federal grants as an experiment in emergency housing for women and children referred to the camp by judges presiding over family criminal abuse cases. Mothers and their children may stay at the camp for an unspecified period or until their case is settled. The issue has received extensive local media coverage for more than a year. Camp Buttress opened this weekend, and a media tour was scheduled although officials asked that details about location, security and current residents not be revealed. Some news media might refuse to cover such an event because agreeing to conceal information from the public raises ethical concerns (discussed in Chapter 17). However, most news media would honor the officials' request to cooperate as long as it was not a prerequisite for covering the opening. Here is the beginning of the main story and sidebar on the camp:

Main News Story

Camp Buttress, the government's experiment to provide family protection to victims of abuse, opened for business this weekend.

Nestled in the pine forests some 10 miles from Centerville, the $500,000 facility has 24 three-room log cabins, a recreation building and an outdoor park with swings and climbing equipment.

"It's a peaceful setting," Mayor Wes Jackson said, "and we intend to keep it that way."

Jackson and six HUD offi-

Sidebar

A 5-year-old boy whose fractured jaws were wired together three days ago, attempted his first smile.

Jane, his mother, said, "This is the first time I've felt safe since my wedding day."

Her son's eyes sparkled in agreement.

The two were among 35 people transferred from a halfway house in the city to a rustic site called Camp Buttress, an experimental protective compound for abused women and children that opened this weekend.

Main News Story (continued)

cials from Washington, D.C.,
hosted a low-key ribbon-cutting
Sunday for Camp Buttress,
which officials asked be kept in
relative obscurity because of its
protective purpose.

However, they pointed to
some high-security devices such
as an iron fence circling the
compound and 24-hour patrols
by armed guards.

Mona Pendergast, a deputy
secretary at HUD, said, "We intend to ensure the safety of
these families and offer them
sanctuary in pleasant surroundings where they can renew their
faith in society."

Pendergast said the Camp
Buttress experiment will "be the
stopgap refuge that protects victims until our legal system provides a more permanent
solution to their problems."

Mayor Jackson said the facility offers the comforts of a rustic home. "There isn't anything
flashy about the place, but
these families seem to feel
happy and safe here. That's exactly what we were trying to
accomplish when we asked the
government to fund this experiment," he said.

Sidebar (continued)

Another mother, call her
Mary, served her two daughters
a pancake lunch on plastic din-
nerware. Dressed in a silk
blouse and designer jeans,
Mary obviously was used to a
more comfortable lifestyle, but
she didn't complain.

Her left cheek was still
swollen from stitches she received in an emergency room
last week.

"I wouldn't trade this place
for a table at the Ritz," she
said. "My girls and I are safe
here. We have what we need,
and we've got a lot of family
bonding to catch up on . . . just
the three of us this time."

Boys and girls, from toddlers
to teenagers, played on the
swings and walked the grounds
discovering their new surroundings and enjoying the serenity
of the pine forest that became
their new temporary home.

Susan, 7, wasn't as lucky as
most of the other children. She
has been in a wheelchair since
her legs were fractured two
years ago.

"I'm going to go out later
and watch them play," she said.
"Mommy will push me."

Ellen, a sister of one new resident, brought some toiletries to
the camp. She said she heard
her niece laugh "for the first
time in a long, long time.

"In that instant, I sensed
what this place is really about,"
she said.

The main story is an inverted pyramid-style news article on the opening of this experimental family shelter. It has facts and figures, and quotes from official sources. The sidebar is a human-interest featurette that gives readers the personal perspective on the news event: what life is like at Camp Buttress, and a hint of what the life that brought them there might have been like.

This example offers several additional clues about possible differences between sidebars and their related main news story. The first is focus. The main story usually contains more straight facts; the sidebar is likely to be more featurized, stressing tone. The news story *tells* the event; the sidebar *shows* it. If the main news story contained a human element mixed with its facts, there would be little need for a sidebar. The Camp Buttress story is a good example. Had it been written as a single story (space considerations often make editors insist on one story), it might have begun:

> A 5-year-old boy whose fractured jaw was wired together three days ago attempted his first smile Monday.
>
> Jane, his mother, said, "This is the first time I've felt safe since my wedding day." Her son's eyes sparkled in agreement.
>
> The two were among some 35 family abuse victims who began temporary residence at Camp Buttress, a $500,000 rural experimental shelter, opened by government and local officials this weekend.

A single story on this human services topic ought to contain some feel for the people at Camp Buttress and why they are there, so a featurized news story is appropriate. However, it's evident from the single story's beginning that combining necessary facts about the camp with the human interest element will reduce the human element's impact. Separating fact in the main news story from feature in the sidebar is a better approach.

Actually, separation is the second clue and one of the key points to remember about news story and sidebar differences. The example indicates that the writer purposely tried to maximize the fact/feature separation between the two stories. Doing so makes perfect sense because separating the two elements reduces duplication. An assumption with sidebars is that the audience will be compelled to read both stories, and that the information in the sidebar is newsworthy enough to deserve separate treatment. Content of the two stories should not overlap.

But complete separation is a grave journalistic error. News media space and time constraints preclude any guarantee that the main news story and the sidebar will be adjacent, although the writer approaches the sidebar task with that in mind. Still, it isn't unusual for the main news story to appear on page one or page six of the paper and the sidebar to run on page four or page 12. There's no guarantee which story readers will see first. Therefore, the sidebar must contain a reference to the main news story, and the reference must be high enough in the sidebar story so readers understand that this story is closely associated with another news story. The example gives that connection in the fourth paragraph of the sidebar:

> The two were among 35 people transferred from a halfway house in the city to a rustic site called Camp Buttress, an experimental protective compound for abused women and children that opened this weekend.

Including this information early in the sidebar is essential for readers to understand that this story goes with another story. We might think that an editor will insert a boldfaced reference to the main news story, such as "See Camp Opening, Page 1," but the writer cannot take such a reference for granted. Instead, the sidebar writer must ensure that readers clearly understand what this children and mothers story is all about by including a link to the main story. True, the reference paragraph in the sidebar does overlap the main news story, but this overlap is crucial. Exactly how much overlapping reference is needed? Just enough—and just high enough in the sidebar—to guarantee that readers will understand that this story is related to another news article.

A third clue to sidebar differences is structure: The main story is likely to be an inverted pyramid news article; the sidebar probably will not be. Both the Oakshadow house fire and the Camp Buttress examples offer inverted pyramid news articles and sidebars with different structures. Oakshadow's was a listing; Camp Buttress was a human-interest feature. While structural differences improve separation of the sidebar and its associated news story, it is certainly possible for a sidebar's structure to match that of the main news story: both could be inverted pyramid articles.

Associated with story structure, length is another clue to differences in the two story forms. While there is no law about length, in most instances the sidebar will be shorter than the main news story. This makes sense because the sidebar, after all, is a secondary aspect of the main news story. Chances are that if the main story was short, the information selected for the sidebar would fit easily into the news story. Its impact would not be compromised by being buried near the end of a long story.

Finally, in case there was any doubt, the main news story can be written by one journalist, the sidebar by another. Important breaking

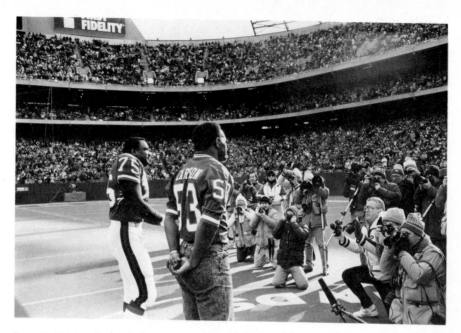

Sports journalists converge on the field to report retirement ceremonies for New York Giants football great Harry Carson (53). The day's main news story will be the outcome of the game. Carson's retirement will be a human interest sidebar that sports fans might remember long after today's score is forgotten.

news stories frequently are covered by two or more reporters, one assigned to do the main news story, the other to do the sidebar. The Oakshadow house fire story is a probable example of such coverage. Monitoring the fire station's citizen band radio channel, an editor might send one reporter out to the scene. That reporter would be instructed to send back a story on the fire. Even before the house actually collapsed at 10:30 p.m., a second writer would be assigned to search the newspaper's morgue files and write the sidebar on the history of Oakshadow.

This general overview of sidebars leads to discussion of several more specific types of sidebar stories.

COLOR STORIES

A wide but amorphous category of sidebars can be placed under the general heading of color stories or featurized approaches to a main news story. Emphasizing the human element of straight news through a sidebar is a time-tested tactic to make the day's news more memorable. A separate-but-associated story frees writers to accentuate the personal perspective without being tangled in necessary news value presentation. Unshackled, the color story pumps emotion at full power.

The "sob story," or empathy sidebar, is one example. Given its head, the Camp Buttress sidebar might have become a sob story. Interviews with disaster survivors or the relatives of victims suggest an empathy color story treatment. By their nature, sob stories rely on heavy human interest appeal although the sidebar themes can be either sad or happy:

> "It was like having him come back from the grave," Becky Nolan said.
>
> "I was so happy when I seen him brought out of the mine, I just fell to my knees and cried my thanks to the Lord."
>
> No one had waited longer or had more at stake than Mrs. Nolan when the foreman of St. George's Mine told her three days ago that her husband of 32 years was trapped in a shaft nearly two miles underground.
>
> No one was as elated as she when John F. Nolan was brought safely to the earth's surface early this morning.
>
> Becky Nolan hadn't slept for 38 hours. Her only comforts were her white cardigan sweater, turned a sooty gray during the ordeal, and a thermos of coffee given to her by one of the rescue workers.
>
> "When Earle told me John was trapped down there, I decided I would wait as long as it took. . . ."

The critical aspect of empathy color stories is that the facts must support the heavy emotive tone. If Becky Nolan's vigil had been less intense, the sob story would be a sham; readers quickly would discern its artificiality. But if Becky's story weren't worth telling, no sidebar would be suggested. The wife's reaction would be captured as part of the main news story. Assuming the facts do prompt a sob story approach, the journalist should exploit every good writing strategy to maximize reader empathy. Don't stretch the truth, but don't be embarrassed to emphasize the sob story's legitimate poignancy.

Another form of color story is called a reaction sidebar. It, too, is an interview-based article, but it usually involves interviews with several people more distant from the story rather than with only one or two people who are very close to it. This sidebar form is similar to street interviews with people who are only loosely related to an important news event.

> "If I knew I was going to get caught up in this thing, heck, I'd have signed up," said Merl Arnett, 30, a Bixby resident who lost six pounds.

Ruth L. Gary, 47, a Bixbian who did participate, said she thought dieting for a cause "beats dieting for vanity. I took off nine pounds, and it's gonna stay off."

Mrs. Gary's nine pounds was the average resident's three-month weight loss that won $200,000 for the Bixby Public Library in Trim'n Slim's national challenge contest.

But winning wasn't a piece of cake for everyone.

"I never thought we had a chance, so I kept falling off the diet," said Barbara Overton, 26, of 311 W. Glade Road. She said she actually gained two pounds by the second week. "I guess my system reacted negatively at first, but I lost nearly two pounds every week I followed the diet after that," she said. Miss Overton finished with an eight-pound loss.

"It made me sick as a dog," said Keith Forsyth, 35, of 405 Duke St. "I'm a proud Bixby native, so I waited until the last two weeks and drank one glass of the stuff every other day. I couldn't hold anything down, so I lost 15 pounds," a triumphant Forsyth said.

*   *   *

They had been a "couple" since kindergarten.

Everybody knew that Jeffery Shaver would marry Tracy Evans as soon as the two 16-year-olds graduated from high school.

Instead the couple was found asphyxiated in the Shaver basement yesterday, bringing the number of teenage suicide victims in the Baltimore metropolitan area this year to six.

"There's just no reason I can think of," said Julie Burson, 16, Tracy's closest girlfriend.

Julie, pallid against her pink housecoat, was under sedation as she tried to answer detectives' questions. But it was a tearful struggle from a dazed and grieving friend with no inkling of why the tragedy occurred.

Others who knew Jeffery and Tracy were equally stunned by their death.

"Those two were inseparable," said Mrs. Susan M. Ward, their ninth grade teacher at Raleigh Junior High. "They studied together so much that they'd get the same score on their tests."

Reaction sidebars often accompany a second-day or continuing news story because of the difficulty in contacting several sources somewhat removed from the incident. However, a wide variety of important news events prompt such reflective treatment as an appropriate method of providing complete media coverage.

The last distinct category of color stories is the mood sidebar. Here, through superior writing, the journalist attempts to capture people's general mood in relation to the main news event.

A story of substantial importance to a local or national audience suggests doing a mood sidebar. For instance, the aftermath news story of a tornado or flood assesses the damage, provides facts about the number of dead and injured, and gives disaster relief information. But the main news story's factual approach can't capture how survivors, methodically picking through the ruins of their homes and possessions, feel about what happened. A mood sidebar can capture those feelings.

However, news events other than disasters also suggest mood sidebars:

> Laughing waitresses carrying manhole cover-size platters of tamales in arms stretched toward the ceiling twisted through the butcher paper-sheathed tables.
>
> Shouts of jubilance rang in Spanish Town's Casa del Pueblo center as couples hugged and toasted friends with 24-ounce glasses of draft beer.
>
> The celebration lasted until dawn: a fitting tribute to the government's decision of amnesty for Hispanic Americans who can prove they have been in the United States more than five years.
>
> Mrs. Tina García of 10407 Herald St. flopped into a folding chair after dancing a spirited reel with her 9-year-old daughter. Her breathlessness was no deterrent to her joy. "Que Dios bendiga a América—God bless America," she said.
>
> José, Tina's husband, said his wife's sister and her three children have been living in fear since 1983.
>
> "No more," he said. "They will be first in line at the court steps Monday morning."
>
> A more somber attitude contrasted the night's revelry at a few tables where toasts were made to those who had been sent back and to those whose time in the United States would not qualify them for the amnesty.
>
> "We salute our compatriots who must wait their turn," said Thomas B. Diago. . . .

The mood sidebar shares several attributes with the other forms of color stories described: (1) more flowery writing; (2) simplicity in presentation; (3) devotion to the facts; and (4) adherence to journalistic honesty in portrayal.

Most of the examples contain more descriptive and flowery writing than is expected in a straight news story. This is acceptable in featurized articles that stress emotion. It is, after all, the basis for calling these sidebars color stories. Still, each of the examples derives its impact from simplicity in presentation rather than a melodramatic writing style. Too much sentimentality in the writing will give an impression of unreality that interferes with the empathy readers should feel. Like using a short lead on a momentous news story, simplicity makes the color story more powerful.

The last two attributes color stories should share are related. Color stories are real news stories and demand adherence to the facts and journalistic honesty. Although the writer is using every legitimate maneuver to evoke audience emotion, the story facts must set the presentation boundaries. If there were 100 people in the Casa del Pueblo, don't paint a picture that suggests there were thousands. Tell readers how many pounds each of Bixby's quoted residents lost during the contest. If Becky Nolan said "seen him brought out of the mine," use her exact words. Color stories allow a little more flexibility in writing style, but journalists aren't given "poetic license" to create a fictitious impression.

Finally, a reminder about repetition between sidebar and main news story. Notice that each of the color story examples contains a linking paragraph to the news story high in the sidebar's lead. The repeated material is concise. It is only enough to let readers understand that this color story is associated with a related story, even if the two stories happen to run side by side. Too much repetition between the two articles will disrupt both stories' readability.

PROFILES

Profile sidebars are not personality profile features that require several hours of interviews with the subject and are intended to be published alone (these are covered in Chapter 15). Instead, the profile sidebar is designed to accompany a news story, one in which the profiled individual plays a prominent role.

Most news stories are about people, and most of those individuals can be portrayed adequately (in proportion to their newsworthiness) in the news story without any consideration of doing a sidebar. But when news events are significant or complex enough to require lengthy coverage, and the person's characterization would interfere with or be buried at the bottom of the news story, a profile sidebar should be considered.

For example, the news story involves the murder of a community leader during the burglary of his home last night. A silent alarm brings police to the man's house in time to catch the fleeing burglar as he leaps over the back fence. There is a car chase that ends with the culprit's vehicle running off a bridge embankment and crashing into a culvert below, killing the man. This news story will be a lengthy, front-page article. It should be accompanied by a sidebar with a picture of the prominent citizen who was murdered. In this case, the profile sidebar will be a death story of the community leader.

If the event is a civic club banquet that includes a speech by a national celebrity and several awards to local citizens, the main news story will cover the banquet and the speech. A profile sidebar on the foremost award recipient might accompany the main news story:

> He remembers the cotton field on which Southgate Mall was built because he spent most of his summers in its furrows with his family.
>
> He says that rubbing the calluses on his palms and fingers still reminds him of picking cotton with the sun beating down on dozens of his neighbors in the rows of that field.
>
> Judge Tyrone Henry Masters hasn't forgotten those days of his youth, but his life now resembles that of a segregation-era field hand about as much as the cotton field resembles the Southgate Mall.
>
> Masters, 56, won the Humanitarian Society's Medallion of Honor last night, the most prestigious distinction given by a Williamsport civic group.
>
> The fourth son among seven siblings, Tyrone was born in the hand-hewn oak bed his grandfather made as a wedding present to Tyrone's parents. The extended family of 12 lived in a three-room "shotgun" shack with tar paper interior walls and a leaky tin roof scavenged from a salvage lot.
>
> "My folks told us all that education was our only chance to make a better life," Masters said. He attended segregated city schools and was Lincoln High's valedictorian in 1954, the year Brown v. Board of Education of Topeka ended school segregation. Princeton gave Masters a full-tuition scholarship. . . .

The profile sidebar will recount major events in Judge Master's life and his foremost accomplishments. As it relates reasons why Masters won the medallion, it provides description, quotes and insights about the man that help readers understand the significance of this news event. The sidebar presents a more complete and personal story than could be woven into the main news story on the banquet and speaker.

Securing the information for the Masters profile is relatively easy. The news media are likely to receive information about the award winner from the civic organization prior to the banquet. A reporter supplements this news release with information from morgue file stories on the recipient. Quotes come from what the judge says when he accepts the award, and a good reporter gets a half-hour interview with Masters before leaving the banquet. This profile sidebar, together with the main story, is a compelling package for local audiences.

How frequently do events prompt profile sidebars? Although profiles are one of the more common forms of sidebars, there are probably more than half a dozen justifiable opportunities to do a profile piece for every one that is written. One reason for the omission, mentioned earlier, is lack of space or time. But the more likely explanation is that journalists too frequently forget that people enjoy learning about other people, particularly those in the news. The person behind the story very often is the real story.

SUMMARY

All mass media use forms of sidebars, color stories and profiles to give audiences the complete story. A sidebar is suggested from a multidimensional news event, when one or more aspects of the event qualify for a separate news story.

Some rules for sidebars are that they (1) relate to a main news story, (2) accompany the main news story and (3) embellish the main news story. These differences between main news stories and sidebars are delineated:

1. Focus. The main story usually contains straight facts while the sidebar is more featurized, stressing tone. The news story *tells* the event; the sidebar *shows* it.

2. Separation/overlap. Although the sidebar writer tries to separate fact/feature and other content between the two stories, every sidebar must contain a reference to the main news story. This brief overlap must be high enough in the sidebar so readers know that this story is closely associated with another news story.

3. Structure. The main story is likely to be an inverted pyramid news article; the sidebar probably will not be.

4. Length. There is no law about length, but in most instances a sidebar will be a shorter story than the main news story.

5. Writer. The main news story can be written by one journalist, the sidebar by another. In fact, this happens frequently.

Through a series of examples, the chapter discusses several types of sidebar stories, including color stories with their subcategories of "sob stories," reaction and mood sidebars, and profile sidebars.

_____ **Thinking it Through** _____

EXERCISE 14.1

Identifying Sidebar Opportunities

For each of these fact sets, first select an element of the story on which a sidebar should be written. Next, identify what kind of sidebar should be written from the list provided here. Finally, list elements of content the sidebar ought to contain.

historic highlights   reaction sidebar
featurette   mood sidebar
sob story   profile sidebar

A Federal narcotics agents seized cocaine with a street value estimated at more than $200 million late yesterday afternoon. Some 60 federal agents with Coast Guard and helicopter backup units surrounded PetCo Industries, a cat food canning plant, at 4:30 p.m. Twenty-eight plant workers were taken into custody. At the same time PetCo was surrounded, agents arrested alleged cocaine kingpin Jack V. Gray at his Robinpoint estate. Gray, known in the underworld as "Crackerjack," has 15 previous drug-related arrests and has been indicted four times in the last 10 years. Agents said records filed two years ago by PetCo showed the firm was purchased by Jackknife Properties, which authorities have insisted is Gray's corporate front for drug trafficking. "We've been after Crackerjack Gray for a long time," Agent Pat Bradshaw said. "This time we've got him where we want him, with two years of records and 20 witnesses to testify."

Best sidebar topic: _____

Type of sidebar: _____

Elements to include:

1.

2.

3.

B Dr. Sylvia Higgins, director of biomedical genetics at Preston Labs Inc., has identified the cause of Lou Gehrig's disease. The degenerative disease, which attacks the nervous system of middle-aged people, primarily males, was named for the baseball player who died from it. Medical term for the syndrome is amyotrophic lateral sclerosis (ALS). A fatal disease for which no cure is known and no cause was known previously, ALS affects more than 30,000 people per year, 80 percent of whom die in under five years. Higgins, 39, who had three other important genetic breakthroughs before being named a Preston research director in 1989, discovered a genetic abnormality in blood samples of persons diagnosed with ALS. Preston officials, in a joint announcement with the Surgeon General's Office, said they believe a cure for ALS is at least five years away, but Dr. Higgins' medical discovery ranks with Salk's polio vaccine in the late 1950s.

Best sidebar topic: _____

Type of sidebar: _____

Elements to include:

1.

2.

3.

C The FBI's five-day manhunt for serial killer Frank W. Grimes, 28, ended this morning when the suspect was killed in a shootout at his motel room here. FBI agents working with local police received a tip that Grimes was in the motel. They called for his surrender at daylight today. Grimes opened fire from the motel room window, and police pumped teargas canisters into the room in an attempt to subdue him. Grimes burst through the front door firing a shotgun. Police returned fire with automatic weapons. Grimes was on the FBI's top-10 wanted list for a series of stabbing deaths of teenage girls. At least 12 victims were found in motel rooms from Idaho to Louisiana, including his latest two victims found in this state last month. Grimes escaped from a federal high-security prison last year where he was serving a 20-year-to-life sentence for second-degree murder.

Best sidebar topic: _____

Type of sidebar: _____

Elements to include:

1.

2.

3.

D It was a sleepy town of 2,300, one of those railroad stops that never quite developed during the 1930s. At that time local businessmen hoped that the thriving little community of 5,000 would become a major link between rail lines, but the war and the decline of passenger service during the 1950s ended those hopes. Instead the interstate highway system missed the place by nearly 10 miles, and the town's largest employer became a school for the blind located just off the Amtrack line in downtown Fairbanks. Then, Saturday afternoon, a 14-car Amtrack train hit a gasoline truck that didn't quite clear the tracks in time. It happened just in front of the school. The tanker truck exploded; the train derailed. Almost one-third of the school building was destroyed in the blast. The death count in the school building was 17; five people on the train were killed. Hospitals in your city, about 125 miles from Fairbanks, received the injured: 22 students and 13 employees from the school for the blind; 18 from the train. It's now late Saturday night. Your editor dispatches two reporters to Fairbanks to send back stories for Monday morning's paper. A colleague will do the aftermath news story; you do the sidebar.

Best sidebar topic: _____

Type of sidebar: _____

Elements to include:

1.

2.

3.

E   A local author's latest novel made the New York Times Best Seller List this week. She is Fern Foster, 50, an English professor at Centennial College. She tells you her new book is the last in a series of novels on her life experiences during the 1960s. Although Foster has authored eight novels, the first four, reflective of her youth and school years, did not receive much recognition or popular success. She began to get some regional attention with her fifth novel about life in the Haight Asbury district of San Francisco. Two others followed about life in Detroit and on a commune in Utah, both books gaining in literary acclaim. The new novel focuses on a group of young people travelling to Woodstock, N.Y., for the music festival. Movie rights to the new novel and portions of her last three works have been purchased by Paramount for $500,000. The main news story will give quotes from Foster, details about the new novel's success, her plans for the near future with the college and making the film.

Best sidebar topic: _____

Type of sidebar: _____

Elements to include:

1.

2.

3.

_____ **Writing Practice** _____

EXERCISE 14.2

Sidebar Leads

Write at least three paragraphs to begin each of the sidebars you described in Exercise 14.1. Be sure to include an "overlap" sentence or paragraph to link your sidebar lead to the main news story.

EXERCISE 14.3

Sidebar Stories

Each of the following exercises contains several paragraphs from a main news story and information that can be used to write a sidebar. Using the facts, descriptions and quotes given in each set, write a sidebar designed to be published at the same time as its associated main news story.

A Main News Story:

A packed coliseum rocked until 11:30 p.m. last night in one of the longest concert performances in the long career of the band "Chicago."

Some 12,000 fans of the 1960s band, which has maintained hit albums through the 1980s, stood and applauded for an hour and a half beginning at 10 p.m. "Chicago" is known for giving few if any encores after a two-hour performance.

Although some fans filed out of the coliseum after 10:30 p.m., exit traffic still jammed the parking lot at midnight.

The band followed its usual selection format of leading with original compositions not yet recorded, then playing its most recent album material followed by a few selections from the 1960s and 1970s hits.

Sidebar Information:*

At 6:30 p.m., you were in the "Chicago" dressing room for interviews with band members prior to the 8 p.m. performance. This is the first experience you've had covering a band that has been touring for 20 years, and you were struck by the nervousness of these seasoned performers.

The dressing room is relatively large for the six performers and two stage managers. It's a well-lighted place with 15 individual dressing tables, a bar, wardrobe racks and three couches. Several large bouquets of flowers from "Chicago" fans adorn the tables, along with some boxes of pastries from a local bakery. Band members pace between the bar, the pastry and the dressing mirrors. They make small talk, worry about their outfits (mostly T-shirts and jeans), joke and talk about stage settings for the performance.

From guitarist Daniel Cummings Jr.: "It's the music. We live for a good performance, even after more than 20 years. When the music is right, it justifies our lives. When it doesn't go so well, which is usually, we feel it. After so many years, you can't expect perfection, but we still try to reach it in every show."

* names are fictional

From drummer Jimmy P. Jaynes: "We know the audience likes it. Whether it's good or not-so-good, they appreciate it. Reviewers usually say the show was outstanding, even when we know it wasn't. But if we just went out there and did our songs, and we didn't care whether it was our best shot, we might as well be selling shoes. It's surprising that after 20 years we can still feel that way, but come backstage tomorrow night and I'll say the same thing."

From trumpet player Neal Graham: "We're not one of these neighborhood garage bands that lucked up and got some good gigs. All of us are serious musicians who went to school or spent some years on the road of hard knocks. We write our own stuff; we orchestrate it. The music means something to us. We don't go in for the theatrics most of the pop groups rely on today: no fireworks, no sequined costumes, no gyrations, no stage props. We could perform outside in the dark and be just as entertaining."

From Nathan Blalock, manager: "That's just how they are. There were a few times back in the 1970s when the guys got disgusted and it was all I could do to get them back on stage after the break. If they hadn't been under signed contracts, they wouldn't have gone back out. So I said, 'Hey, nobody out there heard anything but greatness from you guys. There can't be more than a dozen people in the audience who heard a sour note or a timing error in any song you played.' But these guys are 'Chicago''s worst critics. They want every performance to be studio quality on the first take. That's what makes it right for them."

From Angela Eldridge, sound technician: "It's like Jimmy said. They're the only ones who detect the problems. Yeah, I know too, but I've been on the road with them for six years now. That's long enough to have seen a few good nights when everything went right: the music, the sound, the audience, everything. That's when they do encores, when they want to make it last. But it doesn't happen very often, and they know it. So they get edgy and temperamental before every performance. You could cut the paranoia with a knife."

A stagehand comes to the dressing room at 7:50 p.m. and says, "It's show time." The band members amble out the door to wait in the wings for the curtain to rise. They carry their drinks out with them. Neal Graham returns and walks toward one of the couches. "Forgot my trumpet," he says.

B The National Association of Pawnbrokers holds its annual convention in your town. You are assigned to cover the convention's business meeting today.

Main News Story:

A fund that should exceed $2 million was established to provide rewards in excess of $25,000 for information leading to the arrest and conviction of persons who rob pawnshops.

The action was taken at this morning's business meeting of the National Association of Pawnbrokers convention at Bergin Civic Hall.

Annual dues of $100 were assessed for the 2,600-member NAP after convention delegates narrowly defeated a resolution condemning law enforcement for "failure to ensure the safety and property of pawnshop owners across America."

Although delegates said they were angry that the incidence of pawn shop holdups has increased since 1985, NAP's membership voted against the resolution blaming police for the rise in holdups.

"We're dealing with the general crime problem of the times," said Lloyd D. Connell, owner of six Los Angeles pawnshops. "Our police do a good job for us, but we can't expect special treatment. This resolution is an insult to their efforts."

However, Connell voted for the special national reward fund designed to supplement any local informants program in robberies involving pawnshops.

"We're tired of being the brunt of attack in every city across the nation. . . ."

Sidebar Information:

The City of Bergin has had several pawnshop robberies since 1985, with the worst incident in 1986. Two masked gunmen robbed Northbridge Loans Inc. in daylight, killing the owner, Vincent S. Childs, 63, and a clerk, Lee Dougherty, 29. Jewelry worth more than $75,000 was taken. No arrests were made.

In 1987, Jolly Pawnbrokers was robbed at night. Professional thieves took some $300,000 in jewelry and merchandise from the store using acetylene torches and a 10-wheel transport truck. Three burglars were caught, tried and sentenced to 10 years in prison, but the merchandise was never recovered. Holly Jolliff, the store's owner, put up a $10,000 reward for the thieves' capture and conviction.

You phone Mrs. Jolliff, who says it's important to offer a large reward in pawnshop robbery cases. "We're in a business that attracts some unsavory characters. Most pawnshops are in their town's most seedy neighborhoods. Even though the vast majority of our customers are perfectly honest citizens, we get more than our fair share of the criminal element or people who are in tough financial straits. They frequently have to pawn their valuables for cash, and they're familiar with the layout of our stores. We're vulnerable to theft, a choice target even with bars on our windows, security alarms and police surveillance.

"Luckily, our trump card is that the criminal element knows what happens on the street. Some of these people would turn their relatives in if the reward was large enough and they could do it anonymously. Check the record on this: The majority of thefts and robberies that end in convictions are those where the pawnshop owners put up sizable rewards. We think if it happens automatically, knowing there's a big reward will reduce the number of robberies."

A robbery attempt in 1986 resulted in the robber being wounded by the pawnshop owner. Oscar H. Smith III, owner of Ace Pawn on Greenwood, shot the thief as the man was leaving his store. The man was in the hospital for two months and is still in prison serving a 10-year sentence. Smith says: "These guys who rob pawn stores are nuts. Every owner and most of the clerks carry guns, and we know how to use them. After all, we rank with liquor and convenience stores as the most frequently robbed businesses in the country. There isn't a single pawnshop in Bergin that hasn't been hit since 1985, and half of them have been hit at least once a year."

Other robberies included:

—1990, two at Benny's Brokerage; $250 cash in one incident, no reward, no arrests; $3,800 in cash and jewelry, no reward, thief arrested and convicted;

—1991, Warren's Pawnshop; $40,000 in jewelry and rare coins; reward, thieves arrested, waiting trial;

—1991, Ace Pawn; $6,600 burglary of musical instruments, binoculars and telescopes; two thieves arrested before reward was posted; in county jail;

—1988, Ace Pawn; armed robber got $150 in cash and costume jewelry; no reward, no arrests;

—1989, Northbridge Loans; $22,500 burglary of jewelry and cameras; reward, no arrests;

—1986, Jolly Pawnbrokers; $8,300 in watches and cash; reward; thief arrested, no conviction;

—1987; Benny's Brokerage; $14,000 in stamps and coins; no reward, no arrests.

C Main News Story:

Barker Products, the city's largest high-tech medical products plant, will cease operations in 30 days, company officials announced Monday morning.

The facility, employing some 500 line workers, 100 managers and technicians, and 50 engineers, was the sister plant of Consolidated Medical in Prairieview, which closed six months ago.

Barker corporate officers had discussed filing for Chapter 11 bankruptcy or ceasing operations. The deadline for a decision was set for today.

"We could see no future for this company, so we are settling with our creditors now and moving the firm's operations abroad," Board Chairman Benjamin D. Acord said in this morning's statement.

The firm, which opened here five years ago, posted losses from the beginning. Last year the company lost $123 million; this year's losses are expected to be $135 million, according to the company's financial forecasts.

Attorneys representing Barker have waged losing battles with the government on patent rights, and have lost major research and development infringement suits against competing medical technology firms. Management unsuccessfully sought wage cutbacks from workers during the past two years.

"Between stiff competition from other medical technology corporations and the U.S. Patent Office, we have decided we can no longer develop and market products based in the United States," Barker said.

Anticipating that today's news would be bad with either decision, your editor sent you to Prairieview two days ago to gather this sidebar information:

Prairieview was a town of 56,000 located 63 miles from your city. Consolidated Medical was the town's second largest employer with 900 employees. It was one of the first high-tech medical products engineering and manufacturing firms in the country, a leader during the early years of corporate expansion in the medical field. Since the demise of Consolidated Medical, Prairieview has suffered population loss (down to about 49,000), and retail businesses throughout the city are closing.

Margie W. Burnett, 42, homemaker: "Two years ago this place was thriving. The schools were filled and there was talk about building new ones. The Welcome Wagon was on every block just about every week. Now there's a house for sale on every block in town. The planned subdivision is like a ghost town with unfinished houses. I guess the worst part was losing your friends. We had several good friends who were with Consolidated, and a few got out early. Those who were still here when the plant closed are pretty bitter about it."

Mayor Linda J. Montgomery: "The tax base will be way down this year. We're having to cut a lot of good programs and put a halt on any new ones. There's no doubt Prairieview will survive this setback, but it won't be without cost, and it won't be soon."

Calvin L. Crenshaw: "I moved here from San Diego for a job at Consolidated. I was an engineer at a computer plant there, and I'm thinking about going back to find whatever work I can. We loved San Diego. I guess we liked it here for awhile when the plant was going strong and there were a lot of other engineers from all over the country who came to Consolidated. Most are gone. We're leaving too, if we can sell our house, but there aren't any buyers."
In a tavern near Consolidated's plant:

A 58-year-old native of Prairieview: "I can't complain. I got nearly 10 years on the line at Consolidated . . . made better money than I ever thought I'd make, and got me a condo in Florida. I'll be retiring there next year and catch some part-time work to get by. I can't complain."

A 25-year-old native of Prairieview: "Well, I can sure complain. I worked on the line six years, just about out of high school. Got a wife and two kids now. We're geared to living on an income we can't make anymore, even if we both had jobs. Point is, neither of us has a job, and I've been out of work six months since the plant closed. Do you know anyone who has enough money saved to live for six months without an income? Neither do I. We borrowed all we can, and I guess I'm just going to have to lower my expectations and our life style. Trouble is, every job I interview for there are 20 other guys waiting in line, and all of 'em are from Consolidated. We may have to leave just to find work at half what I was making last year."

A 62-year-old who came to Prairieview with Consolidated: "Bobby's got a sad story alright, but he's young enough to start over. I kinda feel like it's too late for me. We came here 10 years ago when Consolidated opened; gave up a place in Boston. Three more years and I'd be pensioned, but when a company goes under, there are no pensions. I was a purchasing agent, so I know about spending money, and I know mine isn't going to last long with my wife's medical bills. I figure Bobby there will be back on his feet in five years, even if his wife has to work and his kids have to buy their clothes at K-Mart. But I'm afraid that in five years I may be living with one of my own children's families and taking up space. I'll tell you the truth, I'm just afraid."

Tech-Med Tavern bartender: "A couple of hours in a bar on Saturday afternoon is all you ever need to learn about a place, and Prairieview—this side particularly—is at its worst time in recent memory. I built this place on this lot I inherited from my father, but business is off so bad that I'll probably have to shut down before next year. Besides, off the record, I don't like listening to the depressing self-pity around here. This used to be an upbeat place where plant workers dropped in for an hour after work. In the last six months, some of the guys I serve are pretty far along to becoming alcoholics. I'm just holding on in case the Consolidated property gets sold to another firm and things turn around. Most of us hoped that would happen right after the plant shut, but it looks like that was just a pipe dream. Instead, I think we've all pretty much realized that isn't going to happen. If Barker closes in your city, you tell your readers this: The worst part of what happens down the road is when you admit to yourself that your family has already seen the best days they're likely to see. First you lose your confidence, and then you lose your hope."

D Main News Story:

Graduates of the new computer-assisted literacy program at State Tech received certificates in ceremonies Sunday afternoon.

The 14 students, ranging from age 17 to 53, completed the city's first "programmed" course on computers donated last year by Apple Computer.

According to Dr. Mattie N. King, president of the County Literacy Program, the group of graduates represents "a breakthrough in retention for this county's literacy instruction program." She explained that the average dropout rate for literacy classes is more than half who enroll. "Here we had 16 start the class, and 14 finished," she said. "It's a phenomenal success record."

King said part of the accomplishment is needing only 60 hours of computer contact rather than 100 hours of one-on-one instruction from volunteer teachers. "But the rest of this success belongs to the process itself," King said. "Learning how to read on a computer is fun."

The teaching component of computer-assisted literacy is the result of three years and more than $25 million donated by Apple and other corporations. Using software written by some of the nation's outstanding educational consultants and programmers, students work at their own pace. . . .

Sidebar Information:

When the graduation ends, Dr. King escorts you to the Literacy Lab down the hall at State Tech. The room is sparse but cheerful with colorful posters touting books and reading. The centerpiece poster is a gold-framed reproduction of a GED (High School Equivalency exam) certificate, with "YOUR NEXT AWARD" stamped across it. Sixteen computer stations line the walls. A cubicle of desks in the center of the room is the technician's station.

Sandra Leggett, 31, of 1447 Orchid St. is on duty at the station. Seven students, clad in jeans and sweatshirts and wearing headsets, are at the terminals now. Insulated coats drape over the backs of their chairs. Students stare intently at a full-color screen and punch a button pad with their index finger. There's an occasional muffled groan interspersed with less-frequent muffled laughs. During the half hour you're there, several students come to the center cubicle to exchange computer disks. Every time that happens, the student is smiling. They chat with Leggett, then return to their station—not eagerly, perhaps, but willingly enough.

Leggett: "I just got my computer science degree here at State Tech. I was hired part-time to run the Literacy Lab because I helped set it up as my senior project. There are three other technicians, so we can keep the place open from 6 a.m. to 10 p.m. seven days a week. That's important because most of the students work. They can come here before or after work, or on weekends. Those who work at night come here during the day."

King: "We began the second class four weeks ago, just as soon as we saw that the first class, the one that just graduated, was going to finish so quickly. Now we're actually running eight classes at once, or an initial enrollment of 128 students. At least 100 of them are still with it after four weeks, and most of them will graduate on time four weeks from now. The students put in seven-and-a-half hours a week, so there are no more than about a dozen students here at any time, usually only half a dozen. They work on their lessons in sequence, and they have 15 lesson programs to complete, each of them four hours long. But the beauty of using the computers is that they can work at their own pace. That means some will finish the course in only five weeks, and all will be done in eight weeks."

King and Leggett explain the process:

1. The entire class of 16 gets a two-hour introduction to using the computers at the beginning of the program. "It's very easy to use the computers," Leggett says. "They're really user-friendly, and they talk to students through headphones so no one else is disturbed." After that, there are no formal meetings of the entire group, and every student works on his or her own. They begin the first lesson with disk No. 1 and work their way through No. 60. Depending on their reading skills when they begin the class, they might start with disk No. 5 or No. 15. The first disk is a review of the alphabet; the second is combinations of vowel and consonant sounds, etc. The last disk is a 10th-grade-level novella, "Ivanhoe."

2. When students master each hour-long lesson—each has a quiz at the end—they bring the disk to the technician and exchange it for the next one. The lab has 12 sets of disks.

3. The lessons are interactive. A student performs tasks and gives responses when prompted by the computer. Wrong answers halt progress until the student demonstrates understanding of a word or sentence.

4. Vivid color drawings and moving figures dance on the screens. There's a lot more activity on the screen than in the reading lessons given in primary grades.

5. The later lessons introduce vocabulary, grammar and sentence construction.

King: "Teaching one person how to read used to take at least 100 hours of intensive instruction from a committed, trained volunteer instructor, when we could recruit one. Then there was only a 50-50 chance the pupil would finish. Job, family, transportation problems or slow progress in the lessons interfered with success. And through it all, there was the constant embarrassment of others knowing you were illiterate. It was too much to ask.

"I'm convinced this computer-assisted instruction is the answer, and we're just beginning to tap its potential. Imagine two-week intensive sessions, required and paid for by employers, with hundreds of labs just like this one all over the country. Our dream of wiping out illiteracy in our lifetime could be a reality."

Shelly S. Lewis, 23, a pupil in the lab: "If we had computers like this in school, I would have gotten my degree. I'm sure I would. But when you're 17 and you're still in the ninth grade 'cause you can't read, you feel like everybody's staring at you all the time . . . like they all know. The teachers know, and they treat you different.

"I don't know if young kids can handle the lessons, but if they could, then everybody who can't read in the fourth grade should be put in a class like this one during the summer. That would have changed my whole life. And don't say it would be too hard to tell who can't read in the fourth grade. The teachers all know."

E   Envision what the main news story will be, and write the sidebar accordingly.

Sidebar Information:

"It don't matter so much that we were big shots and now we're not," said Johnny Miller Jr., Toby's 16-year-old brother. "What matters is that Toby was a hero around here, and now they say he's just another black man who got on drugs."

Alma, 40, Toby's mother, agreed. "When he was growing up, there were people who cared about him and us, too. His junior high and high school coaches took him fishing to keep him off the project's playground where the dealers sold to the kids. Johnny sees them every day, but they knew to stay away from Toby.

"Some people came around and gave us clothes and things. John, his father, always had work at the school or at the gyms around town. Toby always had summer jobs, and he got a basketball scholarship at the university. Our family made out all right. But nobody came around to see us after he was arrested."

John Sr., 44, Toby's father: "I don't give a damn about what happens to us. That's not important. Toby is going to jail, and I'm afraid of what it will do to him. I ain't saying he don't deserve it. He ran over that little boy when he was high on cocaine. He has to pay for it. The jury was right today. But that doesn't change my feelings for my son. There's a lot of pressure in professional sports. People don't understand that. They think his life has been easy with all those trophies from the university and the big money he got that first year in the pros. What they don't understand is that Toby was only 21 years old. He's just a kid who couldn't handle the success. He didn't mean any harm."

Alma: "Toby was the oldest, but he's got three sisters and his brother who look up to him. This hurts them all.

"I just wish we could have kept him from it. Between his coaches and his agents, someone should have been with him and kept him from making a mistake. When he wasn't high, he just wanted to play and do for his family and friends. But when he was high, there was just no talking to him. He'd be gone for weeks, and nobody knew where he was. At the trial, they said he stole and he gambled. I don't believe that, but I'm his mother. Maybe when he was out of his head he did those things they said."

John Sr.: "We're going to move back to our old place and go on. With Toby being in jail for three years, we won't have the money to live here, but we can sell the place and do all right. He took good care of us when he went pro, and we'll visit him as often as we can.

"I just worry about what's going to happen to him when he gets out. He may not be able to play basketball in this country anymore. He won't be the same person he was. But, if they put him in a drug treatment program, he may be a better person.

"Three years in jail is a long time when you're 22. It can change a man a lot. But maybe he can still play ball, and maybe everything will be okay then. This family will spend a long time praying for him to get well and to put this thing behind him."

Alma: "We'll be praying for that little boy, too, and for his parents . . . praying they forgive Toby for what he did to their son."

Johnny Jr.: "My friends at school are still my friends. Some of them used to play ball with me and Toby after school, so they know what happened to him. They understand. They're gonna stick by me, even when we move back to the projects. Toby will be back on top when he gets out. He'll be a star again. He'll show those people who say he deserves what he got. You'll see."

News Features

Gaining in popularity in recent years, the news feature is often a more effective story-telling device than straight news presentation. Depending on the topic—aspects of the news event itself—a featurized approach allows more flexibility than the traditional inverted pyramid story structure. The trade-off for flexibility is efficiency: Feature stories increase reader interest, but they usually sacrifice swift information transfer. A journalist deciding between writing a straight news story and a feature should determine whether the sacrifice is worthwhile.

News editors have to make similar decisions. For efficiency and for the "hard news" values, editors prefer the inverted pyramid news treatment. But for "soft news," which is often less time-constrained than the breaking news story, editors may willingly forfeit some efficiency to increase audience interest. Editors also appreciate the contrast gained by juxtaposing the straight news and news feature formats. Finally, editors know that some news topics deserve the additional space and writing time that is required for features. Reporters usually work on feature stories at the rate of one or two a week, in addition to their responsibilities of covering general assignment or beat news. And, while the editor generally assigns the straight news stories, reporters usually develop their own feature story topics with their editor's approval.

FEATURE CONSIDERATIONS

Although it is impossible to say that any story should be a feature rather than straight news, each set of news values suggests one type of treatment.

Practically speaking, writing time might be a primary consideration. It is possible to write an effective feature article in a couple of hours, but doing so is likely to produce less than the best feature. Preparing a good feature usually requires rummaging through morgue files for background information, several interviews, the compilation and verification of supporting facts, and some latitude in writing time. Breaking news rarely allows enough freedom from deadlines to do an adequate feature treatment.

Another important consideration is the news topic, which may not lend itself to featurization. For instance, breaking crime stories, government meetings, announcements of abrupt changes in policy, impending disaster stories, accidents, deaths and many other news topics call for straight news treatment. Audiences will be interested primarily in outcomes, and where outcomes take precedence over deliberation, straight news presentation should prevail.

While it is true that any hard news topic *could* be a feature theme, only unusual circumstances would lead to that decision. Special cases that might call for a feature could be when a breaking crime story fits into a crime wave pattern, a series of related crimes the community is concerned about; when some rare occurrence at a government meeting involves a unique measure; when a policy change can affect people's lives in the future. However, it would be bizarre to featurize an impending disaster story (that should be written as a community warning), an accident or a death.

We think of features more as a way to get behind the breaking news; to humanize it, analyze it or just tell an interesting story with it. So, rather than fitting in with breaking news, the typical news feature topic is likely to be the story of the girl whose heifer won the blue ribbon at the county fair, the restoration of a Victorian house, the sights and sounds of Mardi Gras, or the couple who gave up their comfortable suburban lifestyle to run a riverside shelter for the homeless.

Article length is another consideration. Although there is tremendous variance in the length of both hard and soft news stories, the average feature will be much longer than the average news story. Media space is a hotly contested prize awarded only when editors are convinced that the longer feature stories will have a payoff in reader interest. A reporter/ writer considering a feature story topic should weigh its importance and whether there is enough worthwhile material to hold reader interest through what might be 30-to-40 paragraphs, or four minutes of air time. Frequently the decision to go with a feature depends on the number of facets a story has. If there are only a couple of slants to the topic, it can (and therefore should) be told through a straight news story. Features

Overpowering as a national political convention seems, journalists are at home in this fast-paced news environment. As camera crews cover the action from specially designed rafter perches, writers mingle with floor delegates and look for news features between the main platform events.

usually are topics with several incidents or perspectives that require more extensive presentation for audiences to appreciate the news.

Closely associated with article length is the whole idea of content selection, including writing style. To hold a reader's attention throughout, the feature story must include illustrative and interest-generating material. For example, the following passage might be included in a feature article:

> Ranger Smith has two aerial views of the valley tacked next to one another on the wall behind the desk of his observation tower office. Both were taken from the same angle in a plane at 20,000 feet: the first in 1970, the second in 1990.
>
> The striking difference between the two maps, obvious even from across Smith's desk, is the patchwork pattern on the land. In 1970, the valley is crisscrossed by hundreds of fences that cut the land into tiny squares and rectangles, each with a discrete hue denoting a different crop or planting stage.
>
> On the 1990 map, the valley is divided into fewer than a dozen fenced units. Methodical regularity has replaced the patchwork pattern. Where there were a hundred small farms, farm families and crops, now there are 10 large corporate cultivators.

The comparable passage in a straight news story might be:

> In 20 years, the valley has seen a hundred individual farms, farm families and crops replaced by only 10 large corporations planting on massive tracts.

There is considerable difference in content selection and writing style. In the feature passage, a reporter has gone to extremes to select material that illustrates the point. The passage leans heavily on description and attention to detail: reader interest-building devices. The straight news passage offers a single factual concept, the same concept, in one sentence. However, there is no doubt about which passage has greater impact. Although the feature passage is far less efficient, readers are certain to understand it, and they will remember it.

FEATURE STRUCTURE

The single overriding difference between a feature and a straight news story is that the feature is written to be read all the way through. Recall that an inverted pyramid-style news story is built with all of the necessary facts at the beginning of the article. Each paragraph is written so that all paragraphs beneath it could be deleted without omitting more-important information. A feature, on the other hand, has a distinct beginning, a body that has some logical ordering and a distinct ending. The assumption is that readers will read from beginning to end.

Figure 15.1 is a diagram of the four parts of a news feature story. It emphasizes the structural differences not found in a straight news story.

The basic components shown in the diagram are (1) an interest-grabbing lead, (2) some early reference to the news element that is the theme of the news feature, (3) the body of the story and (4) an ending. Each component is covered separately in the following discussion.

FEATURE LEADS

Although simple or summary leads do appear on feature stories, they belong only on stories with topics that sell themselves. For instance:

> A diamond ring worth $10,000 was uncovered on Municipal Golf Course yesterday by a man using a homemade metal detector.

Few such automatically compelling topics exist, although some possibilities include buried treasure, dreams, the secrets of eternal youth or beauty, ghosts and UFOs, magic and miracles, small children and cuddly animals, how to get rich quickly, chocolate desserts and sex. The point here is that a summary lead is acceptable for a feature story in which

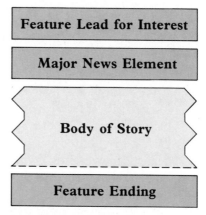

Figure 15.1 Feature story structure

reader interest can be assumed; it should not be used for less-compelling feature topics.

The chief purpose of feature leads is to draw the reader into the story by stirring the reader's interest. This can be done by arousing curiosity, challenging accepted beliefs, teasing, exciting, offering humor or creating a compelling mood.

A secondary but important aspect of feature leads is that they should match the rest of the feature: The lead should be consistent with the body of the feature. Consistency is achieved when the lead matches the feature's tone and length. For instance, an upbeat feature should have a light or humorous lead; a descriptive or narrative lead belongs on a feature about a ferry boat's last crossing. Longer feature stories can sustain long leads; short leads should be used on shorter feature stories. But mismatching, writing a long lead for a short feature or writing a quip lead for a serious feature, weakens the feature by deceiving readers' expectations.

Chapter 3 presents a list of lead types, some of which are used primarily on feature articles. The following review offers a slightly different categorization of these leads, with brief examples.

Tried-and-True

Three types of feature leads are tried-and-true: narrative, descriptive and quotation. A narrative lead is most effective for action or adventure features:

> They actually tiptoed up the last flight of stairs to the landing and moved gingerly toward Room 308. Standing on either side of the doorjamb, they drew their revolvers quietly. Jerry looked at Bill, who nodded that he was ready. This was the moment of truth.
>
> Then both officers made a two-step leap at the door, crashing into the room together. Jerry came through first, in a low crouch; Bill held the backup's standing position. As their eyes and weapons darted across the blackened interior, a burst of explosive gunfire lighted the room. This time they were the targets.
>
> Both officers were wounded in what narcotics agents now call the "Up Against the Door" game approved by the City Council last year, a drug enforcement tactic to surprise suspected crack house dealers. However, a *Tribune* analysis of local police records shows that since its inception the procedure has become the leading cause of death and injury.
>
> "They always seem to know we're coming. . . . "

Descriptive leads are most appropriate for features that will contain a lot of description:

At 7 a.m. the mist hanging over the still water blocks the view of the other bank . . . it might as well be an ocean as a river. An electric winch slowly raises the ferry's tailgate as rusty chains creak over the rollers.

Although the old tub only holds eight automobiles, it seems huge with its high steel sides and towering pilot house. Forget exploring

Personality Profile Features

As the most frequently written type of news feature, a personality profile is a long piece, usually the result of extensive interviews with the person being written about.

Interviews may extend over two or more sessions and in a variety of settings: the subject's office, home, favorite relaxation spot or other familiar location. Choose a setting that will put the subject at ease and allow you to see his or her usual surroundings. The following are suggestions for a personality profile feature.

1. Relate the personality profile to a news peg, if there is one. In most cases, a news event spurs the profile: a job promotion, election to office or other major accomplishment. But profiles are also prompted by less immediate news: How is the university's president doing after the first year? What were the major life experiences of this town's most prominent philanthropist (or farmer or doctor), and what does that person see for the future?

2. Build the personality profile around a theme. Look for one that might not be evident in the record. For instance, during a two-hour interview, it becomes apparent that the tycoon considers herself a successful player in the male-dominated business world; the politician's life really revolves around his family; or the singer owes her career to her pastor and to her early

years in the church choir. But it isn't necessary to find a story-behind-the-story theme. More often, the person's record is the theme of a personality feature.

3. Let the subject's quotes constitute the core of a personality profile feature. Readers should expect a lot of direct quotes and paraphrases. Let the subject's words tell the story.

4. Back up the quotes with verified facts from published sources. Know this information before the interviews begin. Impress the subject by doing your homework.

5. Talk to other people, perhaps many others, who know the subject. Talk to family members and more distant relatives, work associates, housekeepers and the people who water the plants in the office at night. Discover the subject's foibles and strengths.

6. Color the story with pertinent descriptions of the surroundings, with the subject's physical characteristics and mannerisms. Readers should get a visual image of the subject in that person's habitat, even if a photograph will accompany the story. But don't overdo these color touches. News media audiences aren't expecting a novel, so limit the depth of character portrayal to what will hold the audience's attention.

7. Don't forget to get anecdotes, the lifeblood of any feature article.

the decks, because the big white sign with fading black stenciled letters says: "Passengers are required to remain in their cars for the duration of the trip," so there isn't much to see or do on the ride.

Then the mist lifts, and the passengers' eyes widen as they see the massive pilings of the James F. Grady Bridge, gargantuan in comparison to the tiny ferry boat. Seen from the below, the superstructure of the six-lane bridge is colossal. With the early morning sun glinting off the bridge, it looks like the highway to heaven.

The ferry, so plausible in the mist, is an anachronism in the clear light of day. Looking at the two, there is no doubt that the 56-year-old ferry would be retired the day traffic began crossing the new bridge.

The last form of tried-and-true feature lead is a quotation lead, appropriate for features that will lean heavily on facts or viewpoints told through quotes. Remember that quote leads for features should adhere to standards governing the use of any quote lead: The quote should be strong, succinct and theme setting. If the "Up Against the Door" feature was to be told primarily through quotes, the following lead would be effective:

"They always seem to know we're coming, so we're losing a lot of good men needlessly," said Jerry N. Tate, a narcotics squad detective.

His partner, Sgt. William H. Richards, agreed. "I felt like one of those targets in a shooting gallery," Richards said. "We were framed in the doorway like sitting ducks, and they just pumped shots into us."

The two officers are recuperating from injuries they received 10 days ago in a drug enforcement procedure designed to surprise those in suspected crack houses, places where crack cocaine is made and sold.

Approved by the City Council last year, the tactic has become the leading cause of patrol officers' death and injury, according to a *Tribune* analysis of police records.

But Police Chief Aubrey Baldwin defends the "Up Against the Door" procedure as an effective weapon in the local fight against drugs.

"The City Council gave us the authority to break down doors of suspected crack houses. . . . "

Narrative, descriptive and quote leads qualify as tried-and-true feature leads because they are used frequently and because they are straightforward writing devices: There's nothing fake about them. These lead types can be contrasted with the remaining categories, both of which are gimmicks.

Gimmicks That Work

Two types of leads fall into this category: teaser leads and freak leads. Both are gimmicks because the feature writer "manufactures" them to increase interest in the story. A teaser is designed to arouse interest, to make readers want to keep reading so they can learn what the article is about. This is an obvious gimmick in which the writer purposely teases the reader into reading more by withholding information, and the reader tacitly agrees to the ruse.

Let's consider a brief set of feature story facts: It's April 8, one week before federal income taxes are due, and you're assigned to write a feature on what happens to the actual forms, the documents taxpayers file. You find:

1. from the mailbox to oblivion takes seven years;
2. the IRS doubles its staff the week beginning April 16 just to open the envelopes;
3. money, including checks or money orders, is separated from the forms and deposited every evening . . . the government can begin spending the money the next day;
4. forms are put into categories of taxpayers so statistical information can be computed;
5. the arithmetic on each form is checked;
6. there is a check for irregularities;

and there are about a dozen more steps to mention in this feature article.

This is not a particularly exciting feature topic, so some reader stimulation is required from the outset. Here are a few teaser examples:

April 16. It's the day your troubles are over and the Internal Revenue Service's troubles are just beginning.

No sooner than you send it, they spend it.

It's called one of the two sure things in life, and although this one is painful, it beats the heck out of the other choice. The other sure thing is death.

These teaser leads will stir reader interest better than a direct, informative lead even when it's slightly humorous:

> The long and short of it is that it takes about 18 steps and seven years for your federal income tax form to reach oblivion.

However, all of these leads seem to break the two "matching" rules about feature leads. This feature article is likely to be a longer article and serious in tone. These leads possess neither of those properties. Let's turn to another fact set example.

You happen to catch two competitive mouthwash commercials while watching television, and you decide to do a feature on mouthwashes. You read some Federal Trade Commission reports and market studies that say mouthwash firms contend their product prevents colds and sore throats. Other research indicates:

1. 72 percent of the adult population uses mouthwash regularly;
2. total sales is $650 million annually;
3. critics of Americans' buying habits call the figures an "insecurity quotient," a measure of how insecure people feel about themselves
4. Listerine is the leading seller, with almost one-fourth of the market;
5. an advertising agency executive says, "Bad breath is big business"; and
6. doctors have mixed views: mouthwashes are antiseptics that may kill some germs, but the effect is short-lived, and some people get sores from using mouthwash . . . nobody seems to know if mouthwash users really have fewer colds.

Again, it's a topic that will need some interest boost from the lead:

> A bottle of mouthwash is to many Americans what a fuzzy blanket is to Charles Shultz's Linus, or so Madison Avenue would have us believe.

> Americans spit $650 million down the drain each year.
> That's the annual price tag for mouthwash, which doctors give mixed reviews because of their short-lasting effect. Still, 72 percent of adults in this country believe the social security of mouthwash is worth the price.

Don't breathe a word of this, but personal security may not be the sweet smell of success you always thought.

Insecurity will lead many Americans back to the bottle this year.

These teaser leads should help increase reader interest, and with a topic like mouthwash, they do a better job of matching the probable tone of the feature story.

The other gimmick-that-works type of feature lead is a freak lead: something so unusual that readers are challenged to continue reading the story just to make sense of the lead. Weirdness is the key here. Freak leads—perhaps poems or riddles—belong on feature stories with peculiar topics.

For instance, as a police beat reporter, you decide to do a feature on the fellow who is the night clerk in the city morgue. Entering the glass-paneled door that says MORGUE, you find a brightly lit, antiseptically clean room with white-tiled walls and a highly waxed linoleum floor. Two gunmetal gray file cabinets and a desk and chair set are the only appointments in the room. The clerk, 22-year-old John Smith, wears a white hospital orderly's uniform. Some freak lead examples are:

> He is never wanting for company, and he gets no back talk from his clientele.
> All in all, it's a quiet sort of job.

> This bodyguard can talk all night without getting a single response. At least he hopes not, because there really isn't a soul to keep him company.

> **ƎUƆᴙOM**
> Few people actually see this word, but John Smith stares at it often.
> Smith is the night clerk at city morgue. . . .

Although these freak leads fit a feature story about a clerk in the city morgue, several of them attempt to spin humor. Those that don't are the better choices for this feature topic, which isn't likely to be humorous.

Desperation Gimmicks

The final category of feature leads should be considered only in desperation. These are the gimmicky leads that may increase reader interest but at the same time stand out as gimmicks, possibly defeating their purpose.

Included in the category are question leads and direct address leads, both of which can sometimes qualify as teaser or freak leads. The distinction of the desperation gimmick category is that the question or direct address is simply that and nothing more. Here are a few question and direct address leads that compare favorably with the teaser and freak leads:

> Pretend you are inside the envelope that is licked, stamped and mailed with your own 1040 income tax form. The long journey ahead is almost inconceivable.

> If you are worried about the accuracy of your arithmetic on your income tax form, worry no longer: the IRS will check it for you.

> That bottle of Listerine on your bathroom shelf may not prevent a cold or sore throat. It might not even make your breath smell fresher for very long, but it probably will make you feel more secure.

> Do mouthwashes really do what they are supposed to do?
> With total sales of $650 million a year, it's apparent many people believe that they do.

> If you breathed on your grandmother, would she wither away?
> Most mouthwash firms hope you are concerned about the possibility. That insecurity is yielding $650 million every year in mouthwash sales.

> Would you like a job where the customers never disturb you?
> John Smith isn't bothered by the noisy night life at his oh-so-quiet job as clerk in the city morgue.

These may be among the better examples of question and direct address feature leads, but each of these is more self-indulging than the less intrusive gimmicks that work. Use the desperation gimmicks when all else fails. The single exception is the "how-to" feature, for which a direct address lead that involves the reader is appropriate. If the topic is finding bargains at flea market sales, lead with the feature's objective of helping readers discover good buys.

MAJOR NEWS ELEMENTS

Several of the preceding longer lead examples show how the major news element follows the feature lead. In the "Up Against the Door" feature, it's this paragraph:

Both officers were wounded in what narcotics agents now call the "Up Against the Door" game approved by the City Council last year, a drug enforcement tactic to surprise suspected crack house dealers. However, a *Tribune* analysis of local police records shows that since its inception the procedure has become the leading cause of death and injury.

After raising reader interest through the narrative lead anecdote, the feature tells readers the topic and theme of the article. Topic is one aspect: The feature is about "a drug enforcement tactic to surprise crack house dealers." But theme is another aspect: "The procedure has become the leading cause of death and injury." A feature article should include both aspects in the major news elements segment. In the ferry boat feature, it's this line:

Looking at the two, there is no doubt that the 56-year-old ferry would be retired the day traffic began crossing the new bridge.

The topic is the ferry boat's retirement; the theme is that the boat is an anachronism that may have served well in its day, but that day is past. We may pause here to reconsider the ferry boat story's theme. The theme is more likely to be "an anachronism that served well during some glorious days of this town's history." If the ferry boat story is, in fact, a historic object feature on the boat, another line is needed in the major news element paragraph:

Looking at the two, there is no doubt that the 56-year-old ferry would be retired the day traffic began crossing the new bridge. But the Beaver Gorge Ferry owes no apologies in its half century of service.

Now the paragraph sets the proper theme for the article. It achieves what a major news element graf in a feature story is designed to do. It tells readers, in effect, "If you read the rest of this article, here's what you're going to learn." To understand what the feature is about, readers need this information relatively early in the story (the interest-building lead may not give it). Readers also need to justify investing a lot of time in reading a longer feature article.

In one of the shorter feature lead examples, the main news element follows the one-line opening lead:

Americans spit $650 million down the drain each year.
That's the annual price tag for mouthwash, which doctors give mixed reviews because of their short-lasting effect. Still, 72 percent

of adults in this country believe the social security of mouthwash is worth the price.

Here the main news element paragraph is very similar to a topic sentence in a theme. It tells readers exactly what points will be made in the remainder of the feature article. A superior topic-and-theme paragraph like this one, early in the story, also serves as an efficient device for writing the rest of the feature. It becomes an outline for maintaining the theme throughout the feature's body.

BODY OF THE STORY

Almost all of the feature article is contained in the body of the piece, diagrammed in Figure 15.1 as the portion shaped like an accordion bellows. Only three pleats are shown in the truncated model, but there might actually be a dozen pleats in the body of the feature, each one representing a major concept or viewpoint. The body of a feature is little more than a logical ordering of concepts or viewpoints strung together with transitions. Figure 15.2 is a close-up depiction of the feature body model:

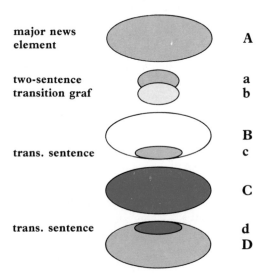

major news element   A

two-sentence transition graf   a b

trans. sentence   B c

C

trans. sentence   d D

Figure 15.2 Aspects of a feature article body

The figure shows four concepts, labeled **A, B, C** and **D,** and transitional elements labeled with lowercase letters. A "color" scheme in the model represents the separation and interlocking of concepts. For example, the dark gray of segment **A** indicates it is one concept, and **a** is a transition between segment **A** and another transition, the lighter gray **b.** Lowercase **b** is a transition to concept **B,** and so on.

To suggest how the model actually correlates with building a feature body, Figure 15.3 depicts paragraph fragments from the "Up Against the Door" feature topic.

This detailed presentation simplifies the writing of longer feature articles. The body of the story is no more than several logically ordered elements:

    A. Chief Baldwin praises the procedure, saying it is effective;

    B. anecdotal incident on Gates family;

Major News Element	The two officers are recuperating from injuries they received 10 days ago...tactic has become the leading cause of death and injury, according to a Tribune analysis of police records.
A	But Police Chief Aubrey Baldwin defends the "Up Against the Door" procedure as an effective weapon in the local fight against drugs. "The City Council gave us the authority to break down doors of...Those records ignore our success rate in shutting down crack cocaine production in the city."
a	The Tribune's study shows that the monthly figures doubled from four successful raids against crack houses to eight busts per month.
b	However, the figures also show that the victories had a toll in human life and injury, and not just among narcotics agents.
B	Joseph and Martha Gates of King Arms, Apt. 5, were eating dinner with their two daughters at the kitchen table March 20. "We heard a crash...glad to be alive," she said.
c	The Gates Family attack is one of six such incidents, including two accidental deaths of innocent residents, but the numbers for narcotics agents is staggering in comparison.
C	Four police officers have been killed since the law went into effect. One incident in April cost...22 officers have been injured, making the tactic more lethal than high-speed chases.
d	In spite of the toll, authorities defend the procedure, which has received attention in national law enforcement magazines. "Narcotics officers are trained in teams of two for no less than
D	12 hours...by any standard, it's the most effective procedure in the country," he said....

Figure 15.3   **Feature body paragraph fragments**

    C. inventory of police deaths and injuries; and

    D. full explanation of procedure.

Each of these feature article elements is connected by transitional sentences that end one segment or begin the next. In the case of **a–b,** two transitions are contained in a separate paragraph that takes readers from concept **A** to concept **B.** There might be a dozen or more elements in the feature body, all arranged in a similar manner, and each of these major elements could be four or five paragraphs in length.

Although the example makes the writing process look easy, building a 20-to-40-graf feature story isn't simple. For instance, some of the elements are placed in strategic positions specifically to increase reader interest through a long story. The lead pulls the reader in, and then two paragraphs of factual material follow. Just when the reader is about to move on to another article, the Gates family incident pulls the reader back. The Gates anecdote is a little human-interest story within the feature story. Recognizing that the anecdote is an effective device for holding reader attention, the feature writer places it between drier, more passive elements such as Baldwin's praise and the inventory of police deaths and injuries. Anecdotes and passages that are heavily laden with quotes help rekindle reader interest throughout a long feature. Their placement in the story should serve the interest-building purpose.

Transitions are the cement that binds the content bricks of a feature article. Without transitions, there would be no flow to the piece. Readers would have to force their way through instead of being carried smoothly from one concept to the next. Figure 15.3 offers a few clues about transitions in feature articles:

1. Transitions are used to connect the major content elements.

2. Because they are connectors, transitions usually are found at the beginning or end of discrete content element blocks. However, as seen in the a–b paragraph, transitions can form a separate bonding unit.

3. Transitions usually are short. Actually, brevity is a byproduct of a transition's requirement not to draw attention to itself. As a link between major concepts, the transition is only a bridge, a writer's device to improve readability and understanding. If the transition is too long, too contrived or too blatant, it obstructs rather than expedites its subtle linking assignment.

4. Transitions are no more than the usual writing tactics of comparison and contrast, offering examples, moving from general to specific (or vice versa), introducing lists, and linking by time or magnitude or sequence.

5. If the transition between elements is too difficult to write or too

obtrusive when it is written, the journalist should reevaluate the sequence of content elements in the feature body. Difficult transitions usually mean that the two elements being linked don't go together well. Readers may have trouble following the logic, a prompt to a writer that the order should be changed.

FEATURE ENDINGS

Straight news stories have no endings. They trail off with the least important piece of information. A feature article's ending is important, but not necessarily because of the information it transmits. The ending's purpose is to make readers feel satisfied that they read the story. "Satisfied" merely means that before readers turn to another article, they sense the slightest twinge (even subconsciously) of gratification: "I'm glad I read that."

Feature endings are a natural wrap-up to the whole feature topic. Like the feature lead, an ending should match the article in length and tone. Also like the lead, an ending should be rewritten several times to ensure that every word is in place; that it belongs. Inappropriate or awkward endings destroy reader satisfaction.

From these general guidelines about endings, a few specific suggestions follow:

1. Perhaps the most frequently used feature ending is called a tie-back. The idea is to make a connection between the feature's ending and its lead. An analogy is tying a ribbon around a gift, making it a tidy and satisfying package. If the lead is descriptive, try ending with a similar descriptive passage. If the lead is an anecdote, use another anecdote for an ending. Repeat some key words or phrases from the lead so the reader recalls the whole. Cause the reader to reflect on the entire feature with a tie-back ending.

2. A summary ending also is appropriate for a feature story. In a paragraph or two, reiterate the main points of the feature article. Summarizing has the disadvantage of being repetitive, but achieves the satisfaction effect by reviewing the main concepts of a long story.

3. Another possibility is a look toward the future. One of the feature sources might have provided a quote that points to solutions or anticipated directions for this feature topic. Save the quote and use it as part of the ending.

A real danger that occurs in writing feature endings is the tendency for journalists to moralize or draw their own conclusions to the article. The inclination to do so must be avoided at all costs. A news feature article may contain a high degree of writing maneuverability, but it is still a news article bound by the facts, by clear attribution and by journalistic objectivity. The writer, pressed for a satisfying ending, must not succumb to the tempting lure of creative writing. A soft news article is no excuse for straying from journalistic integrity.

SUMMARY

News features allow more writing flexibility than does the traditional inverted pyramid story structure, but the trade-off for flexibility is efficiency. Features increase reader interest at the expense of swift information transfer.

Each set of news values suggests one type of treatment rather than another, and other considerations include: (1) time available for writing the story, (2) the topic itself, (3) article length, (4) content selection and (5) writing style.

A news feature article requires an entirely different structural approach from a straight news story because the feature is written to be read all the way through. Few topics interest readers automatically, so writers begin building interest with the feature lead. Types of feature leads are the tried-and-true, including narrative, descriptive and quotation; gimmicks that work, including teaser and freak leads; and desperation gimmicks, including question and direct address leads. The chapter presents examples of the types of feature leads in each of these categories.

A model of the parts of a feature story shows placement of the segment containing the major news elements; the body of a feature with transitions linking discrete story elements; and the feature story's ending. Each of these aspects of news feature article writing is discussed in detail.

Thinking it Through

EXERCISE 15.1

Building Feature Stories

For each of these feature story fact sets, arrange story elements in a logical and readable manner by using the letter that corresponds to each fact block. For instance, if you believe the lead should use points B and F; the major news element, point K; and the feature body, points A and C followed by M, and so on, the pattern might look like this:

Lead:	B, F
Major news element:	K
Body:	A, C
	M
	E, G

As you arrange elements, particularly in the body of the feature, try to combine similar elements where possible, as the example suggests. One objective is to place related elements on the same line, indicating these would abut, thus reducing the number of transitions that will be required in the feature. If you decide some elements are not needed in the feature story, omit the letter of those elements.

A You cover a photography opening and are struck by an exhibit of explosions. You jot down the name of the photographer and give him a call. He's happy to hear from you, gives you some information and invites you to the next meeting of his club, the Shooters. Twelve guys show up and talk you through their scrapbook before you go out with them on a "shoot."

A Began three years ago when Patrick L. Engel, 27, took photos of fruit shot by a rifle and showed the pictures to friends. Several camera buffs met on the weekend, went to the woods and shot artichokes and tomatoes.

B Two of the original fruit shooters talk about how they set up tripods, and used time exposures and high-speed film advance. These people are serious photographers.

C There are about 20 members of the informal club of photo buffs in the city who like to get together to take color photos of something they explode. Explanation of how the club is organized, a few leaders, dues, etc.

D Members admit a little drinking goes on at the shoot site, "but that's only natural," said Matthew B. Patterson, 22. "Most of the guys hunt, so we're used to having a little booze when we're in the woods."

E Is it legal? "Well, a policeman and a lawyer are in the club," Patterson says. "Our guns are licensed, and we sign for the over-the-counter explosives we buy."

F Patterson says supplies for a shoot might cost $200–$500; most cost less than $100. Everyone contributes.

G Six female photographers are regulars with the club, and a few wives and girlfriends also attend some shoots. "Women shooters come up with the best ideas," Engel says.

H Chad D. Adkins, 31, explains how shoots evolved from shooting rifles at fruit to the exotic recent shoots: 1) shotguns at pumpkins; 2) junk cars run into trees; 3) flammable material loaded into junk trucks that are run off cliffs; and 4) the explosions of antique salvage furniture pieces such as mirrored bureaus.

I On the shoot, you witness a lot of revelry, except with the pictures; that's serious. Safety prevails, partly because of the danger to the camera equipment. Obviously these guys will do anything for an exciting photo.

J On shoot, guys dig 6-foot trench and fill it with an explosive. An old wooden canoe loaded with gallon cans of paint covers the trench. From 50 feet, you're awed as a multi-hued fireball roars from the ignited trench.

K The museum curator invited Engel, a freelance commercial photographer, to submit some photos for the current regional exhibit. Seeing the explosion pictures, the curator selected a series of six to hang.

Lead: _____

News element: _____

Body: _____   Body contd.: _____

_____   _____

_____   _____

Ending: _____

B A recent prison reform concept is placing first-time offenders under age 25 in a boot-camp environment rather than a state penitentiary. The idea is that younger criminals have a better chance of being rehabilitated if they are separated from the hardened multiple offenders. Also, if the first offenders are taught discipline and given basic educational skills, their chances of being repeat offenders decrease.

Your county has a new boot-camp facility, a converted boy's military academy that was closed for five years, but reopened as a prison boot camp last year. Your editor sends you out to do a feature article on the camp concept.

A Prisoners' daily routine: 5 a.m. wake-up, breakfast, exercises, camp cleanup, morning classes, lunch, afternoon vo-tech training in production plant, drill, dinner, camp cleanup, free time, lights out at 9 p.m.

B Col. Andrew L. Farleigh, 53, retired Army infantry officer, now heads the facility. He's called "commandant," not warden; was a boys' military school commander last 10 years in the Army.

C Head drill Sgt. Richard C. Avery, 37, explains the three goals of Camp Talon: discipline, education, vocation.

D All of the boot camp's goals are accomplished through traditional military training procedures. Sgt. Avery explains why this approach works for young men.

E Camp Talon is a boot-camp prison, now marking the end of its first year of operation in the county. Concept of boot-camp prison explained.

F Only bars are the iron gate at the front of the camp, built in 1920. Six-foot stone wall rings the entire site. The inmates sleep in barracks, not cells. More description of the place.

G Does it work? Commandant Farleigh: "We've only been open a year, and the earliest scheduled parole is still two years away. It's sometimes hard to remember, but these men are convicted felons. We have very high hopes that upon release, they will remain in society."

H Criminal Court Judge Michelle Grisanti explains conditions under which a convicted felon might be offered Camp Talon rather than prison.

I The day you're at camp, it's 90 degrees. Some 200 prisoners in starched khaki uniforms stand in formation for nearly an hour; no complaints. Platoons drill for next half hour. No rifles, but it looks just like a military academy.

J Lights out. Bugle blows taps. Muffled sounds come from the barracks, but these end soon. "After a day at camp, the men look forward to a night's rest," Sgt. Avery says.

K Prisoner Jules R. Burke, 22, says, "If they give you a chance to come here rather than the state prison, you take it. Once you go there, you can't come here. If you leave here, there's no coming back."

L Commandant Farleigh: "We've had no escape attempts and no discipline problems requiring a man's being sent to the state prison. They aren't all good apples, by any means, but they're making the most of this opportunity."

Lead:	_____			
News element:	_____			
Body:	_____	Body contd.:	_____	
	_____		_____	
	_____		_____	
		Ending:	_____	

C You are writing what is likely to be an 8-page feature article on a local manufacturing company that makes large, helium-filled balloons and dirigibles for Disneyland, Disney World, amusement parks, and for companies that want to attract attention during sales by floating one of these balloons in the air above the store. Here is the information you've gathered for your feature:

A Owner Robert Breed is the father of eight; says he'll be a millionaire before he's 50; now 45.

B Quotes and factual information by foreman of the rubber manufacturing unit.

C Two years ago, a small ship carrying an order to Brazil began to sink. Crew inflated some balloons in the cargo department and kept ship afloat until rescue was made.

D Quotes from head artist, who designs the balloon shapes.

E Breed says orders have nearly doubled every year; plant now ships about 200 balloons a year.

F Quotes and factual material from marketing department head, who gets business from around the world.

G Rubber "mixer" describes why different mixes are needed, depending on the job.

H Breed says he wants his employees to appreciate what they're doing, so he sends them—on rotation basis—to make customer deliveries. Some go to Disneyland, some to Montreal, some to Rome.

I In Canada last year, a balloon hit a power line and hurt two people. Firm using the balloon was sued; paid some $250,000 in damages.

J Breed used to work for Disneyland and was surprised how long it took (and how much it cost) to order a balloon from abroad. That's how he got the idea.

K Rubber "dyer" explains how complicated it is to get each job's color right.

L Shipping foreman says balloons weigh from 300 to more than 2,000 pounds; average 600 pounds. They're tricky to pack; sometimes takes two days to pack one properly.

M Breed says process begins with the order, then artists do the design, then forms are made for the design; rubber is mixed to the right consistency, the rubber is colored, the balloon is formed and then powdered so the rubber doesn't stick; after a two-day wait, there's a test inflation, then deflation, packing and shipping.

N Artist tells you he's really a structural engineer with a degree from Rice University, but he got tired of doing someone else's interior girder designs for buildings.

O Raw material for rubber comes from India and South America; other mix chemicals are from U.S. and France.

P Toughest design he's ever done was of a giraffe, artist says. Balloon was for Toys-R-Us. Had to figure out how to keep the neck from drooping.

Q Breed says customers pay $4 a pound for balloons, plus design and form charges for originals. Most stock orders cost about $2,500; special designs might cost $8,000 more. He gets about 50 new design orders a year.

R Shipper says some balloons have to be packed in dry ice to prevent melting if they're going to hot climates.

S Biggest balloon was King Kong replica to advertise mid-1980s movie remake. It was 60 feet high, done in six sections, weighed 15 tons and cost the ad firm $75,000. "They thought they got it for bananas," Breed says.

T Eddie McGregor, who makes the forms, gives some quotes and says he learned his trade in graphic productions and machine tool technical schools.

U Marketing head says the firm is always seeking new business. "We could double our output. We're idle almost three months a year, off and on." He says amusement parks are opening all over the world, so he thinks the business will be there before too long.

V Strong smell of chemicals in the mixing area; mixer has to wear a special oxygen-fed mask.

W Plant has about 35 employees. They've been working for last two months to make three animal balloons for local children's park; employees of firm are donating the balloons in a presentation scheduled for Saturday.

X The entire plant area is very clean. Foreman says they can't afford to have any sharp objects around because the balloons are easily damaged.

Y Last year a balloon burst in the plant during a test. No one was hurt, but now the plant follows a safety procedure every time there's a test.

Z Breed is short and rotund. He's highly energetic and moves quickly despite his weight. "I'm the original model for the Pillsbury Dough Boy," he says.

Lead: _____

News element: _____

Body: _____   Body contd.: _____

_____   _____

_____   _____

                                                         Ending: _____

Writing Practice

EXERCISE 15.2

Transitions

For each exercise in 15.1, write transitions between the major content elements in the **body** of the article you built. A portion of your finished exercise might look like this:

Body:

C, G

That was how its mission began five years ago. Today, the organization raises funds for a variety of educational projects for the music profession.

P, F, L, D

Projects like these require substantial financing, so the group spends half its energies raising funds through community projects and donations.

A, E

. . . the single most successful fund-raising effort the group has had, but only a fraction of the amount members anticipate in their next event. . . .

<u>B</u>

. . . assuming the event draws at least 2,000 people. Such assumption is reasonable based on the group's own membership growth.

In 1975 . . .

<u>O, H</u>

EXERCISE 15.3

Leads and Ends

Write **only** a lead and an ending for each of the following fact sets. Label the type of lead and ending you use according to their chapter definitions.

A Karen Sue Williams, a 21-year-old junior at State College, works weekends at a nearby outdoor theme park called Wilderness Park. She works in the wild animal section as an animal keeper. The public relations agent for the park calls about an incident this past Sunday involving Karen. You go for an interview and get the following information:

Karen works in the cheetah section and says these are the most aggressive animals at the park. "The lions have lost much of their hunting instinct because of the heat and because we keep them well fed, but there are about 20 cheetahs now and they still move around a lot. Maybe it's because there's only a chain-link fence between them and the antelope section. The antelope are constantly running, so the cheetahs follow after them against the fence. Anyway, it was kind of cool Sunday morning, and the cheetahs seemed more restless than usual."

What happened was that a motorist—they drive through the animal sections at 5 mph with their windows closed—was already close to the fence when his foot slipped off the brake, hit the gas and crashed his vehicle into the fence. Karen was parked in a safari-type Jeep nearby. "We're trained for such situations, but it didn't work the way we practiced it in the drills. I was supposed to call for a rifleman to be ready with a stun gun on the antelope side of the fence. But instead I got out of the Jeep and tried to throw some food on the ground to keep the cheetahs on their side."

She explained that the excitement of the car hitting the fence was too much for the cheetahs, who sensed an opportunity to get to the antelope. A pack had already formed, and none of the cheetahs was interested in the food she threw. Instead, they cut off her retreat to the Jeep and threatened to attack her. She could see some of them jumping around the car, looking for a way through the fence. One was even on the car roof trying to leap the fence. She dove under the visitors' vehicle to temporary safety.

While the passengers remained in the safety of their car, Karen knew only she was in trouble. But she didn't realize her peril until a couple of cheetahs began nosing under the vehicle at her. The pack near the car was wild with excitement, and their howls goaded the others to try to get through the broken fence by going under the car. Soon Karen was watching in terror as half a dozen cheetahs began inching toward her, snarling, their teeth and claws bared.

"As they got nearer, I knew my only chance was to use my small size to advantage. I could move around a little bit under the car. I began shouting at them and waving my hand in their faces. They were too crouched under the car to make any lunges at me, but it seemed the more I tried to keep them back, the more angry and excited they became. Some were only a foot away by then, and they were snarling and snapping at my waving hand, trying to bite it." She shows you two fresh scratch marks on her wrist. "I didn't even realize one of them had clawed me. I was so sure I would be dragged out, mangled and dead before help ever came. It was all happening so fast, it seemed like it had been only a few seconds."

Then, before the first cheetahs could grab her hand firmly, the motorist began honking his horn. Apparently from underneath the car the noise was loud enough to frighten the cheetahs out. "I imagined it was Gabriel at first, but then I saw the cheetahs scramble away and join the rest of the pack at a distance from the car."

The horn alerted other keepers in the section and brought the stun gunners, who used their weapons on two of the cheetahs, enough to drive the others away. Karen had to be helped from under the vehicle by the Wilderness Park personnel. She was badly frightened, but regained her composure enough to thank Bernard K. Packard, 276 Chestnut, Chicago, both for not moving the car and for honking his horn the moment he did.

"He saved my life. I know enough about cheetahs to know I would have been killed if they had another few seconds to reach me under there."

You ask if she's quitting the park. She says, "No. What happened was freaky. It's going to teach me to pay more attention during our drills and to have more respect for the animals I'm watching. I just wasn't thinking when I left my Jeep under those conditions."

Karen is the daughter of Mr. and Mrs. George Williams, 119 Cherry Ave. She got her job through her biology teacher at State College where she is a pre-veterinary science major. She's been working at the park for almost a year with no previous incidents. In fact, there have been no animal-related injuries reported at the park since its founding in 1978.

Miss Williams is blond, 5-foot-1-inches.

B After circling a major fire by helicopter at 6 a.m., you cover a Lions' Club breakfast meeting (where the guest speaker selects you as his opponent in a judo demonstration). When you get to the office, they've lost your copy from yesterday's robbery, so you have to rewrite it by 9 a.m. Then it's off to the mayor's press conference, followed by lunch at the Octoberfest (with perhaps too much beer). You were supposed to be off for the afternoon, but instead you're sent on overtime to participate in a Civil Defense earthquake emergency drill (you became a stretcher bearer for a 200-pound panic victim who overplayed the part). Dinner is at the Jamaican Centennial Celebration, where there is a 45-minute traditional dance for all assembled (and rum and cola is the only drink available). At 7:30 p.m., you're back on your own beat for the regular City Council meeting. After an hour of debate and discussion by members on zoning, you fall asleep.

You are awakened by cold air and bright lights. You sit up, look around, and find you are on an open sliding drawer in the city morgue. A clock on the wall shows it's 5 a.m. Your death certificate is pinned to your lapel. The only personal belongings on you are a marriage license showing you were lawfully wedded last night to an 83-year-old whose name you've never heard; a warrant for your arrest for DWI and leaving the scene of an accident; two used tickets to Tijuana; and an identification bracelet that indicates you are mentally incompetent.

Just as you begin to remember having fallen asleep at the meeting, two night watchmen find you and arrest you for breaking and entering, and vagrancy. You get booked and spend the rest of the night in a holding cell of the local jail.

At 8 a.m., Councilman Harvey DuBois of Northwood gets you released into his custody, gives you your personal effects and takes you to breakfast, where the remaining Council members are gathered laughing. They explain you've written many articles about their shortcomings during Council meetings, making some of them look foolish, so they decided to get revenge when you began to snore at last night's meeting. When they finished business, they decided to invoke the power of local government by contacting night judges and other city officials for the documents and to continue the prank.

During impromptu speeches, you jot the following quotes:

Edna Wilson of Edgemont: "We may be boring, but we don't tolerate snoring at City Council meetings."

DuBois: "You should be pleased. It takes most people four days to obtain a marriage license."

Bill McDonald of Glen Cove: "With a little more time, we could have had you buried or cremated."

Chris Denton of Northwood: "When the power of the press has been abdicated, it must be laid to rest."

EXERCISE 15.4

Leads and Ends

Write **another type** of lead and ending for each of the fact sets in Exercise 15.3. Label the new lead and ending you use according to chapter definitions.

Localizing National News Stories

Try this one-day experiment: Read your local newspaper; catch CNN's headlines; read a national newspaper; listen to a radio news report; read a news magazine; watch the evening national and local newscasts. You'll find extensive overlap in stories, especially in the most important stories. Are the mass media copycats?

Actually, some "copying" does occur. For instance, almost all news media subscribe to wire services, and journalists attend to the major networks and newspapers as part of their daily business routine. But the overlap in stories isn't exact duplication; often it's extension of the news elements.

This text's chapters on rewrites, continuing stories and sidebars cover some perspectives on developing and extending news stories. However, a separate presentation on localizing national news is appropriate because localization is such an important aspect of augmenting reader comprehension. These articles often form the major, front-page news series critical to local interests, and they frequently become the entries for reporting awards.

There is nothing mysterious about localizing national news. Trends and events that merit national attention also deserve local scrutiny. In fact, research shows that the news media set people's agenda of what is important, called the agenda-setting theory.[1]

---

[1] Donald L. Shaw and Maxwell E. McCombs, *The Emergence of American Political Issues: The Agenda-Setting Function of the Press* (St. Paul, Minn.: West, 1977). See also: Shanto Iyengar and Donald R. Kinder, *News That Matters: Television and American Opinion* (Chicago: University of Chicago Press, 1987); Lutz Erbring, Edie N. Goldenberg and Arthur H. Miller, "Front-Page News and Real-World Cues: A New Look at Agenda-Setting by the Media," *American Journal of Political Science* 24:16–49 (February 1980).

National issues, such as presidential elections, and local issues, such as property taxes, begin to receive attention in the media. After a while, the issues dominate the news and become the focus of public discussion. Social scientists who study the phenomenon report that the top half dozen issues that get the most space in the news media are likely to be the same half dozen issues people say are important. Each of us is aware of the major public issues, and our set of issues constitutes virtually the same set other people believe is important. The set of critical issues we carry in our heads is put there by the mass media. So, even if the media don't tell us what to think (persuasion), they do tell us what to think about.[2]

Agenda-setting theory offers a rationale for the confluence of major national news stories and explains the interest local audiences have in knowing as much as possible about important issues. Journalists provide a necessary service to readers by localizing national news.

Two types of national news stories suggest localization: news events and news trends. The difference between the two is similar to that of breaking, hard-news stories versus soft news or feature stories. For the local reporter-writer, the distinction relates primarily to initiative: how much resourcefulness and enterprise localization requires.

NEWS EVENTS

The international hostage crises of the early 1980s are examples of national stories with local slants. United States embassies were held, along with several dozen of their personnel; cruise ships were captured; gunmen boarded airplanes and threatened passengers' lives. In all, hundreds of American citizens became victims of terrorist acts and were held as bargaining chips for periods ranging from several days to several years. Some remain captive today.

Depending on the severity of the situation, these hostage crises dominated the national mass media for extensive time spans. The stories led evening newscasts and made banner headlines daily. In most instances, teams of reporters were dispatched to the scene of the incident, and others were sent to cities across the United States to report reactions from the hostages' families. After the national media left, local reporters took up the vigil because the hostages' relatives remained important news sources until after the episodes were resolved.

As in the hostage crisis stories, national news events frequently can be

[2] Maxwell E. McCombs and Donald L. Shaw, "The Agenda-Setting Function of the Mass Media," *Public Opinion Quarterly* 36:176–187 (1972).

localized by focusing on local sources who are associated in some way with the event. Sometimes the connection is the family link described, but more often it is an occupational link. A local businessman piloting his small aircraft misjudges an approach at the Indianapolis airport and hits a taxiing jetliner, causing both planes to explode. Of course near misses and accidents occur several times a year, but this one is likely to remain in the headlines for a few days. People in your community are certain to ask themselves, "Could a thing like that happen here?" So you call your local airport commissioner, the head of traffic control and the president of the local private pilots association. Your story addresses the local problems with overcrowding air traffic, airport terminal safety and private pilot licensing.

But a superior reporter should not wait for crisis-level news to think about localizing. A Pittsburgh police captain replaces patrol officers' sidearms and nightsticks with electronic stun guns. The national news media carry a story marking the first year without fatalities in the captain's district. You wonder if your local police have thought of using stun guns, so you call the chief and ask. The chief says that there's a lot of debate about stun guns' effectiveness in deterring crime and protecting officers. . . . You have a start on a good local story that answers the question many of your readers will want to know: "What about using stun guns here?"

Figure 16.1 depicts a national news event, the passage of a controversial Congressional bill aimed at controlling loan defaults by licensing bank officers. Five story ideas are suggested to localize the national event: to help local readers understand how the new federal law may affect the area's banking industry.

Most breaking news stories that are important enough to qualify for national media attention ought to spur local reporters to consider whether the story has implications for local audiences. The following is a short list of possibilities.

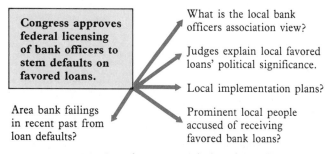

Figure 16.1   **National event with local implications**

1. A man walks into a Cleveland fast-food restaurant at 7:30 a.m. and opens fire with an automatic weapon: How easy is it to obtain an automatic weapon locally; has there been a similar tragedy here; are fast-food restaurants doing anything about security; can a local psychiatrist explain such incidents?

2. A successful transplant occurs in Houston using a new mechanical heart device: Are surgeons at your hospitals still performing transplants; would they if this new device proves successful?

3. Congress censures a national political figure for exceeding the personal income limits from lecturing fees: Who are your state's busiest political speakers; what do fees average; what do politicians talk about to justify charging fees; how are speaking arrangements made?

4. A singer's debut album wins a Grammy award in Las Vegas this year: How have her album sales been here; does she have a local following or a fan club?

5. A multiple fatality happens at a poorly marked railroad crossing in Kansas City: What is your county's accident record at rail crossings; are the warning devices computerized, safer; is there any advice from local rail officials to motorists?

None of these examples involves duplication of the national story, but all are extensions of the news event topic directed to local audience interests. In each case, a discrete news event triggers journalists' thoughts about a tie-in between the national event and the local situation. But how can journalists be expected to look for local angles to national events when their hands are full in just meeting their daily job responsibilities? The answer is that a competent journalist always considers a local tie-in to any important news event. Sometimes the link is only a reaction comment from local authorities; often it is a separate story, as the list of examples implies. Frequently, an editor whose job is to initiate story ideas, assigns localization stories in response to important national news.

For every item on the list of news event possibilities, several alternative localization approaches should occur to you, and even a beginner will recognize that there are hundreds of national news events begging for localization stories.

NEWS TRENDS

Trend stories require more reporter initiative than does localization of a single national news event, but they offer greater reader interest potential. The shooting at the fast-food restaurant is a discrete news event, but it is also part of a trend. For example, the news media have reported several incidents of disturbed people going berserk and shooting at innocent bystanders. But only as recently as the past few years have people—under psychiatric care or merely depressed—gone amok in fast-food restaurants. Is it a response to violent Hollywood films that depict shootouts in diners? Do crazed people, bent on destructiveness, seek familiar, crowded places without security guards? In short, is there a trend, why is it happening and what (if anything) is being done about the problem? Answers to such questions make a worthwhile local story even if the story appears several weeks after the national news event. However, in this instance and many others, the local reporter has to make the trend connection.

The process of making such connections is depicted in Figure 16.2. After reading several unrelated stories, published in perhaps a variety of mass media and business journals, a local reporter recognizes a trend. Innovative business people are being supported through a government "incubator," or management consultant office, that provides office space, financial counseling and grant coordination. None of the triggering stories focuses on local firms, but a business reporter should have no difficulty determining if there is a local tie-in for this trend. Countless such trends exist.

1. Some recent trends in the health care field:

A few years ago, minor emergency clinics were popping up across the country as a response to high costs of care at hospital emergency rooms. Then the hospitals waged price and quality wars with the new clinics through advertising campaigns in the mass media. Most recently, the clinics have been closing. What has happened? Have emergency rooms

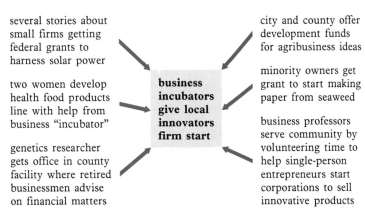

Figure 16.2 **National trend with local implications**

lowered prices? Did hospital advertising successfully persuade people that in a real health emergency, only the hospital facility was equipped to deal adequately with the crisis? Were minor emergency clinics only a passing fad, or is there some other explanation for their early success and later dissipation?

Everyone is aware that people are living longer, and that greater longevity has implications for health care. Homes for the elderly, with an on-premises medical staff, are a growth industry. However, annual inspections result in authorities finding some homes in violation of health care laws. Everyone should be concerned about the quality of these facilities locally, if not for members of their family or themselves, simply for humanitarian reasons. A story evaluating the homes, comparing costs and quality of care, ought to be at least a biannual undertaking.

Treating young people with alcohol or drug dependency problems is another recent health trend. Again, hospital treatment centers—facilities that didn't even exist a decade ago—now advertise on television. Treatments at some of these clinics cost families $25,000 for a 90-day program, and health insurance may cover only one such treatment. How effective are the programs? What happens to families when the insurance runs out? What are the implications for medical insurance premiums?

2. Trends in education:

In the last five years, some colleges of education dropped their undergraduate teaching degrees to offer only education master's degrees to students who already possess a baccalaureate in another field. This change was a response to countless national trend studies indicating that American education was losing ground. Part of the blame fell on education colleges that stressed the principles of teaching rather than emphasizing the teacher's future subject areas. Is the change working? Are education master's graduates better prepared for the classroom? Are school principals more pleased with their new hires? Do Parent-Teacher Associations approve of the change?

Hardly a day goes by without some national story about discipline problems in the elementary and secondary schools. We associate these incidents with the public schools in big cities, but a closer inspection might reveal the problem is more widespread. What's happening locally? What are the current local policies governing student discipline? Are they being followed? Why are there more discipline problems today? What do teachers and psychologists say?

Perhaps the single most important recent concern in subject matter is high-tech education. Computer literacy, math and science education in the United States is considered below par in comparison to that being offered by other nations. Is it true? If so, what's being done locally about improving high-tech education? Are there some success stories that might be imitated?

3. Trends in business:

The work force is shrinking. During most of the 1980s, jobs were difficult to find, particularly as manufacturing was being replaced by service industries. In the 1990s, "Help Wanted" signs appear in store windows, and larger corporations are hard-pressed to find capable employees. This trend is almost certain to continue as the population of working-age people diminishes. Businesses are "adopting" schools, cooperating with universities to develop better training programs and offering employee incentives to hire and retain workers. How is the trend affecting local business? What's being done to combat the problem? What are the implications for the future?

White-collar crime, from embezzlement to petty theft, is on the rise in spite of measures to fight it. Increased corporate security in the form of surveillance, psychological testing of employees, computer inventory control and uniformed armed guards attests to businesses' concern. Is the problem evident locally? If so, what precautions are being taken? What do managers and workers think?

Obviously, the list of societal trends is endless. Government, the family, religion, crime, drugs, marriages, housing, poverty, school dropouts, working women, illiteracy, waste control, taxes—virtually all of the national news concerns have implications for local audiences. However, while these issues often make the headlines, they usually aren't accentuated by a single compelling news event. Instead, a journalist must initiate local stories by consolidating less-conspicuous events from a longer time frame to identify a trend. Once identified, the trend must be matched with the reporter's knowledge of local conditions and audience interests. Finally, the reporter has to do some research and legwork to ensure that the trend localization story is applicable and worthwhile.

Trend localizations aren't feature articles. They don't capture readers' interest unless a compelling case can be made that the information is important. However, from the examples suggested, it should be evident that the localization topics are more important news items than this season's largest pumpkin or the firm that imports plaster yard ornaments shaped like animals. In fact, the trend topics being suggested for localization qualify as more important news than a local convenience store robbery or a fire in a boarded vacant house. These are the stories that help people make sense of their environment, that get discussed at local civic group board meetings and that eventually shape government policy.

RESEARCH REPORTS

A fertile field for trend localization is found in the proliferation of research studies sponsored by government agencies, universities, businesses and associations. Research reports provide the data on which policy decisions are made. Medical breakthroughs, social program improvements, prison reforms, import-export policies and water use programs, to name only a few developments, are founded on the results of statistical studies. These usually appear first in reports to the sponsoring agency, which may or may not release them to the media. Some of the

Pouring through magazines and journal indexes, searching library files and computer databases, reporters try to make sense of national trends that affect their local readers. This behind-the-scenes research isn't glamorous, but it can lead to prize-winning journalism.

research reports appear in scholarly publications or become the basis for stories in trade journals. For instance, *JAMA,* the *Journal of the American Medical Association,* reports medical research findings and is a primary source of major news stories on the latest discoveries and practices in medicine.

Thousands of periodicals carry research reports that rarely receive the media attention and localization their content deserves. Sponsoring agencies also send copies of the research reports, or news releases summarizing the reports, to the mass media. However, local reporters read them infrequently, and seldom use them to develop local news stories. Some of the reluctance is understandable and perhaps wise:

1. Although beat reporters should stay abreast of research reports in their specialty area, time constraints often prevent sufficient background reading.

2. A cautious journalist should weigh research reports with some degree of skepticism, recognizing that the results might be tainted by special interests of the sponsoring agency. For example, a research report about a product isn't likely to be sent to the media unless the findings show the product in a favorable light. A political candidate isn't likely to release a poll that shows the candidate's opponent is ahead. Similar reservations should be attached to many research reports that may be biased in favor of the sponsoring agency's special interest.

3. Often, a research report doesn't contain enough information so that anyone can assess its accuracy or legitimacy. Journalists wanting to use the information might have to expend considerable time and effort to verify the report's honesty. Incomplete research reports should raise warning flags of doubt.

While these are legitimate objections to using research reports, the main reason journalists shun statistical data is lack of comprehension. Too often, the value of research findings is obscured by cumbersome figures and tables, and by scientific jargon in the text of the reports. Additionally, most journalists aren't trained in statistics or scientific method, so they often are unable to interpret the data or evaluate the worth of research findings. Fortunately, as the reports proliferate and the media come to rely more on them as a source for important news, more reporters are being trained in social science research methods. If the national media run a story from a government census report that reveals a continuing trend for young adults to marry later in life, local media today are likely to develop a separate story for their readers. A Wisconsin newspaper might build a story based on the government report's figures for marrying ages in Milwaukee or statewide, along with comments from local sources about the implications of later marriages.

The amount of initiative required for a reporter to localize research reports falls between that required for news events and trends. The research report itself is an "event," but without the attention-grabbing impact of a major news occurrence. Although journalists must interpret the findings in relation to local audience interests, research reports frequently contain a plethora of comparative data and an implications section that make the inherent trends rather explicit. Much of the reporter's direction for localizing the story is contained in the research report. Consider the following possible report topics:

1. A city housing report provides figures on the number and average income of below-poverty-level families in the metropolitan area. It gives data on the number of low-income dwelling units and the number of units completed in each of the past five years. The report compares these figures with statistics for comparable-size cities and concludes that the number of homeless families in this area is higher than that in comparable cities.

2. The Federal Aviation Administration releases a study of airline fares that shows average round-trip costs by distance of flights. Costs at the largest 100 airports are compared. Prices for flights from your state's major airport (65 miles away) are among the top ten in the nation.

3. A sanitation inspection report for the meat-packing industry is released. The report contains statistics on which firms have paid fines for violations, how much was paid and how many violations were recorded for each company. A table in the report also shows the incidence of wholesale shipment recalls and the number of restaurant food poisoning cases related to spoiled meat. Your newspaper is located in a beef-producing state.

4. The annual meeting of governors receives a consulting firm's report that has tables of city government employees per capita. The governors will use the data to reduce matching dollars to municipalities that employ significantly more than the average number of workers per population levels. Your city has far fewer than the average number of employees, and in some municipal departments the number of workers is the least in the nation.

5. A *Chronicle of Higher Education* article reports a study from the Department of Education that shows the average length of term in office for college presidents and academic vice presidents. A comparison is made between public and private colleges, and a breakdown is given by university size categories and by tuition cost categories. Finally, a table shows differences in length of terms by whether or not the administrator held a doctorate

degree. The article points out that terms of non-doctorate administrators are shorter, and that non-doctorates are likely to be political appointments.

As with the news event and general trend examples, these illustrations of possible research report localization stories suggest only a few topics among thousands of potential major news stories of interest to local readers. A journalist should have little difficulty convincing an editor to allot time to develop these stories, and space to publish them. In fact, by recognizing their value to readers, the journalist who initiates localization stories will quickly earn a reputation as a credit to the staff and to the profession.

SUMMARY

National news stories localized to augment reader comprehension often are the major front-page news series, and they frequently become the entries for annual reporting awards.

The overlap in national news reports suggests that the mass media purposely copy one another. Although there is duplication in the day's news, much of this repetition is due to reader interest in major news events. A mass media theory called agenda-setting explains why media and the public interest result in a spiraling attention to the same important topics.

Two types of national news stories suggest localization: news events and news trends. For the local reporter-writer, the distinction relates primarily to initiative: how much resourcefulness and enterprise localization requires. National events can be localized by focusing on local sources associated with the event. Sometimes the connection is a family link, but more often it is occupational. With trend stories, the local reporter has to make the trend connection, but these stories offer greater reader interest potential. A third category of localization stories are those taken from research reports. Reporters often have difficulty using research reports, but their value as the basis for important news makes learning how to interpret and evaluate them worthwhile.

The chapter presents a host of examples of news event, news trend and research report localization. However, it emphasizes that the illustrations are only a few suggestions from the thousands of important topics about which local stories can and should be written.

_____ **Thinking it Through** _____

EXERCISE 16.1

News Event Localization

For each of these story fact sets, determine what the local story is likely to emphasize. Then list sources you would use to develop the local story.

A An explosion at a Wyoming power plant releases toxic gasses resulting in 10 deaths, at least 30 injuries and the evacuation of the town. Power plant officials say the gas emission was the result of a relatively new substance the company has been using to lower machinery resistance during power generation.

Local story topic:

Sources: 1. _____

2. _____

3. _____

B A bloc of Eastern European nations purchases $2 billion in wheat, soybeans, corn and rice from U.S. stockpile reserves. The government announces that the deal will lower the national deficit, and negotiations are now taking place for several more deals in the next five years. The government is reconsidering its current farm subsidy program. It anticipates excellent near-term sales for food staples and other farm products, including vegetables, fruit and cotton. The European sale means a bonanza for farm-belt communities.

Local story topic:

Sources: 1. _____

2. _____

3. _____

C A married couple in Jacksonville, Fla., is arrested for espionage. The couple lived in the community for eight years and they have two children attending public schools, yet the FBI is accusing them of being agents of a foreign government that trained them to infiltrate the United States as high-tech industry spies. He worked for IBM; she was a secretary in a National Aeronautics and Space Administration office.

Local story topic:

Sources: 1. _____

2. _____

3. _____

D Colleges will be permitted to pay as many as 30 athletes up to $25,000 per student, according to a new ruling by the National Collegiate Athletic Association. The policy change is a trial designed to acknowledge that collegiate sports is a major money-maker for most schools and that "amateur" status for players is no longer realistic under the present system that has seen countless violations of rules that are impossible to police.

Local story topic:

Sources: 1. _____

2. _____

3. _____

E Drug enforcement officials made their largest bust ever at the Texas border when truckloads of marijuana with a street value in excess of $200 million was seized today. Customs officials said detecting the drug was the easiest part of the bust. South American and Mexican fields were sprayed last year with a chemical that has no effect on the plants or marijuana users. However, the chemical can be detected in concentrations of marijuana from distances of several miles. Customs officials said, "We expect to close down the import of this illegal substance by next January."

Local story topic:

Sources: 1. _____

2. _____

3. _____

EXERCISE 16.2

Trend Localization

For each of these story fact sets, determine what the local story is likely to emphasize. Then list sources you would use to develop the local story.

A

1. Two runners in the New York Marathon died of heat exhaustion this year.

2. An entrant in a "fun-run" in Dayton sued the sponsoring charity for injuries received in a fall during the race.

3. A corporate sponsor withdrew from a 10-kilometer charity run in Knoxville, Tenn.

4. The Arthritis Foundation issued a directive to local chapters advising them to have volunteer runners sign a waiver against damages before being allowed to run in charity races.

Local story topic:

Sources: 1. _____

2. _____

3. _____

B

1. The American Civil Liberties Union opposes a police tactic designed to prevent motorists from driving under the influence of alcohol. The tactic, called "spotting," allows police to stop suspicious drivers, talk with them and force them to take a breath test if they appear intoxicated.

2. Following use of the spotting tactic, highway patrol units in four states reported July 4th auto fatalities decreased by more than 10 percent this year.

3. Police in Atlanta and Omaha are requesting permission to use the "spotting" regulation in efforts against drug suspects. They want to stop and search vehicles of suspected drug dealers.

4. A cache of machine guns is discovered in the truck of a man stopped at a highway "spotting" point. The arrest is ruled illegal and the case is thrown out of court.

Local story topic:

Sources: 1. _____

2. _____

3. _____

C

1. New York City apartment owners form a coalition to bargain against rent control statutes. Owners say they want to repair their dilapidated and haz-

ardous property, but they cannot afford to do so without some increase in the amount of rent they can charge.

2. A Housing and Urban Development report shows that 35 percent of the apartment units built before 1960 are uninhabited and beyond restoration. It recommends the buildings be razed and the land be sold or new apartments be constructed.

3. In Phoenix, a government loan enables low-income housing tenants to purchase their 200-unit complex. Residents say they will begin repairs.

4. A corporation in Providence, R.I., purchased a vacated government housing project and established a shelter for the city's homeless. Several of the city's civic groups are helping the new occupants restore the project. Police have volunteered assistance because the housing project has reduced crime in the harbor area.

Local story topic:

Sources: 1. _____

2. _____

3. _____

D

1. Several incidents have been reported of children treated for chemical burns to their feet and legs after playing in their front yard.

2. One case has been reported of a 4-year-old being blinded after playing on a Slip-and-Slide water skid in the front yard.

3. A hospital near a fashionable Denver suburban neighborhood reported a dozen separate cases during the summer of skin rashes, swelling and blisters on children's hands, feet and legs. Doctors said the injuries resembled acid burns.

4. A Davenport, Iowa, lawyer filed a $1 million personal injury suit against a lawn chemical spraying firm after the lawyer's child was hospitalized. The 7-year-old had an allergic reaction and stopped breathing during a picnic in the front yard.

Local story topic:

Sources: 1. _____

2. _____

3. _____

EXERCISE 16.3

Research Report Localization

For each of these story fact sets, determine what the local story is likely to emphasize. Then list sources you would use to develop the local story.

A A federal audit of government construction projects in Washington, D.C., shows that a disproportionate share of contract jobs and dollar amounts goes to eight firms in the District of Columbia area. In each case, the firms are owned by relatives of public officials, although these officials have no connection with the agencies that let the contracts. Six of the eight firms are the largest construction companies in the District; two are average-sized firms of about 50 employees. The report alleges no legal infractions or breach of ethics. However, it suggests that agency directors may be influenced by the family association between the contracting firms and the politicians.

Local story topic:

Sources: 1. _____

2. _____

3. _____

B The third report in a series by Stanford University's Institute for Communication Research indicates that children's television viewing hours has no adverse effect on their school achievement in the fourth through 10th grades. The report shows that matched samples of heavy and light television viewers in four U.S. cities achieved the same standardized test scores. However, the study shows a weak negative correlation between television viewing and test scores in grades one through three and grades 11 and 12. Researchers say they suspect these latter correlations will be erased when the data are analyzed for family demographics in the early grades and for psychological profiles of students in the two higher grades.

Local story topic:

Sources: 1. _____

2. _____

3. _____

C　A trade publication for a growers association carries an article based on a survey of its membership. The article shows that a majority of chicken and catfish farms are now owned by multinational conglomerates. Ten years ago, 70 percent of both industries were "mom and pop" operations with fewer than 20 employees. Today, only 45 percent of the annual yield in chickens and catfish is being produced by the small American firms. Additionally, the multinational corporations are exporting almost one-third of their yield while virtually none of the small firms is exporting any of its annual yield.

Local story topic:

Sources: 1. _____

2. _____

3. _____

D　A study by the League of Women Voters shows that more than 95 percent of the national elected officials are incumbents. Beyond the substantial benefit of name recognition, the report says, these are other factors leading to reelection by incumbents:

1. ability to raise campaign funds;
2. mailings paid for by the government through elected officials' franking privileges;
3. connections with state and local party machines after their first election;
4. ease in getting speaking engagements through their political positions; and
5. challengers' fear of entering a campaign against an incumbent.

Local story topic:

Sources: 1. _____

2. _____

3. _____

E　An article in an environmental journal charts the flow of toxic waste from its source to federally approved waste sites. The national map of these routes shows that 80 percent of the mileage matches the miles of interstate highways. According to the article, alternate routes that avoid the more populated areas and the high-traffic interstates should be used. Another 10 percent of the mileage matches the routes of commercial railroad freight, which also travels through populated areas. The article urges use of secondary rail routes through more rural areas.

Local story topic:

Sources: 1. _____

2. _____

3. _____

Legal and Ethical Considerations

Knowing your legal responsibilities and rights as a journalist is vital to success in the profession. The quickest way to exit from the field is to be tagged as a person who regularly gets involved in legal problems; to a nervous employer, twice means regularly. Understanding the ethical implications of reporting and writing is vital to your self-respect. Again, your career in journalism is only as firm as the confidence your sources and colleagues have in you.

Placing this chapter at the end of a basic newswriting text is not intended to diminish the importance of the topics presented. In fact, you will have discussed this chapter's substance throughout the term, probably extensively, because so much of the reporting and writing process is intertwined with legal and ethical considerations. Some instructors will have assigned these contents earlier in the term, or will have suggested reading the sections on libel or copyright when errors on assignments showed the need for better understanding.

However, this chapter presents only a cursory look at legal and ethical concerns. It is a truncated overview of both of these broad and indispensable aspects of journalism. The scope of topics covered is incomplete because each of these two subject areas constitutes a separate course in journalism education. This discussion is limited to only a few of the most critical legal and ethical concerns a beginning reporter or writer is likely to face.

LEGAL CONSIDERATIONS

Six areas of law are identified as being most important in news reporting and writing:

- libel
- invasion of privacy
- open records and meetings
- free press/fair trial
- confidentiality
- copyright.

Libel

Always the profession's single greatest legal concern, libel is not well-understood by the public or, unfortunately, by journalists. What journalists do understand is that libel actions against the media have become the first line of defense by politicians, public figures and organized crime. When media investigations launch reports of improprieties, a libel suit is almost sure to be filed. It's partly done to indicate publicly that the alleged impropriety is a false accusation and partly to silence the media: to halt further reports. Often the strategy succeeds because the recent history of jury verdicts in libel cases shows juries tend to favor the plaintiff (party bringing the complaint) and tend to award huge monetary damages. While damage awards are frequently reduced on appeal, the media's real predicament with a libel suit is the cost of fighting it: Whether you win or lose, you lose.

Libel is defined as anything disseminated (printed or broadcast) that defames someone (the person need not be named) in one of three ways:

1. It damages the person's good name or reputation in the community by suggesting the person has done something illegal, immoral, contemptible or ridiculous.
2. It damages the person's livelihood by suggesting the person is incompetent, unreliable, bankrupt or unethical.
3. It reduces the person's enjoyment of normal social activity by suggesting the person is stupid, insane, gay or has a contagious disease.

Obviously the range of possibilities is too encompassing to offer you an easy guide for guarding against libel. Perhaps the best advice is to be wary of writing something that you would resent having someone write about you. That doesn't mean you shouldn't write it, but you should be alert about possible libel before you do.

Libel law contains several additional stipulations a journalist should know. For instance:

- a person can collect damages in a libel suit without having to prove that a financial loss was suffered;
- a libel suit can be lost even when the journalist had no malice (intent to harm); identifying a person incorrectly through a wrong address might result in a lost libel suit because journalists are held responsible for being competent . . . for taking appropriate precautions to check facts;
- journalists are held responsible if they publish libelous statements made by others; so even if a libelous statement appears in a direct quote, the media can still lose a libel action;
- basing a libelous story on a "confidential," or unnamed, source can be considered "reckless disregard" for the truth and grounds for losing a libel suit; many editors justifiably refuse to publish stories that contain unnamed sources for this reason.

With so many possibilities for libel actions, how can a journalist protect against libel? Clearly, the best protection is accuracy. Check your facts scrupulously so you don't make any mistakes. But no one is perfect. Before you find yourself in purgatory on a potentially libelous story, go through the checklist of defenses shown in Figure 17.1.

1 – Is the statement true; can I prove it?

2 – If I can't prove it's true, is it privileged?

 3 – If it is privileged, is the account fair and accurate?

4 – If 1 and 2 above can't be proved, is it criticism of a public figure?

 5 – If it is criticism of a public figure, is the statement part of the figure's public presence?

6 – Is the statement "fair comment and criticism"?

7 – Has the person consented to publication, or is the person replying to a libel?

8 – Should I consult an editor if there's any doubt?

Figure 17.1 Checklist of defenses against libel

At the risk of burdening beginning journalists with more detail about libel than may be needed, this checklist embodies most of the general principles of libel law, the single greatest area of journalistic legal concern.

First, ask yourself if you can prove that the potentially libelous statement is true. *Knowing* that the statement is true is easy; being able to prove it in court can be extremely difficult. There is some indication that the law is changing on this point as courts require the plaintiff to prove the statement is false in topics of public concern. Which party has the burden of proof is often critical to winning the case. Still, a journalist would be wise to think in terms of having to prove a statement's truth.

However, if you can't prove the statement is true, perhaps it is privileged. *Privilege* is a legal term meaning that certain official proceedings and records are open to publication without question. If you base your story on a privileged statement, you aren't likely to lose a libel case. An example of privilege is a statement made on the floor of the U.S. Senate or one made during a jury trial. The main problem with privilege is that not every "official" document or proceeding is legally privileged. For instance, the record of arrestees booked into the city jail may not be privileged, and neither are all court transcripts. A journalist has to know which statements are protected by privilege.

But privilege doesn't take journalists off the hook entirely. The written account of privileged statements must be a fair and accurate representation. To report only the prosecution's trial testimony without including needed balancing testimony from the defense would curtail the protection of privilege. The rationale for this rule is to protect against misrepresentation by selective omissions from privileged statements. The accuracy requirement is that a report from privileged material be accurate in its essential facts.

If truth can't be proven in court, and the statements aren't privileged, a protection may exist if the alleged libel is criticism of a public official or a public figure. This is a relatively new area of libel law: a special category recognized by the courts only during the last generation. To maintain a free flow of debate on public policy issues, the courts have recognized a distinction between "private" and "public" persons. Public persons are those in the news because they hold public office or because they are celebrities. The idea behind recognizing such a category was to allow the media some latitude in reporting on officials' job-related activities without abnormal media concern about libel. Notice that the public figure protection provides only a little more leeway in reporting, and the subject matter must be related to the public-interest aspects of public persons, not their private lives.

Problem areas for the journalist involve deciding who might be recognized as a public person (unless the person holds public office, this can be a close call) and determining that the potentially libelous statement is in fact related to the figure's public interest area. Additionally, the courts won't protect a journalist who makes libelous statements with actual malice, which is prior knowledge of a statement's falsity, or with "reckless disregard" for the truth. We know already that basing stories on unnamed sources can be considered reckless disregard; so also is failing to follow reasonable journalistic procedures to ascertain accuracy before publication.

Another possible defense against libel is if the statements constitute fair comment and criticism. This is the area of libel that protects editorial opinion, music and theater reviews, and news analyses. However, journalists must be sure that the defamatory words are reasonable conclusions based on the facts rather than statements of facts masquerading as opinion. For instance, you quote someone who says, "I think Coach Smith got roaring drunk before the big game last night." That's a statement of fact pretending to be an opinion, because no facts are furnished. However, you could write: "The fifth of whiskey that dropped from his pocket onto the field, and his crawling back to the bench after the coin toss, indicated he might have been drunk before the game." Here the underlying facts are supplied.

Two other possibilities exist that might help protect a journalist who is unable to prove truth or privilege. The damaged person may have consented to publication in some way. While such circumstances are unusual, they do occur. Perhaps the injured party told the reporter, "Talk with Joe Smith. He witnessed the whole thing." The other possibility is when a person quoted in the libel is replying to a statement in which he or she was libeled. Here the person is exercising the right of self-defense, which offers a protection for the journalist writing the story. However, in both of these situations the journalist should already be alerted to the possibility of a libel suit, so there is little excuse for making a serious error at this point or placing yourself in a position that requires relying on either of these legal protections. Actually, these protections generally are accepted only in conjunction with other defenses.

The final consideration in Figure 17.1 is not a defense but a precaution. Should you consult an editor if you have any doubt about the accuracy or verifiability of what you're writing? Obviously, you should always alert your editor to a potentially libelous statement.

Invasion of Privacy

Under the privacy area of law, the truth of a statement is not the issue being presented, so libel is not part of the problem. Instead, an invasion of privacy action involves the right of a citizen to be left alone. Journalists have become almost as concerned about the area of law governed by privacy statutes as they are about libel. There are four main categories of invasion of privacy: (1) intrusion on solitude, (2) violations of private matters, (3) casting a person in a false light and (4) using a person's name or likeness for commercial gain.

Intrusion on solitude. Court decisions have established a body of limitations beyond which reporters may not go to gather information for a story. The limits are the same for all citizens. But, as applied to this profession, the rules bar reporters from the following activities:

- trespassing illegally on private property
- placing a "bug" or listening device on private property
- using a false identity to gain access (for instance, claiming to be a police officer)
- going to "unreasonable" lengths to obtain a photograph
- unreasonably harassing a person for information, regardless of whether that person is in a private or a public place.

While no ethical individual would attempt such intrusions (some are illegal), journalists occasionally have been asked by their superiors to breach these limits or have done so on their own initiative in the heat of pursuing a story. The best way to avoid temptation is to remember that no laws afford journalists any more rights of access than those granted to all other citizens. But, just like any other citizen, you do have the right to engage a person in a public place, as long as you don't harass.

Violations of private matters. This area of law presents problems for journalists, who frequently must provide background in their stories. You may provide background, but it should be pertinent to the current news element in the story. For instance, if a woman is a candidate for mayor, publishing the fact that she had an abortion when she was 18 years old would be a violation of private matters, under most circumstances. If the woman is running for an elected juvenile court judgeship on an anti-abortion platform, her early abortion experience becomes a pertinent aspect of today's news.

Casting a person in a false light. Journalists should assume nothing, yet we often make the same erroneous stereotypes that others do. For instance, the fact that a man has a ponytail, wears a leather jacket and rides a motorcycle does not necessarily mean that he is a member of a motorcycle gang. Making such an assumption (this one actually happened) can cast a person in a false light and result in an invasion of privacy action. Journalists get into false light difficulties when they embellish or distort quotes (another reason for accuracy in quoting) and thereby depict the source as saying something erroneous or foolish. The difference between libel and false light is subtle, but libel implies serious damage to reputation, whereas false light damage might be only for embarrassment caused by inaccurate portrayal.

Using a person's name or likeness for commercial gain. Photographers and free-lance writers must guard against violating this privacy statute. The rule is that people have a right to the monetary rewards their image or name brings in commercial (non-news) uses. Publishing a famous model or celebrity's picture in a news story is fair use, but the celebrity is entitled to be paid if that picture later appears in an advertisement or on a magazine cover.

Caveats and defenses. Although invasion of privacy is a rapidly expanding area of legal entanglement for journalists, people who sue must prove that the publication would be considered highly offensive to a reasonable person. This guideline leaves much private material open to publication without fear of losing a lawsuit.

Also, there are two defenses against some invasion of privacy suits. First, did the person consent to the invasion? Consent is pertinent in intrusion, private matters and commercial gain cases. Permission can be either written or oral, although a journalist who anticipates possible legal action should try to have a witness for oral consent. Unless the consent is in writing or corroborated by witnesses, it's difficult to guess how a court might rule on this first defense.

The second defense is newsworthiness, or being able to prove that publishing the material was necessary to the public interest. Newsworthiness is pertinent in violations of private matters and commercial gain. If relying on the newsworthiness defense, a journalist should ask: (1) will the information being sought serve any significant purpose by being published—does the public need to know, and (2) is the material relevant to the story?

Although the privacy area of law deals primarily with how information is obtained, the remaining four areas of law that concern reporters and writers focus narrowly on access to information. Reporters who most frequently face problems with these laws are those who cover the courts, government and public affairs issues. But editors expect every journalist to know these areas of law. A reiteration of an earlier point is appropriate here: No laws grant rights specifically to journalists. Instead, rights of access to information are granted to the public, so a journalist has only as many rights to information as does any other citizen. However, the journalist is more likely to exercise those rights as a representative of the public.

Open Records and Meetings

Each state has its own laws governing the kinds of records and the portions of those records that are open to the public. The most encompassing law in this area is the federal Freedom of Information Act, which itemizes what kinds of records are closed to the public, but allows the public access to all other official documents. The FOI Act says the public may have copies of the records by paying the costs for making copies, and the law specifies that government agencies in charge of the records must provide them to the public on request within a reasonable period of time. However, if public officials seek to thwart journalists' efforts to obtain documents, they may take several months to process the copies and hope that the documents' news value will wane.

In the 25 years the FOI Act has been in effect, several presidential administrations have tried to restrict access to documents under the act. These attempts have failed, and the media remain successful in securing documents by filing FOI requests. In fact, the FOI Act has been a dominant force in obtaining crucial records of everything from international espionage to local political corruption to misappropriation of funds by registered charities.

But the FOI Act is national in scope, and state governments have enacted public records laws that often impede the intent of the federal law. Journalists must know their state's laws on official documents; otherwise they run the risk of being bullied by every minor public servant who feels empowered to deny access to records.

Closely associated with open records is the problem of open meetings. Open meetings laws are called sunshine laws, suggesting that meetings at which government officials decide public policy questions should be open to public scrutiny: Such meetings should take place with "the sun shining in" rather than happen behind closed doors. The rationale for such laws goes to the heart of governing by democracy. If the majority is to rule, then decisions by the elected representatives must be open to full public debate.

Today, the mass media serve as society's main conduit of information. The public depends on the media to report government decision making. Consider a city council debating whether to raise its members' salaries 25 percent. Every taxpayer in the city has a vested interest in the council's decision, but if the council holds its debate behind closed doors—barring both the public and the mass media from attending these meetings—the public is denied its right to know about how the decision was reached. In fact, the public might not even learn which council members supported or opposed the raise. Government bodies often debate sensitive issues, and their members occasionally attempt to avoid public inquiries by closing the meetings.

The only federal laws governing open meetings are those directed at public bodies on the national level. But most states have enacted their own sunshine laws directed at state and local governing bodies. Some state laws are extremely restrictive: Closed meetings are rarely allowed. Other states are far more permissive, allowing government bodies to close meetings frequently. These are some topics of public business that often result in closed meetings:

- personnel matters such as the hiring, firing and misconduct of public employees
- real estate transactions and the discussion of bids on public works projects
- discussions of pending law suits against the government body
- labor negotiations.

The discussion of many of these topics does seem to justify a closed meeting. For instance, the city council loses its negotiating effectiveness if union employees know the council is willing to grant them across-the-board annual salary increases of 7.5 percent. However, most states permit closed meetings to discuss a variety of less critical subjects, and many governing bodies close meetings to hide debate that might be embarrassing rather than because it is crucial to conducting public business. Further, the sunshine laws prescribe minimum penalties, if any, perhaps only a reprimand or a $100 fine to a public official who illegally closes a meeting. The power of these laws lies in any perceived harm to an official's career from being marked as a person who illegally barred the public from knowing what transpired at a public policy meeting.

When barred from a meeting, journalists must assert their right to be present as members of the public and as surrogates for the public interest. Most press associations provide printed sunshine law cards that journalists carry and from which journalists read aloud if a public meeting is about to be closed. Public officials may refrain from closing a meeting when confronted with the law and a reporter willing to challenge them, or they may be inclined to risk public consternation and close the meeting anyway.

Free Press/Fair Trial

The free press versus fair trial area of law exists because the First Amendment freedoms of an unrestricted press are often pitted against the Sixth Amendment guarantee of a fair trial. The First Amendment seems to allow full coverage of any jury trial. Generally, what happens in open court is considered accessible to press coverage. But the Sixth Amendment requires that a defendant be given a fair trial by an impartial jury of peers, and judges worry that press coverage of the trial might interfere with impartiality.

These conflicting Bill of Rights guarantees have resulted in a host of judicial restrictions on trial coverage, including closing the trial to the press and the public. The extent of press restrictions often depends on the nature of the case, a judge's assessment of how much leeway the law allows to control the courtroom and, sometimes, the judge's current opinion of the media.

Judges' most frequent restriction on the press involves prejudicial, pretrial publicity, or statements that appear in the mass media that may not be admissible in court. Pretrial publicity can include anything published about the case from the time the crime is committed to the beginning of a trial. For instance, a graphic description of the crime scene might result in community outrage against any suspect who is later charged with the crime, or publication of the prosecutor's statement, "We have this villain's confession to this murder and four others," may preclude the selection of an unbiased jury among community residents. Judges issue "gag orders" restricting pretrial reporting, and they occasionally rule that the media may not publish anything about the case. The outcome is that the public loses its source of information about the crime, the arrest, police procedures in the case and even trial coverage.

Penalties for not abiding by the judge's ruling can range from the publication's being fined to the journalist's being held in contempt of court, which might mean going to jail. In instances where the media believe the judge's restrictions are within the law, the rules are followed. When the media believe the judge has breached the press's freedom to report, the media appeal the judge's ruling to a higher court.

Many state bar associations and press associations have established guidelines that all parties follow for trial coverage. A journalist should know these rules but should work closely with an editor in any free press versus fair trial conflict.

Confidentiality

The confidentiality area of law involves keeping the names of sources, and possibly other facts, hidden. Imagine that a source agrees to give you a story only on the condition you don't divulge her name. She tells you that a house on the outskirts of town is being used to store drugs. You do some investigating, find out that the story is true and write an article about the house. The police raid the place, but discover the drugs were removed the night before. Chances are the police will want to talk to you about where you got the information. If you refuse to divulge your source, you could find yourself testifying before a grand jury and being faced with jail for your refusal. Instances such as this don't occur frequently, but reporters do get a lot of information from sources they would rather not name simply because the source might not provide information again.

There is no federal law that protects a reporter from having to reveal information when required to do so by the proper legal authority. A reporter has no more right than any other citizen to keep information secret. In fact, if police had found a body in the house, the reluctant reporter might be withholding information in a murder case.

Many states have enacted "shield laws," or statutes that do give reporters the right not to reveal information. Some state shield laws are broad: they protect a reporter in a variety of situations. But the shield laws generally are designed to protect reporters from being harassed for information when the information could be secured another way. None of the states' shield laws would protect a journalist in either of the two situations described because both involve the possible commission of a felony.

Again, a journalist must know the state's laws. However, confidentiality problems can be avoided in two ways: (1) don't promise your sources confidentiality unless you're prepared to go to jail for the story . . . very few stories are worth it, and (2) don't use unidentified sources in your stories. Actually, most editors refuse to publish stories that contain unidentified sources. They justifiably believe that unnamed sources reduce media credibility, and they don't want to be put in the position of having to defend a reporter's secrecy for anything other than a major investigative piece. Even for a major story, editors usually insist on two sources to corroborate facts, or they want to know who the unnamed sources are.

Journalists can avoid confidentiality problems by adopting the habit of naming sources in all their stories. In fact, a journalist must know what the newspaper or station's policy is on confidentiality. Editors often insist on knowing the confidential source's name as part of a policy in which only the media organization, not the reporter, has the right to grant confidentiality.

Copyright

The last area of law that consistently concerns reporters and writers is copyright, or the protection against infringement of literary property. Writers often must quote copyrighted sources, which is usually no problem if the quoted material is short and is properly attributed to the source. Failure to properly attribute is called plagiarism.

Unfortunately, recent evidence suggests that few journalism students know what constitutes plagiarism, and they are surprised when they are told their stories contain plagiarism.[1] The evidence also indicates a high frequency of plagiarism. However, there should be little reason for a writer to have plagiarism difficulties if only one thing is remembered: It's illegal to use someone else's published words as your own. Note that ideas may be used; it's only the words themselves—the way they were put on the page—that can't be used without direct quotes.

Admittedly, you aren't likely to be sued for plagiarism. You are likely to be fired and have difficulty finding another job in journalism, but you probably won't be sued. Copyright lawsuits usually are brought against the media only when the author or owner of the original work believes that revenue was lost by the illegal publication of part of the work. For instance, a celebrity publishes an autobiography, and advance copies of the book are sent to the media for review or other publicity purposes. A major newspaper excerpts three of the most exciting pages of the book. If sales of the book go badly, the publisher might sue the newspaper, claiming that by publishing copyrighted material, the newspaper hurt book sales. Notice that a copyright suit can occur even when the source of the material is given proper credit. The issue in most copyright cases is that the work's value was reduced because it was illegally reproduced.

In such a situation, the newspaper would have to prove "fair use" of the material. Fair use depends on four factors: (1) how was the work used, (2) what is the nature of the copyrighted work, (3) how much of the copyrighted work was used in relation to the whole and (4) what effect on the potential market value of the work did the copyright infringement have? As is evident from this list, a jury might award damages in a wide variety of circumstances, even in cases in which the offending publication clearly had no intent to cheat the owner of the original work.

Of course, the best way to avoid copyright problems is to get permission to use the work, even if it means paying a fee. Journalists run into the problem of not having time to get permission. When time is an issue, consider the following guidelines to avoid copyright litigation:

- limit quoted material to fewer than 100 words from a book

---

[1] Bonnie J. Brownlee, "Coping with Plagiarism Requires Several Strategies," *Journalism Educator* 41:4 (Winter 1987): 25–29. See also: David Shaw, "Plagiarism: A Taint on Journalism," and "Recycling the News: Just Laziness or Plagiarism?" *The Los Angeles Times* (July 5 and July 6, 1984, respectively); and Jerry Chaney and Tom Duncan, "Editors, Teachers Disagree about Definition of Plagiarism," *Journalism Educator* 40:2 (Summer 1985): 13–16.

- limit quoted material to less than one or two paragraphs from a magazine article
- remember that even one line from a poem or a song might result in a copyright infringement suit.

ETHICAL CONSIDERATIONS

The three dimensions of ethics are: individual, organizational and societal. At the expense of a more philosophical approach to ethics (meta-ethical questions about why reporters should be ethical), this presentation views laws as the minimum standards by which societies are maintained. Although a society has laws covering specific ethical areas, what is legal may not be ethical and vice versa. Reporters and editors may have higher individual standards than either organizational (media) policy or society's laws. Ethical considerations involve the moral values people hold . . . a

Editors faced an ethical dilemma after Pennsylvania State Treasurer R. Budd Dwyer called a press conference prior to being sentenced on a kickback conviction. When the media assembled in his office, Dwyer drew a gun and committed suicide as the press recorded the entire act. Editors across the nation had to decide if grisly photos of this sad scene were appropriate to use.

level beyond society's minimum standards. Because journalists are power brokers—their work influences public policy and can drastically affect people's lives—they face ethical dilemmas nearly on a daily basis.

Slanting and Editorializing

Perhaps the single most frequent ethical consideration a journalist faces is how to be fair in reporting and writing. Objectivity and fairness are discussed in Chapter 1, where it was pointed out that objectivity is an ideal: No one can be totally objective. Yet journalists must strive to be as fair as possible. A story may be absolutely accurate (every fact in it is verifiable), but the overall impression of the article might be false or misleading. The story is slanted. Journalists realize this happens, and that their personal professionalism can reduce its frequency: thorough reporting that reveals all facets of a story, and effective writing that discloses those facets in the article. However, a conscientious journalist has the ethical plight of worrying about having done enough.

Editorializing is similar to slanting, but the term implies that a journalist is altering the story purposely. Actually, beginning news writers stumble into editorializing by carelessly including their opinions in the story: "Smith mistakenly called our student elections a popularity contest." This sort of error is easily caught, but editorializing errors also stem from the writer's decision of what to emphasize, deemphasize or omit.

Slanting and editorializing clearly are unethical behaviors if you purposely alter a story's fairness. Even if a reporter believes that one candidate is a crook and the other is honest, the journalist's evaluation should not influence the fairness of a news story. If you do your best to provide fair coverage but fail, then the problem is a professional shortcoming, not an ethical dilemma.

"Cleaning up" Quotes

Changing quotes is probably the second most frequent reportorial-writing ethics consideration. Every journalist must grapple with decisions about correcting sources' grammar or changing words from what a speaker said to what a speaker meant: "proposal is lucrative" to "proposal is ludicrous." The Chapter 6 section on handling quotes discusses this ethical dilemma and suggests the opposite poles of ethical decision making: an absolutist position versus a situational position.

Figure 17.2 describes and defines the two ethical dimensions. The absolutist follows a set of rules that are applied in every ethical challenge, and by following established rules (even if they are personal rules such as never changing direct quotes), the absolutist has few ethical dilemmas.

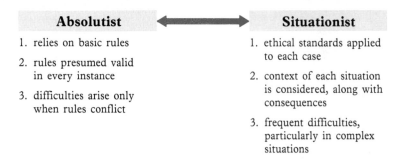

Absolutist	Situationist
1. relies on basic rules	1. ethical standards applied to each case
2. rules presumed valid in every instance	2. context of each situation is considered, along with consequences
3. difficulties arise only when rules conflict	3. frequent difficulties, particularly in complex situations

Figure 17.2 Ethical perspectives

However, the absolutist runs the risk of being traumatized when rules conflict. A situationist is plagued by constant reassessment of values, standards and outcomes reflected in ethical decisions. For instance, is it okay to clean up a college president's quotes and leave a high school lineman's quotes intact? The situationist has many ethical dilemmas, but strives for equity among these conflicts.

Gifts and Favors

Although it may seem strange to list gifts and favors as the third most frequent ethical consideration, journalists often are offered gifts. If a gift is defined broadly as a privilege or an object of any value, most journalists face the dilemma nearly every day.

As recently as a generation ago, every reporter on the news staff received a bottle of liquor as a Christmas gift from at least one politician . . . some reporters might receive an entire case. Of course, no such obvious distribution of gifts occurs today, but countless more subtle gifts, called freebies, remain at issue: (1) free meals at civic club meetings and banquets the news media cover; (2) free tickets to review concerts or plays, or tickets to ballgames sports writers will cover; (3) a corporation sponsoring a journalism conference reception; (4) books and record albums sent for review; (5) T-shirts sent to promote a charity's 10-kilometer run; (6) a cup of coffee paid for by a source during an interview; and hundreds of others. Most media organizations have policies about accepting gifts. The policies range from absolutist (nothing even of the slightest value) to situationist, including possible acceptance of all items mentioned in the preceding list. Some policies set dollar limits: nothing over $25 in value.

The ethical standard is that nothing of value should be accepted. It's evident to anyone that the business reporter who accepts a new Chevrolet from a local car dealer may feel bound to write favorably about that dealer. But compromise of principles is less evident if, during a 10 a.m. interview, the city manager pours two cups of coffee and hands you one. Do you say, "I don't take bribes!" Do you politely refuse? Do you drink the coffee?

In the gift or favor area, a journalist should follow company policy, at a minimum, and may set higher personal standards.

Individual Causes

The topic of individual causes is a return to the issues of slanting and editorializing, but it is not as frequent a dilemma. Here the question is at what distance should a journalist remain from a favored cause. For instance, should a reporter belong to a civic club, serve in public office or join a social issue cause? Many people consider such participation a responsibility of being part of the community, but many editors and journalists believe such activity gives the impression that news relating to such causes will be biased. The ethical dilemma of joining causes is similar to that of accepting gifts; for example, a music reviewer who accepts two free tickets to a concert may feel no obligation whatsoever to the sponsor and may in fact write a review panning the event. A journalist who belongs to or supports the National Organization of Women may be able to write an unbiased story on a NOW-sponsored rally, but the public perception of fair coverage is likely to suffer. Editors prefer that journalists not report about causes on which they hold strong feelings, and journalists usually agree to step aside.

However, a legislative reporter is certain to form very strong opinions about individual state politicians after a few years. Should this reporter, the staff's political expert, be removed from the legislative beat to avoid any public perception of bias? Journalists are supposed to be able to ignore their personal feelings, but can anyone really reach this ideal? The difference is that the legislative reporter's biases are part of an expertise demanded by the job; the non-work-related individual causes are a compromise that can be avoided.

Other Ethical Dilemmas

Other ethical dilemmas occur less frequently, but most journalists have had experiences such as these:

- paying for information . . . most media organizations have a policy against purchasing information, but the rule might be broken in some situations;

- failing to identify yourself as a journalist, or concealing your purpose when interviewing sources;
- obtaining information by suggesting to sources that you already know the information and are merely confirming;
- filching a document or a picture;
- interviewing sources who are under great emotional stress immediately after an accident or because of their bereavement;
- reading documents that are left on a source's desk.

Actually, this list of ethical considerations could extend for several more pages without mentioning all of the possible moral dilemmas a journalist will encounter on the job. In all, reporters and writers should stay within the law and follow media organization policies. Beyond that, journalists should behave as professionals who set high ethical standards to maintain self-respect.

SUMMARY

The chapter is an abbreviated discussion of the legal and ethical considerations that reporters and writers face most frequently. Six areas of law covered include:

- libel—anything printed or broadcast that defames someone by damaging a person's good name or reputation in the community, the person's livelihood or the person's enjoyment of normal social activity. The chapter discusses libel pitfalls and the defenses against libel.
- invasion of privacy—the right of a citizen to be left alone, including (1) intrusion on solitude, (2) violations of private matters, (3) casting a person in a false light and (4) using a person's name or picture for commercial gain. Each of these invasions is defined and discussed.
- open records and meetings—the federal Freedom of Information Act and state laws on official documents and "sunshine laws" identifying which meetings must be open to the public.
- free press/fair trial—the First Amendment freedoms of an unrestricted press pitted against the Sixth Amendment guarantee of a fair trial. These Bill of Rights conflicts have resulted in a host of judicial restrictions on trial coverage.

- confidentiality—keeping the names of sources or other facts hidden. The chapter suggests conditions under which journalists might use unnamed sources, and reviews aspects of protection such as state "shield laws."
- copyright—the protection against infringement of literary property rights. The chapter mentions plagiarism and the legal boundaries of copyright, including the defense of "fair use." Guidelines are offered to avoid copyright infringement.

Ethical considerations involve the moral values people hold . . . a level beyond society's minimum legal standards. The chapter discusses slanting and editorializing, cleaning up quotes, the absolutist versus situationist approach to ethics, gifts and favors, individual causes and other, less frequently encountered, journalistic ethical concerns.

Thinking it Through

EXERCISE 17.1

Legal and Ethical Decisions

The following sets are legal or ethical decision points. For each, mark whether it is a legal or an ethical decision, and then write the category of law or ethics in which it belongs.

A As a news reporter, you discover that a state official's 12-year-old son has $120 in delinquent library fines. You had begun investigating library fines when police arrested three city residents for having outstanding fines of more than $100 that were more than a year in arrears. The son's fines are more than a year in arrears. The circulation librarian tells you the son's records must have been overlooked.

legal   ethical _____

Legal:	**Ethical:**
libel	slanting/editorializing
invasion of privacy	cleaning up quotes
open records and meetings	gifts and favors
free press/fair trial	individual causes
confidentiality	other ethical decisions
copyright	

B You just wrote the following paragraph in a story you're about to submit to your editor:

Jones said she had to go to work at age 15 to help support her family. "I has two childrens now of my own," she said, "and I'm gonna make sure they gets their high school diploma and maybe go on to the city college."

legal   ethical _____

> **Legal:**   **Ethical:**
> libel   slanting/editorializing
> invasion of privacy   cleaning up quotes
> open records and meetings   gifts and favors
> free press/fair trial   individual causes
> confidentiality   other ethical decisions
> copyright

C You donate $100 a year to the Sierra Club, an international organization dedicated to environmental issues, including preservation of wildlife. Your editor asks you to interview a fishing boat captain who was fined for killing dolphins while netting tuna in your state's coastal waters.

legal   ethical _____

> **Legal:**   **Ethical:**
> libel   slanting/editorializing
> invasion of privacy   cleaning up quotes
> open records and meetings   gifts and favors
> free press/fair trial   individual causes
> confidentiality   other ethical decisions
> copyright

D You just wrote the following paragraph in a story you're about to submit to your editor:

"I think the guys in Sigma Theta were serving alcoholic beverages to underage girls," Johnston said.

legal   ethical _____

> **Legal:**   **Ethical:**
> libel   slanting/editorializing
> invasion of privacy   cleaning up quotes
> open records and meetings   gifts and favors
> free press/fair trial   individual causes
> confidentiality   other ethical decisions
> copyright

E Federal authorities are conducting negotiation hearings to settle a strike at a local plant. You are sent to report on the hearings but are turned away at the door.

legal   ethical _____

Legal:	**Ethical:**
libel	slanting/editorializing
invasion of privacy	cleaning up quotes
open records and meetings	gifts and favors
free press/fair trial	individual causes
confidentiality	other ethical decisions
copyright	

F You just wrote the following paragraphs in a story you're about to submit to your editor:

The plaintiff's attorney paused near a water fountain outside the courtroom. He shook his head in disgust and said his client was as good as convicted.

"My entire case rests on an eyewitness whose testimony has been ruled inadmissible," he said.

legal   ethical _____

Legal:	**Ethical:**
libel	slanting/editorializing
invasion of privacy	cleaning up quotes
open records and meetings	gifts and favors
free press/fair trial	individual causes
confidentiality	other ethical decisions
copyright	

G An alcoholic has been a good tipster for you. You meet him at a bar to get another story tip, but he asks you for $10 this time because, he says, he hasn't eaten in two days.

legal   ethical _____

Legal:	**Ethical:**
libel	slanting/editorializing
invasion of privacy	cleaning up quotes
open records and meetings	gifts and favors
free press/fair trial	individual causes
confidentiality	other ethical decisions
copyright	

H You just wrote the following paragraphs in a story you're about to submit to your editor:

> Winning first prize for lyrics was "Too Long Without You."
> The song's refrain is: "Island sands are washed by the blue; I hear the waves say 'too long without you.'"

legal   ethical _____

Legal:	**Ethical:**
libel	slanting/editorializing
invasion of privacy	cleaning up quotes
open records and meetings	gifts and favors
free press/fair trial	individual causes
confidentiality	other ethical decisions
copyright	

I A trusted source tells you that a candidate for mayor is having an affair with a married man who is 20 years younger than she.

legal   ethical _____

Legal:	**Ethical:**
libel	slanting/editorializing
invasion of privacy	cleaning up quotes
open records and meetings	gifts and favors
free press/fair trial	individual causes
confidentiality	other ethical decisions
copyright	

J You just wrote the following paragraph in a story you're about to submit to your editor:

> Smith said our political system is doomed because we permit the wealthy to influence the electoral process.

legal   ethical _____

Legal:	**Ethical:**
libel	slanting/editorializing
invasion of privacy	cleaning up quotes
open records and meetings	gifts and favors
free press/fair trial	individual causes
confidentiality	other ethical decisions
copyright	

K A source you need for an important story says she would get a big raise if your paper published a story about her company's new program. She hands you a news release and asks you to pass it along to the right person at the paper.

legal   ethical _____

Legal:
libel
invasion of privacy
open records and meetings
free press/fair trial
confidentiality
copyright

Ethical:
slanting/editorializing
cleaning up quotes
gifts and favors
individual causes
other ethical decisions

L You just wrote the following paragraph in a story you're about to submit to your editor:

Councilman Webber spent nearly an hour talking to a lobbyist for the Dairy Association, a consumer group member said.

legal   ethical _____

Legal:
libel
invasion of privacy
open records and meetings
free press/fair trial
confidentiality
copyright

Ethical:
slanting/editorializing
cleaning up quotes
gifts and favors
individual causes
other ethical decisions

M Although the list of arrestees at Central Precinct showed James L. Roberts is being held on assault charges, you discover the arrestee was really James R. Roberts.

legal   ethical _____

Legal:
libel
invasion of privacy
open records and meetings
free press/fair trial
confidentiality
copyright

Ethical:
slanting/editorializing
cleaning up quotes
gifts and favors
individual causes
other ethical decisions

Writing Practice

EXERCISE 17.2

Fairness

Here is the transcript of testimony by a husband and wife during a divorce custody case. Write a portion of the story (no lead or ending) that would present this testimony in a <u>fair</u> manner.

Jerry: Shelia is an exotic dancer at one of the clubs by the airport. She's out from 7 at night until 3 a.m. That's no example to be setting for our 6-year-old daughter. Sure, the money's good, I guess we'd have gone on welfare a couple of years ago without it. I wasn't bringing in much these last few years after being laid off. But I still don't think it's right for Ashley to be there with Shelia. Once I'm out of the hospital, I want Ashley to live with me. Shelia can help with the support until I'm back on my feet again. I know it's unusual for the father to ask for custody and child support from the mother, but that's our situation.

Shelia: If it wasn't for his addiction problem, I might agree with everything he said. But going back four or five years, it's clear where the blame lies. He got hooked, and then he got fired from his job. And he hasn't been able to hold a job since. We'd have starved if I didn't find work at the club. Now Jerry says he's ready to check into a drug detoxification unit. Why didn't he do that four years ago? He wants me to pay for Ashley's support. Well, I'm doing that already, but I don't see why he's any more fit a parent than me. My work held the family together until his drug problem led to this divorce. There's no guarantee he will be helped, and no guarantee that he won't go back to the drugs even if he is. Should Ashley be put in that kind of risk?

EXERCISE 17.3

Quotes

Write a portion of a story (no lead or ending) that presents the following quoted passage's information in a <u>fair</u> manner, <u>without</u> cleaning up the quotes.

Speaker is Billy Harris, 19, lead guitar player of "The Hammers," a local band that has a hit record and a popular video on MTV:

"It's not like this happened overnight or anything like that, man. You got to go back about five years to when we played together in John Durand's garage every afternoon after school. Other kids were playing sports or doing their homework, but the four of us never did nothin' but practice our songs. And we took a lot of grief from our folks and our teachers. I guess that's why we bailed out of school as soon as we could and started lookin' for gigs, even if we had to play 'em for nothin'.

"When you get a hit, man, everyone thinks you're instant oatmeal. I could tell you stories about what it's like to be thumbin' rides in the rain and sleeping in flop houses. We done that for just about three years.

"Then we're playin' this gig in Baltimore and—what can I say—we get a lucky break from a New York rep. Two weeks later we have a record and a contract, and now we're on the charts. It kinda goes to your head, man, but it's still too new for us to feel like we've made it. We ain't been there long enough yet."

Stylebook

In newswriting parlance, *style* usually refers to the nationally accepted, systematic use of words or punctuation. The most recent Associated Press or United Press International stylebook is the recognized authority, and should be a close companion for anyone earning a living in newswriting. Although each newspaper, magazine or station may have adopted some different style guidelines, a writer who knows AP or UPI style will only have a few changes to learn.

How important is it to know style? The best answer is simply that using recognized journalistic style is the mark of a professional; not knowing style is the mark of an amateur. But learning accepted news style isn't easy. The good news is that style follows most of the basic rules of English grammar and spelling. The bad news is that there are numerous exceptions designed for the reader's ease, and these must be memorized.

The following guidelines deal with the four major categories of newswriting style. These are only the basics. You need to examine the latest edition of the AP or UPI stylebook for further details about these general rules.

CAPITALIZATION (C)

The major mistake with capitalization is that we think we know when to capitalize, so we don't pay much attention to it.

Novices over-capitalize to emphasize importance. A news release from a local church auxiliary may read:

> The Men's Auxiliary of The First Methodist Church Congregation will hold its Annual Fundraising Sports Event at 9 A.M. Friday at the Church's Soccer Field, announced Bert Wiley, Auxiliary Publicity Director.

Being involved with the event, this writer believes that everything about it is important, so everything is capitalized. Journalists try to be more objective and more judicious with their capitalization. A general rule for journalists is that unless there's a reason to capitalize a word, don't capitalize it.

A second general rule is to capitalize titles before a name, but use lowercase for titles after a name or titles standing alone.

Here are some specific capitalization rules, the ones most frequently used by journalists. For further details, see the AP Stylebook entries referred to at the end of each rule.

C-1. Capitalize proper names of a specific person, place or thing: John Smith, Cincinnati, Lincoln Tunnel. Lowercase common nouns without unique identification: the judge, at the intersection, the monument (see capitalization, food, planets, plants and revolution).

However, hundreds of proper names have become so commonly used that writers forget they are actually trade names that must be capitalized: Band-Aid, Coke, Dacron, Deepfreeze, Jell-O, Seeing Eye dog (see brand names, service mark and trademark).

C-2. Capitalize formal titles only when they immediately precede names: President George Bush, Mayor Lucille Davis, Associate Dean Ginger McGregor. But: Ginger McGregor, associate dean; or the associate dean. Don't capitalize false titles, or job descriptions used as titles: attorney Dana Spence, deliveryman Dick Jones or rookie pitcher Ben Olson (see judge, judicial branch, nobility and titles).

C-3. Capitalize most U.S., state and city government titles, including: U.S. Congress, Louisiana Legislature, Federal Bureau of Investigation, Adams County, the Supreme Court, Minneapolis City Council, House of Representatives. In subsequent references to the specific government group, capitalize Congress, Legislature, County, Supreme Court, City Council, House (see capitol, city council, congress, county, federal, foreign governmental bodies, governmental bodies, legislature, senate, state, and Supreme Court—both entries).

C-4. Capitalize the formal name of a committee or subcommittee: Congressional Ethics Committee, Legislative Banking Subcommittee (see committee and subcommittee).

C-5. Capitalize the proper names of buildings, including the word building or its synonym if that is part of the proper name. To decide what is part of the proper name, try to imagine what might actually be written on the front of the building: Wrigley Building, Akron Civic Center, Chandler Music Hall; but Chemistry building, Smith Bros. warehouse, K-Mart store. Similar problems occur with the names of organizations such as Rotary Club, Pi Phi sorority (see building, fraternal organizations, monuments, mountains, office, organizations and institutions, and police department).

C-6.   Lowercase all academic departments except those that are proper nouns: journalism department, English department, the department of sociology. But capitalize administrative offices: Academic Affairs, Business and Finance, Registrar's Office (see academic departments, Department of Agriculture, organizations).

C-7.   Lowercase compass directions: "He went south on his vacation." "The band sat on the east side of the stadium." But capitalize all recognized geographic regions: "She went to the South on her vacation." And capitalize regional geographic areas such as Upper Michigan, the Oklahoma Panhandle, Mid-South, Northern California, Upstate New York and South Chicago (see directions).

C-8.   Capitalize the first and the last word; all principal words; and prepositions or conjunctions of four or more letters in the titles of books, films, lectures, plays, poems, songs, speeches, television shows and works of art (see composition titles and music).

Capitalize (and look up these stylebook references):
C-9.a.   holidays: Easter, Thanksgiving, New Year's
C-9.b.   historic periods: Prohibition, the New Deal
C-9.c.   wars and battles: World War I, Battle of the Bulge (see war)
C-9.d.   references to the U.S. flag: Old Glory, Stars and Stripes; and references to the U.S. Constitution; but lowercase *constitutional*
C-9.e.   religious titles, religions and the names of holy days: the Rev. Billy Graham; Catholic, Jewish, Methodist; Christmas, Hanukkah
C-9.f.   direct references to the deity and the Bible: God, Old Testament, Holy Scriptures; but lowercase *his* or *biblical* (see Satan)
C-9.g.   proper names of medals and awards: Medal of Honor, Purple Heart, Heisman Trophy; minor awards with official titles such as Tiger Alumni Medallion; but lowercase *blue ribbon, first place* or *alumni award*
C-9.h.   names of political parties or direct references to members of that party: Republican Party, Communist, Socialist Party; but lowercase references to a political philosophy: democracy, communism
C-9.i.   names of U.S. military units: Navy, Air Force
C-9.j.   names of specific rooms: Room 202; Oval Office
C-9.k.   names of nationalities, races and tribes: Indians, Asian, Caucasian; but lowercase *black* or *white*
C-9.l.   personifications: Easter Bunny, Tooth Fairy

Lowercase (and look up these stylebook references):

C-10.a. common noun elements of names in plurals: Mississippi and Ohio rivers; corner of First and Main streets

C-10.b. seasons: autumn, spring

C-10.c. school classifications: freshman, senior

C-10.d. titles without names, even if they sound important: priest, president, first lady, federal, government

ABBREVIATION (A)

While they restrict their use of capitalization, journalists use abbreviations more frequently than is usual in other forms of writing. This is done for conciseness: To use Department of Housing and Urban Development throughout a story wastes space that can be saved by using HUD. However, conserving space never justifies confusing the reader, so all journalistic use of abbreviations is designed to be concise without being confusing. Here are a few general guidelines that apply in most cases.

Most titles before proper names are abbreviated if these titles are ever abbreviated.

Titles after a name or standing alone are never abbreviated.

These words are never abbreviated: alley, assistant, associate, association, attorney, building, circle, department, district, drive, fort, government, president, professor, road, secretary, square, superintendent, terrace and treasurer.

Acronyms give journalists fits because there are so many, and acronyms are used frequently. A guideline that may help is that if the letters of an acronym spell a word, use periods; if they don't spell a word, omit the periods. Hence AWOL (absent without leave) but M.A.S.H. (Mobile Army Surgical Hospital); mph (miles per hour) but c.o.d. (cash on delivery).

The guideline for acronyms should be a perfect example of using abbreviations in ways that don't confuse readers; unfortunately there are far too many exceptions. For instance, Woodmen of the World is WOW, the National Organization for Women is NOW and the Cooperative for American Relief Everywhere Inc. is CARE. In fact, most of the all-capital acronyms are used without periods, and that's probably a safer rule than the spell-a-word guideline. But the safest rule—especially when the Knights of Columbus fraternal organization is K of C, and R.S.V.P. does have periods—is to look it up.

In almost all cases, acronyms are not used until the second reference— after the writer has spelled the words fully the first time so the reader won't have any doubt about what they mean—but the most common acronyms, such as FBI and mph, may be used on first reference.

Each of the following specific rules for abbreviation is listed separately in the stylebook, and follow-up reading should be done there.

A-1.   Before names, use abbreviations for titles such as Dr., Gov., Lt. Gov., Rep., Sen. and many of the military ranks. Some of the more frequently used military titles are: Gen., Col., Lt. Col., Maj., Capt., 1st Lt., Sgt. Maj., Staff Sgt., Sgt., Spec. 5, Cpl., Pfc., Pvt.; Adm., Cmdr., Petty Officer 1st Class (see military titles, many of which require memorization; legislative titles; and titles). To abbreviate a legislator's political party identification, set it off with commas as follows: "Sen. Albert Gore Jr., D-Tenn., sponsored the bill" (see party affiliation).

A-2.   Journalistic use of courtesy titles such as Mrs., Mr., Miss and Ms. has received much commentary in the past 20 years, but the current stylebook offers these rules:

1. omit courtesy titles with first and last names together
2. don't use courtesy titles on first reference
3. never use *Mr.* without also using *Mrs.* (Mr. and Mrs. Joe Jones, but never Mr. Joe Jones or Mr. Jones);
4. use a married woman's first name and her husband's last name on first reference: Wanda Smith; in subsequent references use Mrs. Smith or, if she prefers, Ms. Smith or Smith;
5. in second references to a single woman, use Smith, Miss Smith or Ms. Smith, according to the woman's preference; and
6. if a woman wishes to be addressed as Ms., include her marital status only if it is necessary to the story.

A-3.   Avoid abbreviating academic degrees, but in lists of individuals with their degrees, use: B.A., M.A., Ph.D., etc. Spell out formal academic titles such as professor and chairman (see academic degrees and academic titles).

A-4.   Abbreviate avenue, boulevard and street in numbered addresses: 102 Main St. Abbreviate compass points in numbered addresses: 5700 E. Front St. N.W. Spell out all of these words when used without a street or building number: West Lincoln Avenue (see addresses).

A-5.   Abbreviate company, corporation, incorporated, limited and brothers when used in the firm's name: Nottingham Ltd., Smith Bros. No comma is used before these designations (see company and incorporated).

A-6.   Abbreviate junior and senior after a name, without a comma between the name and the designation: John Q. Williams Jr. (see junior).

A-7.   Abbreviate U.N. and U.S.—no space between the initials—only as adjectives; spell out as nouns (see United Nations).

A-8.   Abbreviate initials in people's names: H.G. Wells, L. Thomas Brandon. Note that there is no space between two initials appearing together (see initials and middle initials).

A-9.   Abbreviate states only when they appear with cities, never when the state name appears alone. Eight state names are never abbreviated: Alaska, Hawaii, Idaho, Iowa, Maine, Ohio, Texas and Utah. A rule to help you remember: Don't abbreviate states that aren't attached to the continental United States or states with fewer than six letters (see state names).

A-10.   Use the proper abbreviations, not the two-letter postal codes, for states that are abbreviated with cities. The following abbreviations should be memorized: Ala., Ariz., Colo., Ky., Md., Mo., Mont., Neb., Ore., Pa., Vt., Wis., Wyo. (see state names).

A-11.   Abbreviate Saint in city and other names: St. Thomas, St. Christopher, Sault Ste. Marie (see saint).

A-12.   Abbreviate bullet and gun sizes: .22-caliber pistol, 12-gauge shotgun, 9mm pistol, Colt .45-caliber revolver (see weapons).

PUNCTUATION (P)

Journalistic style uses punctuation to increase reader ease and understanding. Punctuation should help the reader grasp ideas quickly and reduce reader confusion. In virtually all instances, journalistic style follows English grammar punctuation usage. The problem for journalists is that we're not a whole lot better at English grammar than other people. The stylebook has a separate section on punctuation, with the subheadings also used here, each of which should be studied for a brief review of grammar.

Periods

P-1.   Use a period at the end of every declarative sentence and at the end of an indirect question: She asked how to get home.

P-2.   Periods are used inside parenthetical elements when they form a complete sentence; outside when the material isn't a complete sentence. At the end of any such sentence, put the period outside the closing parenthesis (*as in this example*).

P-3.   Most abbreviations take periods; most all-capitalized acronyms do not.

Commas

Use of commas is the bane of all writers, not journalists alone. As part of the design for reading ease, use commas only when there is a rule calling for their use or when they are needed for clarity. Unfortunately, there are many rules, and some can be close calls.

P-4. Possibly the single most notable difference between English grammar and journalistic style is the omission of a comma before the conjunctions *and* and *or* in a series of three or more elements. In a short-phrase series, omit the comma: The building was old, crumbling and unsafe. Also omit the comma in a non-complex longer-phrase series: He grabbed the steering wheel with both hands, pumped the brakes with both feet and skidded the car safely into a snowbank.

Use the comma before the conjunction if one of the elements of the series contains a conjunction: She dressed for the outdoors using ear muffs, a coat and hat, and insulated boots.

P-5. Use a comma before a conjunction connecting two complete sentences: Her father became ill, and she was forced to consider a nursing home.

P-6. Set off a person's age with commas: William Elliott, 37, was killed in the crash (see party affiliation and academic degrees).

P-7. Omit the comma before *of* in this use: Joe Jones of Cleveland. However, if a hometown isn't preceded by *of*, use commas to set it off: Joe Jones, Cleveland, and Jane Smith, St. Louis.

P-8. Separate what was said from its attribution (who said it) with a comma:

> Local police will add 50 new patrolmen, Mayor Gene Smith announced today.

> Job specifications will be posted, she said.

> The jobs, he said, will require six months' training.

However, no comma would be used in the following:

> He said the pay will be more than $20,000 a year.

P-9. Set off appositives with commas: The robber, described as being bald, escaped through an alley.

P-10. Use a comma after clauses or phrases that begin sentences when those clauses begin with such words as <u>since</u>, <u>because</u>, <u>if</u>, <u>when</u> and <u>although</u>. Use a comma before non-essential clauses that begin with <u>which</u> and <u>who</u>.

P-11. Use a comma before a direct quote containing a complete, single sentence: Baker said, "I am confident the jury will find me innocent." Omit the comma if the quote is shorter than a complete sentence: Baker said the jury "will find me innocent."

P-12. Use a comma to separate a city and state name or abbreviation. Use a comma after the state name or abbreviation (except at the end of a sentence or when city-state units in a series are separated by semicolons instead of commas): Madison, Wis., was the scene of a tornado.

Many large cities such as Boston, Chicago, Houston, Milwaukee, Seattle and others don't require a state designation: She was from Minneapolis. However, Washington, D.C., should be distinguished from Washington state by using the D.C. initials.

P-13. Set off people's names with commas in the following sentence structures:

> The district attorney, Wanda Cramer, lead the hearing.

> Her brother, John, was married.

P-14. Use a comma to separate equal adjectives. Identify an equal adjective by determining if the word *and* could replace the comma without changing the meaning: She drove a clean, shiny car. But: She drove an inexpensive new car.

P-15. Put a comma after *yes* or *no* used to describe a person's response or action: She said yes, it was her scissors. "No, I won't go," he said. Yes, they would make the trip together.

Semicolons

Semicolons are used infrequently in newswriting, with one exception: in a complex series that includes commas. These series appear in news stories on topics such as awards, organizations and groups of people, and obituaries. There's a pattern to this use of the semicolon that has to be learned.

P-16. Here's a series that requires semicolons, with a step-by-step approach for its punctuation:

> Cheerleaders were Rose Wright Boston Bob Black of Dayton Ohio a French major Sue Small a 19-year-old finance major from Jackson Mississippi and Tim Taylor 21 Sacramento California.

The first decision to make is how many people there are. Once you decide the units you're dealing with, the punctuation will be easier. There are four people, not five or six. Wright is from Boston, Black is a French major from Dayton, Small is 19 and from the South, and Taylor is from the West Coast.

The rule is: Use semicolons to separate the major units, in this case the four people with all of their age, major and hometown baggage intact. Also, do use a semicolon before the conjunction *and*. Here's the paragraph with the semicolons added:

> Cheerleaders were Rose Wright Boston; Bob Black of Dayton Ohio a French major; Sue Small a 19-year-old finance major from Jackson Mississippi; and Tim Taylor 21 Sacramento California.

Here it is with the commas and abbreviations added:

> Cheerleaders were: Rose Wright, Boston; Bob Black of Dayton, Ohio, a French major; Sue Small, a 19-year-old finance major from Jackson, Miss.; and Tim Taylor, 21, Sacramento, Calif.

Notice that there's a comma between the city and the state, and a comma after the state (unless a semicolon or period replaces the second comma). Notice also the commas separating names from ages, and separating the appositives that give more information about the person (a French major; a 19-year-old finance major from Jackson, Miss.). There is no comma between "Bob Black" and "of Dayton" because *of* takes the place of the comma.

If the example seems difficult, memorize the procedure for punctuating it, the rules involved and the punctuation structure that results. Early in your newswriting career you will face the need to use paragraphs of this type in about 5 percent of the articles you write.

P-17.   Also use a semicolon to link two independent clauses (complete sentences) from which the usual conjunction has been omitted: The jury returned to its place; a hush fell over the courtroom.

Colons

P-18.   Use a colon to introduce a list or a long statement. In the cheerleader example, the colon appears after *were* to introduce the list of people and their identifications. It would also be used as follows: "Smith was caught with the property: a television set, two radios and a dozen VCR units, all still in factory boxes."

P-19.   Use a colon to introduce a quote of more than one sentence: She said: "My reputation is on the line here. I don't want to go to the grand jury with this one unless we're sure."

P-20.   Use a colon to introduce a question: She said she wanted to know: Which suspect will be indicted?

Quotation Marks

Quotations are a mainstay in newswriting. Most articles are based on interviews, press conferences or speeches, and direct quotes comprise at least half the material in these stories. There's nothing particularly difficult about using quotation marks. The other punctuation used with quotations is usually the source of any problems writers have in this area.
P-21.   Consider that people who use the English language write from left to right across the page (or the computer screen). Therefore, anything to the left precedes, or "comes before," anything to its right. If you think of writing as sequential, then remember that other punctuation usually comes before quote marks. Here's an example:

> "I think," Col. Adams said, "that the weapon should be for use only by the military." He added, "There is no reason for a civilian to own this device."

Note that in every instance involving other punctuation, the commas and periods come before, or to the left of, the quotation marks. The grammar rule is that commas and periods always precede the closing quotation marks. However, question marks, dashes and exclamation points go before the quote marks only when they're part of the quoted matter. And semicolons go after the quotes. Fortunately, journalists rarely use these other forms of punctuation, so the rule about punctuation going before quotes will be accurate 95 percent of the time or more.
P-22.   Use quotes to enclose titles of songs and books, movies and TV programs, and lectures and speeches. Capitalize newspaper and magazine titles, but do not enclose them in quotes.
P-23.   Use quotes for nicknames such as: J.P. "Jimmy" Jones. Use quotes sparingly with slang or eccentric expressions.

Apostrophes

P-24.   The most frequent use of the apostrophe is in a possessive noun: Dr. Ortega's patient was the only survivor.
P-25.   Use an apostrophe to indicate that one or more letters is missing from a word, the usual manner of forming contractions: She didn't have insurance.
P-26.   Use an apostrophe to form the plural of a single letter: She earned A's throughout high school. But omit the apostrophe with multiple letters: He already knows his ABCs.

Dashes

P-27. Journalists seldom use dashes because they disrupt sentence flow. Use dashes to separate an abrupt change of thought in a sentence, to indicate a heavily emphasized pause, or to set off a phrase containing a series:

> He raised his card—it was his first auction—and bid on the painting.

> A 300-passenger airliner crashed—no one was injured.

> Jones was a three-time loser—assault, armed robbery and manslaughter—who needed to plea bargain.

P-28. Use dashes to introduce separate segments of a list, particularly to include minor news events at the end of news stories. Introduce such lists with a colon, capitalize the first word after the dash and use a period at the end of each line listing:

> In other action the Council:
> —Purchased five acres of land south of town.
> —Approved $15,000 in repairs to the City Hall building.
> —Tabled a motion to increase parking meter rates.

Hyphens

P-29. Use hyphens to join two or more words used as an adjective or compound modifier: Company-hired guards with foot-long billy clubs kept order in the smoke-filled room. However, omit hyphens with the word *very* and adverbs ending in *ly:* Scantily clad natives hurriedly paddled toward the eagerly waiting tourists.

P-30. Use a hyphen to join prefixes to words: co-owner, ex-convict. Except for *cooperate, coordinate* and other permanent forms, use a hyphen when the vowel ending of the prefix is the same as the beginning vowel of the word: pre-eminent. Note that the word *vice* is not hyphenated: vice president, vice chancellor, vice versa. (See also prefixes.)

P-31. Compound words used as nouns rarely take hyphens, but it's a good idea to look these up individually: statewide, weekend, back yard, sit-down, etc.

P-32. Hyphens are used frequently in forming numbers, but see the Numbers section, which follows Punctuation, for specific examples.

The camp opens March 15, 1994, and closes Oct. 15, 1994.

The play is scheduled at 8 p.m. Nov. 3–9.

The play will open Nov. 1.   (not "1st")

Books will be sold at half-price during February.

The target date is February 1994.   (no comma before year)

Afternoon and evening editions of newspapers allow use of *today, this morning, this afternoon, tonight,* etc., but other papers expect the day of the week to be used if the date is within seven days of the current date. If the date is not within seven days, use the month and a figure for the date. Avoid redundancies such as: last Monday, next Wednesday (see time element, today, tonight, tomorrow, yesterday and months).

N-7. Money.   Money is another frequently used topic in journalistic writing. Amounts of money are almost always in figures. There are several distinct rules to be followed, without exceptions, starting at the smallest amounts:

a. Amounts below $1 are figures without decimal points: 15 cents; 25-cent stamp; 50 cents (instead of half a dollar); 89 cents.

b. Amounts of $1 and more use the dollar sign—which replaces the word *dollar*—and a decimal place for dollars and cents: $1.25; $5.50; $2.75-tickets. If the amounts include no cents, omit the decimal and zeros: $1; $5; $600; $30-tickets.

c. A comma is required in all figures of more than 999, so in dollar amounts: $1,000; $37,465; $500,000; or $10,525,750.

d. For reader ease (it might be difficult to recognize that last amount as ten million, five hundred twenty-five thousand . . .), large numbers are rounded to the first or second decimal place: $10.53 million; $1.25 billion; $1.5 trillion GNP (no hyphen in $1.5 trillion GNP or $400 billion budget).

In giving ranges, be sure to include the word *million* after each figure: She is worth $2 million to $3 million.   (not $2 to $3 million) (See millions.)

e. Do not use figures for money amounts when the amount is a casual reference to money rather than an exact dollar amount:

He said he has lost thousands of dollars at the track.

The heiress was worth millions.

N-8. Percentages.   Use figures for all percentages: 8 percent; 1 percent; 65 percent; 5.5-percent tax; 17-percent tip. *Percent* is one word (see percentages).

N-9. Ordinals.   Ordinal numbers follow the nine-and-below, 10-and-above rule when *first* through *ninth* stand for time sequences or locations: first place; Sixth Amendment; eighth from the rail; 10th racer; 22nd place. The rule applies as well to century date references, with the word *century* lowercase: fifth century; 13th century. The rule also applies to street names: Second Avenue; 12th Avenue; 109 Sixth St.; 100 23rd St.

However, when ordinals below 10 are used as names other than street names—in political, military and judicial designations—use figures: 6th Ward; 3rd Fleet, 8th Division, 1st Sgt. (see addresses, century, court names, numerals and political divisions).

N-10. Speeds.   Use figures for all speeds: 6 miles an hour; 4 knots; 250 mph (see speeds).

N-11. Scores, odds, proportions and ratios.   Use figures for all scores, odds, proportions and ratios. Hyphens are required for most of these forms (see betting odds and ratios):

The Cardinals defeated the Pirates 5-3.

The Tigers took a 36-6 trouncing from the Bulls.

Jones had a 3 on the 18th hole and finished 5 below par.

8-5 odds; the odds were 3-2 against him; odds of 5-to-4

mixture of 2 parts lemon to 8 parts water

the ratio of 3-to-1; a 3-to-1 ratio

N-12. Temperatures.   Figures are used for all temperatures except zero. For temperatures below zero, use the word *minus*, and use the word *degree* instead of a degree sign: minus 4 degrees Fahrenheit; it was 8 degrees.

Temperatures don't become warmer or colder; they become higher or lower: Tomorrow is expected to be 10 degrees higher than today (see temperatures).

N-13. Priority.   To show priority, use *No.* instead of the word *number*, and use a figure: He was the No. 5 choice. She was the No. 1 candidate.

N-14. Elections.   Vote totals greater than 999 votes on each side are done with sets of figures connected with the word *to*, not with a hyphen: Smith won 245,873 to 193,661 (see election returns and vote tabulations).

N-15. Highways.   Routes and highway numbers are figures. Here are some forms: U.S. Highway 5; State Route 101; Interstate Highway 95; Interstate 20 (on second reference, I-20); U.S. Route 3A (no hyphen when a letter is appended to a number). (See highway designations.)

N-16. Fractions.   Fractions require a special rule because some printing equipment may not include body type for fractions. So instead of using figures, spell out numbers less than one in news stories. Connect the parts of a fraction with a hyphen: one-fourth; two-thirds; one-half.

N-17. Roman numerals.   Use letters instead of figures: World War II, Richard III, Pope John XXIII (see numerals and roman numerals).

N-18. Serial numbers.   When letters and figures are used in a series, no hyphen is required: U.S. Route 333A, Patent No. 914B075Z. However, many abbreviations do require hyphens: I-95, M-16, 3-D (see serial numbers).

The numbers section ends this stylebook presentation. In the four sections there are 76 numbered rules (and several unnumbered ones), with about half in the punctuation section. It's important to spend some time with these rules and to spend even more time looking at examples in the suggested sections of the most current stylebook edition. Much of the material doesn't have to be memorized; knowing the major rules is sufficient. But many examples should be memorized. A news writer, sooner or later, will learn style through constant reliance on the stylebook. It might as well be sooner.

Copy Editing Marks

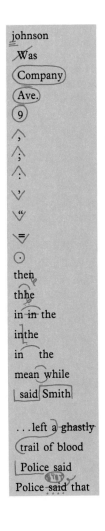

johnson	capitalize	three parallel lines under letter
Was	lowercase	slash mark through letter
Company	abbreviate	circle (do it the other way)
Ave.	spell full word	circle (do it the other way)
9	spell out number	circle (do it the other way)
⌃	insert comma	caret indicates where to add
⌃;	insert semicolon	
⌃:	insert colon	
⌄	insert apostrophe	
⌄"	insert quotes	
=	insert hyphen	
⊙	insert period (also: ⋀)	
then	delete	
thhe	delete and close	
in in the	delete and close	
inthe	separate words	(also in the for insert space)
in the	close extra space	
mean while	close up space	delete space; spell as one word
said Smith	reverse order	(squared or rounded; may be used to reverse longer elements)
...left a ghastly		delete and continue on next line
trail of blood		
Police said	new paragraph	(also: ¶ Police said...)
Police said that	stet (let it stand)	ignore deletion; let stand as typed

433

insert quotes; abbreviate	Lawrence "Bull" Durham, 34, Number 6 on the
insert apostrophe; delete word	FBIs most-wanted list, was was arrested at
delete words; spell out number	11 a.m. this morning after holding 5 people
delete letter; lowercase letter	captives in the Bank Of Commerce.
new paragraph	Police said none of the hostages was hurt,
let stand as it was; insert hyphen	and Durham surrendered his sawed off shotgun.
uppercase letter (capitalize)	The FBI said Durham was repeating a july
transpose letters; transpose words ④③ reverses order of two grafs change words; insert comma	robbrey in which an bandit armed escaped ④ from a Dallas bank with over $200000.
spelling is correct; spell full word	Amy G. Swiff, 26, Westbrook Ct., Apt. 202,
insert comma, delete several words and continue on next line	a bank teller who began working six months ago, ③ tripped a silent alarm when Durham brandished the
close up; insert colon; new graf	shot gun in the lobby at 930 a.m. FBI officer
insert period; insert word	Leslie J Lott said all banks were under heavy
transpose letters; delete and close	surviellence becuase sources said Durnham

Copy Editing Test 1

Governor Bobbie R. May was reported in good condition following an emergency appendectomy at City General Hospital Thursday night.

Mae 47 was rsuhed to surgery at 730 p.m. last night after she fainted during the pledge of allegiance at the tenth annual awards banquet for state employeees.

Doctor Ahmed L Rama who led sergical team, said, The governor came through the operation like a twelve-year-old. Rama said it is unusual for an adult of Mays age to have apendicitis, "but it isn't dangerous if treated quickly. Aides said May will remain at city General 3 days for recovery.

Copy Editing Test 2

A conference of business leaders looking for ways to safely recycle polystyrene materials agreed Monday to disband.

After the 2nd day of discussion, the the\ business people voted to stop wasting precious time and to end the conference

We will stop using polystyrene and seek alternative packing products said Timothy G Horn president of xerox. Horn said a $500000 research fund the organization raised will be donated charity. The final report given by Ronald D. King Junior PhD. idicated recyclable polystyrene might require twenty more years of research. King siad the scientific community recommends banning plastic packing now.

"Regardless of any futurerecycling

success" King said, "Polystyrene production

pollutes the atmosphere."

City map

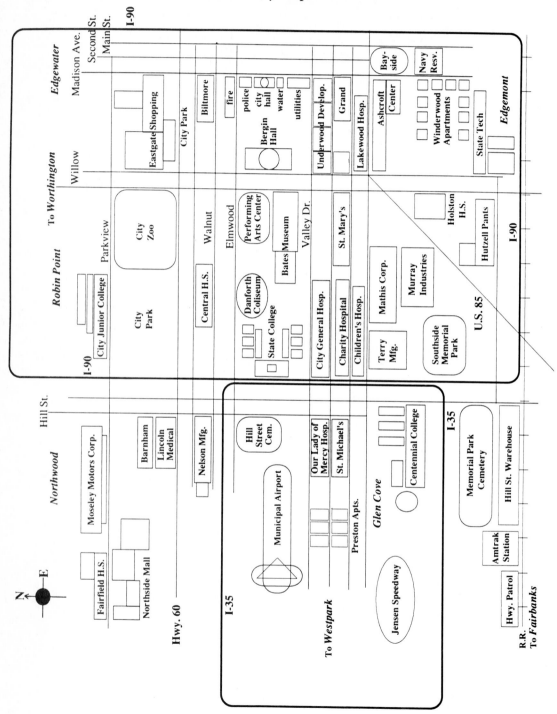

City Directory

Use this directory as if it were a telephone book for the hypothetical city referred to in the chapter-end exercises. For instance, this City Directory should be used to verify names and addresses given in every exercise assignment in the text. In virtually every exercise, there is an incorrect spelling, middle initial or address. Journalism teachers lower a grade substantially if the story contains a factual error in a name or address; many underscore the accuracy principle in journalism by failing a writing assignment with a single such factual error. In time—and it should be a very short time—you will automatically verify all facts in the directory before you begin writing.

City Directory information supersedes any information contained in the exercises. An exercise might identify a story source as Bennie R. Acord, vice president of Baker Products. Checking the directory, you find that the source's full name and identification are wrong: He is Benjamin G. Accord, chairman of the board of Barker Products. There are five factual errors in the exercise's use of Accord's name.

However, there are many instances in which a fact appearing in an exercise cannot be verified in any of the directory material. For instance, an exercise may include a speech given at the Elk's Lodge. There is no Elk's Lodge in the City Directory or on the map. If a piece of information cannot be verified through the directory, it should be considered as accurate.

Additional information is found in the separate listings at the end of the directory and on the accompanying city map. Two exercises follow the directory. Completing these exercises is a valuable introduction on how to use the City Directory to verify information.

Inclusions in the City Directory follow this format:

1. last name
2. full first name

3. middle initial (if there is one)
4. junior or senior (if pertinent)
5. spouse's first name and middle initial if known
6. occupation of the person listed
7. address of the person listed.

If an address does not end with the abbreviations Ave., Rd., Blvd., etc.,
it is a street. The following special abbreviations are used consistently
throughout the directory:

Abbreviations

admin.—administrator
adv.—advertising
assoc.—associate
asst.—assistant
atty.—attorney
Ct.—Court
dect.—detective
Dev.—Development
dir.—director
div.—divorced
educ.—education
exec.—executive
fin.—finance

Gr.—Grove
Hosp.—Hospital
Ln.—Lane
mgr.—manager
phil.—philosophy
pr.—public relations
pres.—president
Prods.—Products
prof.—professor
psych.—psychology
rev.—Reverend
tech.—technician
v-pres.—vice president

A A-Plus Advertising Inc., 417 2nd

AMTRAK Station, 3314 Illinois

Accord, Benjamin G. (Connie), board chair Barker Prods., 1101 Cedar Ave.

Ace Pawn Co., 606 Greenwood

Acme Products Inc., Speedway Rd.

Adkins, Chadwick D. (Stacy), accountant, 4040 Blueline

Adler, Ronald (Vivian), X-ray tech. St. Michael's, 1341 9th

Akers, Judy N. (Keith), M.D., researcher Cardiovascular, 337 Preston Apts.

Alexander, Barry C., asst. prof. phil. Centennial, 811 Atlantic, Apt. 16

Altimer, Simon (Winnie), conductor Civic Symphony, 819 Glade

American Medical Association, 2101 Lions Head Dr.

Applegate, Jack P. (Gail), chief psych. Oakhill Clinic, 274 Quince Ave.

Armstead, Novell (Kate), city council, 626 Central

Arthur, Eugene D. (Susan), M.D., Charity Hosp., 2183 Lexington

Arthur, Julie (Terrance), commodities broker, 1747 Pine

Arthur, Terrance (Julie), adv. acct. exec., 1747 Pine

Ashcroft Shopping Center, 540 Avery

Avery, Richard C., head drill sgt., Camp Talon

B Baker, Diana L., ticket agent, 219 3rd

Barker Products Inc., 525 Ridgemont

Barlow Auditorium, 505 Elmwood

Barnes, Scott J. (Glenda), pilot Federal Express, 615 Apple

Barnham Research Lab, 1110 Hill

Bates Museum, 1015 Central

Battered Wives Inc., 1435 Main, Suite 392

Baxter, Wayne G., v-pres. purchasing Terry Mfg., 993 Lionel

Bayside Auditorium, 1000 Main

Beale, Robert C. Sr. (Sally), foreman Nelson Mfg., 918 6th

Beckwell, Louise M. (widow), seamstress, 2205 Elm Parkway

Beckwell, Mabel S., court clerk, 2430 10th, Apt. 57

Beckwell, Rex W., cantor, Gates of Prayer, 712 9th W.

Beckwell, Richard E. (Judy A.), deputy dist. atty., 1641 American Ave.

Benny's Brokerage, 2101 Madison Ave.

Bergin Civic Hall, 600 Willow

Bergin Hall Board Room

Better Business Bureau Inc., Bergin Hall, Room 203A

Biltmore Hotel, 507 Madison Ave.

Black, Lena R. (Gerald), police officer, 2310 8th

Bonner, J.D. (Linda), florist, 1011 Main

Boritosky, Benjamin (Ginger), owner Gourmet Cafe, 414 Front

Boritosky, Guido (Leona), retired, 391 Preston Apts.

Boy Scout Troop No. 15, 1756 Talbert Dr.

Boy Scouts of America, 1455 Union

Breed, Robert (Donna), owner Global Balloons, 380 Bee

Brighton Mortuary, 109 Fort

Bryant, Earl R. (Jennifer), atty., 717 High

Bryant, Jennifer E. (Earl), WKNW-TV consumer reptr., 717 High

Bursin, John B. (Vera), M.D., Our Lady of Mercy, 709 Robin Roost

Butler, Nancy L. (Brian), staff sgt. Navy Reserve, 892 Quincy

C Caldwell, Ginger, receptionist, 1240 Arrow, Apt. 8

Camp Talon, 3270 Old Harper Rd.

Cardiovascular Research Lab, 1219 Hill St.

Carter, Al (Nikki), caretaker Memorial Park, 1117 Winderwood Apts.

Centennial College, 3400 Pacific Dr.

Central Episcopal Church, 1357 Longwood

Central High School, 552 Walnut

Central Housing Authority, Bergin Hall, Room 226

Chamber of Commerce, Bergin Hall, Room 154

Charity Cotillion Inc., Bayside Auditorium, Suite 112

Charity Hospital, 1855 Lions Head Dr.

Child Abuse Prevention Center, City Hall, Room 115B

Children's Home, 702 Highpoint

Children's Hospital, 1860 Lions Head Dr.

Childs, Vincent S. (Phyllis), owner Northbridge Loans, 139 7th

Chung, Lillie (Shu G.), Ph.D., supt. city schools, 4401 Maple

Chung, Shu G. (Lillie), M.D., Children's Hosp., 4401 Maple

City Employees Union, 2119 Hampton

City General Hospital, 1355 Arrow

City Hall, 570 Madison Ave.

City Junior College, 1780 Parkview

City Utilities, 707 Madison Ave.

City Water Service, 630 Madison Ave.

City Waterworks, 5710 Old Harper Rd.

City Zoo, 500 Hwy. 60

Claremont Mortuary, 1447 Hill

Clemmons, Patrick E. (Betty), director CHA, 443 Central

Cobbins, Jack Y. (Sherry), rev., pastor Second Street Church of Christ, 2487 Hickory

Cocroft, George M. (Susan), unemployed, 159 Underwood Dev.

Coleman, Hank Y. (Vanessa), mgr. Jensen Speedway, 201 Tarpon

College of Arts and Sciences, State College

College of Business, State College

Commerce Building, 200 Main St.

Convention Bureau Inc., Bayside Auditorium, Suite 26

Cooper, Wilson (Angela), dishwasher, 673 Winderwood Apts.

County Highway Commission, Bergin Hall, Room 280

County Literacy Link Inc., Performing Arts Center, Suite 221
Cox, Lester C. (Nicolle), bartender, 1493 Easthaven
Craig, Calvin S. Jr. (Melanie P.), owner Craig Plantation
Craig, Catherine M. (widow), retired, Biltmore Hotel
Crimestoppers Inc., 404 Line
Cutler, Mary M., student Centennial, Pearson Hall

D Dade, Jack L. (Carol), insurance sales, 1016 Ashley Way
Danforth Coliseum
Daniels, Bonnie P., stylist, 2154 9th
Davis, Oscar S. (Inez), mgr. Hillcrest Savings, 3558 Denton Rd.
Deloach, Charles W. (Hattie), retired farmer, 21 Oak Manor Ct.
Denton, Christopher (Beth), city council, 1851 Trenton
Department of Public Safety Building, 500 Madison
de Witt, Frank N. (Pauline), police capt., 1440 Elmwood
Dickerson, Mary T. (Charles), court clerk, 401 8th
Diet Deli Health Restaurant, 618 Center
Dillard, James J. (Loretta), retired mayor, 713 Preston Apts.
Dougherty, Leah J. (div.), clerk Northbridge Loans, 809 Underwood Dev.
Dozier, Thomas (div.), dect. sgt. vice squad, 316 Maple
DuBois, Harvey (Alice), city council, 1904 Cherry Ave.
Dulles, C. Robert (Geraldine), 222 Birch
Duncan, Charlie V. (Sara), tech. Children's Hosp., (Westpark)
Durand, Dennis O. (Sharon), contractor, 2966 Foxview
Durdem, Helen V., dir. County Immigration Bureau, 129 Preston Apts.
Dyson, Jerry K., owner Robo Wash, 1326 Trenton

E Eastgate Shopping Center, 300 Willow
Edwards, Charlene, student State Tech, 799 5th
Edwards, Charles E. (Gloria), painter, 857 Horton
Edwards, Sherry G., florist, 1962 Beech, Apt. 5
Eisenhower, Camp, U.S. Army
Elite Jewelry Inc., 1705 Plaza
Ellrod, Harry D. (Cecile), owner Diet Deli, 5521 Heath Rd.
Engel, Patrick L., clerk camera store, 1592 4th
Estes, Donald (Nancy D.), consultant Mathis, 3405 Pacific Dr.
Estes, Nancy D. (Donald), pres. Centennial, 3405 Pacific Dr.

Evans, Doyle W. (div.), police officer, 941 Dunlap

Evans, E. Clinton (Brenda), travel agent, 566 Oak

Evans, Jacob A. (Robin), tech. Lincoln Medical, 2229 Bayside

Evans, Marjorie A. (widow), retired, Lyons Apts., No. 330

Everett, Samson T., student State Tech, 210 Bledsoe, Apt. 5

Ezernieks, John W. (Sandra), lab tech. Children's Hosp., 493 7th

F Fain, Clarence, student State Tech, 1479 Winderwood Apts.

Fairfield High School, 3593 Parkview

Fallstaff, Harvey (Evellyn), pres. First National, 449 Robin Way

Familytime Games, 3095 Hwy. 60

Farleigh, Andrew L., commandant, Camp Talon

Farmer's Co-op, 3519 Old Farm Rd.

Farris, B.L. (Lois), machine operator Nelson Mfg., 2035 Watson

Federal Express Corp., 1090 Airway Dr.

Ferguson, Scott B. (Cindy), 1st lieut. U.S. Army, 484 9th

First National Bank, 344 Main

First Presbyterian Church, 212 Hamilton

Fisher, Jo Ann (Blake), clothing sales, 210 Oak, Apt. 4

Fitzgerald, Donald B., student State Tech, Applegate Apts., No. 7

Fitzgerald, Jerry "Cotton" (Deborah), cook The Spoon, 3954 Flag Rd.

Fitzgerald, Walter H., retired, Longview Retirement Home

Ford, Eugena C., typist, 131 4th, Apt. 22

Forderhase, Gregory J. (Dale), M.D., St. Michael's, 2006 Overton

Forrester, Fern, prof. English Centennial, 411 Preston Apts.

Fowler, Heather, receptionist, 588 Line

Fox, Michael P. (Tilda), lt. commander U.S. Navy, 1477 9th

Franklin, Effie B. (John), stockbroker, 2645 Gardenview

G Gabriesheski, Bob M. (Bonnie), computer programmer, 397 Locust

Garcia, Albert P. (Abbie), bail bonds, 519 Douglas

Garcia, George Hector, packing Moseley, 4100 Talbert Dr., Apt. 219

Gardner, Louise K., receptionist, 573 9th

Garner, Peter B., police sgt., 812 Ivory

Garvin, William T. (Faye), barber, 1302 Winderwood Apts.

Gates of Prayer Temple, 945 Walnut

Gemignani, C.R. (Carolyn), carpenter, 546 Cotton

Gentry, Bonnie, waitress White Castle, 1344 Central

Gibson, Alicia K., retired, 4420 Glen Place, Apt. 15

Gibson, Larry D. (Aubrey), sanitation supervisor, 697 Blake

Gibson, Lawrence H. (Arlene), city council, (Westpark)

Gillespie, Donna, v-pres. operations Huron Petroleum, 1116 12th

Girl Scouts of America, 930 2nd

Golden, Marshall N. (Naomi), rabbi Gates of Prayer, 3222 Avery

Goodman, Mark U. (Rose), M.D., psychiatrist City General, 1248 Trenton

Goodwin, James P. (Ruby), officer Immigration Bureau, 513 5th

Gourmet Cafe, 694 2nd

Grand Hotel, 1500 Madison Ave.

Grant, Leslie G. (Catherine), teacher, 947 10th

Gray, Jack V. (Pat), owner Jackknife Prop., 14 Point Estates

Greene, Jackie W. (div.), receptionist, 429 Underwood Dev.

Greenpeace Inc., 1834 Hampton

Grimes, William C. (Mary), travel agent, 535 Riverside

Grisanti, Michelle, judge Criminal Court, 2344 Timbers

Gwinn, David N., cashier Safeway, 609 5th

H HAVEN Inc., 803 2nd

Ha, Tan K. (Kim), M.D., radiologist Our Lady of Mercy, 1565 Clear Point

Hadley, Herbert T. (Loraine A.), laborer, 2111 Oakmont Gr.

Haines, Horace P. (Kimberly), playwright, 210 Oak Haven Ct.

Hale, Wayne C., staff sgt. U.S. Army, 484 Walnut, No. 16

Haley and Associates Engineering, 2711 Adams

Halstrom, Bart N. (Dottie), pr. asst. Great Northern, 457 Line Ave.

Hammond, Desderia, police lieut., 2626 Valley Dr.

Hancock, Hiram (Gracie), rev., pastor First Presbyterian, 519 8th

Hardgrip Tires Inc., 2715 U.S. Hwy. 85

Hargrove, Irene, v-pres. pr. Our Lady of Mercy, 1481 Lexington

Harris, Gregory L. (Alma), mechanic, 1194 9th

Harris, William C., student State Tech, 3035 Willow, Apt. 7C

Heart Association, The, 1903 Parkview

Henderson, Keith L., sanitation, 2203 12th, Apt. 423

Henderson, Paul G. (Anna), dect. vice squad, 716 Terrance

Hickman, Mrs. Holly (widow), pres. Mathis, 404 Fox Point

Higgins, Jesse G. (Marjorie), air traffic controller, 809 U.S. Hwy. 85

Hill Street Cemetery, 1437 Hill

Hill Street Warehouse, 2710 Hill

Hill, William T. (Dale), waiter, 768 4th

Hillcrest Savings Inc., 1507 12th

Hillside Industrial Park, (Westpark)

Hocker, Daniel U. (Ida), retired, 4675 Hillsboro Lane

Hodges, Odell (Helen A.), clothing sales, 414 Round Tree

Hoevelman, Sarah V., reporter WKNW-TV, 493 8th, Apt. 12

Holmes, Jean N., student State College, 2209 Elmwood, Apt. 310

Holmes, Jerilyn, student Centennial, Pearson Hall

Holston High School, 2416 Central

Homeless Care Center, 157 Main

HopShop, 512 Valley Dr.

Horton, Eva G., teacher, 1012 Wayne

Huron Petroleum Corp., 200 Main, Suite 500

Hutzell Pants Manufacturing, 502 Front St.

Hwang, Ho, engineer Moseley, 1849 Kings Rd.

I Iannucelli, Anthony G. (Katherine), tv repair, 719 4th

Immigration Bureau, County, 909 Willow, Suite 325

Internal Revenue Service, 1220 2nd

International Extras, 2819 Hwy. 60

Iwasaki, Tina L., computer programmer, 131 Willow Way

J Jabkowsky, Viola, owner Office Cleaning Service, 292 Heart

Jackknife Properties Inc., P.O. Box 724

Jackson, Harvey W. (Daisy), butcher Kroger, 684 7th

Jackson, Henry P. (Anita), Ph.D., head geography dept. State College, 117 Preston Apts.

James, Mary E., waitress, 421 Underwood Dev.

Janes, Richard L., col. USAF base commander, Wakeley Field

Jennings, Wilbur N., police officer, 1650 Willow, Apt. 4

Jensen Speedway, 1580 Atlantic

Jerman, Kathy P. (widow), piano teacher, 885 Lester Ln.

Johnson, Victor G. (Jean), foreman Moseley, 3483 Billings

Jollif, Hazel M., owner Jolly Pawn, 1015 Newcomb Ave.

Jolly Pawn Brokers, 1703 Willow

Jones, Brenda F., student State College, Watson Hall

Jones, Danny A. (Clara), bank teller, 427 10th

Jones, Erma Jean, maintenance Barnham, Lyons Apts., No. 330

Junior Chamber of Commerce, Performing Arts Center, Suite 202

K Kabacinski, Johnathan (Debra), farmer, 5726 Hwy. 60

Kallup, Joseph (Dorothy), owner Safety First, 680 Preston Apts.

Kelly, Louis G. (Vivien), mgr. Terry Mfg., 2658 Riley Rd.

Kelly's Used Cars, I-35 Bypass

Kemper and Hart, law office, 305 Main

Kennedy, Tommy C. (Lucille), teacher, 307 9th

Kerr, Samuel D. (Vicky), car sales Kelly's, 361 Elm

Killebrew, Theresa I., nun and city council, 905 Hill

King, Mattie N., Ph.D., pres. Literacy Program, 604 Preston Apts.

King, Vernon L. (Roberta), city editor Star, 859 Nottingham

Kirkpatrick, Eugene B (Ethel), hosp. adm. Children's, 578 Hightower

Kirkpatrick, William R., draftsman, 1505 Racine, Apt. 22

Klodzinski, Joseph (div.), plumber, 2644 Heather

Kramer, Julius (Bess), owner Elite Jewelry, 588 Robin Way

Kuykendall, Lois G. (Lonny), supervisor Hutzell, 414 Hickory

L Labarreare, Robert (Peggy), realtor, 276 Beacon

Laffiteau, Lenoir (widow), owner Bootheel Shoe Repair, 1641 Shady Grove

Lakeside Nursing Home, 2121 Old Harper Rd.

Lakewood Hospital, 440 Highpoint

Lane, Stephanie D., secretary, 2098 Kyle Rd.

Lane, Vincent T. (Joyce), deputy State Highway Patrol, 2897 Old Farm Rd.

Langley, Wayne G. (Josie), retired, 821 Blueline

Langsford, Carlton G. (Karen), v-pres. fin. State College, 1974 Lilly Dr.

Lawrence, Donald L. (Kara), D.D.S., 716 5th

Lee, Bobby M. (Rosetta), tool and die Murray, 2388 Lemon

Leggett, Sandra, computer tech. State Tech, 1447 Orchid St.

Lehman, Dennis G. (Virginia), owner nursery, 5114 Pine

Lehman, Virginia (Dennis G.), Ph.D., prof. educ. State College, 5114 Pine

Lemon, G. Walter (Rosalind), city council, (Westpark)

Lettermen's Club, 605 Valley Dr.

Lewis, Shelly S., attendant service station, 302 Underwood Dev.

Limpert, Arnold (Gloria), fire chief, 845 Cherry Ave.

Lincoln Medical Clinic, 3112 Hwy. 60

Lions Club, 303 Main

Lipscomb, Chauncy (Jane), rev., deacon St. James Episcopal, 1443 Walnut

Littlejohn, Hattie S., landscaper, 805 Benton St., Apt. 10

Logan, Barry A. (Susan), orderly St. Michael's, 434 4th

Long, Flora N. (George), teacher, 319 Harper

Loudon, Jessie D. (Dora), pres. Hardgrip Tires, 390 Robin Way

Lupardus, Bettye G., accountant, 514 Eagle Trail

M Machinists Union, Grand Hotel, Suite 290

Maffessoli, Roy E. (Pearl), shipping clerk Mathis, 1833 Quincy

Malone, Taylor Jr. (Ruth), police chief, 1060 Orchid

Malone, Taylor Sr. (Maxine), prof. speech, 994 Broad

Marcum, James R. (Patsy), owner Familytime Games, 414 Edgewater Blvd.

Marquette, John (Anna), owner Marquette Motors Co., 2720 Clear Point

Marquette Motors Co., 3030 Hwy. 60

Marshall, Daniel G. (Molly), city atty., 1198 Lincoln Ave.

Martin and Young Funeral Parlor, 806 Park Dr.

Martin, Edwin K. (Julie), bus driver, 539 7th

Mason, Gilbert S., student Centennial, Lane Hall

Masons, The, 116 Central

Masters, Bernard H., co-owner Woodworks, 108 Old Farm Rd.

Masters, Lionel F., appliance sales K-Mart, 208 Estate

Masters, Marilyn P. (Nathan), reporter Times, 2084 Granger

Masters, Melvin E. Jr. (Kate), co-owner Woodworks, 675 Northbrook

Masters, Melvin E. Sr., retired carpenter, Lakeside Nursing Home

Mathis Corporation, 1700 Avery

Matthews, Lee Y. (Helen), M.D., Children's, 1790 Valley Dr.

May Festival Inc., Performing Arts Center, Suite 226

Mayfield, Rita H., unemployed, 221 Winderwood Apts.

Mayor's Action Council, Bergin Hall, Room 240

McConnaughey, Paul C. (Yvonne), driver Hutzell, 555 Underwood Dev.

McDonald, William H. (Ethel), city council, 404 Atlantic

McGregor, Edward (Leslie), artist Global Balloons, 207 5th

McGuire, Alex I. (Doreen), v-pres. County Bank, 1645 Robin Hood Rd.

McQuesten, Dean M. (Mabel), musician, 1739 Albany

Memorial Park Cemetery, 2204 Hill

Miller, John Sr. (Alma), security guard, 2206 Central

Miller, Toby R., pro basketball player, 119 Preston Apts.

Miller, Tony R. (Elsie), sanitation, 619 Underwood Dev.

Moseley, Louise, Ph.D., owner Moseley Motors, 775 Hightower

Moseley Motors Corp., 3333 Parkview

Mulberry Park Golf Course, I-35 Bypass

Mullikin, Gary T., foreman Hutzell Pants, 915 W. Cannon, Apt. 3

Municipal Airport, Airway Dr.

Murray Industries, 403 U.S. Hwy. 85

Murray, Larry R. (Dee), appliance sales Sears, 2219 Gilbert

N Nabakowski, Darline, quality control tech. Westwheels, 187 9th

Navy Reserve Armory, 1222 Main

Neil, Jasper C. (Anna), retired dairy operator, Rt. 6, Box 33

Nelson Manufacturing, 1250 Hill

Netters, Angela, student State College, Leggett Hall

Nicks, Christine, exotic dancer Danny's Place, 1118 7th

Niles Funeral Home, 418 Center

Noordermeer, Hugh W. (Ida), mgr. Northside Mall, 2677 Winter Rd.

Northbridge Loans Inc., 3214 Hwy. 60

Nyalakonda, Ashok (Tammy), M.D., radiologist City General, 963 Quail

O Obergfell, Sven L. (Marta), gen. mgr. WKNW-TV, 3086 Hampton

O'Conner, Patricia M., dir. Tourist Dev., 756 Lexington

Oliver, Maggie B. (James), real estate broker, 2112 Cove Ln.

O'Malley, Patrick H. (Wilma), D.D.S., 1403 North Gate

Optimists Club, 104 Madison Ave.

Osborn, Betty, comptroller Terry Mfg., 219 Preston Apts.

Our Lady of Mercy Hospital, 1600 Hill

Overbeck, Stanley (Blanch), 308 Walnut

Owens, Joe W. (Page), teacher, 1009 5th

P Paavola, Winston D. (Devaiah), machinist, 2929 Westgate

Panyanouvang, Khamla (Nhom), chef, 433 9th

Parker, Jerry L. (Cynthia), tech., Lincoln Medical, 111 5th

Patterson Brothers Funeral Home, 1919 Beacon

Patterson, Matthew B. (Lisa), pipefitter, 550 Central, Apt. 13

Payne, Marlin G. (Vickie), police officer, 1492 Clearview

Pennwaite, Thomas K. (Brenda), head coach State College, 4220 Walnut

Performing Arts Center, 505 Elmwood

PetCo Industries, 2668 Industrial Rd.

Phillips, Steven J. (Alice), chauffeur, 638 9th

Pierotti, Christine M., nurse City General, 553 Estate

Pipe Fitters Union, International, 1559 Avery No. 12

Pokornsky, Jacquelyn, utilities line repair, 2540 Holston, Apt. 11

Porterfield, Samuel (div.), driver Beacon Co., 734 Winderwood Apts.

Powell, Ernest C. (Nadine), bell captain, 522 4th

Prestige Dry Cleaning Co., 1165 Willow

Preston Apartments, 3530 Lions Head Dr.

Princeton, Oliver, student Centennial, 1491 Winderwood Apts.

Products Pricing and Safety Council, 1104 Avery

Punyashthati, Supakorn, press operator Moseley, 2247 Leader Ln.

Q   Qualls, Albert G. (Mae), sales Huntzell, 1677 Hampton

Quick, Lisa R., patrol officer, 816 9th

Quinn, Christy, mayor, 357 Willow

Quinn, Peter D. (Christie), electrician, 2629 Old Farm Rd.

Qureshi, Saleem (Tarikka), D.V.M., veterinarian, 490 Castle

R   Ragghianti, Lester A., student Centennial, 304 Glenview, Apt. 208

Raintree, Jerome V. (Susan), orderly Charity Hosp., 115 Underwood Dev.

Raleigh, G.R. (Barbara), mgr. HopShop, 1689 Pleasant

Rarick, George X. (Tess), owner International Extras, 2249 Plaza Dr.

Ray, Sharon R. (James), teacher, 747 Alpine Rd.

Recycled Cycles, 4113 Hwy. 60

Reedy, Norma (Ralph K.), Ph.D., v-pres. academic affairs City Junior, 2710 Needle Point

Reedy, Ralph K., assoc. prof. biology Centennial, 2710 Needle Point

Reedy, Sharon V., student Centennial, Pearson Hall

Reform Memorial Cemetery, 3794 Lions Head Dr.

Reschenberg, Wayne R. (Sandy), air conditioning repair, 308 9th

Richardson, Dale, stockroom Murray, 4743 S. Madison Ave.

Richardson, Susan B. (Timothy), line supervisor Terry, 3191 Valley Dr.

Rico, Mickey (Diane), judge, 4217 McLean

Robertson, Alfred L. (Lottie), welder Nelson Mfg., 1506 Front

Robinson, Dean C., police officer, 627 Birch

Rotary Club, 1045 Wildwood

Russell, Shawn W., gardener, 770 8th

Rutherford, Deborah (widow), asst. prof. history State College, 1330 Trenton

Rybczyk, Wallace H. (Evelyn), bookkeeper, 2319 Cedar

S Sachenbacher, Mike (Roberta), welder Nelson Mfg., 283 7th

Safety First Inc., 200 Main, Suite 1456

St. James Episcopal Church, 105 Center

St. John's Catholic Church, 1072 Hill

St. Mary's Academy for Women, 1420 Central

St. Michael's Infirmary, 1700 Hill

Salvation Army Inc., 910 Main

Sanders, Gloria H., maid, 659 Winderwood Apts.

Sangilantoni, R.T. (Emma), atty., 488 Hampton

Save Our Zoo Inc., 505 Elmwood, Suite 12

Schnadelbach, Leroy P. (Joanne), sales Moseley, 509 Longview

Scott, Lucy A., tech. Lincoln Medical, 611 Park, Apt. 7

Scruggs, Herman (widower), retired, 945 Parkview

Second Street Church of Christ, 213 2nd

Sengsavang, Boualy (Anita), parts dept. Mathis, 555 9th

Shadyview Memorial Park, 1942 Rawlings

Sherman, Barry Jr., pr. dir., Huron Petroleum, 808 Pine

Simmons, Martha D., 2nd. Lieut. U.S. Air Force, 1466 Ridge Rd.

Simms, Otis N. (Eulah B.), laborer, 293 Underwood Dev.

Simpkins, Brad G. (Tracy), dir. City Tax Collection, 4777 Memorial Dr.

Simpson, Billy L. (Samantha), stock clerk Barnham, 1843 9th, Apt. 10

Sims, Glenda M., owner Pet's Pride, 956 Evergreen

Sims, Gloria (div.), waitress, 617 Cherry, Apt. 6

Skorupa, Cornelius (Joan), financial consultant, 3042 Pecan

Smith, Bradley J. (Adele), trooper State Hwy. Patrol, 518 Ardmore

Smith, Gilbert R., press operator Hutzell, 265 Underwood Dev.

Smith, Oscar H. III (Greta), owner Ace Pawn, 1635 Northampton

Smith, S. Troy Jr. (Isabelle), baker, 2292 Gilmore

Smith, Wanda T., pharmacist, 788 10th

Smythe, Edward C. (Grace), retired, 793 Preston Apts.

Southivongsa, Sop (Beverly), clothing sales, 919 9th

Southside Memorial Park, 2942 Line Ave.

Spoon Restaurant, The, 706 Hwy. 60

Spring Fling Inc., Bayside Auditorium, Suite 181

Stampout Inc., 404 Line

Stanley, Sandra O., rev., pastor First Presbyterian, 703 Mills

State College, 1500 Line Ave.

State College Alumni Club, 1214 Elmwood

State Highway Patrol, 3316 Illinois

State Tech, 3000 Willow

Stevenson, Greta O., draftsman, 565 7th

Stewart, Ruby C., paramedic, 894 Parkway, Apt. 19

Student Government Association, State College

Sullivan, John Z. (Stefanie), contractor, 433 Beech

Swensen, Benjamin J., tech. bloodbank, 854 Lexington

Swensen, Frank (div.), engineer Haley Assoc., 902 Easthaven

Swensen, Lottie M. (div.), salesclerk, 1431 Oakmont Grove

T Taegtmeyer, C.H. (Lillie), payroll clerk, 772 Summer

Tankersley, Kenneth B. (Judy), M.D., researcher Cardiovascular, 337 Preston Apts.

Tate, Naomi K., assoc. prof. business State College, 303 Yellowstone

Taylor, Francis G., commercial artist, 1110 Lincoln Ave.

Taylor, Homer Y. (Fannie), clothing sales, 495 Walker

Terry Manufacturing, 1860 Avery

Terry, Theodore S. (Jean), owner Terry Mfg., 1001 West Point

Thomas, Kent O. (Ethel), private investigator, 316 7th

Thomason, Randolph (Blair K.), M.D., St. Michael's, 3105 Greenvalley

Thompson, Julia D., police officer, 3187 Oak

Thorpe, Edgar (Joy), judge 6th District, 436 Robin's Nest Ct.

Throckmorton, Randy (Linda), insurance sales, 644 5th

Thurman, Brenda F., v-pres. personnel Mathis, 1754 Gerrard

Thurmond, R.G. (Ella), owner Hutzell Pants, 218 Cherry Ave.

Tough Love Inc., 627 Central, Suite 410

Tourist Development Office, Bayside Auditorium, Suite 100

Trent, Aston (Mary P.), police dect., 592 Elmwood

Trent, Wallace (Bernice K.), bank teller, 385 Washburn Drive

Tubular Products Inc., 409 Walnut

Turner, Nolan R. (Myrtle), fitter Moseley, 744 Hillbrook

Twardzik, Thad (Judy), mgr. Jensen Speedway, 3434 Jackson Ave.

U Uchamasky, Peter (Loraine), supply clerk Terry Mfg., 838 9th

Uhlhorn, Linda L., Th.D., rev., pastor Good Shepherd Methodist, 905 Preston Apts.

Underwood, Alan C. (Joyce), designer Murray, 1859 Hampton

Underwood Housing Development, 900 Willow

United Way, 333 Main

Uyumaz, Ali T. (div.), security guard, 611 5th

V Vaccaro, Van W. (Nina), asst. prof. zoology City Junior, 987 Castle

Valdez, Gerald M. (Tonya), police dect., 2014 Central, Apt. 5

Valdez, Maria U., architect, 2753 Beacon

Vaughn, Allan D. (Ronnie), foreman Hardgrip Tires, 832 Oak

Veterans of Foreign Wars, 215 2nd

Victor's Steak House, 2404 Hwy. 60

Vincent, Philip C. (Anita), rev., pastor Central Episcopal, 308 Trenton

Vinson, Winston H. (Sadie), M.D., research dir. Barnham, 1525 Pointview

Vredingburgh, Ruth (Basil), computer graphics Mathis, 741 9th

W WKNW-TV, 1474 Center

Walker, Lincoln G. (Carole), insurance sales, 1366 Beech

Walker, Nancy W. (Jim), teacher, 493 Watson

Waits, Rusty M. (Kim), state treasurer, 8220 Fox Point

Wakeley Field, U.S. Air Force base (Edgemont)

Ward, Samuel B. (Mary), capt. U.S. Army, 2192 Trenton

Warner, Elliot, deputy State Police, 3154 Cramer

Warren, Daniel R., paramedic, 616 Holly, Apt. 32

Warren, W.C. (Pamela), punch operator Moseley, 414 7th

Warren's Pawn Shop, 1410 Avery

Watson, Paul J. (Sonya), bailiff, 3753 Kings Rd.

Waxman, Herbert L. (Virginia), retired, 3484 Riverbend Rd.

Waxman, Virginia (Herbert L.), dean Faculty Senate State College, 3484 Riverbend Rd.

Weller, David G. (Alicia R.), retired, 404 Valley Dr.

Weller, Wayne G. (Stella J.), M.D., City General, 2027 Hartway

Wells, John C. (Hillary), musician, 856 Winderwood Apts.

Wentzel, Nina O. (R. David), head City Utilities, 9119 Leigh

Wentzel, R. David (Nina O.), mechanic Murray, 9119 Leigh

Westgate Holiday Inn, I-35 Bypass

Westside High School, 1012 Old Farm Rd.

Westwheels Manufacturing Co., 5535 Old Harper Rd.

White, Clinton H. (Rose), Ph.D., assoc. prof. geography State College, 315 Parkview

White, June G. (div.), cook, 304 Underwood Dev.

White, Martha L., Ph.D., pres. State College, 901 Elmwood

Wilderness Park, 4800 U.S. 85

Williams, George (Mimi), mortician, 119 Cherry Ave.

Williams, Henry (Della), sales Nelson Mfg., 694 Merton

Williams, Karen S., student State College, Leggett Hall

Wilson Fabricating, 2116 9th

Wilson, Robert A. (Edna), city council, 3830 Central

Winderwood Apartments, 2650 Madison Ave.

Woodworks, The, 1676 Hoover St.

Worstead, Olin (Bernice), farmer, Rt. 7 Box 202 (Summervale)

XYZ Xaypany, Bounyouma, pharmacist, 477 Walker

Yang, Cheng Tun (Jill), chemical sales, 581 9th

Zitzelberger, Ida (widow), retired, Longview Retirement Home

Zumbahlen, Mike C. (Diane), sheriff's deputy, 978 Grover

City and State Officials

Beckwell, Richard E., deputy dist. atty., 1641 American Ave.

Clemmons, Patrick E., director CHA, 443 Central

de Witt, Frank N., police capt., 1440 Elmwood

Grisanti, Michelle, judge Criminal Court, 2344 Timbers

Limpert, Arnold, fire chief, 845 Cherry Ave.

Malone, Taylor Jr., police chief, 1060 Orchid

Marshall, Daniel G., city atty., 1198 Lincoln Ave.

May, Bobbie R., governor

Quinn, Christy, mayor, 357 Willow
Rico, Mickey, judge, 4217 McLean
Simpkins, Brad G., dir. City Tax Collection Division, 4777 Memorial Dr.
Waits, Rusty M., state treasurer, 8220 Fox Point
Wentzel, Nina O., head City Utilities, 9119 Leigh
White, Martha L., Ph.D., pres. State College, 901 Elmwood

Government Offices

Bates Museum, 1015 Central
Bergin Civic Hall, 600 Willow
Bergin Hall Board Room
Camp Talon, 3270 Old Harper Rd.
Central Housing Authority (manages UHD project)
Chamber of Commerce, Bergin Hall, Room 154
Child Abuse Prevention Center
City Employees Union, 2119 Hampton
City Hall, 570 Madison Ave.
City Junior College, 1780 Parkview
City Utilities, 707 Madison Ave.
City Water Service, 630 Madison Ave.
City Waterworks, 5710 Old Harper Rd.
City Zoo, 500 Hwy. 60
County Highway Commission, Bergin Hall, Suite 280
Department of Public Safety Building, 500 Madison
Immigration Bureau, County, 909 Willow, Suite 325
Mayor's Action Council, Bergin Hall, Room 240
Municipal Airport, Airway Dr.
State Highway Patrol, 3316 Illinois
State Tech, 3000 Willow
Tourist Development Office, Bayside Auditorium, Suite 100
Underwood Housing Development, 900 Willow

State College, 1500 Line Ave.

College of Arts and Sciences, State College
College of Business, State College

College of Education, State College
Danforth Coliseum, State College
Student Government Association, State College

Federal Government

Eisenhower, Camp, U.S. Army
Internal Revenue Service, 1220 2nd
Navy Reserve Armory, 1222 Main
Wakeley Field, U.S. Air Force (Edgemont)

Hospitals

Charity Hospital, 1855 Lions Head Dr.
City General Hospital, 1355 Arrow
Children's Hospital, 1860 Lions Head Dr.

Directory Test 1

1. What is the complete address of the Mayor's Action Council?

   _____

2. Who is E. Clinton Evans' wife? _____

3. What is Ernest Powell's occupation? _____

4. Her first name is Ruth; her last name begins with *V*. Spell her last name:

   _____

5. Her name is Faye Garvin. What is her husband's occupation?

   _____

6. What is Rex Beckwell's middle initial? _____

7. How many public hospitals are there in the city? _____

8. What is the Junior Chamber of Commerce's suite number? _____

9. In which kind of business is Haley and Associates? _____

10. What is the correct name of Frank N. Dewitt? _____

11. Which city facility is adjacent to City Park? _____

12. What is UHD? _____

13. What does the abbreviation "Gr." stand for? _____

14. On which city street is the Ashcroft Shopping Center (hint: it isn't Madison Avenue)? _____

15. What is the correct name of the Hilltop Industrial Park?

   _____

Directory Test 2

1. What does the abbreviation "pr." stand for? _____

2. Is Thomas Dozier married? _____

3. What is Marilyn Masters' husband's name? _____

4. Two corporations are listed under the "T" section of the directory. Which are they? _____

5. Where does Lillie Chung's husband work? _____

6. Does Henry Williams have a middle initial in his name? _____

7. Who is police officer Black? _____

8. His first name is Sop; hers is Beverly. Their last name begins with S. Spell it correctly: _____

9. What is the name of the U.S. Air Force base near town? _____

10. On which road is the Westgate Holiday Inn located? _____

11. She might be incorrectly identified as Ruby Stuart in an exercise. What is her real name? _____

12. Who is the city's fire chief? _____

13. What is the full name and address of the city's police department?

    _____

14. U.S. 85 ends at which intersection in town? _____

15. Assuming Bayside Auditorium had a Madison Avenue address rather than its Main Street address, would the address be odd or even? _____

Glossary of Terms

Active voice Structure in which the subject acts on the object of a sentence; news stories should be written in the more forceful active voice: "the board approved" (active voice) versus "the measure was approved by the board" (passive voice)

Add "Additional" page; the second page of a news story is headed "add 1"

Advance Story written about a coming event, such as a story about a speech to be given later in the week

Agenda Formal listing of the order of business to be undertaken; most official meetings follow an agenda of activities from call to order through adjournment

A.M.-P.M. Morning paper, with deadline usually near 11 at night; afternoon paper with deadline usually near 11 in the morning

Anecdotes Shorter stories inside a longer story, usually a feature

Angle Focus or slant of a story

Anonymous (unnamed) sources Sources who provide information on the condition their name will not be used; avoid granting anonymity

Assignment Writing or reporting duty given by an editor to a staffer

Attribution Reference to a source in a story

Backgrounding Information gathered prior to an interview; any information that reviews previous events related to the current news story

Beat Reporter's continuing assignments such as coverage of schools, politics, police, etc.

Blind lead Lead that identifies a person who is not actually named until the second or third paragraph; also called delayed identification lead

Body Main portion of a news story, which follows the lead

Boil Tight editing of a story done to reduce length or to streamline it by deleting minor details

Breaking news Unexpected events that cannot be anticipated, such as fires; often the event is still in progress or has occurred within hours before deadline

Bridge Transition in a news story designed to take the reader smoothly from one aspect of the story to another; a sentence or paragraph between the lead and the body of a news or feature story, frequently used in brights

Bright (brite) Short, featurized version of a news story; frequently contains a humorous or odd twist

Bureau Satellite news office away from the main newspaper office, usually in an outlying circulation area or in a major news site such as Washington, D.C.

Buried lead Lead that does not contain the most important aspects of the story

Byline The writer's name appearing at the beginning of a newspaper article; often bylines are awarded to page-one stories or those that show some special reporter enterprise

Caps Uppercase or capital letters

Chain Two or more newspapers under the same ownership; also called a group

City editor Editor in charge of local news and local news staff; sometimes the highest-ranking, hands-on editor in the news room

Clips Stories cut from newspapers or taken from videotape, including stories from competitors

Closed-ended questions Questions designed to elicit a short, specific answer such as yes or no

Color story Featurized aspect of a news story usually run as a sidebar to accompany a news story, e.g., a story about the newly elected mayor's family

Column Vertical body of type in a newspaper; also an opinion article or standing feature such as a medical or gardening column

Copy desk Area of news room or station at which copy editors work

Copy editing marks Editing marks used on hard copy (paper) story to indicate article changes; no copy editing marks are used in a VDT system

Copy editors Usually desk editors who read the reporter's finished story draft and make, or suggest, changes, question verification, write headlines, etc., to prepare articles for publication

Correspondent A staff member who is based away from the paper

Courtesy titles Mr., Mrs., Miss, etc., preceding a name

Crash Malfunction that renders a computer inoperable

Cub Rookie reporter

Cursor Spot of light or blinking symbol on a computer screen indicating the point at which the next letter will appear

Cut Edit or eliminate portions of a story; usually done to reduce its length

Data All text material stored in a computer

Data base Directory of information accessed by computer through telephone lines or cable; a service to provide information, such as stock prices or law cases, which is usually paid for by a subscription fee

Dateline City in which the story originated: "Milwaukee—" appearing at the beginning of a non-local story

Deadline Time at which the story must be completed to be included at its intended publication time; deadlines must be met

Death story News article about a person's death that reviews the person's life and accomplishments

Dig Intense effort to gather complete information

Direct quotes Actual words a source said, in quotation marks

Directory List of stories in a computer file, usually by story slug

Disk (hard disk) Storage device used in a computer; floppy disk is removable, but hard disk is permanently connected to or inside the machine

Edit Change the story, usually to tighten it, improve it, correct it

Edition One press run of a newspaper (many larger papers have several editions per day, perhaps one for the region or state and a later edition for the city)

Editor News room manager who directs the entire news product of a newspaper or news broadcast, and the news room people who produce it

Editorial Opinion piece on the editorial page designed to persuade or to educate

Editorialize Inappropriately express the reporter or writer's opinion in a news article; editorializing must be deleted

Editorial matter All news and opinion copy, columns, weather, etc.; all non-advertising newspaper content

Embargo Future time before which a wire story or news release may not be published

Enterprise story Story that reflects extra effort on the part of a reporter or writer and usually carries a byline; often the story idea is originated by the journalist and approved by an editor

Ethical consideration Moral decision about news that a journalist makes based on professional competency and personal honor

Fair comment and criticism Expression of opinion that is protected from libel, written about the performance or abilities of someone in the public eye

Feature Soft news story; usually a longer, non-deadline article; also, non-news matter such as horoscopes, columns or puzzles that run regularly in a paper or on a newscast

Featurize Emphasize a human interest or novelty aspect of a news story

File Send a story to the news room from outside, usually by phone or modem; an article stored in the computer; the paper file of articles on a subject stored in the morgue

Filler Short news article or unusual fact used primarily to fill out space on a newspaper page

First Amendment The first article in the Bill of Rights to the U.S. Constitution, which protects freedom of speech and of the press

Five W's and H   News values in the lead of a story: who, what, when, where, why and how

Folo   Short for "follow up"

Font   Family of type

Fourth estate   Power of the press, after that of clergy, nobility and commoners (English Parliament)

Free-lancer   Writer who is not affiliated with any publication, but who sells work to media

Futures book   Editor's calendar of coming events from which to make reporter assignments

FYI   Memo or note: for your information

Gag order   Presiding judge's directive that media not publish stories about a trial

General assignment reporter   Reporter without a specified beat, who covers any story assigned by an editor

General manager   Executive responsible for the business operations of a newspaper or station

Graf   Journalese for paragraph

Guild   News room employees' union (Newspaper Guild)

Hack   Incompetent staffer

Handout   Publicity release sent to news media

Hard copy   Copy typed on paper

Hard news   Breaking news; opposite of soft news or features

Human interest   News value element; aspects of a story, usually about people, that appeal to audience emotion

Identification (ID)   Full identification of people named in a news story, including full name, title, age, address, occupation, etc.

Indirect quote   Any quote other than the full, exact words a source used; not placed in quotation marks

Input   To keyboard data (story) into computer; also, the data itself

Insert   Portion to be included in a news story already written

Invasion of privacy   Breaching an individual's right to be left alone

Inverted pyramid   News story written with the most important facts first; all of the more important facts precede all of the lesser details of the story

Investigative reporting   Extensive assignment designed to uncover crime or corruption

Issue   One day's edition of a newspaper or periodical

Jump   A story that is continued to another page in the paper

Justify   Align right margin of story to even line length as in a column of type

Kill Delete a story or decide not to run a story

Lead (lede) Opening of a news story, usually the first paragraph, although the lead might extend two or three paragraphs into the story

Lead story Article given the most prominent position at the top of page one of a newspaper, or the first story of a newscast

Leak Provision by an anonymous source, often a member of a public body, of information the group intended to be kept secret; information obtained in this way

Legman, legwoman Field reporter who gathers news and phones the information to the newsroom

Libel Defamatory, false information published about a person

Localize Emphasize the local aspects of a story

Lowercase Change from a capital letter to a non-capitalized letter

Malice Reckless disregard for the truth, a condition of libel

Managing editor Chief administrative officer of the news room

Media Plural for two or more news and entertainment outlets: books, newspapers, magazines, radio, television, movies, etc.; "the media are," "the medium is"

Modem Electronic device used to send data (a story) through telephone lines, usually from a portable computer at the scene of a news event to the news room

More Word centered at the bottom of a hard copy page to indicate that another take follows

Morgue Library of files that contains past articles on all topics; reporters rely on these past stories to background current stories; newspapers today are converting files of clipped articles to stored electronic data

News hole Part of the paper available for news and editorial matter

News peg The current event or central aspect about which a news story is written

News values Elements that constitute news: consequence, prominence, proximity, timeliness, action, novelty, human interest, sex and humor

Nut paragraph Paragraph high in a news article that contains the kernel or essence of what is important in the story

Obit (obituary) Story on a person's death; appears in a column of such stories and is written in a very specifically prescribed manner

Off-the-record Relating to a source's remarks that are not given for publication; avoid granting permission for the source to go off-the-record

Ombudsman Person who is paid by a media outlet to critique the job it is doing as an advocate of the public

Op-ed page Page facing the editorial page of a newspaper; carries columns, cartoons, letters to the editor, etc.

Open-ended questions   Questions designed to elicit a long answer given from the source's own frame of reference

Output   Typeset version of a story that is printed out of the computer

Pad   Unnecessary information in a story, usually designed to lengthen it (avoid padding)

Paragraph   Unit of information in a story, which should average about four typed lines in length

Paraphrase   Put what the source said in the writer's words without direct quote marks; the usual goal is to shorten and to clarify what the source said

Partial quotes   Short passage of a source's exact words, used in the story and placed in direct quotation marks (avoid using very short partials)

Password   Code to access computer file

Personality profile   Depth story on a person designed to capture the person's character for readers

Play down; play up   De-emphasize or emphasize an aspect of a story; move an element lower in the story or move an element higher

Police log (blotter)   Police department's list of the day's activities; record of arrests, etc.

Press   Formerly the print media, now the term applies to all news media

Press conference   News conference called by a news source to announce or explain a news event to all media at the same time

Press release   News story written by a public relations source and sent to the media; these should be used as background information if their news value warrants a possible story

Privilege   Right of government representatives to speak in their official capacity without fear of libeling; some documents such as court transcripts are privileged and may be quoted without fear of libel

Proofreader   Person paid to read typeset stories and catch typographical and grammatical errors; often the last person to review an article before it is published, although frequently proofreader's corrections are reviewed by an editor

Public figure   Person who is prominent enough to be considered in the public eye; journalists have more latitude under the law in reporting about such people

Public relations   As it pertains to newswriting: at its best, the process of assisting to inform the public about an organization; at its worst, an attempt to receive free publicity

Publisher   Owner or chief operating officer of a newspaper or magazine

Q. & A.   Question and answer; interplay between source and reporters after opening statements at a press conference; also a form of story presentation designed to give verbatim query and response, usually reserved for court testimony or personality profiles

Queue   Lineup or list of stories in computer memory

Rewrite   Process of improving a story by making extensive revisions such as a new lead, resequencing paragraphs or changing story structure; a rewrite might even involve gathering additional information

Rewrite desk   News room station of writers who take information called in by field reporters and write finished stories

Roundup   Several related recent news stories tied together in a single new story: "rash of robberies brings residents together to form neighborhood watch"

Running story   Events and associated stories that continue over several days or longer

Schedule   List of stories to be published in the paper or aired on the newscast

Scoop   An exclusive story, one the other media did not get

Scroll   Roll story lines above or below the visible computer screen

Second-day story   Follow-up or outcome story on a news event that originally was reported when it was in progress the first day

Series   Two or more articles on a topic, usually published on consecutive days

Shield laws   State laws that give reporters the right not to reveal sources under certain circumstances

Sidebar   Related story, usually a color story, accompanying a news story and often adjacent to it

Slant   Emphasis or focus of a story; e.g., the slant is on the speed chase; also may indicate that the story contains bias or inappropriately heavy emphasis on one aspect

Slug   One or two words indicating the subject of the story so it can be identified as it is processed through the news room: "bullet" or "Smith fire"

Sob story   Story designed to evoke great empathic emotion, usually a human interest story

Soft news   Feature story or other non-breaking or non-essential news story

Software   Computer program that instructs the machine how to process data

Spike   Kill a story

Spot news   Unanticipated, breaking news; hard news

Stet   Editor marks copy for a change, then decides the original was better; editor writes "stet" near the original copy, indicating "let it stand"

Stringer   Contributing writer who is not a staff member; usually paid by the story or a flat monthly fee

Style (AP or UPI); stylebook   Conventions to make words, titles, punctuation and treatment of numbers consistent throughout the paper; book of style instructions; use of accepted style conventions indicates a non-fiction writer is a professional

Summary lead   News story lead that includes the five W's and H, providing an overview of the essential elements of a news story; also called a simple lead

Tag line Attribution statement associated with a quote: "according to police"

Take One page of copy

Thirty (-30-) Newswriter's symbol to show the story end; also (#)

Time copy Story that has no specific deadline and can be held

Transition Writing device designed to take readers smoothly from one topic area of a story to a different, loosely related, topic area

Tube VDT screen

Typo Typographical error: "teh"

Update News story that brings a previous story up-to-date by including more recent material; to revise a story in this manner

Uppercase Capitalize a non-capitalized letter

VDT Video display terminal; the desktop computer that has replaced typewriters in the news room

Wire copy Stories that arrive at the paper or the station via telephone or computer lines or satellite transmission, usually from press or wire services

Index